MILITARY INTERVENTION AND PEACEKEEPING

By the same author

The War of the Rising Sun and Tumbling Bear
– The Russo-Japanese War 1904-5

The Republic of the Ushakovka – Admiral Kolchak
and the Allied Intervention in Siberia 1918-20

Military Intervention in the 1990s – A New Logic of War

Shrouded Secrets – Japan's War on Mainland Australia 1942-44

Celebration of Victory

The Nature of Future Conflict

Descent into Chaos

MacArthur and Defeat in the Philippines

Military Intervention and Peacekeeping

The reality

RICHARD CONNAUGHTON
Centre for Defence and International Security Studies (CDISS), Lancaster University, UK

Ashgate
Aldershot • Burlington USA • Singapore • Sydney

Published by
Ashgate Publishing Limited
Gower House
Croft Road
Aldershot
Hampshire GU11 3HR
England

Ashgate Publishing Company
131 Main Street
Burlington, VT 05401-5600 USA

Ashgate website: http://www.ashgate.com

British Library Cataloguing in Publication Data
Connaughton, R. M.
Military intervention and peacekeeping : the reality
1.United Nations - Peacekeeping forces 2.Intervention (International law) 3.Pacific settlement of international disputes
I.Title
327.1'72

Library of Congress Control Number: 2001094285

ISBN 0 7546 1802 1

Printed and bound by
Antony Rowe Ltd, Chippenham, Wiltshire

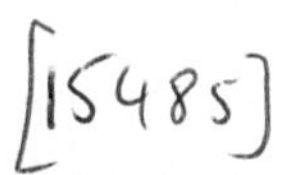

Contents

Preface *vii*
List of Abbreviations *ix*

1 The Origins 1

2 Embroidering the Tapestry 15

3 Doctrine for Expeditionary Conflict 31

4 The Heart of the Matter – The Fundamentals 53

5 Operations in Iraq 1990-91 and their Consequences 81

6 'If you liked Beirut, you will love Somalia'
– Ambassador Smith Hempstone 111

7 Rwanda – 'Tropical Nazism'
– Boutros Boutros-Ghali 139

8 Kosovo – 'Only a bunch of bad options'
– Bill Clinton 191

9 East Timor and Sierra Leone – A Coming of Age 241

Select Bibliography *267*
Notes *269*
Index *285*

Preface

This book represents an accretion to my writing and thinking over the past ten years on the subject of military intervention and peacekeeping. The UN Charter makes no provision for peacekeeping and its progress towards finding its niche post-1945 has been ad hoc and largely interest driven, so much so that it has been driven into areas never intended.

To introduce an essential element of order to the concept of collective security it has been necessary to deconstruct what has developed previously under the auspices of UN 'peacekeeping' with a view to producing a new paradigm more appropriate to face today's challenges. This is not an exercise in disparaging the UN. The UN's substantial achievements are acknowledged but so too is the Organisation's far too prevalent habit of entering environments it has neither resources nor expertise to manage.

The first four chapters establish a foundation built upon philosophy, doctrine, definitions, principles and decision-making processes. Having laid out the stall, the new thinking is tested by reference to scenarios drawn from Iraq, Somalia, Rwanda, Kosovo, East Timor and Sierra Leone. It was at Cambridge 1989-90 that I wrote *Military Intervention in the 1990s – A New Logic of War*, an attempt to establish a collective memory for military intervention in *inter*-state conflict.

I was in Northern Iraq in 1991 during the conflict there when the reality dawned forcibly upon me that we were witnessing a tectonic shift in our thinking about state sovereignty. We had to think through our attitude to external involvement in *intra*-state conflict, something which the UN was never established to consider. Unfortunately a new phenomenon emerged on the back of the assumed victory in the Gulf, namely the Peace Profession. Instead of developing a new doctrine relevant to changed circumstances the UN actively encouraged the writing of new doctrine aimed at maintaining the status quo, that is, to continue to relate to relations *with* states rather than *within* states. Thus, no longer were traditional peacekeepers' interests confined to monitoring peace lines and peace agreements but they were drawn inexorably into other states' civil wars with what were the forecast devastating consequences.

The UN has to restore its credibility. Only then will the states upon whose support it so vitally depends be prepared to resource that which falls within the realms of possibility. An exercise in public relations between the UN and the USA and its Congress in particular is urgent and overdue. In examining who does what, when and how, this book offers a number of ideas appropriate for a world not as it should be but as it is.

Most of what I have written here has already been rehearsed with people I have met in strange, isolated, sometimes dangerous, inhospitable places throughout the world. The book is founded upon theory and practice. In getting behind the scenes, however, it is particularly intended to explain to a wider audience the conduct of the political and military processes involved in military intervention and peacekeeping. After Iraq, my research continued, taking me into Rwanda, Burundi, Bosnia, Croatia, Kosovo and Sierra Leone, and was supported by targeted study into the UN's operations in Somalia and East Timor. Along the way I was privileged to meet many dedicated, professional, brave people – civilian and military – who gave one hundred per cent to their enterprise. By the same token I also met many who were less impressive.

A work such as this is a synthesis arising from the experience of such encounters. I am no longer certain who would thank me for acknowledging their help and assistance and will therefore resort to the simple expedient of thanking all those who helped me put these thoughts together. They know who they are.

Richard Connaughton
Nettlecombe
June 2001

List of Abbreviations

ABM	Anti-Ballistic Missile
APC	Armoured Personnel Carrier
ASEAN	The Association of South East Asian Nations
CDS	Chief of the Defence Staff
CEE	Central and Eastern Europe
CENTCOM	Central Command (US)
CIA	Central Intelligence Agency
CIMIC	Civil-Military Cooperation
CJFO	Chief of Joint Force Operations
CJFORT	Chief of Joint Force Operational Readiness and Training
CJO	Chief of Joint Operations
CMOC	Civil Military Operations Center
COS	Chief of Staff
CST	Civil Support Team
DART	Disaster Assistance Response Team
DMZ	Demilitarized Zone
DPKO	Department of Peace Keeping Operations
ECOMOG	Ecowas Monitoring Group
ECOWAS	Economic Community of West African States
ERRF	European Rapid Reaction Force
ESDI	European Security and Defence Identity
ESDP	European Security and Defence Policy
EU	European Union
EUCOM	European Command (US)
FBI	Federal Bureau of Investigation
FCO	Foreign and Commonwealth Office
FEMA	Federal Emergency Management Agency

FINABEL	France, Italy, Netherlands, Germany, Belgium, Spain and Luxembourg
GPS	Global Positioning System
HIC	High Intensity Conflict
HUMINT	Human Intelligence
ICP	Integrated Contingency Planning
ICRC	International Commission of the Red Cross
IED	Improvised Explosive Device
IFOR	Implementation Force (NATO – Bosnia)
INTERFET	International Force East Timor
JET	Joint Essential Task
JFHQ	Joint Force Headquarters
JRDF	Joint Rapid Deployment Force
JRRF	Joint Rapid Reaction Force
KDOM	Kosovo Diplomatic Observer Mission
KFOR	Kosovo Force
KIM	Kosovo Implementation Mission
KLA	Kosovo Liberation Army
KPC	Kosovo Protection Force
KVM	Kosovo Verification Mission
LIC	Low Intensity Conflict
MACA	Military Assistance to Civil Authorities
MIC	Mid Intensity Conflict
MNB	Multi-National Brigade
MPRI	Military Professional Resources Inc
MSC	Military Staff Committee of the United Nations
MTA	Military Technical Agreement
NAC	North Atlantic Council
NATO	North Atlantic Treaty Organisation
NGO	Non-Governmental Organisation
OAU	Organisation of African Unity
OLRT	Operational Liaison and Reconnaissance Team
OOTW	Operations Other Than War
OPEC	Organisation of Petroleum Exporting Countries
OSCE	Organisation for Security and Cooperation in Europe
PDD	Presidential Decision Directive
PJHQ	Permanent Joint Headquarters
POLMIL	Police-Military
QRF	Quick Reaction Force

RFA	Royal Fleet Auxiliary
RM	Royal Marines
RPF	Rwandese Patriotic Front
RUF	Revolutionary United Front
SACEUR	Supreme Allied Commander Europe
SDR	Strategic Defence Review
SFOR	Stabilisation Force (NATO – Bosnia)
TA	Territorial Army (UK)
TOC	Tactical Operations Centre
UN	United Nations
UNAMET	United Nations Mission in East Timor
UNAMIR	United Nations Advisory Mission in Rwanda
UNAMSIL	United Nations Mission in Sierra Leone
UNDP	United Nations Development Programme
UNHCR	United Nations High Commission for Refugees
UNMIK	United Nations Mission in Kosovo
UNOMUR	United Nations Observer Mission Uganda-Rwanda
UNOSOM	United Nations Operation in Somalia
UNPROFOR	United Nations Protection Force
UNREO	United Nations Rwanda Emergency Office
UNSAS	United Nations Standby Arrangement System
UNTAET	United Nations Transitional Administration in East Timor
USMC	United States Marine Corps
WEU	Western European Union
WMD	Weapons of Mass Destruction
WTO	World Trade Organisation

1 The Origins

People often study history less for what they might learn than for what they want to prove. This is one reason why so much is known about internationalist theories since the end of the Middle Ages. Vast efforts have been made, innumerable books have flowed, from the wish to cite Dubois or Dante, Crucé or Sully, as forerunners of the League of Nations or United Europe or the United Nations experiment - and from the even more curious supposition that it was necessary to study these early writings for guidance in creating, improving or saving these twentieth century projects.

F.H. Hinsley, *Power and the Pursuit of Peace,* 13.

It suits our purpose to note what Professor Hinsley wrote above to identify and cite a more recent clutch of war-management philosophers in order to examine war or, more recently, armed conflict, in the context of international organisations and state sovereignty. This chapter represents a short guide as to how inter-state security relationships developed from the seventeenth century to the beginning of the Cold War. Attitudes to war had remained unchanged from the fourteenth century when Dubois and Dante were alive through to the eighteenth century when Kant, Bentham and Vattel were writing on the subject. Realism was the dominant perspective of an international order which exuded social Darwinism and supported a thesis set out in a letter originating from the Athens/Sparta War whereby 'the strong take what they will, the weak yield what they must'. This was not a revolutionary theory but a reflection of a long-lasting reality that international relations were dominated by considerations of power. In October 1648, after the conclusion of the Thirty Years War, the Westphalian concept of international relations became established in Europe. It was a system which remained virtually intact for three and a half centuries and was founded upon set principles, namely:

> the sovereign right of the state to act as supreme arbiter within its national borders and to be the absolute priority of the interests of the state (*raison d'état)* and maintenance of security within the parameters of the balance of power - were the universal fundamentals of European and later world politics.[1]

The strategist Clausewitz, of approximately the same period as Immanuel Kant, Jeremy Bentham and Emmerick de Vattel, might also have been speaking for Hegel and Marx when he wrote 'war is an extension of politics by other means'. A postscript to which could be added by Marx to the effect that 'nations are strengthened as a result of war'. With the benefit of hindsight, Tsar Nicholas II, who embarked upon the disastrous 1904-05 Russo-Japanese War, would not have agreed.

The mid-eighteenth century saw an outpouring of thinking which set aside mediaeval aspirations of a united Europe whose orderly structure it was assumed would automatically guarantee peace. It had been an *aspiration* because Christian and realist views oscillated alternately between dialogue and conflict from Constantine's time onwards. The new Europe was to be a collection of independent sovereign states within an international system. Kant and Bentham entered the debate at this point insisting that peace was not in prospect unless states first recognised that they were part of the international system and second, drew up a regime of international law to regulate collaboration between states. Where Kant and Bentham differed was in the length of time they believed it would take to establish the new world order. Bentham believed sooner rather than later while Kant believed later rather than sooner.

Kant shared his optimism for greater morality in politics with Jean-Jacques Rousseau (1712-78) but their point of separation lay in the latter's pessimistic assumption that international organisations could not constrain the independent sovereign state, a point upon which Thomas Hobbes agreed. In *Leviathan* (1651), Hobbes recounted how international order lacked a central government and cohesive purpose:

> Yet in all times kings and persons of sovereign authority, because of their independence are in continual jealousies and in the state and posture of gladiators, having their weapons pointing and their eyes fixed on one another, that is their forts, garrisons and guns, upon the frontiers of their kingdoms; and continual spies upon their neighbours, which is a posture of war.

The predominant doctrine in Western Europe of the seventeenth to nineteenth centuries therefore was essentially a Realist policy of grab what the state's strength would permit. There was no internationalism to speak of: international law applied to states.

> They may choose to bind themselves but accept no higher authority. The duty of those who serve and direct them is to promote the national power and influence in each case and under the doctrine of *raison d'état* statesmen cannot

be bound in public affairs by the same morality they would respect in private life.[2]

The linkage between state sovereignty and international law appeared in Vattel's *Le Droit des Gens.* Drawing on the thinking of others who asserted the sovereignty of the state and the resultant cohesion formed through common interest, Vattel endorsed the notion of the independence of states but also emphasised their common rights and duties. His first principle of natural law was the sovereignty of the state. *Le Droit des Gens,* written in French, the language of diplomacy, was widely read and achieved considerable status within states. Vattel's insistence upon the sovereign equality of states would lead to quarrelling states, irrespective of their size, claiming equal rights. Vattel also underpinned the historical doctrinal understanding that states, by virtue of being states, retained their right to use force to go to war. It was remarkable that a Swiss national should have taken the initiative to formalise what had previously been an understanding. Vattel was mindful of what he was unleashing and sought to limit the right to go to war to instances where such action was unavoidable and in reminding states that they had duties in addition to rights, which involved a duty to behave with restraint. Vattel also codified and drew upon the example of the balance of power as evidenced as a post-1815 development in the Concert of Europe as a means of maintaining peace and order. The point is that there was a clear notion of the balance of power in the eighteenth century: it was not a nineteenth century construction. The equilibrium which was the essential component of the balancing act evolved as a form of compromise to states' failure to achieve a preponderance of power.

The mechanics through which equilibrium was achieved were through the device of a Security Council or Directorate which met periodically. The members devised a set of rules and conventions, in other words a Charter, as to how the Great Powers were to relate one to another. Any change or amendment to the Vienna Settlement at the end of the Napoleonic Wars (1815) required the unanimous consent of the five powers. It was in the Powers' interest to act with self-restraint and through meeting regularly and recognising that their interests and those of Europe were best served through the maintenance of balance. Kant and Bentham were not disposed to a *carte blanche* to go to war but saw in the development of workable, international law the encouragement for states to set aside their rights to go to war. Nevertheless, it was the device of the Balance of Power which would keep Europe free from major regional conflict for the best part of a century. States came to recognise their duty to maintain peace through the means of the balance of power that they had created but without prejudice to state sovereignty. As Professor Hinsley explained:

> The technique was the conference of powers; the basic operating principle was that the great States must submit their interests to devices of peace by way of the technique of the balance of power designed to create equilibrium. They maintained the balance by self restraint, meeting and the recognition of themselves and Europe being served by maintaining that balance.

It became evident that the maintenance of international peace and order became impossible as long as individual states retained the right to go to war. After 1890, the desire for peace became subordinated to the aspiration among some states for a larger distribution of power while, concurrently, competition between alliances increased. What ultimately triggered the First World War was the assassination in Sarajevo on 28 June 1914 of Archduke Franz Ferdinand of Austria by a young Bosnian anarchist, Gavrilo Princip. Although a Bosnian and therefore a subject of Austro-Hungary, there was a strong suspicion that Princip and others had been encouraged and equipped by senior military officers in the Serbian Nationalist association, Narodna Odbrana or Black Hand. 28 June is an emotive date in the Serb calendar for it was on that day the Turks defeated the Serbs at Kosovo in 1389.

One of the most telling consequences to arise at the end of the First World War was the subordination of Realism to a new, almost universal mood emphasising Idealism and Utopianism. The Great War of 1914-18, the war to end all wars, was never to be repeated and, if that goal were to be achieved, there had to be a fundamental overhaul of the international system. The obvious target for attention was a state's right to go to war. The difficulty in formulating the rules to limit a state's right to go to war lay in the recognition that there had to be an enforcement mechanism.

When the League of Nations was founded, it was part of the Treaty of Versailles, a derivative of the 1919 Paris Peace Conference. It had its origins, in the same way that the United Nations had in the 1941 Atlantic Charter, in allied conferences and coordination during the First World War. The aim of the new organisation was the promotion of international cooperation and peace and security. America's contribution appeared to be very positive. Ex-President William Howard Taft established a shadow organisation in Philadelphia and one of President Woodrow Wilson's 14 points had been the requirement to form a general association of nations. The draft Covenant was put before the Peace Conference in April 1919.

Collective Security, 'a design for preserving the integrity of the anonymous victim of attack by the anonymous aggressor, it is no respecter of states, but an instrument to be directed against any aggressor, on behalf of any violated state'[3] was placed in the hands of the League together with a supervisory role which the UN (Security Council) would not have. Sir Eric Drummond set about the recruitment of the necessary staff for a Secretariat that was administrative rather than political and, when the Peace Treaty was ratified, the League of Nations came into being. For Woodrow Wilson, however, the Peace Conference was seen as a personal defeat because the Treaty became uncoupled from his 14 points, leading to a more stringent peace being imposed upon Germany than he intended. The overwhelming sense in Germany was one of betrayal, and herein lay the seeds of the origins of the Second World War. There was however an indication in America's coolness towards the League of Nations, an attitude towards international organisations, which also accounts for the tensions which would arise between the United States and the United Nations.

Wilson's peace initiative became ensnared in domestic politics. The Republican Cabot Lodge attacked Wilson for his independent action and for his failure to cooperate with the Allies. The American casualty list fostered the same repugnance to war within the United States as was the case throughout Europe. In the 1918 Congressional Elections, the Republicans won control of both Houses which established the not unusual conflict between the Administration and the Executive, or what Neustadt described as 'separate institutions that share power'. In the spring of 1919, the consideration of domestic politics meant that Wilson had to make concessions to the allies in order to generate support for his concept of the League of Nations. But these were Allies who each had their own separate agenda. Britain sought to maintain freedom of operation on the high seas and was not greatly enthused. France's priority was to engineer security against future German attack. Exasperated, Wilson threatened to withdraw from the peace process; a gesture not well received by US public opinion and a contributory factor in opposition being generated towards their not joining the League of Nations.

The new Republican Senate was heavily influenced by isolationism and there was the enormous difficulty of the Democrat Administration to achieve a two-thirds majority to have its proposed legislation accepted. While Cabot Lodge was not an isolationist he deplored Wilson's moralising foreign policy. For his part, Wilson saw in the League of Nations the embodiment of a universalist Foreign Policy, but national self-interest among the major parties adversely affected the terms of a Peace Treaty inextricably linked to the League of Nations. Between the summer of 1919 and the spring of 1920, US public opinion and attitude towards the League of Nations began to shift. They wanted nothing more to do with Europe's problems and, as though to emphasise that point, the Senate repudiated Wilson's American mandate. The question arose as to what benefit would accrue to an America warned against entangling commitments in joining the League of Nations and wedded to the primacy of national sovereignty as implicitly understood in 'America First'. The benefit to be derived from an American presence in the League was a difficult question for Wilson to answer, particularly since he promised the continuation of America's separate diplomacy. The League of Nations became seen as a threat to the American way and to America's freedom and was therefore repudiated. Washington's decision not to join the League weakened the organisation at the outset. Germany joined in 1926 and was made a permanent member of the Council. In 1934, the Soviet Union also joined and also became a permanent member of the Council, as a result of which Spain and Brazil withdrew.

The purpose of the League of Nations was the maintenance of peace; the subject of 10 of the League's Articles. The prevention of wars through collective security, the peaceful settlement of disputes through arbitration and the Permanent Court of International Justice and through Reports of the Council was seen to be the way forward. The proposal of South Africa's Field Marshal Jan Smuts of the establishment of a three month cooling off period was adopted within a regime which sought to achieve unanimity in both the Council and Assembly. Where this was not achieved, as was often the case, various ploys were used to fudge the reality that unanimity on important issues was a virtual impossibility. There were too many irreconcilable interests.

Under Article 10, for example, each member state undertook 'to respect and preserve as against external aggression the territorial integrity and existing political independence of all Members of the League', yet no procedure was put in place to enforce such a guarantee. This shortcoming was recognised by the French who sought to have established an international General Staff with Standing Forces at their disposal. Wilson rejected this initiative because he objected to any measure which might appear to be throwing the League into an undesirable alliance. When the League did finally emerge onto the international stage, it contained no machinery to impose rules to stop war although provision had been made for appeasement and conciliation. The League sat uneasily in the middle ground between collective security and peace processes. Provision had been made for the imposition of sanctions, but there were two vitally important gaps in the procedure. First, there was no guarantee that war could be avoided and second, there was no obligation to go to war in the pursuit of peace. Whereas territorial guarantees were explicit, no procedure had been established for their enforcement. The gaps were recognised at the time the League was launched but it was assumed that the problems would be resolved in the fullness of time, for otherwise the League would be doomed.

There was an attempt outside the framework of the League, which had the support of the United States, to circumvent Kant's observation that no international organisation that seeks to discipline states is compatible with the nature of states. He believed that the onus should be on states to discipline themselves. In 1928, by which time attempts to fill the gaps in the structure of the League had failed and attempts at evasion were at their most creative, there arose a bilateral pact between the United States and France - the Pact of Paris, or the Briand Kellogg Pact. The idea was that Pact signatories would only solve disputes by pacific means. Sanctions were not permitted. Order would be maintained through the promises of the signatories. Conceptually it was very idealistic.

The gaps in the League of Nations were never filled and the concept of collective security was exposed as a sham when Japan occupied Manchuria in 1931. The League was reluctant to operate in the Far East without the support of the United States. In 1935, Italy invaded Abyssinia. The League did nothing of consequence (they imposed minor sanctions) because of British and French concerns that too overt an action would drive the Italians into a coalition with Germany. Hitler had withdrawn from the League and the Disarmament Conference in 1933. So too had Japan. Hitler's re-militarisation of the Rhineland (1936) transgressed the Locarno Treaty which guaranteed the French-Belgian-German borders and was met with no substantive response. The Spanish Civil War (1936-39) drew in Italy, Germany and the Soviet Union as well as volunteers drawn from throughout the world. The Soviet Union's attack on Finland, 30 November 1939, led to her expulsion so that the revisionist powers of Germany, Italy, the Soviet Union and Japan, who all had reason to dislike the 1919 post-war settlement, were no longer members of the League. Because the League had been an extension of Versailles the post-war relationship with Germany did not change significantly. Germany was still regarded as the underdog in a victor/vanquished relationship. The glimmer of a new benevolent direction of events was wrecked by the great depression which brought Hitler to power.

Only Britain and France remained as the League's significant powers as the world prepared to enter the darkness of a second world war in the first half of the twentieth century. The League ultimately failed because it was founded upon a moralistic and vindictive peace settlement and was ultimately rejected by too many important, powerful states.[4] Moreover the post-war environment was too unstable to accept into the international system a profoundly new international organisation founded upon affirmative action yet one which opposed alliances and balance of power and which resisted attempts at the restoration of stability.

The United States was at the forefront of states who believed a new international organisation responsible for collective security was required at the end of the Second World War but one that had to be more effective than the League had been. The League was tainted by failure and therefore required a new title. 'United Nations' had been Roosevelt's idea in recognition of those states who had been united in war against the axis powers. The allied powers met during the war at Dumbarton Oaks and San Francisco to draft a new Charter which would rectify the mistakes so obviously apparent in the League. The United Nations Charter was signed in San Francisco on 26 June 1945, six weeks before VJ Day, and was thus never part of a peace treaty. The League of Nations Secretariat moved over with much of their administrative expertise to the United Nations in New York. The US Senate Committee for Foreign Relations was reasonably satisfied with the end result:

> While it may be that this is not a perfect instrument, the important thing is that agreement has been reached on this particular Charter, after months and even years of careful study and negotiation, between the representatives of 50 nations.[5]

The League and the Charter had much in common but action had been taken to close recognised gaps. The Peaceful Settlement of Disputes and enforcement procedures were incorporated into Chapters VI and VII of the Charter respectively. States were obliged to act as part of the collective security guarantee but while states did agree to be bound by this undertaking, when a tension occurred between that undertaking and national interest, national interest was rarely subordinated to an international aspiration.

Article 2(4) of the new Charter set aside a state's historic right to go to war in so far as the members 'shall refrain in their international relations from the threat or use of force against the territorial integrity or political independence of any state'. Article 2(7) appeared to preserve the notion of domestic sanctity but there was an important caveat: 'Nothing contained in the present Charter shall authorise the United Nations to intervene in matters which are essentially within the jurisdiction of any state...*but* this principle shall not prejudice the application of enforcement measures under Chapter VII'. The notion that a state could do as it wished within its own borders did not receive automatic endorsement. It was more to do with the fact that in the new post-war relationship between states there was no clear vision as to the precise place of domestic sanctity in world order. That much was admitted in 1945 by John Foster Dulles:

> Article 2(7) is an evolving concept. We don't know fifteen, twenty years from now what in fact is going to be within the jurisdiction of nations. International law is evolving, state practice is evolving..... Let's just let things drift for a few years and see how it comes out.

The Charter's forceful settlement clauses were also made more flexible and less legalistic while the concept of a cooling-off period was abandoned. Whereas the League had charged states through their individual undertakings to preserve world order and peace, a new supranational authority, the Security Council, had been established in the United Nations to guide and coordinate the actions of its members. Observance of Security Council decisions, resolutions or mandates was made obligatory. Unanimity was abandoned and replaced by the requirement for the affirmative vote of 7 of the 11 members. Only the Security Council was empowered to initiate armed conflict. The only exception the Charter permits is the inherent right of states to claim self-defence under Article 51, but with the rider that such action is to be referred subsequently to the Security Council for confirmation. The new Charter did require states to refrain from the threat or use of force yet the Security Council offered no collective guarantee that it would respond on behalf of states in difficulty. States' guarantees were therefore reciprocated by what can only be described as the Security Council's conditional guarantee.

The five permanent members of the 1945 Security Council were the victors of the Second World War: the United Kingdom, the United States, the Soviet Union, Nationalist China and France. Germany and Japan were referred to as the 'enemy' and, since the Charter has not been amended, that still remains the case when the permanent membership remains what it was in 1945. What the drafters of the Charter had done was to restore the Concert of the Great Powers and the understanding that global rule was the gift of the Great Powers. However, as was the case of the membership of the Concert there was a disparity in the power of the individual members. The war marked the end of any aspiration Britain might have had to be regarded as a long-term superpower, not that it was a fact recognised at the time. In the ten years from 1946 when she was the most active of the western powers until Suez, she had been a major player. After 1956, Britain's power simply evaporated. She had, in Correlli Barnett's words, 'become the warrior satellite of the United States'. As early as 1943, London had identified Russia as being the principal post-war threat but increasingly began to feel that the United States could not be relied upon.

US troop levels in Europe fell from 3.5 million in 1945 to 200,000 in June 1947. During the war, Vichy France collaborated with Germany and with Japan in Indo-China but became a permanent member of the Security Council at Churchill's insistence. During the immediate post-war period there were fears that France and Italy might embrace Communism. Eventually, in 1958, the Free French General, Charles de Gaulle, gained power and pursued a line independent of the Anglo-Saxons. General Chiang Kai Shek's *Kuomintang* had its attention held by the intensifying civil war against Mao Tse Dong's Communists. In 1945, the United States dominated a western-orientated, colonial era, United Nations and exercised her national interest through a pliant Secretary General, the Norwegian Trygve Lie. Harry S. Truman had become President on Roosevelt's death but he suffered the disadvantage of not knowing the wartime leaders, particularly Stalin. It was the emerging power-play between the west as represented by the United States and the eastern bloc as represented by the Soviet Union which reflected the reality of the existence of a balance of power system. In the early years, the Soviet Union discovered that it could redress the disparity in balance through the means of exercising the veto. In later years, the United States replaced the Soviet Union as the predominant state in the use of the veto, a right which could be exercised by each of the permanent 5 on the Security Council. If a crisis could not be resolved by peaceful means, and where there existed a threat to peace, breach of peace or an act of aggression, the Security Council was empowered to 'take such action by air, sea or land forces as may be necessary to maintain or restore international peace and security'.[6]

The provision of the veto has often been cited as the reason why the United Nations never rose to what was expected of it but in reality there are two avenues of thinking. One is that in the transition from the Covenant to a Charter which embodied the veto provision, states had exchanged one system which might not have worked for one that will not work. What the Charter had achieved was the extension of the sovereignty of the principal powers. Alternatively, there was the view that the drafters of the Charter were being entirely realistic in recognising that since the Security Council was the source of so much power and the sovereignty of the great states an inescapable fact, the United Nations could only be effective if the principal powers were prepared to cooperate. Such pragmatism was extended to the field of international law whereby the international community continued the historic motions of a body of law, *jus ad bellum*, which circumscribes the right to use force and one for application once hostilities begin, *jus in bello*.

The book published in London and written by the British Realist E.H. Carr, *The Twenty Years Crisis,* identified Idealism as a principal cause of the Second World War and the Holocaust. The 1920s-30s had been a reformist period in an attempt to distance parties from balance of power, arms races and alliances. Carr had observed how:

> The advocate of a scheme for an international police force or for collective security or some other project for an international order generally replied to the criticism not by an argument designed to show how and why he thought his plan would work but by a statement that it must be made to work because the consequences of its failure to work would be so disastrous.[7]

Carr's rival principles did gain ground but the impetus came from Hans Morgenthau in the United States. The reason Realism had this great revival post-1945 was due to the Idealists having ignored the inescapable reality of international relations - power. Realists believed that International Organisations were founded upon Great Power supervision. The dominant mechanism is spheres of influence where intervention occurs at will, for economic or military reasons, and order is maintained through the balance of power which provides equilibrium within International Organisations. The Charter paradigm was a repackaged form of Idealism, founded upon International Organisations such as the United Nations and its Charter. The principal philosophies were based upon state sovereignty, non-interference and non-intervention. States retained domestic sanctity and abode by international law. The Charter concept was thus far removed from the dominant Realist concept which had emerged all-powerful in 1945. 'Realism', wrote Robert Rothstein,

> is always a doctrine which takes for granted the primacy of foreign policy and the dominance of the security issue defined in terms of simple notions of power. It is, in sum, not only the classic version of a state centric doctrine but also an affirmation of the rightful dominance of the Great Powers and the autonomy of their foreign policies.[8]

The signatories of the UN Charter undertook to put armed forces and facilities at the disposal of the Security Council, who were to be advised and assisted by a Military Staff Committee (MSC). The MSC was capable therefore of providing to the UN the General Staff functions which France had wished to see included in the League of Nations. The first problem the MSC had to face was to decide upon the strength and composition of the separate components of the UN Collective Security Force and the proportion of the overall strength that should be provided in the first instance by the five permanent members (the other members would provide forces later). With the exception of the United States, the numbers recommended by the other four members were broadly similar, being sufficient to deal with what would now be considered a regional aggressor. The United States proposed land, sea and air forces which were more appropriate for use against a major power, being generally twice the strength proposed by the other members. The Soviets continued to insist that the principle of equality should govern the contributions of the permanent members and demanded a clear definition of the conditions under which force could be used.[9] The divergent opinions of the United States and the Soviet Union could not be reconciled and the questions of command which were, according to the Charter, 'to be worked out subsequently', were not considered. There was thus no requirement to tackle the even thornier problem of who was to pay. What is clear from the discussions, however, is that what was being considered was a multinational force drawn from member states and commanded by a nominated commander under the strategic direction of the MSC, the latter being responsible to the Security Council. Nowhere was the Secretary General mentioned. The structure proposed for the MSC was not dissimilar to that created in NATO.

The first of three tasks given to the MSC by the Security Council on 25 June 1947 was to submit an estimate of the overall strength of the armed forces which should be made available to the Security Council. General R.L. McCreery, the British Chairman of the MSC, replied to the Chairman of the Security Council:

> Inasmuch as unanimity could not be achieved on the question of the overall strength and composition of the United Nations Armed Forces, it was, *a priori,* impossible to consider Items II and III of the programme of work, dealing with the contributions by member nations.[10]

Part of the problem was the Soviets who, although goaded by the United States, did not want to see a USA-dominated United Nations wield such considerable military power. The ideological divide between east and west could not be bridged. The Soviet Union was an entrenched though expansionist Marxist-Leninist state retaining its traditional fears of encirclement by hostile powers. The comprehensive destruction of Germany and the collapse of political authority in Central and Eastern Europe (CEE) created a vacuum into which were drawn the competing aims of the Soviets and the Americans. Germany and Japan, the enemies upon which the Allies had focused their attention, had been neutralised. But now the Allies did not have a common enemy to keep them up to the mark and 'the Charter assumed, with a stunning lack of political realism, that they would stay united in supervising, and if necessary enforcing world peace'.[11] NATO was created in 1949, the Warsaw Treaty in 1955, and the UN assumed a special function not provided for in the UN Charter but one which sat comfortably under the umbrella of Chapter VI, *The Pacific Settlement of Disputes,* namely peacekeeping.

2 Embroidering the Tapestry

There ought to be a rule to the effect that no one should discuss military intervention or peacekeeping without first defining their understanding of the terms. 'Peacekeeping' in particular has been so heavily influenced by creative interpretation and loaded with considerations of interest that it means different things to different people. Military intervention is a political concept where the definition can change with the debate. Military intervention will often occur when armed forces confront an opponent against the wishes of the *de facto* or *de jure* government. Where military intervention occurs at the invitation of the incumbent government, it will invariably suppress the perceived right of self-determination of that proportion of the population challenging the interests of the government. Military intervention is therefore closely linked to coercive interference and occasionally, as occurred with the Soviets in Czechoslovakia, it is difficult to separate the act of intervention from the act of invasion. There is no template for an interventionist operation. That it can be escalatory in terms of commitment is emphasised in these three stages:

> The first stage is characterized principally by the provision of material and financial assistance..... The second stage of intervention is characterized by the limited participation of the supporting power in military operations..... But in order for the intervening power to get effective control, it is necessary to proceed to the third stage. Then the intervening forces become the dominant element in the war effort of the supported side.[1]

This example was true of Vietnam and, in 1999, stage two had been reached in US assistance to Colombia, but not of the Falklands and the 1989 Panama interventions which proceeded directly to the third stage.

It is equally true to say that non-intervention, as was the case of capable parties in the Spanish Civil War, could also be described as a form of intervention. In addition, an act of intervention justified as a form of self-defence may appear to be nothing more than a blatant act of reprisal. Military intervention is a broader concept than the term that has emerged as a politically correct alternative, namely 'peace support operations'. Peace support operations evolved as a derivative of a discredited concept known as 'wider peacekeeping' which established the vogue of inserting the word 'peace' into every available activity. Military intervention will not always have as its aim the support of peace. More often than not, there will be no peace to support. There is therefore no easy, neat and precise definition which overcomes the complexities of international politics. It is best defined by declaring what it is not.

The warning by Alan James[2] that the term 'peacekeeping' as applied to the United Nations has a variety of meanings suggests we are no further forward. Indeed, the International Peace Academy demonstrated the scope for confusion by describing peacekeeping as a form of intervention:

> the prevention, containment, moderation and termination of hostilities between or within states, through the medium of peaceful third party intervention organised and directed internationally, using multinational forces of soldiers, police and civilians to restore and maintain peace.[3]

Alan James made the distinction between military intervention and peacekeeping:

> Yet when compared with military intervention, there is a distinction between the two (which) was seen to lie in their attitudes towards the associated issues of force and consent, collective security relying, ultimately, on the mandatory use of force, while peacekeeping eschewed force, except in self defence and required the consent of the host state for the admission of UN personnel.[4]

The original peacekeepers who first appeared in 1947 were the observers the UN employed in Greece and also the military attachés in Indonesia recruited to observe the ceasefire between the Dutch and Indonesian freedom fighters. This period of de-colonisation ran concurrently with the Cold War, the new states generally achieving independence when they were deemed to be ready. When states were given their freedom too soon, as happened in the Congo, chaos ensued. Some former colonies chose to align themselves in the polarising east or west camps while many maintained a policy of strict non-alignment. The problem facing many of these newly emerging states who came forward to join the UN - an organisation with its *raison d'être* founded upon inter-state relationships - was their artificiality. Most had had their boundaries drawn up with pencils and rulers in the foreign ministries of Europe, ignoring ethnic realities out on the ground. The new states' attitude, however, was that they should persevere in perpetuity with the new borders and create a new sense of nationalism. This understanding became enshrined in the 1964 Cairo Declaration and, with few exceptions,[5] was only challenged in more recent times. The UN Charter gave the new states virtually a free hand to resolve their own domestic security problems while they sought to find their place in an international order in which the concept of global collective security had been frozen out by the developing Cold War. 'Cold' did not simply describe the frigidity which had developed in east-west relations. It was an apposite adjective with which to describe the concurrent, suspended animation in which many potentially difficult and divisive border issues had been sidelined.

The United States was unquestioningly the dominant power to emerge from the war. A representative of the new world had arrived to redress the balance of the old. America's people and economy had been jointly developed to become the dominant factors in the defeat of both Germany and Japan. The political tradition of avoiding entangling commitments and alliances was set aside because America found herself out in front in an unassailable leadership position in international politics. Isolationism became subordinated to the ideal of bestowing upon shattered if not defeated nations the American Way. But America needed a strategy or doctrine with which to plan the future. Serendipitously, Hans Morgenthau had already penned out his theory of Realism, a paradigm that was seized upon as the way forward. Morgenthau was the architect who gave to post-war realism its heavy Central and Eastern European bias. The Central and Eastern Europeans, mostly Jewish emigrés, understood the shortcomings of the old world order in which they had played a part but they also saw how power had to be marshalled to influence change. This truism was reflected in the performance of Henry Kissinger who understood international politics and, more recently, Madeleine Albright who arguably had a less good grasp. Both however were academics seduced by ambition and the attraction of power. Of Kissinger, it could be said that he often operated in lieu of the Secretary of State whereas of Secretary of State Albright it could be said that she operated foreign affairs independent of the President.

The first major conflict to arise over the ideological differences, as represented by America on one side and the Soviet Union on the other, came in Korea when, on 25 June 1950, seven North Korean divisions crossed the 38th Parallel and invaded the South. The 38th Parallel had been an artificial device introduced at the end of the Second World War. The Soviets accepted the surrender of Japanese to the north of the line and the Americans those Japanese to the south. The 38th Parallel became a *de facto* border despite a wartime declaration at the Cairo Conference and reaffirmation by the Potsdam Proclamation that Korean freedom would be restored. The Soviets set about the training of the North Korean Army, building a highly capable force around a hard core of 25,000 veterans of the Chinese Communist campaign in Manchuria. Mao had secured his victory over Chiang Kai Shek in 1949, thus rendering the Korean mercenaries redundant. The United States trained the significantly smaller South Korean Army but not in the comprehensive and dedicated manner in which the North Korean Army had been prepared to take over the militarily less capable South.

The UN Security Council reacted to the rapid gains of the North Koreans through their Resolution 82 of 1950 and two days later made recommendations that troops should be made available. The 70 year old General Douglas MacArthur was at that time commanding US Forces in the Far East and it was to him, on 28 June 1950, that President Harry S. Truman gave the order for the United States' *air* and *maritime* forces to support the South Koreans. The Administration aspired not to use ground forces because such a move represented a quantum leap in political risk-taking. It was only after a matter of days that it became evident that US ground forces would have to be committed. Meanwhile, in the UN Security Council, the members requested the United States to lead a unified command under a US commander under a UN flag. On 7 July 1950, President Truman appointed General MacArthur Commander-in-Chief, United Nations Command. Forty-eight of the then sixty members offered assistance while twenty-two states volunteered armed forces, of which fifteen ultimately supported UN military action in Korea. This was the earliest example of the UN establishing a *sanctioned* command, commanded and controlled by a 'framework' or 'lead' state. It also established a command principle which became more apparent in the post-1990 expeditionary period whereby the major shareholder in terms of risk and commitment would vote the majority of the stock. The United States provided fifty per cent of the land forces, eighty-six per cent of the naval forces and ninety-three per cent of the air forces.

When politicians and diplomats consider international military options there is, among the less experienced, an assumption of sameness among the national contributions or insufficient weighting given to the profound differences in terms of training standards, education, morale and commitment. For example, the reservoir of experienced American manpower available in 1945 had been depleted not just in size but also in military skills. Post-war recruitment emphasised the benefits of travel and learning a trade and neglected to point out, on occasions, the need to make the supreme sacrifice. After an armed conflict it is usual for the victor's ground forces to undergo a qualitative decline. The initial military contact made between the armies of a hardened North Korea and American reinforcements from a cosseted existence in Japan was, for the latter, a sobering experience. America, however, was less sensitive then vis-à-vis casualties than she is now. This caused some difficulties among lesser partners whose correspondingly smaller armies often comprised conscripts. Even in the 1990-91 Gulf Conflict, a major consideration of the commander of the British contingent was not to lose a substantial part of what represented a high proportion of the total force and its equipment.

It had been possible for the Security Council to avoid the Soviet veto due to a temporary boycott by the Soviet Permanent Representative, Jakob Malik, but, by virtue of his absence, it had not been possible to use the offices of the MSC to organise and supervise the UN's military response to the invasion of South Korea. Malik had been away from the Security Council since January 1950 but returned on 1 August 1950 to preside over the Council. From that point, the Security Council became ineffective. Power was delegated to a pliant General Assembly through the means of the Uniting For Peace Resolution in order to break the impasse over Korea. On only one other occasion was the General Assembly invited to overturn a veto by weight of numbers and that was in 1956 following the Suez fiasco.

As the Korean crisis intensified, it became evident that the UN had no political or strategic control over the United States. MacArthur, who was supposed to furnish the Security Council with situation reports, largely ignored UN Headquarters in New York, dealing instead directly with the Pentagon in Washington. In 1951 hearings before the Senate Committee on Armed Services and Foreign Affairs, the General announced his association with the UN as having been 'purely nominal... no direct connection whatsoever'. MacArthur's independent nature and right-wing inclinations had also given rise to increased concerns in a Democratic White House. His anti-Communist opinions were oft expressed but the Soviet Union, the political, military and economic sponsor of North Korea, was a nuclear power which the political Washington could not ignore. While China did not have a nuclear capability she had such a large quantity of disposable manpower that she represented a significant regional threat. One contemporary writer wrote that these differences in outlook caused: 'difficulties because of controversial decisions of military strategy and the laxity of US civilian control over General MacArthur. It also led to a situation where military operations thus became identified with the policy of the United States'.[6] British Prime Minister Clement Attlee's worry was due to both the absence of a clearly enunciated Korean strategy and concern about where a strong-willed, apparently out of control commander would lead his multinational forces. As the British Foreign Secretary explained in his cable to the British Ambassador in Washington:

> Our principal difficulty is General MacArthur. His policy is different from the UN. He seems to want war with China. We do not. It is no exaggeration to say that by his public utterances, he has weakened public confidence in this country and Western Europe in the quality of American political judgement and leadership.[7]

Britain's regional focus was particularly influenced by the continuing possession of her colony of Hong Kong. After the Americans had bombed the Yalu River power stations, Britain sought from her major partner greater political and military control over the course of a war she intended should remain a limited war. In that endeavour, as a lesser partner, she was partially successful: '...the Allies that Dean Acheson was able to line up, notably the United Kingdom, were able to influence American policy on the Korean War far out of proportion to their input on the battlefield'.[8] Even in 1950 it would have been possible to suggest that the day of the truly sovereign state was over although, as now, some states remained more sovereign than others.

By the mid 1950s there were only two remaining superpowers on the world stage, the United States and the Soviet Union. Despite Mao's victory in 1949, China's seat in the Security Council was occupied by the feeble Nationalist regime now confined to Formosa and a number of smaller islands in the South China Sea. Britain's and France's behaviour on the world stage was as though they were still great powers, but both would get their come-uppance in 1956 through an unlikely, temporary alliance of the Americans and Soviets. What we were witnessing was the exercise of Realist power play in a context of the survival of the fittest, ultimately won by the United States as evidenced by the conclusion of the Cold War.

The continual attempt to increase spheres of influence, to gain some advantage or concession, was played out in dangerous and conflictual circumstances. The participants were competitors in a game partly political, economic and military and it was known by its devotees as the Great Game. The pursuit of power between Britain and Russia in the Near and Middle East, an activity in which France was not a disinterested observer, was an important feature of conflict in the nineteenth and twentieth centuries. One of the last remnants of Anglo-French colonial power in the Near East was the Suez Canal. On 26 July 1956, President Nasser of Egypt made an announcement in Cairo that, as he spoke, the Suez Canal was being taken over and nationalised. The jointly owned Anglo-French canal and its equipment were due to be handed over gratis to Egypt in 1968 on the expiration of the original hundred year old concession. The Suez Canal Company's administrative offices were in Paris but it had been established under Egyptian law with its head office in Egypt. The Egyptian president had therefore nationalised an Egyptian company. Nasser advised that compensation would be paid based on the company's value on the stock market, but such payment would only be made upon the surrender of all the company's assets.

British Prime Minister Anthony Eden's obsessive view that Nasser was becoming a dangerous, destabilising force in the Middle East was a view shared with Washington. Dangerous obsessions have a habit of appearing in modern conflict and can have a seriously adverse effect on the political and military decision-making processes. President John F. Kennedy became obsessed with Castro, Bush with Saddam Hussein, Boutros Boutros-Ghali and Albright with General Aideed of Somalia and Albright with President Milosevic. The American Administration had earlier withdrawn financial support of the prestigious Aswan Dam project. The Baghdad Pact, founded in 1954, included Britain, Pakistan, Iran, Iraq and Turkey. The United States was an associate member of the Pact yet was represented on the economic and defence sub-committees. Ostensibly, the Baghdad Pact was an anti-Soviet alliance aimed at preventing Soviet expansionism and at protecting the Middle East's oil wealth. From the British position, however, the Pact was very much an anti-Nasser instrument. It was also a device of the Great Game. The Soviet Union was sympathetic to the nationalist aspirations of the Egyptians to a degree not reflected in Central and Eastern Europe. A rising Soviet academic devoted his doctoral dissertation to Nasser. His name was Yevgeni Primakov. Eden had not been impressed by Nasser whom he regarded as another Hitler or Mussolini threatening British interests. Nasser went on to wreck the Baghdad Pact and used his influence on the young King of Jordan to dismiss Glubb Pasha (Sir John Bagot), the British commander of the Arab Legion. During the currency of the previous Attlee government, Mohammed Mossadeq nationalised British oil interests in Iran. Now, Nasser was imitating that affront to Britain's prestige and position in the Middle East.

The British Cabinet had made an early decision to regain the Suez Canal from Egypt. Although France was preoccupied with events in Algeria, she was of a like mind. But not all of Eden's ministers were pro-intervention. Anthony Nutting wrote:

> My suggestion that at least the Foreign Office legal adviser, Sir Gerald Fitzmaurice should be brought in on a matter which involved taking the law into our own hands met with the flattest of negatives. 'Fitz is the last person I want consulted', Eden retorted. 'The lawyers are always against us doing anything. For God's sake keep them out of it. This is a political affair'.[9]

A secret meeting at Sèvres on 22 and 24 October 1956 was attended by representatives of the British, French and Israeli governments. Those attending the meeting endeavoured to have Egypt 'set up' so as to lend legitimacy to the proposed intervention. It was proposed by the three parties to give Egypt (and Israel) what proved to be, for the former, an impossible ultimatum - to cease hostilities and to withdraw ten miles from the canal. Nasser's predictable refusal provided Britain and France with what would be argued to be their justification for intervening. (A similar ploy was used against Milosevic to justify intervention in Kosovo.) 'Our intervention would be defensible in international law; for we should be intervening to prevent interference with the free flow of traffic through the canal, which was an international necessity.'[10] Fitzmaurice warned those who might wield influence over the Cabinet that armed intervention would be contrary to international law. The future international judgement that the Suez intervention was an illegal act was made without the awareness of the secret connivance at Sèvres. It is the fact that military intervention will invariably stretch the understanding of international law or breach it that is a conspiracy-rich environment. States invariably wish to be seen as acting within the law.

A high price was paid for that ill-advised intervention. Britain suffered her greatest humiliation since the war in the Far East. A run on the pound occurred, which the USA proposed to allow to continue until all the interventionists agreed to withdraw. Throughout the Middle East, British influence and authority were undermined, not least in Iraq where the pro-British government was overthrown. The United States, in a providentially opportunistic and systematic move, filled the vacuum created by the demise of Anglo-French fortunes in the Middle East. Concurrently, in Europe, the Soviet Union had the benefit of the diversion of the Suez affair to put down the Hungarian uprising.

The ramification of Suez was to see two weary Titans fall out from the line of march, leaving the United States and the Soviet Union to attempt to steal a march over one another. What the world was seeing now was, firstly, important events dominated by the superpowers within spheres of influence, meaning the external domination within a region by an external power and, secondly, low key events in world affairs which fell under the loose management of neutral and non-aligned states. Among the more stable regimes post-1945 were those dominated by one or more of the superpowers. The new bilateral relationship and the development of recognised spheres of influence should, in theory, have taken those areas out of the competition. That was not the case of Cuba, 1962.

Cuba produced a classic scenario for the study of the decision-making processes. The leading work is Graham Allison's *Essence of Decision.* Allison wrote how the decision-making process could be explained in simple Realist terms in so far as the Soviets put missiles into Cuba in furtherance of their own national interest and had therefore acted rationally. Similarly, the USA had made rational decisions based upon the threat posed by the missiles. Washington analysed the options, made calculations in the form of an appreciation of the situation and acted upon the resultant plan. The Cuban Missile Crisis was essentially resolved through the realisation of the parties that it was more important for the US to have the missiles removed from Cuba than for the Soviet Union to keep them there. In both the Berlin and Cuba crises the winner was the power which made the shrewdest and most imaginative assessment of the adversary's will in a particular situation.[11] However, Allison also suggests that the manner in which the crisis was managed could be explained as an intervention of bureaucratic politics. Examining what happened in 1962 could be argued not as rational decision-making but as the interplay of the separate interests of bureaucratic organisations. There is therefore the pursuit of the player's interest rather than the national interest. Rational choice can be subordinated through political evolution to the obsession, whim or interest of a key bureaucratic player.[12]

In October 1962, US reconnaissance flights first produced incontrovertible evidence that Soviet intermediate ballistic missiles were being installed on the island of Cuba. Photographs revealed that some were already *in situ* while others were *en route* aboard Soviet ships. Given the historic Monroe Doctrine, enunciated to warn Europe away from ambitions in the Americas, Nikita Khrushchev's initiative seems at first sight difficult to comprehend. The Soviet Union also had a Doctrine to describe their own sphere of influence and the limited sovereignty of those within it, although it was not until 12 November 1968 that it was spelt out. The Brezhnev Doctrine was applied as a rationale for the 1979 intervention in Afghanistan. Although Afghanistan had historically been an aspiration of the Tsars in their Great Game, its doubtful place within the Soviet sphere of influence undermined the justification for Soviet intervention. The Soviets' principal concern was that the development of Muslim fundamentalism, as seen in Iran and Afghanistan, might percolate through to the southern Muslim republics in the USSR. At the Fifth Polish Party Congress, Leonid Brezhnev declared that 'when a threat to the cause of Socialism' arises in a given country, 'it becomes not only a problem of the people of the country concerned, but also a common problem and the concern of all Socialist countries'.

But America had a young and untried President. Robert Thompson has suggested that if Nixon had been President, Khrushchev would not have made a move on Cuba.[13] Nevertheless, the Soviet threat was something that US strategy found untenable. The legal arguments did not rise to much prominence because decisions ultimately were based almost exclusively upon a political rationale. From a technical point of view, Cuba's action in putting missiles on her own sovereign territory did not contravene international law. It could be said, and it was said, that US missiles in Turkey represented a similar threat to the USSR. There is no law to prevent Cuba entering into an alliance with the USSR nor one which places limitations on the type of weapons Cuba could deploy. What the USSR had done, however, was politically unacceptable to the USA for it threatened to destabilise the balance of power in a particularly sensitive sphere of US interest. A blockade was imposed around Cuba but, since the term has warlike connotations, the action was described more passively as a 'quarantine'.

At the time of the Cuban crisis in 1962, Dean Acheson made a typically Realist comment which still has resonance today:

> The propriety of the Cuban Quarantine is not a legal issue. The power, position and prestige of the United States had been challenged by another state, and law simply does not deal with such questions of ultimate power - power that comes close to the sources of sovereignty.[14]

The eminent American international lawyer, Professor Henkin, reacted to Acheson's statement by commenting that 'such a view would indeed be a negation of law that no legal system could tolerate'.[15] In fact, the selection of the less confrontational of the plausible options - to invade, launch an air strike or blockade - had much to do with a legalistic rationale. Similarly, legal arguments were adduced to justify the action to NATO and to the Organisation of American States. 'It demonstrates', wrote Schachter, 'that states require a basis of legitimacy to justify their action to their citizens and even more, to other states whose cooperation or acquiescence is desired'.[16]

As a comment on the Cuban Missile Crisis, Professor Henkin wrote: 'But by 1962, in Latin America surely, the day of unilateral intervention by the United States seemed over, replaced by collective judgement if not by truly collective action'.[17] Although, progressively, this observation did prove to be generally correct, it did not happen immediately. The USA intervened unilaterally in the Dominican Republic in 1965 on the whim of President Lyndon Johnson, because someone had shot at the US ambassador. The underlying reason had been a typically US fear of leftish regimes, as would be the case in the 1983 Grenada intervention. In the former case, however, there was no serious attempt to legitimise the intervention because Johnson believed that what happened in the Dominican Republic could not be of concern to any other important state.

Cuba showed that international order was subjected to the influences both of the balance of terror and the balance of power. The two principal nuclear powers recognised that the prospect of nuclear war was so ghastly, they used their power to ensure they did not seek recourse to the ultimate weapon system but also actively engaged in the prevention of other aspiring states from becoming nuclear powers. America's growing preoccupation with South American politics meant that she was unable to extend the Pax Americana throughout the world and, for that reason, sought the creation of a balance of power through détente with the Soviet Union and called the People's Republic of China to the high table of power, to the disadvantage of China's Nationalists. Such a display of pragmatic politics did not mean, however, that America and the Soviet Union could resist point-scoring or more or less covertly frustrating the political goals of their opposite number in a new chapter of the Great Game.

The superpowers believed that they could control the lesser states within their hegemony. When this proved not to be the case, the automatic assumption was that of the devious interference of the other superpower. But that was also not always true. In the lead-up to the 1973 Middle East war, the Soviet Union supported the Arab states against an Israel supported by the United States. As became clear, neither of the client states was answerable to its respective superpower sponsor. Détente had not been a good experience for Egypt who, unable to obtain defensive weapons from the Soviet Union in 1972, asked the superpower to leave Egypt. Egypt's President Anwar Sadat decided that the only way he was likely to derive the requisite power and weaponry within the region was through the creation of a crisis which risked undermining superpower détente.

At the outbreak of the Arab-Israeli war or *Yom Kippur*, both superpowers acted in harmony through the Security Council to impose a ceasefire upon Egypt and Israel. Israel has never been the most dedicated observer of UN Security Council Resolutions which again, on this occasion, both she and Egypt ignored. The Egyptian Army overreached and found itself threatened with annihilation. The Soviet Union came to the aid of its client in the UN with an ultimatum; either the UN act multilaterally to enforce the ceasefire or the Soviet Union would act unilaterally. The United States responded by ratcheting up its nuclear alert in a regional crisis which undermined the superpower management of international affairs through détente. Détente would evaporate in the early 1980s with the onset of the second phase of the Cold War.

The competition among the superpowers to bring non-aligned, friendly nations under their respective umbrellas worked against the superpowers because it gave would-be clients the leverage to trade one superpower off against the other. Some who had strategic assets which the superpowers coveted found themselves in a strong position from which to strike bargains. Whereas in the 1950s-60s arms transfers had given the superpowers the upper hand over regional clients, that situation began to change from the 1970s onwards when the emergence of a buyers' market reversed the leverage position. What really frustrated the superpower-client relationship was the former's eventual securing of its goal, very often after long, patient and expensive negotiations, only to find the head of government with whom the deal had been struck removed in a *coup d'état.*

Vietnam was never within the sphere of interest of the United States. Washington's attention was held by the progress the Communists were making there and elsewhere in the South East Asia region. Proponents of the domino theory explained how, if Vietnam should fall to the Communists, there would be a knock-on effect whereby all the neighbouring states would also fall. America's engagement in the conflict followed the traditional, three stage pattern of the provision of material and financial support, the provision of military advisers and the intervenors becoming the dominant element in another power's civil war. Understandably, the Soviets and Chinese did all they could to thwart

America's political and military success, even though there has been a traditional enmity between China and Vietnam. One lesson from Vietnam was, despite the great wealth of disposable military power, it was insufficient to guarantee success against the most inferior opposition. The USA dropped a greater number of bombs on North and South Vietnam than in the European theatre during the Second World War. The 200,000 casualties the USA suffered in Vietnam, including 58,000 dead,[18] were greater than during the entire course of the Pacific War. The war cost $190 billion. The effect the legacy of Vietnam had upon domestic public attitudes severely circumscribes military options to this day - particularly the deployment of ground forces. The American press is widely regarded as having been responsible for negative attitudes towards the Vietnam conflict but, in reality, they were reflecting the views of the increasing numbers of communities that had suffered losses, that politically and militarily the Vietnam intervention was not working and could not work. One truism that has remained in America's collective political memory is that elections are not *won* on foreign policy issues but they can be *lost* on foreign policy issues. Most American leaders, from F.D. Roosevelt onwards, have been so sensitive to public attitudes towards foreign engagement that they have been led by opinion polls rather than set the mood, tone and leadership for the country.[19]

Understandably, the USA was not prepared to allow the Soviet Union an easy ride in Afghanistan. The Mujahadeen were supplied with money and weapons. The then Soviet Armed Forces comprised 60 per cent conscripts. As casualties began to mount over the 10-year war, mothers who lost what was in many circumstances an only son, agitated to end a war not seen as being in the Soviets' interest. The intervention was finally drawn to a conclusion by the 1988 Geneva Conference. 13,310 Soviet troops died in Afghanistan. The politicians and military vowed Afghanistan would never happen again and blamed Brezhnev who had died in 1982. But then there was Chechnya I 1994-96 and Chechnya II 1999-2000, part of the Former Soviet Union's (FSU's) Near Abroad and most decidedly within the FSU's perception of her sphere of interest. All these aforementioned military interventions and limited wars occurred at a different level from the concurrent traditional peacekeeping activities of neutral and non-aligned states.

It was in 1956 that peacekeeping procedures were standardised into a format that is recognisable today, to be improved upon in 1973 in the matter of command and control when a peacekeeping force was deployed into Egypt and Sinai following the war of *Yom Kippur*. The precedent was established that peacekeepers were not normally drawn from among the permanent membership of the Security Council and they confined the use of lethal force to self-defence. There were two implicit understandings: first, peacekeepers were to act *impartially* at all times and second, their presence required the *consent* of the parties to the dispute. Peacekeeping therefore set out as an interstate phenomenon on behalf of established governments or regimes who comprehended the meanings of impartiality and consent. The temperament of the blue berets was more important than their military skills; their patience and non-threatening presence enabled them to hold a line until a political solution could be found to the local difficulty. (As the UN Force in Cyprus (UNFICYP), set up in 1974 shows, political solutions can take a long time to be reached.) It was not long, however, before traditional Chapter VI peacekeeping became compromised as the Force in the Congo was used to coerce Katanga back under Congolese national authority. From that point, the obligatory abstention from the use of weapons other than in self-defence - in the growing number of environments where the settlement of disputes by armed force had become the norm - became increasingly difficult to sustain.

Peacekeeping evolved as a low-grade, zero-conflict, military operation *sponsored* by the United Nations under the aegis of what would become the Department of Peacekeeping Operations (DPKO). The DPKO is the operational arm of the UN Secretary-General, responsible for the day-to-day management of peacekeeping operations. Although national contingents were under the nominal command of a designated UN commander who reported to the DPKO or its predecessor, the federal nature of traditional peacekeeping meant that national commanders often consulted their own governments before anything other than routine operations were undertaken. This structure could not function where traditional peacekeepers might find themselves in hostile, complicated environments where the military of the host and neighbouring states enjoyed a higher level of military skill and competence than they. As the nature of UN-sponsored operations began to change, the UN found it had neither the cohesion nor the expertise to cope.

'Six, yea seven' was a Hebrew phrase understood to mean an indefinite number, as is evident in Job Chapter 5 verse 19: 'He (God) shall deliver thee in six troubles, yea in seven...' In modern common usage, to be 'at sixes and sevens' has two meanings. Spoken of *things*, it means confusion, and spoken of *persons* it means in disagreement or even hostility.[20]

Preservation of national, institutional and individual interests which spawn so much disagreement and at times the hostile reluctance to embrace reform, the insistence of clinging to the status quo and not desiring to differentiate between peacekeeping and intervention are all symptomatic of a society at Chapters VIs and VIIs with itself. The device through which order might be brought to an environment in which disorder prevails is tested, tried and relevant military doctrine.

3 Doctrine for Expeditionary Conflict

The British have had a traditional disdain for doctrine, regarding it as prejudicial to their intuitive and innovative spirit. If we look back to the middle of the nineteenth century (1859), to identify the centres of military thinking, we find that approximately half the literature was produced in Germany, a quarter in France and one per cent in Britain.[1] In 1924, J.F.C. Fuller recalled a conversation with the Chief of the Imperial General Staff, who 'considered it to be contrary to military discipline for any officer on the active list to write on military subjects. I hear, on good authority that he is against the creation of a War College'.[2] War Colleges came, but their effectiveness was brought into question. 'Since the advent of war schools native genius has been crippled by pedantry, not because sound military education is in itself detrimental (such a contention would be absurd), but because the easiest thing to do in a school is to copy the past and the past is something dead and gone, and frequently a thing which was misbegotten.'[3]

Today, there is still the thread of anti-intellectualism running through British military thought processes and too frequently a continuing failure, in Fuller's words, to 'probe into the viscera of living war'. Where there is a poverty of knowledge there remains the tendency to copy the thinking of others, not just the past but also the present, without applying the requisite tests and challenges to that plagiarised thinking. There are few military enterprises more personality dominated than doctrine and, of the moral qualities, personality traits can lead to calamitous difficulty.

The purpose of doctrine[4] is 'to establish the framework of understanding of the approach to warfare in order to provide the foundation for its practical application'.[5] The formulation of Doctrine should follow three evolutionary stages, namely *debate, decision* and *execution.* There is an unbreakable link between doctrine and training since commanders are expected to train their men in accordance with current doctrine. Although the British Army had this tradition of doing 'what we thought', a great deal of doctrinal guidance was to be found in what were the building blocks of military doctrine, namely the training manuals. 'The Infantry Battalion in Battle' and 'Keeping the Peace Parts 1 and 2' contained very much more doctrine than the doctrinal cynic would have cared to admit. The British and French ways in counter-insurgency operations were framed very much through their respective experiences in policing their colonial empires. Substantial numbers of British and French troops have been sacrificed in the past in distant colonial territories. The reason the British and French approaches to low level conflict are fundamentally different from that of the Americans is that the latter became the world's pivotal, though not fully hegemonic, power without the experience of policing an empire.

It would be reasonable to suggest that future military interventions launched in the interests of peace and international security will continue to involve the armed forces of one or more of the principal interventionist states: the United States, the United Kingdom and France. The culture, traditions and methods of operations of the military components of these states will conspire to create some difficulties in the maintenance of consensus, cohesion and cooperation within a coalition. The sensible use of boundaries to mark the delineation of respective areas of responsibility can overcome many of these states' idiosyncrasies. However, there is one aspect arising from military operations which separates the United States from the UK and France and that is something described here as the body bag syndrome.

Today, none of the three states is blasé towards casualties but, for reasons already adduced, the United Kingdom and France have a relatively more relaxed attitude towards the prospect of taking casualties than is the case in the USA. The British public will not condone pointless casualties but they do see the function of the military as having to fight and view casualties as an occasional, regrettable inevitability. Since 1945 there have been at least 16 conflicts in which 2,724 British servicemen have been killed on duty. France is more reserved in her attitude to casualties arising among conscripts and has ensured that her ground interventionist forces comprise regular soldiers. Only naval conscripts may participate in interventionist operations. Paris is in the process of phasing out conscription with a view to reducing the size of her armed forces from 500,000 to 350,000. The process will be completed in the year 2002.

While America's casualty aversion is partly political in so far as it involves risks, and politicians who desire to be re-elected avoid risks, it is also inextricably tied in with the doctrine of warfighting. The traditional function of America's armed forces has been to fight America's wars or, more precisely, two Major Regional Conflicts (MRC). That there has not been a declaration of war since 1945 suggests that there is some new, original thinking to be done, particularly since the end of the Cold War occurred over ten years ago. But still, it would be true to say that the emphasis has not shifted substantially from the notion that the function of troops is to deter rather than to be used. There was, for example, the salutary lesson to emerge from the Divisional Phase of the Advanced Warfighting Experiment at Fort Hood, Texas in November 1997. During this Command Post Exercise, the 4th US Division suffered 40-50 per cent casualties fighting a Combined Arms Army in NATO's Central Region without raising an eyelid. Yet on real operations, as in Rwanda, there was that unofficial aim posted in the US Army tactical headquarters in Kigali 'to suffer no casualties'.

The question to be addressed is, why is it acceptable to suffer unlimited casualties when fighting the nation's 'wars' but not in pursuit of a national interest during Implementation Operations? There is a difference of political perception between the two cases but also the reality that what the 4th Division was engaged in was make-believe, something that is not going to happen. Forces in being are there to be used. If they are not, they lose their cutting edge. The truth is that, in a democracy, it matters not greatly the quality of a state's armed forces for that, by itself, will never overcome the absence of political will. The answer to the question asked by French General Philippe Morillon cannot be avoided indefinitely. 'What good', he asked, 'are members of an armed force who are permitted to kill but not to die?'

The United States still has such a wealth of disposable power that she can not be described as the latest of the weary Titans, but she can be reasonably described as a wary Titan. America is too important, has too many unique capabilities and assets to take a back seat in the unavoidable necessity for the establishment of world order. There has recently been some beneficial research at West Point analysing the intellectual muddle that exists between the concept of winning the Nation's Wars and what is described as Implementation Operations. In the conflict spectrum, Implementation Operations fit between traditional Chapter VI peacekeeping and traditional Chapter VII military intervention or limited war. We will expand upon these three distinct areas later in the chapter. From the chart below at Figure 3.1[6] it can be seen that Washington's politicians want to have their cake and eat it; senior military leaders are not unanimously disposed towards Implementation Operations, while the mid and lower officer corps, many of whom have no Cold War experience, do not see Fighting the Nation's Wars as a credible option.

The generals' continuing support for the maintenance of full general war capabilities is not simply a reflection of military conservatism among a group wedded to the concept of big wars and the dangers of the long peace. There is an undeniable dichotomy here. It is true that armed forces trained to the standard required for big wars can be retrained to fight lesser wars with little difficulty. However, the reverse is not true. If a state allows its forces to be trained and equipped and permanently committed to lower levels of conflict there is no easy, inexpensive way back to fight at higher levels of intensity. High technology plays a part in the dichotomy because its high cost and entry into service has been at the expense of manpower. Yet high intensity conflict is not as manpower-intensive as Implementation Operations where high technology cannot be utilised to best effect. The danger in such a high proportion of defence expenditure being allocated to platforms and means irrelevant to Implementation Operations is that funds will not exist to provide the equipment and training that is required for the type of operations to which western forces are well nigh exclusively being committed. One important first step is to cease describing expeditionary conflict in the minimalist term of Operations Other Than War (OOTW) because it is going to be the principal form of armed conflict for the foreseeable future. This struggle to find a balance between resources, capabilities and obligations in not new. The tension between apparently irreconcilable requirements had been debated in 1879:

AN INTELLECTUAL MUDDLE		
FIGHTING AND WINNING THE NATION'S WARS – OR MILITARY OPERATIONS OTHER THAN WAR (MOOTW)		
	Big Army, Big War	MOOTW
Political Leaders	Yes	Yes
Military Leaders	Yes	No … Perhaps Yes (1997)
Mid-, Lower- Officer Corps	No, Not Credible	Yes

Figure 3.1

> The most perfect expression of our military wants is a small army in time of peace, a large army in times of war, and yet a larger army for purposes of defence; and yet what is wanted are not three armies but one.[7]

The truth is that technology has not produced the anticipated manpower savings. A core reason is that it attracts a heavy training bill. Commanders interviewed at both Forts Irwin and Hood in the USA were still inclined towards the belt and braces. The map board was still in evidence alongside the computers in the Tactical Operations Centers (TOCs). 'We may be unwise to depend too much upon technology', admitted a brigade commander. 'It could be that we no longer have the time to teach basic infantry skills. Soldiers may soon forget to use the compass because they have become dependent upon GPS (global positioning system). But GPS can be jammed.' One of the lessons of the Gulf Conflict is that a lesser opponent will not engage the west in a full-blown conventional conflict but in asymmetric conflict. It is because the effect of armed conflict has become relatively less severe that the likelihood of its occurrence has increased.

AN ANALYSIS OF U.S. CASUALTY AVERSION		
	IS THE U.S. PUBLIC CASUALTY AVERSE?	WHY?
Political Leaders	Yes	Intervention is High Risk
Military Leaders	Echo	High Risk; Less Preferred Form of War
Junior Military Officers	No	Willing to Sacrifice
American Public	No	Will Accept, Under Two Conditions

Figure 3.2

An analysis by the same team, of US casualty aversion (please refer to Figure 3.2)[8] reveals that America's military leadership is out of step with the public and junior officers in that they echo the political aversion to casualties. The reasons why this might happen are many and diverse. The senior military are beholden to their political masters for the allocation of their Service's budgets and, understandably, those who belong to a profession where obligatory retirement comes relatively early in life will have their own next step uppermost in their minds. The political/military divide became apparent during disagreement as to what to do with the 24 AH-64 Apache attack helicopters sent to Kosovo. Junior commanders insisted that the use of the helicopters would have saved lives but senior officers in the Pentagon and White House politicians refused to countenance the use of the helicopters for fear of attracting casualties. 'Instead', wrote the *Washington Post*'s Dana Priest, 'the vaunted helicopters came to symbolise everything wrong with the Army as it enters the twenty-first century: its inability to move quickly; its resistance to change; its obsession with casualties; its post-Cold War identity crisis'.[9]

The two conditions under which the American public will accept US military casualties are, first, they have to be convinced by their political leaders that the operation is in America's national interest and, second, there should be a political consensus among political leaders to see the operation through to a successful conclusion.[10] What is interesting in the international environment is that the public do not identify the people of the belligerent state as their enemy but rather the leadership of that state or sub state. The public also react to casualties on *both* sides. Public support in the Falklands War and the Gulf Conflict dipped on the occasion of the sinking of the *Belgrano* and the 'Turkey Shoot' which brought to an end the first phase of the allies' conflict with Iraq. Potential opponents will be able to manipulate this sensitivity to their advantage. It is of interest that the sinking of *HMS Sheffield* in the Falklands War caused British public opinion to harden in favour of the war, not against.

The depth of America's problem came into focus during the overt phase of her involvement in Vietnam, 1965-75, a time nevertheless when her principal commitment remained with NATO. One of the key indicators used to persuade the politicians and the public that the war was progressing in the right direction was the body count of the enemy. The body count also served as a reassuring comparator to be set against the increasing number of American casualties as exemplified by media images of body bags often stacked like cordwood at airstrips for repatriation. Firepower was used as by tradition to reduce risks to own troops. (The first city to have to be destroyed to be saved by the Americans in modern warfare was not in Vietnam but Manila in the Philippines in 1945.) Vietnam became an expensive and humiliating sideshow, never again to be repeated.

Conceptually, America intended to concentrate upon fighting the nation's wars and tried to resist forays into expeditionary conflict. It was easier for one of the then two major world powers to establish as an objective than to achieve in practice. On 23 October 1983, a truck bomb destroyed a USMC accommodation block in Beirut, killing 241 US Marines, the heaviest loss of life suffered by the Marines in one day since Iwo Jima. On 28 November 1984, the Secretary of Defense, Caspar Weinberger, outlined six major tests to be applied when considering the deployment of US combat forces abroad. The first was that combat forces should not be committed abroad unless 'the particular engagement or occasion is deemed *vital* to our national interest or that of our allies'. Nowadays, the word 'vital' is not the determinant it used to be.

What began to emerge was an understanding that American lives must not be risked on non-'warfighting' operations. There developed a feeling of military impotence among armed forces who were not to suffer casualties. 'For pay and other benefits we expect these people (the military) to risk - and sometimes lose - their lives to do what we will not or cannot do ourselves', protested a *Washington Post* journalist in December 1992. 'We have a volunteer military.'[11] The American General Johnston, commanding the United Nations Task Force (UNITAF) in Somalia in 1993, is alleged to have negotiated a no-casualty withdrawal agreement from Mogadishu with General Aideed but, as will be demonstrated, the follow-on force, UNOSOM II, was not so lucky.

On coalition operations, comparisons are always inevitable and often invidious. Of their operation in Rwanda, the French commander, Major-General Lafourcade, said: 'My men had no helmets, no flak jackets, and kept their weapons out of sight'. The excessively protected American forces and their ultra caution prompted one correspondent to observe:

> ..... when women were driving through the countryside, alone, as were the rest of the NGO personnel, one begins to wonder whether or not this particular application of 'security' is appropriate. Many recall the curious juxtaposition between unarmed NGOs going anywhere they wanted and the armed-to-the-teeth (US) military having to be in before dark while not being allowed in the refugee camps at all.[12]

This author can recall being met at Sarajevo airport in the late summer of 1996 by a British Army, female Captain in skirt and blouse, and an American military driver in full combats, flak jacket and helmet. In coalitions, comparisons are inevitable. In 1999 Bosnia, British troops could be seen patrolling in their area of responsibility on bicycles while the Americans were still committed to a full personal protection policy. The point is that these limitations placed upon military performance are unnecessary, misconstrued, and embarrass the military. There is substantial evidence to support the West Point studies.

In a 1995 poll conducted by Maryland University, people were asked what their reaction would be to seeing 'the bodies of Americans on television'. Only 16 per cent said that they would want to withdraw all American troops.[13] The assertion that the American public will not stand for casualties on Implementation Operations is not borne out by the evidence. The sensitivity seems to be among the ranks of politicians with little or no military experience. The 1989 Panama intervention, for example, witnessed more fatalities than in Mogadishu but it caused little domestic consternation because President George Bush, a veteran of the Second World War, did not allow it to do so. It is true, however, that when Madeleine Albright was US Permanent Representative at the UN she had disagreements with General Colin Powell, the then Chairman of the Joint Chiefs of Staff Committee, over his reluctance to support the deployment of American forces on UN operations. That was certainly a crucial view of a crucial General in a crucial position but, at that level, Generals are virtually politicians. The presence of the political sensitivity is borne out by a RAND study:

> The simplest explanation consistent with the data is that support for US military operations and the willingness to tolerate casualties are based upon a sensible weighing of benefits and costs that is influenced heavily by consensus (or its absence) among political leaders.[14]

There is evidence that the display of an undue sensitivity to casualties can stimulate a self-fulfilling prophecy in that opponents will see this weakness as the intervenor's centre of gravity, which they will attack with the express intention of taking lives in order to force a withdrawal. The *Interahamwe* forced the Belgians out of Kigali in such a manner, just as Aideed had forced the Americans out of Mogadishu. If there is an assumption that inflicting casualties upon an interventionist force is a means of achieving the withdrawal of that force, then a policy which appears intolerant of casualties arguably places troops at greater risk than they might otherwise be. Sensitivity to taking casualties has an undue influence upon military operations. *The Sunday Times* encapsulated this particular situation at the time when the arrest of indicted war criminals in Bosnia was being examined closely:

> In a domestic jurisdiction, we would never accept the rationale that the police could not apprehend armed criminals for fear of risk to their own men. IFOR, the NATO-led peace implementation forces in Bosnia, have suffered fewer casualties in seven months than the New York Police could expect to sustain in as many days.[15]

The Bosnia Implementation Force (IFOR) and Stabilisation Force (SFOR) operations underlined the depth of the problem of the body bag syndrome. Britain and France consistently stated their position that their presence in Bosnia was conditional upon a continuing US presence. In deferring to a US lead, Britain and France placed themselves under the same level of vulnerability as that affecting the USA. If, during the course of the operation, and as occurred in Mogadishu in 1993, US forces suffered levels of casualties that were unacceptable to Washington, British and French troops would join the Americans in the withdrawal from the Theatre of Operations. It is not a very reassuring situation - politically or militarily.

In the foregoing circumstances, the potential risks suggest the adoption of a policy of non-involvement in other states' affairs but, sometimes, responsible states find it impossible to act out the role of disinterested bystander. If forces are to be committed, it has to be understood that their function is to fight: there can be no half measures or wishful thinking. Today it seems so often that we are attempting to nail jelly to the wall and miss the certainties and the predictabilities that were so reassuringly evident in the recent past. The central problem lies in finding a middle way between those larger states who have the capabilities but so often not the intentions and a United Nations that has the intentions but little by way of capability.

In the heady days after the Gulf Conflict there was no shortage of states volunteering their armed forces to serve under the UN - as many as 80,000 servicemen were engaged on military operations on behalf of the UN. There was, however, a paradox. The likelihood of the early repetition of the Chapter VII Limited War type conflict in the mould of Korea 1950-53 and the Gulf 1990-91 was remote, and examples of traditional Chapter VI peacekeeping were also few and far between. The question therefore is, on what basis and under what understanding was the UN employing so many servicemen? The answer is that a gap, a large gap, a Grey Area, had opened up between the norms and understanding of Chapters VI and VII. As a consequence, the normal functions of peacekeeping and military intervention were extended and drawn into the vacuum, which colloquially became known as Chapter VI½ although this is not the meaning intended by Dag Hammarskjøld, the man who coined the phrase. The UN therefore found itself in a situation of needing to sponsor or sanction military operations in a broad new band of military activity for which there were neither rules nor doctrine.

It became apparent to a small number of observers that a review of the UN's 'peacekeeping' *modus operandi* was overdue. There was no overt intention to marginalise the UN, but rather to make it more relevant and better able to respond to contemporary challenges. As Sir Brian Urquhart said, 'The United Nations has many shortcomings and is weak in many respects, but it is still the best, perhaps the only framework in which we can try to develop some kind of effective world order'.[16] However, the UN, 'the palace of the status quo[17]... insisting on using systems where they cannot be used', was unable and unwilling to reform or re-order its military operations. Peacekeepers in New York still sought visibility in environments where they were not qualified to be. There was an urgent need for a positive external stimulus. Unfortunately the stimulus that did come was extremely negative but welcomed in New York because it enabled the Organisation to paper over the wide cracks in its façade.

The adoption of a timely, realist doctrine was frustrated by the UK's Headquarters Doctrine and Training developing in 1991 an essentially idealist doctrine described as Wider Peacekeeping. 'I believe', said Sir Brian Urquhart, 'that the doctrine of Wider Peacekeeping is very misleading. It is dangerous nonsense.'[18] Conceptually, the doctrine was out of date before its presentation, thereby seemingly supporting something J.F.C. Fuller once wrote:

> The military man is the most conservative creature on earth. It is really dangerous to give him an idea because he will not adopt it until it is obsolete and then will not abandon it until it has nearly destroyed him.

Chastened by the criticism, Wider Peacekeeping was quietly dropped and resurrected in a second generation form, Peace Support Operations (PSO) which retained the logical holes of the former.

It was self-evident to those self-interested parties supporting the furtherance of peacekeeping that they had to demonstrate that the two core components of peacekeeping, *consent* and *impartiality*, its DNA, were transferable into the fields of enhanced military activity. While consent and impartiality may be understood in societies which have established the place of the umpire, as in cricket or baseball, they are not concepts universally understood by the parties in the conflicts in which interventionist states will be called upon to intervene. We cannot apply our perceptions and standards universally to every environment with the conviction that they are bound to be appropriate. The inapplicability of consent in operations beyond peacekeeping is receiving wider recognition, albeit grudgingly and with little positive application to actual events. In intra-state environments, consent tends not to be a constant but a variable. And as laudable as operating impartially may be, it is a two-sided consideration. It is one thing for interventionists to believe they are acting impartially but quite another to convince the parties to the conflict that that is the case. Political events prior to military intervention may well damn the soldiers and present them as partial actors. The EC's early recognition of Croatia during the Bosnia crisis, for example, meant that forces from EC countries would not be recognised as impartial by the Serbs. Humanitarian aid delivered to one party in the conflict is a less overt form of partiality in comparison to that of arming and equipping the Muslim forces in Bosnia post Dayton.

The term 'Peacekeeping' is routinely applied to environments where there is no peace to be kept and the substitution of the term 'peace enforcement' for military intervention when not all military interventions will have as their aim the enforcing of peace.

'Peace Enforcement' therefore is a misnomer, for very rarely will it be possible to enforce peace. Organisations or states with such an intention through interest or conscience will require a clear understanding as to *how* peace is to be enforced, *by whom* and for *how long*. The decision-making process will be dominated by three considerations: low risk, low cost and short duration.

The examination of operations in Somalia (UNOSOM II), Rwanda (UNAMIR), Bosnia pre and post Dayton, and Kosovo, indicates that the historic concepts of *consent* and *impartiality* are virtually untransferable into the Grey Area because they relate only to benign peacekeeping environments. Analysis of the data indicates the emergence of new Grey Area criteria, among which, for example, might be the need for intervention forces to be *independent* of action in the process of securing *leverage* over hostile parties.

The 1994 Rwanda Crisis was unique for in a country the size of Wales or Maryland there were three separate, ongoing, military operations. France took part unilaterally in what was, in effect, a Chapter VII operation. The United States also entered the fray unilaterally, on a mission 'which is not peacekeeping (but) an humanitarian operation'. The UN did insert a force, the United Nations Advisory Mission in Rwanda (UNAMIR). A 400-strong Belgian Parachute Battalion that had been in a quiet area of Somalia on a Chapter VII mandate in 1993, found itself in 1994 in genocidal Kigali with a Chapter VI mandate. For the UN commander, the situation in Kigali was an impossible mission because he was unable to offer protection to the minority Tutsis if it depended upon the continuing consent and cooperation of the majority, belligerent Hutus. The UN military in Kigali had information of arms caches prior to the descent into mayhem and chaos, and asked the UN for permission to seize them. 'They refused', said the commander in Kigali, 'because UNAMIR was deployed under a Chapter VI mandate - traditional peacekeeping. New York argued that a cordon and search was an offensive operation for which permission would not be granted'. In the scale of activities, Rwanda was a Grey Area event for which there were no rules or understanding because it had not been in the UN's interest to grasp that nettle. How, in the face of genocide in Rwanda, could the Belgians remain impartial, as was expected of them on this traditional peacekeeping mission? In fact they became inextricably involved in the crisis when ten of their number were taken into captivity by the Hutus and hacked to death. The Hutu intention was to get the Belgians to leave Rwanda, a ploy that worked. For the UN, Rwanda was its most shameful experience and is examined in detail in Chapter 7 as a case study.

Meanwhile, in Bosnia 1993-95 there had been problems with the concept of Safe Areas (Sarajevo, Gorazde, Zepa, Srebrenica, Tuzla and Bihac). 'We made our reservations known from the very beginning', said British Foreign Secretary Malcolm Rifkind, 'not on policy grounds but on capability grounds. There was a serious mismatch in terms of numbers of troops, apart from Britain and France who made a very large contribution'. It seems that Safe Areas were implemented without any concept of operations or 'end game' considerations. Britain and France went along with the idea to maintain consensus in the Security Council and to maintain NATO integrity. The author Tim Ripley recorded how, by the spring of 1995,

> the cheer leader of the 'safe areas' policy was US Ambassador to the UN, Madeleine Albright. She was always long on rhetoric about standing up to Serbs despite President Clinton's well known aversion to actually sending any Americans to fight for Bosnia.[19]

Western troops deployed to safe areas became hostages to fortune because concerns for their safety effectively paralysed their governments.

The Safe Haven in northern Iraq had worked because there had been the clearest indication of a willingness to defend it in strength and the ability to effect that defence with support drawn from contiguous Turkish territory. 'Peacekeeping', wrote Henig and Both,[20] 'was extremely popular in the Netherlands'. The Netherlands suffered the well nigh universal problem of having traditional peacekeeping in mind when in reality, pre-Dayton Bosnia was another vicious Grey Area environment. But the Dutch government had discovered in this post-Cold War period that military power could be used in support of foreign policy goals despite their own military advice that they should not get involved.

What happened is history, a testimony to muddled thinking and ignorance. A senior Bosnian Serb officer complained to the author that: 'Serb territory was being attacked from the Safe Areas on a daily basis. Even before we liberated Srebrenica, terror groups entered our villages to burn them down. We asked UNPROFOR to control the situation, to disarm the Safe Areas, but they did not'. The Dutch government had gone out of its way to put a battalion into Srebrenica in eastern Bosnia with its 40,000 Muslim population but, according to the former journalist Martin Bell, 'they were from a conscript-based army, ill-prepared for the hardships of Srebrenica… but there was also surely a loss of nerve which would not, or should not, have occurred in a professional battalion disciplined in the tradition of soldiering-on in adversity'.[21] What Bell is emphasising is the reality that there is no common military standard upon which to impose a detailed, universalist doctrine. When troops are put into a conflict environment, it is wise to deploy them, if the option exists, according to the principle 'forces for courses'. More often than not, as was the case in Kigali, no such latitude exists. 'I found it utterly unacceptable that fifty per cent of the personnel in my command were non-operational',[22] said the UN commander in Kigali. As the experienced UN traditional peacekeeper General Gustav Hagglünd said in differentiating between Peacekeeping and the conflict environment such as in the Grey Area, 'it simply requires different forces and a completely different concept. An intention to deter and enforce requires forces that are as frightening as possible. For this kind of mission great-power battalions, professional soldiers and all the means at their disposal are preferable'. To which he might also have added that they require a mandate appropriate to their mission. The Dutch had a totally inadequate mandate for the eighteen months they were in Srebrenica before retreating in 'disarray and dishonour', leaving the Muslims to the attention of the vengeful Serbs.[23] It was for the UN their most humiliating experience in the Bosnian conflict and the most devastating doctrinal failure in modern military history.

In view of what was to come to pass in Kosovo in 1999, it is as well to remember that in July 1995, the commander of the NATO force in Bosnia, the American Admiral Leighton Smith, applied to the UN to use NATO bombers (the dual key system was in operation at the time) to break up a Serb tank attack advancing on the UN-designated safe area of Srebrenica. The initial request was denied. It has been alleged that up to 8,000 Muslims died at the hands of the victorious Serbs. 'I hated the dual key. I thought it was the worst thing we could possibly have become involved in', said the Admiral. The Srebrenica atrocity was, the Admiral said, 'an abomination that should not have occurred'.[24] In terms of the pursuit of future sanctioned military operations under a UN mandate, it seems that the UN can rightly expect an input but not to have a right to influence the conduct of military operations being executed within the terms of the UN mandate.

Few military experts would have agreed with the Admiral that air power alone could have saved Srebrenica. The UN's resistance to the Admiral's wishes did generate another unwelcome opportunity to criticise the UN, but that is not to deny that there were fundamental questions in search of honest answers. What would have happened if the Serbs had continued their advance in the face of NATO air attacks? Would they have spared the women and children after they had taken Srebrenica? How many examples in history are there, in the prevailing circumstances, of 500 lightly-equipped troops successfully controlling and defending an area the size of Srebrenica? Quantity and quality do count. In the report investigating the Srebrenica massacre, Kofi Annan blamed the Security Council, the Secretariat, himself, UN Peacekeepers and the six nation Contact Group overseeing the Balkans (UK, USA, France, Russia, Italy and Germany). 'The cardinal lesson of Srebrenica is that a deliberate and systematic attempt to terrorise, expel or murder an entire people must be met decisively with all necessary means, and with the political will to carry the policy through to its logical conclusion.'[25] It is a fair summary, easier to put into words than into effect but the starting point is to get the doctrine right.

Henig and Both point out the reality, that the Netherlands 'did not have the means, the wherewithal, or finally the will to make it (the Srebrenica Safe Area) work'. In addition, the

> second basic problem with the UN operation was that it relied on the cooperation and consent of the interested parties and that it was driven above all things by the desire to remain impartial... Very few politicians and soldiers ever questioned this premise of impartiality... But the fact is that relying on the cooperation and consent of the Bosnian Serbs meant that the Eastern Safe Areas could not work.[26]

On 18 September 1999, an international fleet of warships departed Darwin Harbour bound for East Timor on what the press, a significant number of the military and the UN described as a 'peacekeeping mission'. East Timor is examined in detail in Chapter 9. Muslim religious leaders in East Timor had meanwhile called for a *jihad,* a holy war, against the UN-mandated force. One of their leaders explained that the *jihad* against what he correctly described as *a foreign intervention* 'should be understood as a spontaneous heroism'.[27]

Australia, the framework state for the East Timor operation (supplying 4,500 of the 8,000 troops) had been singled out by East Timor rebels for threats and vilification. Australia, which had originally recognised the Indonesian acquisition of East Timor, also suffered the disadvantage of being predominantly of European origin. Prime Minister Howard accepted the possibility of Australian casualties and threatened that if attacks occurred, 'then that in turn would provoke a much stronger level of intervention and retaliation, including, I believe, a much stronger involvement by countries that are now giving important support but not massive support'.[28] The United Kingdom's over-commitment in Northern Ireland and the Balkans confined her support to the provision of a frigate, support aircraft and a Gurkha Company from Brunei. Highly trained, acclimatised, protected to work in a malarial environment and of Asian origin, they were an essential adjunct to the force and a factor to concentrate the minds of would-be terrorists. Military intervention requires a higher level of training than that which is suitable for peacekeeping duties. Quality counts rather more than quantity. 'Indonesian intellectuals hope that the first troops to land will be the Gurkhas, their formidable reputation bringing hope that this trauma for the world's fourth largest country can be relieved.'[29] These are all considerations which lend weight to the bones of sensible, applicable doctrine.

Collaborated and agreed definitions of the new peace-oriented terminology are difficult to find. Accepting that military intervention and UN peacekeeping are political concepts wherein the definition can change with the debate, this is perhaps understandable. There probably is no neat and tidy definition that will overcome the complexities of international politics. One of the most recent Doctrine publications is *British Maritime Doctrine,* second edition.[30] The ubiquitous Peacekeeping is defined as: 'Measures by third parties to achieve and maintain peace taken with impartiality and with the full consent of parties involved'. The definition describes traditional peacekeeping but is silent on the abstention from the use of lethal force. The definition of Peace Enforcement indicates that its umbilical link to *peace* renders it only a partial form of military intervention. Peace enforcement is defined as:

> Action including the use of military force on a multilateral basis to maintain or restore international peace previously agreed to be belligerents who may now be in *combat*; and to compel compliance with agreement to which parties have conferred *or implied consent.*[31] Peace enforcement may entail the enforcement

of *sanctions* and/or direct military intervention to impose peace by the threat, or the actual use of force.

Peace Support Operations (PSO), the second generation of the discredited *Wider Peacekeeping*, are all things to all men, heavily laced with the word *peace* yet many so-called PSO have been launched where there has patently been no peace to support:

> Multi-functional operations involving military forces and diplomatic and humanitarian agencies. They are designed to achieve humanitarian goals or long term political settlement and are conducted *impartially*[32] in support of a UN or OSCE mandate. These include peacekeeping, peace enforcement, conflict prevention, peacemaking, peacebuilding and humanitarian operations.[33]

Thus it seems that the peace professionals have made an unchallenged assault on military understandings of peacekeeping and intervention, rendering the straightforward complex and what was simple, a science. There remain strong interests in describing all military activity short of general war as peacekeeping. Not only is this nonsense but extremely dangerous.

Arguably, it does not take the wit of a modern major-general to understand that, as a rule, impartiality cannot be a feature in enforcement situations. The question as to whether it is possible to intervene with consent might at first sight appear less restrictive but that would be the case in only the rarest circumstances,[34] despite the fact that towards the end of the Cold War the USA and USSR, by their actions, implied that intervention with consent was legitimate. All these interventions occurred within what were considered to be respective spheres of influence. The USSR justified their intervention in Hungary in 1956 and Afghanistan in 1979 as having been at the behest of the legitimate government. The USA invoked consent as their reason for intervening in the Dominican Republic in 1965 and again in Grenada in 1983.

The problem with intervention by consent lies in the reality that the would-be intervenor can recognise as the legitimate authority whomsoever it chooses. In 1956, the USSR responded to an invitation from Kadar to intervene in Hungary despite the fact that the established government prior to the disturbances was that of Imré Nagy. At first sight, the USSR intervention into Afghanistan appeared to be impeccably correct. However, any individual or party who resisted the wishes of the Soviets was removed and replaced by a pliant puppet. Any individual who did not comply risked being shot. This state of affairs is therefore political, subjective and beyond the control of international law.

In both the Dominican Republic and Grenada, the USA produced letters of invitation to intervene which were both of doubtful validity and signed by individuals of doubtful authority. There is, in addition to the absence of a controlling influence, the reality that the act of intervention prevents a proportion of a population from determining its own political future. They will be opposed by parties who resort to armed conflict as a means of determining *their* political future, something that is not illegal under international law. This reminds us, therefore, that the act of intervention by consent may be an illegal act. Moreover, there is the risk that intervention by consent will escalate, so that a domestic issue becomes an international crisis.

The principal difference between *Wider Peacekeeping* and *PSO* is the quiet but unsubtle acceptance in *PSO* of the grey area or Chapter VI½ but then this gentle capitulation is ruined by describing the middle ground as 'peace enforcement'. Institutional interests and meal tickets all conspire to encourage the British doctrinal establishment to persist with idealistic, flawed doctrine, lending credence to Liddell Hart's observation that one thing more difficult than getting new ideas into the military mind is getting old ones out. The arguments about the lessons to be drawn from intra-state conflict and the search for better ways of doing things must continue. The only certainty is that we shall do better by all those who will be sent in to put their lives on the line if the doctrine to which they work is built upon the evidence as a whole rather than the evidence being selected to fit a doctrinaire framework.

The litmus test of any doctrine is that it must be believed. The original mistake was to suppress the debate of the initial concept of *Wider Peacekeeping*. The second mistake was to fail to make any intellectual investment in developing the doctrine. The third mistake once *Wider Peacekeeping* had been buried was to exhume it rather than 'take up a fresh piece of paper'.[35] Despite the vindictiveness and the almost paranoid attempts to restrict discussion and keep the lid on the pot, the number of doubters - and particularly those prepared to express their extreme reservations concerning *Peace Support Operations* - has grown.

It is policy which underwrites doctrine, but bad doctrine supported by a hard-sell regime can foster irrelevant policy. As part of the research of this subject, a view was presented to a Departmental Head at the Foreign and Commonwealth Office that we had the reality of a situation whereby there was a spectrum of military interventionist activity anchored at both ends by traditional Chapter VI peacekeeping and Chapter VII intervention, with a broad, grey, undefined area in between. He conceded that this was a correct interpretation but added, 'it is not policy'. Policy is shorthand for government doctrine. All the contributing inputs into interventionist operations are steered by their own doctrine. Some are more susceptible to change than others, which reflects a kind of pecking order. For example, and in general terms, doctrine associated with international law takes precedence over government policy, which in turn takes precedence over military doctrine.

That we should be persisting in the maintenance of an irrelevant, status quo policy without the benefit of political steering might appear curious. It is not a situation requiring courageous decisions. The reason we have seen no positive activity may have something to do with the fact that much of today's political life revolves around the avoidance of those debates governments do not want to discuss. In that respect, UN and Conflict is similar to European Monetary Union. What seems to worry and perplex our chattering classes is their discovery that their enemy's enemy may well not be their friend. Few of yesterday's past reassurances can be carried forward into today and tomorrow. Things are not as black and white nor as easily identifiable as they used to be, but have become diffused in a blanket of grey mist. Modern conflict is no exception, but its very nature demands an end to political prevarication. It would be nothing short of a military crime not to define the Grey Area and what it involves. States no longer understand where they are in this new environment and understandably their ardour to support UN Resolutions has cooled. The Grey Area is undoubtedly a conflict environment where there is no peace to be kept. *The military activity that takes place in the Grey Area must not be described as Peacekeeping - it is not.* If remedial action is not taken to address that reality, then the lessons from Mogadishu, Kigali and Srebrenica will have been ignored. That is a political and military crime.

The requirement goes somewhat further than replacing *Peace Support Operations.* The whole environment is in a state of flux and desperately needs assessment and definition as a total package. We talk of 'warfighting' when there has not been a declaration of war since 1945, but we cling to the vague concept of 'warfighting' because it is from this that the rationale for force structuring and equipment flows. However, as has already been mentioned, the notion of preserving 'warfighting' is nonetheless valid, for, in the range of military conflict, it is true that the skill required by armed forces trained at the general global and regional levels of conflict do cascade down to lower levels, whereas the reverse is not true. We have in the past categorised conflict into levels of intensity. Mid Intensity Conflict (MIC) differed from High Intensity Conflict (HIC) principally because weapons of mass destruction did not feature as a consideration in the former. Today, it is possible that weapons of mass destruction could be introduced into what used to be described as Low Intensity Conflict (LIC). The understanding of what comprised a Low Intensity Conflict became severely undermined when it was realised that Russia's bloody intervention in 1994-96 and revisited in 1999 upon her neighbour in her 'near abroad', Chechnya, was categorised within the system as LIC.

There is also the consideration of what NATO's role is going to be in support of the UN as a sanctioned organisation. NATO has shown a propensity to utilise the non-autonomous air arm in conflict resolution because the political risks of putting infantry on the ground can be a tricky threshold to negotiate. NATO's role has expanded since the July 1990 London Declaration, to include not only collective defence but also collective security. The recent extension of NATO into Central and Eastern Europe, pushed through despite the considerable weight of informed protest, lends credence to the view that here we have an organisation still in search of a proper post-Cold War role. If it pushes too hard to become a global strike force it is likely to self-destruct. NATO's original intervention in the pre-Dayton Grey Area of Bosnia was due to the UN's peacekeepers' failure to stop atrocities in Sarajevo, Srebrenica and Zepa. Not so long ago, it was thought unlikely that NATO would operate outside Europe on Grey Area missions. At the December 1998 NATO Conference, Secretary of State Madeleine Albright told the NATO allies that future NATO missions would take them further afield.

It behoves anyone who argues that a doctrine is irrelevant, poorly structured and simplistic to recommend the manner in which it should be superseded. It has become apparent that there is a requirement for an overarching, general doctrine to bond all the components within a coalition operation. There is also a case for a specific, detailed, national doctrine which will relate the general doctrine to the participants' way of engaging in conflict, usually within operational boundaries. In outline, the new overarching doctrine will need to be in four parts. The first part will establish principles, definitions, the structure under which the various levels of doctrine function, and the actors to be found in these environments (government organisations, agencies and NGOs). The remaining three parts apply doctrine top-down, as stand-alone entities, not envisaged as being of similar length, at the Military Strategic, Operational and Tactical Doctrine levels. It might be appropriate to subdivide, or alternatively to produce separate documents which examine Chapter VI peacekeeping, the Grey Area, and Chapter VII military intervention. Of the three, it is the Grey Area which has to be addressed urgently, so that soldiers and civilians will no longer die due to the preservation of vested interests and political and military ignorance. The time for someone to take charge of this process is long overdue. The recognition and the making available of some of the wherewithal to engage in expeditionary conflict is the beginning not the end of the process. The United Kingdom should resume the lead in developing a sensible and relevant doctrine as a framework of understanding of the approach to expeditionary conflict in order to provide the foundation for its practical application. When Peace Support Operations are revised, they have to be seen as a constituent part of military doctrine and not something that is separate. It is essential to avoid 'freezing' the new doctrine in a particular set of attitudes rather than to acknowledge its evolutionary nature to reflect evolving realities.

Wider Peacekeeping and its derivative Peace Support Operations were born in the crucible of Bosnia, for that was the sum of the then British experience. That the new doctrine did not fit the circumstances then prevailing in Bosnia, not to speak of the other two dozen or so major conflicts ongoing in the world, did not give rise to questions of substance. In referring to the 'Mogadishu Line', General Sir Michael Rose, formerly the Commander of the UN Protection Force (UNPROFOR) in Bosnia, described it as 'the line that separates peacekeeping from war fighting'.[36] It was General Rose who observed that it was not possible to fight from white-painted vehicles but he implies support for the doctrine of Wider Peacekeeping despite it being responsible for much of his difficulty in Bosnia. The General provides no definition of his understanding of peacekeeping or war fighting. Arguably it is more important to put war fighting in its rightful place in the spectrum of conflict than to bother having to define it. It infers a level of intensity of conflict to be found in limited and general war. War fighting would therefore be an appropriate term to embrace Traditional Military Intervention as seen in Korea and the Gulf and flow into General War. It also follows, therefore, that a single line separating peacekeeping from war fighting is too stark a choice, too immediate to be sensible.

If conflict were to be related to understandings associated with the UN Charter, the starting point would be Chapter VII, traditional intervention or limited war. Next there is a non-conflict situation, Chapter VI traditional peacekeeping. Between Chapters VI and VII is the gap, Chapter VI½ or, the Grey Area. The Grey Area is a conflict environment which requires troops of the requisite calibre. There will be movement along and within the spectrum of the Grey Area which will have manning and logistical implications reflecting increasing or decreasing tension. Once the original conflict has been resolved, it would be reasonable to anticipate, with the consent of the parties involved, an adoption of traditional peacekeeping duties. As a worst case, the Grey Area operations could escalate into traditional Chapter VII Limited War, or full-blown military intervention. Grey Area operations have been variously described: Chapter VI½, Aggravated Peacekeeping or Implementation and Stabilisation Operations. Since such operations will invariably be in support of a UN Resolution, it is proposed that Grey Area operations be known as Implementation Operations. Implementation Operations are conflict operations spanning the spectrum of proportional response to the taking of all necessary measures.

We therefore find ourselves with three competing spectra of conflict. The *theoretical*, shown diagramatically as *Wider Peacekeeping*, Figure 3.3, and *Peace Support Operations*, Figure 3.4 and the *reality* shown below at Figure 3.5.

Wider Peacekeeping

Mogadishu Line

Peacekeeping	War Fighting

Figure 3.3

Peace Support Operations

Peacekeeping	Peace Enforcement	War Fighting

Figure 3.4

Reality

Chapter VI	Chapter VI½ Implementation Operations	Chapter VII	
Traditional Peacekeeping - Cyprus	Military and Humanitarian Intervention short of Limited War[37] - Bosnia	Traditional Intervention - The Gulf Crisis	General Regional and Global War - The Second World War
Non conflict	Conflict assumed	Limited War[38]	Unlimited War

Figure 3.5

Armed conflict in the Reality model also fits within the area described as Implementation Operations. This can be a broad area with wide variations of intensity under the rubric of armed conflict. Conflict will move up and down this range and into adjoining zones. This has implications for troop numbers, skills and logistics. The less accomplished military can be accommodated at that end of the spectrum where the intensity level is closer to peacekeeping while the better-trained military will be required for implementation operations short of limited war. By recognising this truth, much of the misconception, misunderstanding and self-interest can be set aside so that never again, as in UNPROFOR, will up to 300 'peacekeepers' die in a fruitless attempt at 'peacekeeping' when there was patently no peace in place to be kept. To this broad doctrinal outline there are now a number of fundamental truths to be examined as a part of the building process.

4 The Heart of the Matter – The Fundamentals

Under normal circumstances, the UN Secretary-General or other interested organisations or states begin the process of forming an interventionist coalition with a request to states to participate. Unilateral military intervention will be a rare occurrence. This exercise is essentially of a quantitative nature, essentially a numbers game, which has been found wanting. There is an important qualitative dimension which cannot be ignored if commanders on the ground are to be given the best chance of achieving their goals. Where there are no treaty obligations, the recipient governments of such a request will enter into a process of analysis before coming to a decision. Often, that decision-making process will be abbreviated as states intuitively decline to become involved in another state's civil war. More often than not, the final decision will be based upon a finely balanced assessment of the factors. There will be domestic and international factors to consider and they will rarely move in harmony. For example, United States' foreign policy is more often than not formulated upon domestic considerations. Demands will exceed assets, so choice will feature prominently. It may be the case, however, as was the situation in 1999 with the British government, that commitments in Northern Ireland, Bosnia, Kosovo and East Timor meant that other than reservists there were no further military resources to be allocated elsewhere.

Understandably, the decision-making process will begin with an assessment as to whether national interests are at stake and, if they are, whether they are vital interests (which will be rare) upon which the government has a duty to act. In the United States, the presence of a clear, unequivocal, national interest is a prerequisite in achieving the support of a public which will invariably be asking 'why us, why there and why now?' Modern intervention is conducted for two basic reasons: out of interest or as an outpouring of conscience. In responding to demands to 'do something', conscience then translates into an interest as a government elects to appease the electors. Rarely will interventions be launched unless there are clear and unambiguous headline threats to people's lives and limbs. If vital interests are not at stake, the government has to reflect upon its international responsibilities and also consider the disadvantages of not intervening. For example, if State A declines to be associated with an intervention into, say, Africa, in which State B had a national interest, it might present problems in the future if State A wished to solicit the support of State B for an intervention which was in State A's interest.

Legality will be discussed in greater detail later in this Chapter but it is an essential consideration vis-à-vis intervention. The would-be interventionist government will invariably require assurance that there are unequivocal moral and legal grounds for the putative operation. The national aim must be agreed and this could involve a compromise as the *coalition's* political aim and military mission have to be finessed among the parties involved. This is a vital step because coalitions can only be held together where there is unity of purpose, an unequivocal aim and an agreed mission statement. In order to avoid so-called 'mission creep' the aim must be rigorously applied until it is amended.

The maintenance of the aim is crucial for so long as the factors which collectively led to the selection of that aim are still of relevance. There has to be a willingness and agreement among the parties to change the aim if circumstances so require. In 1918, General William S. Graves led an American expeditionary force into Siberia. With him he took an *aide-mémoire* typed personally by President Wilson. That it was out of date before he had landed at Vladivostok had not occurred to the general. His determined pursuit of a mission no longer applicable hugely complicated the allied intervention into Siberia. It is incumbent upon the modern leader to be sensitive to changing circumstance which may render the aim or mission to which he is working no longer relevant.

Inevitably the coalition should come to a collective decision as to how success or failure should be measured and defined. An assurance of success is vital. All interventions will invariably be argued as being justified - just causes - but if there is little prospect of success, they should not be entered into. The constituent coalition governments will have in the front and back of their minds the political and military consequences of failure.

Given that it is much more difficult to prepare and execute an exit strategy as opposed to an entry strategy (it's easier to get in than out), a clear perception of the end game is vital. Despite the availability of the most sophisticated decision-making machinery, the USA intervened unilaterally in the Dominican Republic in 1965 on the whim of President

Johnson. Governments will be acutely aware of the ultimate failure of the majority of military interventions and will, even at the risk of proceeding half-heartedly, seek to avoid the danger inherent in descending the slippery slope of expanding commitments. They will be more forthcoming and timely in deciding upon intervention in situations which do not require the insertion of ground forces. Sea and air resources are capable of operating, when necessary, without violating state sovereignty, minimising the risk of casualties. Policy-makers will have uppermost in their minds the question whether public opinion can be sustained and the effect national involvement will have upon the standing of the government. Initially the feel-good factor may be strongly felt but we should reiterate the defining criteria for military intervention if serious political risk-taking is to be avoided; low risk, low cost and short duration. There are seven fundamental questions to be considered as a part of the decision-making process towards military or humanitarian intervention:

- Availability – who can we send?
- Is there a national interest or moral obligation to intervene?
- Is there a real threat to international peace, security, the rule of law and humanitarianism?
- Is there a clear aim?
- Can the proposed mission succeed? How is success to be defined?
- Can the conclusion - the end game - be envisaged; is there an exit strategy? How, therefore, may failure be defined?
- Who pays?

It is necessary, for the record, to mention a phenomenon described as a 'rally event'. Analysis of a government's or leader's domestic popularity prior to an act of military or humanitarian intervention often indicates a resultant upward surge, certainly in the initial stages. That this is not just a western phenomenon is evident from the rising popularity shown in opinion polls for Russian President Vladimir Putin's 1999 intervention into Chechnya. The war against Chechnya became the election platform for the man who wanted to succeed Boris Yeltsin as president. It is possible, therefore, that interventions can be launched for ulterior political motives.

One further consideration capable of distorting the reasoned decision-making process is the 'he's taking us on' syndrome. This applies to circumstances whereby an organisation or lead state reacts hastily and without due reasoning to the provocative action of a party considered to be inferior. The presence of this syndrome is found in Suez 1956 with Nasser, in Bosnia and Kosovo with Milosevic and the classic, in 1993 with Aideed. The Mogadishu experience is the more compelling case study because, in 'taking on' Aideed, the USA forfeited her technological advantages by choosing to eyeball Aideed in his own clan's urban territory. Clearly the military advice given to the USA's Permanent Representative and to the UN's Secretary-General was not of the best quality.

One of the least edifying aspects of intervention operations is the well nigh predictability that the official nominated to run the operation will begin the process as though nothing that has gone before is of any relevance, as though there is no collective memory, no lessons learned. A comprehensive package of lessons learned arose out of America's 1956-1975 Vietnam experience. By the time the USA was involved with the Multi-National Force in Lebanon 1982-84, the lessons learned in Vietnam had apparently been forgotten. Lebanon should not have been allowed to exceed the bounds of traditional peacekeeping. Beirut was one urban conflict the Marines were not going to win, as was so painfully made evident. The subsequent debate that opened in Washington would run and run. Should the USA involve herself in overseas operations in which there was no apparent American interest? The subsequent Pentagon enquiry convened to investigate the bombing of the Marines' barracks and to learn from the experience, produced three principal maxims: the military should not become involved in operations which could not guarantee continuing domestic support, they should only involve themselves in conflicts which could be successfully concluded over a short period of time and, the establishment of garrisons should be avoided. 1983 Beirut had similarities with 1993 Mogadishu. The three principal lessons to arise from the Beirut experience were: be impartial, use minimum force and, know your enemy. During the course of collating the American lessons learned from the 1994 Rwanda operations, a plea was discovered from an anonymous army captain that the military should learn from previous lessons learned.

One of the more surprising developments seen in 1999 was the preparedness of a thus far reticent Germany to accept world order responsibilities approaching proportionality with her power and economic situation. The irony is that an intervention of the nature that occurred in Kosovo would probably not have occurred had Chancellor Gerhard Schröder remained in opposition. The mantle of power brings with it new perspectives, perspectives which, for historical reasons, will appear clearer from Berlin than Bonn. Germany's initiative should not be seen, however, as the beginning of an era of Neo-Interventionism but rather as a world power with some catching up to do. This catching-up process is handicapped by the Schroeder government's continual reduction of funds for defence and security purposes. The British and continental European capacity for wider intervention will depend for the foreseeable future upon the willingness of the United States to provide strategic lift capabilities.

It is desirable that the new American administration should produce a new doctrine which will address the conundrum of casualty aversion and the tension which exists between fighting the nation's wars and expeditionary conflict. The bottom-up process of reform is already in train. The so-called new interventionism, however, will still continue to be conditional, at the mercy of political or other interests, so as to resist codification either as a threat or a promise. In the Washington corridors of power, there is talk of 'intervention fatigue'. The National Security Adviser confronted by those who wanted America to become positively involved in preventing the massacre of East Timorese Christians by Indonesian Muslims commented: 'This is like being forced to clean up my daughter's dorm room'.[1]

Similarly, Secretary for Defense Cohen who had set aside the advice of the Joint Chiefs of Staff in proceeding with an intensive bombing campaign against Belgrade and Kosovo - something which *appeared* to be not in America's vital interest - declined to become involved in East Timor because it was not in 'the vital interest of the USA'.[2] There has been an attempt to broaden approaches to humanitarian crises such as East Timor by categorising them as being of *common interest.* But this gives rise to a whole raft of new questions, as put to the UN General Assembly by the Secretary-General on 21 September 1999: 'What is that common interest? Who shall define it? Who will defend it? Under whose authority? And with what means?' America's approach to Kosovo and East Timor underlines just how difficult it is to produce substantive answers and how virtually impossible it will be to achieve fair and consistent responses. Russia's 1999 intervention in Chechnya without raising significant hackles in the way that Kosovo did, suggests the presence of two particular conditions not evident in Kosovo. First, Russia with her 300 Intercontinental Ballistic Missiles is not Serbia and there remains the remnant of an understanding of spheres of influence in so far as what happens in Chechnya is, for Russia, a domestic matter.

Understandably, given the various power centres in Washington, there will be variations in consistency as to perceptions of, and weighting to be given to, American interests. Answers depend upon questions. Thus, overall, Kosovo was a far less weighty interest than the preservation of NATO's credibility, and the reason is to do with the nature of power. A superpower requires an outlet in order to express and underline possession of that power. Leading, controlling and expanding NATO satisfies that need in accordance with the dictum 'if you've got it, flaunt it'. It might seem callous to suggest that it was not humanitarian considerations which sent NATO into Kosovo but principally, it was a perceived need to preserve an organisation which had been painted into a corner through the exercise of mediocre diplomacy. General Sir Michael Rose in Sarajevo wrote of how he received a note from:

> British Chief of Defence Staff, Peter Harding, telling me that UNPROFOR did not have a right to veto NATO air strikes in Bosnia, adding that 'it *will* happen if conditions are not met...he said that I had to understand that the credibility of NATO was more important than peace in Bosnia.[3]

What Kosovo would do would be to render an implausible statement such as this to fall within the realms of the possible. At the end of the first week of the bombing of Serbia, Foreign Secretary Robin Cook told Peter Riddell of *The Times*:

> The whole credibility of NATO is at stake - not just loss of face after earlier commitments, but confidence in our own security. It is in the national British interest to maintain NATO's credibility.[4]

At the opening of the new session of the UN on 21 September 1999, President Bill Clinton appealed for international understanding that there were limits on American actions and, where a back seat was taken, it did not denote American indifference to suffering.[5] The truth is that, at the end of the millennium, and after setting aside standing garrisons, America (active forces of 1,447,600) was no more heavily committed on intervention operations than the United Kingdom (active forces of 213,800). American isolationist sentiments of over-commitment are therefore not valid.

America's political structure will conspire to inhibit the freeing of the doctrinal log jam and more representative involvement in conflicts which are becoming less force versus force than evil forces oppressing civilian populations:

> We have observed, in each of the five continents, that belligerents are increasingly taking care to avoid direct confrontation with each other. Instead, their favoured strategy to gain ground is the exercise of terror against

> defenceless civilians. Their actions, regardless of any reason that may motivate their struggle, demonstrate a shocking disregard for human values.[6]

When a House of Commons Select Committee asked the then British Ambassador to Washington, Sir Nicholas Henderson, what the Administration's view of the Falklands had been, he replied: 'When you say the US Administration, I am sorry to be pedantic but there is the Pentagon view, the State Department view and the White House view'.[7] To which he later added: '...they do not necessarily communicate with one another'.[8] Sir Nicholas made no mention of the all-important Congress view, a Congress which had consistently refused to release to the UN the $1bn it was legally owed by America. The central rationale has been to encourage the UN to initiate financial and personnel reforms, which it has partially done. It is the representatives of these separate institutions which share power in the United States which often serve to dilute and weaken America's responses to given crises. Representative Christopher Smith attempted to saddle the settling of the UN account with anti-abortion language totally unrelated to the national responsibility to pay its agreed share for intervention and peacekeeping operations. The Smith amendment sought to prohibit US assistance to groups involved in lobbying foreign governments to liberalise their abortion laws.[9] *Time* Magazine observed the need for 'more thoughtful and less parochial leadership'.[10] Herein lies the central dilemma of an American leadership fashioned by domestic opinion and opinion polls. It is not leadership but something quite different - followership.

Effective American leadership is to be welcomed. There is the underlying problem that when engaged, the concept of America First drives America's leadership interests but when disengaged, the quality of leadership offered is often viewed as unacceptably indifferent, particularly among the states of Europe. There has been in Washington an assumption of having delivered on effective leadership. Speaking at Georgetown University to mark the 10th Anniversary of the fall of the Berlin Wall, President Clinton urged his successors to ensure America remained involved as the leader in world affairs. A White House spokesman observed how 'we have exerted leadership for the good and we need to continue in that tradition'.[11] But where was the leadership in the Balkans? Leadership has to be wanted. Small wonder that there is a growing tension between America and France who, in Europe, exercises her own nation-centric notion of France First.

One of the more intractable problems of Congress addressing intervention issues - Kosovo attracted greater debate than any other intervention post-Vietnam - is that it resists the kind of order which, within a party, is known as collective responsibility. Intervention issues cross party lines. There is a tendency for the hawks to come from the southern states while the doves are predominantly from the north.[12]

The automatic assumption of an American leading role in world order operations - what Madeleine Albright described as 'assertive multilateralism' - came to an emphatic end in October 1993, after the Mogadishu fiasco. Europe's subsequent attempt to share some of that burden has been tentative but measurable. In Bosnia, for example, the USA provided one third of the total force whereas in Kosovo, American representation was only 14 per cent of the total. Inevitably the juxtaposition of European and American world roles is interrogated in terms of the EU, NATO and the UN. 'You've got to have America in there', said former British Foreign Secretary and NATO Secretary-General, Lord Carrington:

> I genuinely believe that NATO kept the peace of the world in the Cold War and I think it would be rather silly to throw away a good insurance policy… (In Bosnia), the United Nations came in with a force that was not allowed to use its weapons except in self defence, which alienated everyone. The whole business in the Balkans has been mismanaged from the start. It was obvious it was going to blow up.[13]

A recent RAND report indicated that the EU would need to spend seven per cent of its gdp over the next ten years to achieve a combined armed force equivalent to that of the US. Nothing like that level of expenditure is going to be achieved. With a population and economy broadly similar to that of the USA, the EU's defence expenditure is an inefficiently targeted sixty per cent of that of the Americans but they only have ten per cent of America's strategic lift capacity, have limited command and control capabilities and little by way of electronic intelligence gathering. Kosovo has revealed how unprepared Europe has been to set aside Cold War concepts and face the new challenges of expeditionary conflict. If the European Security and Defence Identity (ESDI) is to become a serious proposition, their peace dividends and defence reviews and assumptions require urgent, systematic reappraisal.

The problem for Europe is that left-of-centre policymakers will take the opportunity for European defence integration not to recommend making genuine improvements in capabilities but rather to make savings to fund vote-catching social initiatives. There was one serious suggestion that

Europe's C-130 Hercules and Future Large Aircraft (FLA) should all be based at one airfield, ostensibly for ease of control and maintenance but in truth to permit further defence savings. Collaborative procurement is one area for examination but since Europeans have differing doctrines[14] and because there are significant variables with desired in-service dates, the outlook is not propitious. 'The story of European collaborative ventures is not a particularly inspiring one so far as learning the lessons of history is concerned' riposted the House of Commons Defence Select Committee. 'The new emphasis on the development of a European defence capability makes the need to learn and apply these lessons all the more urgent.'[15]

Although the idea of the EU subsuming the activities of the WEU had been a Europhile idea for some time, the ultimate stimulus to grasp this particular nettle came from Washington. It was Clinton's reluctance to do what was necessary for European Kosovo, coupled with Europe's inability, which provided British Prime Minister Tony Blair with the determination to make an attempt at assembling a European defence capability inside NATO. (The French perception that the European defence capability should be independent of NATO is one of those issues which have not been adequately addressed. The upshot of this is the entirely politically focused European Rapid Reaction Force (ERRF). That Britain should be taking this initiative was significant because Britain is the pivot of the transatlantic relationship. But Blair is the supreme political opportunist with a high perception of himself as a key player on the international stage. Defence and Security issues, which normally cause little domestic upswelling of emotion, are far safer mechanisms through which to demonstrate strong European credentials than European Monetary Integration, the vexed, almost politically taboo subject for a British Prime Minister. The British lead position with ERRF was essentially a bargaining chip to offset Continental Europe's enthusiasm for replacing the veto in favour of majority voting. ESDI had been a central plank of the Blair-Chirac meeting at St Malo in December 1998 where it was proposed establishing a European security initiative dependent upon NATO support. Thus, in replicating the NATO/EU link-up, the EU achieved the duplication that was so apparent in the NATO/WEU relationship. As a *Times* editorial remarked: 'The likely result is less, not more resolute leadership - and illusions in Washington that Europe can be left to its own defence. Europeans should be concentrating on improving their armed forces, not playing their favourite war games, redesigning institutions'. George

Robertson, the then British Secretary of State for Defence recently admitted, 'you can't go to war on a wiring diagram'.

Although there was an earlier degree of empathy among the principal European Socialist governments, this was due to a determination to maintain a vestige of consensus fully aware that NATO should not be permitted to stumble and fail over Kosovo. Despite that high duty, the cracks in the facade of unity in vulnerable European coalition governments were apparent for all to see. Domestic opposition in geo-strategically important Italy taxed the harmonising skills of Prime Minister Massimo D'Alema. In Germany, Chancellor Gerhard Schröder, with Green coalition partners to keep on side, publicly dissociated himself from Blair's demand for ground intervention in Kosovo. Each of Europe's sovereign states therefore still retains its own national ideas of defence and security, a fact that tinkering with institutions does not overcome. There is little point giving Europe an independent military capability unless it is backed by the kind of political will and consistent foreign policy that might be found in one unitary sovereign state.

The intention is that the 60,000 corps-size ERRF which, by 2003, is to be 'separable but not separate' from NATO, should be capable of deploying within 60 days for up to two years. *Rapid* is therefore a relative statement. In dissociating the ERRF from any appearance of being a fledgling European military force, Prime Minister Blair said its role was 'peacekeeping and humanitarian tasks: it is not a conflict force'. The UK contributed 12,500 men, 18 warships and 72 combat aircraft to the EU peacekeeping force's capabilities catalogue. Of the European states, only the UK and France at a pinch have plausible rapid reaction capabilities. The danger in setting the membership fee at an attractively low percentage of national gdp defence expenditure in order to attract sufficient members is that insufficient funds will be generated to make the prospect of a strengthened EU defence and security role viable. Much of the responsibility for making the dream become reality rests with the EU's High Representative for Foreign Affairs, the former NATO Secretary-General, Javier Solana.

ESDI comes from the same body of theory as the raft of European legislation which creates a common European standard across Europe's increasingly socialised armed forces. In Pristina in 1999, an officer from one of the smaller European countries walked out of KFOR's multinational headquarters declaring he had completed his contracted hours for that day. This is a situation which promises to worsen as military standards and levels of efficiency among Europe's military degrade. They will become aligned and standardised to conform with the norm within continental Europe's principally conscript armed forces. States which endeavour to maintain professional military standards could be faced with a challenge from discontented citizens who have the right to appeal to the European Court of Human Rights. It could be argued, therefore, that a closer integration of Europe's military may not be in the best interests of all European states. A report from Kosovo commented upon the degradation of professional British military standards as a result of serving among French, Italian and German soldiers. The latter 'preferred the safety of large battalions and their camps', whereas initially, the British 'started off by patrolling on foot, day and night in small teams'. But, 'very quickly, the British troops followed the European example. They stopped their dangerous patrols – and as a result, the British sector was soon no better protected from the ravages of the KLA than any other'.[16]

It has not been unusual for the United Kingdom to be out of step with continental Europe's NATO members. Spain and Italy opposed Britain's efforts to restore democracy to the Falklands and, in the Gulf Crisis, Belgium refused to make heavy natures artillery ammunition available to Britain. In addition, there is the added problem that not all the EU's fifteen members belong to NATO, just as not all of NATO's European members belong to the EU. The six European NATO members not in the EU (Iceland, Norway, Turkey, the Czech Republic, Hungary and Poland) were offended at being excluded from the planning phase of the new EU force. Austria would not allow NATO to over-fly her territory during the Kosovo campaign. Neutral Sweden deplores the prospect of military power being used to secure diplomatic goals, a view which is likely to find support in Ireland but arguably less so in Finland. Greece, a NATO and EU member, witnessed sometimes violent civil opposition to NATO's operations against Serbia. Thus, in seeking to achieve the capability 'to respond to international crises without prejudice to actions by NATO' the EU risks introducing discord where it had previously not existed. In addition, any new military or political orientation which includes France will attract its own in-built conditionality. It has been said that Britain regarded NATO as an organisation designed to keep America in Europe, Russia out, and Germany divided. It could be said that London sees the ERRF's purpose as being to tie Germany in and to prevent France from taking over.

America's desire to share and shed burdens pre-dates the serious discussion of the ESDI but, since that prospect now has the possibility of being translated into reality, there has been an accompanying inhalation of breath and sucking of teeth on the other side of the Atlantic. While America supports the idea of ESDI within NATO, that support is

> guided by the answer to two questions - will it work and will it keep the alliance together..... we would not want to see an ESDI that comes into being first within NATO but then grows out of NATO and finally grows up away from it and could even compete with it.[17]

Europe's oft contradicted insistence that ESDI will operate within NATO, and America's observation that if this is to be the case then the first discussions regarding an intervention operation would be held within NATO, begs the question as to the merit and efficacy of the ESDI initiative. Washington envisages being part of the discussion *ab initio* and, as it unfolded, in a progressive decision-making process known as 'sequencing'. This infers a possible US veto within NATO, even if the USA was not going to commit ground forces. Secretary of State Madeleine Albright's view that the European force would strengthen NATO was described by Caspar Weinberger as an opinion coming from a 'lame duck administration that will be replaced one way or another'.[18]

There is still a hope in Washington that the USA will have what would amount to the final say on putative European operations launched within a NATO framework. America puts great store on the control she can exert over NATO, far more so than over the UN which seems to have been abandoned as a hopeless case. The spectre of Vietnam and Somalia has limited America's desire to risk casualties beyond 'warfighting' to the degree that she has endeavoured nevertheless to keep a foot in the door rather as a wholesaler supplying retailers. This function she can satisfactorily achieve in those areas where the EU has a zero or limited capability but the reality is that it will be the major shareholder who will vote the majority of the stock.

Technically, it is the crisis which creates the coalition. So, whereas it is certainly possible to gather together groups of 15 or 19 kindred spirits in anticipation of forming a future coalition (as is the case with the EU and NATO respectively), individual states' attitudes to a crisis will rarely be the same. Certainly, from previous European examples, the disparity in consensus will be predictably wide. Besides, having 15 or 19 states involved in the decision-making process is too cumbersome, too inflexible and too restrictive. It is a situation that will not improve. The EU is on track to expand its membership to 27 within the next three years and NATO has a large number of states aspiring to join. The membership application of

Argentina may take some digesting but the claims of states who facilitated NATO's success in Kosovo - Romania, Bulgaria, Albania and Macedonia - will be more difficult to turn away. These accessions will further infuriate Russia unless there is a political awakening within NATO. The management of the Baltics' aspirations to join the organisation will require justifiably sensitive handling.

The Kosovo chapter will reveal the serious divisions among the 19 NATO member states. The UK has stated that the European Security and Defence Policy (ESDP) which flowed from the ESDI will only be implemented where NATO as a whole is not engaged. ESDP therefore assumes firstly the non-participation of the USA when in NATO's Kosovo operation the USA proved to be indispensable and secondly, the addition of a further 12 European states to the present 15 who will 'have to agree to any EU-led operation being launched'.[19] It is virtually impossible to secure unanimity among 27 EU members to launch an EU operation, and impossible to sustain it. Nothing, it seems, is being learnt.

If states conduct their own contingency planning in accordance with their national interests and capabilities, carefully monitoring emerging crises and concurrently identifying potential common-interest partners, this is likely to be far more productive than the creation of doctrinaire and potentially fallible institutions. There will, of course, be occasions when a military solution is simply not viable. The bottom line is to identify what works.

The meaningful monitoring of potential crises occurs at an international level in such places as NATO Headquarters, Brussels and also at a national level in Washington, London and Paris. The procedures are much the same as those practised by the British. Their Permanent Joint Headquarters (PJHQ) place potential conflicts into four broad categories - quiescent, stirring, quickening and surfaced, which then fit into three categories of interest. The *normal* state is the lowest level of activity, whereby Intelligence is keeping a watching brief on areas of potential or actual operational interest and maintaining a priority list. Concurrently, the staff planners will be engaged in the joint staff planning associated with the establishment or development of contingency plans. *Step 1* occurs when it becomes evident that a crisis is emerging. A multi-disciplinary Contingency Planning Team (CPT) will be formed at the working level under the overall direction of a senior officer in the Planning Division. Each CPT will be expected to so master the situation under observation as to be able to advise or warn, when authorised, up or down the chain of command.

Not all CPTs will move to the third category of interest, *Step 2*, the formation of an Operations Team (OT). If the crisis evaporates or the political decision is taken that there is to be no operational activity, the CPT may well disband. If the CPT does progress to Step 2, it will become subsumed into an Operations Team headed by a dedicated team leader of a rank appropriate to the scale of operations.[20] The role of the British Operations Team is to deal with all the detail associated with command, deployment, sustenance and, ultimately, the recovery of the assigned force, and to be proactive and responsive on the interface with the Ministry of Defence and the supporting Commands. It remains formed until the operation is declared to be over.

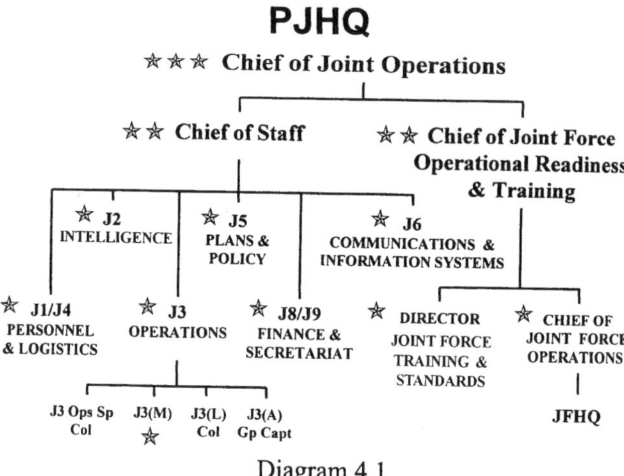

Diagram 4.1

Under the three-star Chief of Joint Operations (CJO) (Diagram 4-1) are two two-star Staff Officers, the CJO's Chief of Staff (COS) and the Chief of Joint Force Operational Readiness and Training (CJFORT). The staff branches under the COS mirror the NATO and USA model from J1 to J9, thus facilitating the proper interaction between similar staff branches within a NATO-organised coalition. (This reciprocity does not exist in UK's MoD. It is not an easy matter, for example, to identify J3 and J5.) A Combined Headquarters is similarly organised with branches 1-9, the principal difference being that it would be staffed by representatives of two or more states. As a development of the 1998 St Malo initiative, an Anglo-French Combined Headquarters exercise was held in June 2000.

The establishment of CJFORT was one of the measures to arise from the 1997 Strategic Defence Review (SDR). His role is to prepare the Joint Rapid Reaction Force (JRRF - successor to JRDF) and JFHQ for operations; to monitor and report on JRRF readiness and the prescription, planning and execution of training at joint level across the five components (Maritime, Land, Air, Special Forces and Logistics) as appropriate. This involves the direction of tier 3 training at the operational and military strategic levels, and the coordination of tier 2 training, at the tactical and operational levels, through the Defence Exercise Planning Process; and the formulation and assessment of Joint Standards and Joint Essential Tasks (JETs) for the JRRF with reference to its manpower, equipment, sustainability and collective performance. This is achieved through monitoring, periodic testing and reporting on training and operations and facilitating joint dialogue between the Services to help them positively exploit one another's training opportunities. The days of sitting in a trench and seeing no air, or flying an aircraft with no land component below, are on their way out. CJFORT therefore finds himself occupying a whole new area, a new space, discovering it to be far bigger than originally anticipated.

The Joint Rapid Reaction Force (JRRF) comprises a pool of combat and support forces from which the UK will meet all short notice, crisis action planned, military contingencies. JRRF's mission is:

> To be a pool of highly capable force elements, maintained at high and very high readiness and trained to the required joint standards. JRRF is to be deployable and sustainable in joint force packages, tailored to meet the operational requirement, in order to conduct operations up to medium scale warfighting, nationally or multinationally under NATO, WEU, UN, OSCE or ad hoc coalition auspices.

The units in the 'pool' are those that are the best trained across the whole range of military capability. This shift away from dependence upon core units and formations is where JRRF differs from its predecessor. The inclusion of Special Forces in the pool is another. The pool units are configured into two echelons according to readiness requirements. First Echelon Forces' readiness varies from 48 hours for Spearhead Forces and the Joint Task Force Headquarters (JTFHQ) to completion within 10 days, followed by the Second Echelon's more substantial capabilities with a phased entry within 11-30 days – far quicker than any European state can achieve.

Subject to availability and commitments, the First Echelon could represent a very potent force. It might contain a maritime task group around an aircraft carrier with frigates and destroyers, cruise missile capable attack submarines, maritime patrol aircraft, mine warfare protection forces and RFA support ships. The naval element might also include an amphibious task group. In addition to light forces, the army could be represented by lead battlegroups from 1 (UK) Armoured Division with their parent brigades in the Second Echelon. The successful positioning of these army assets is dependent upon the force's alignment with the strategic lift required to move it so as to be in place in time to deal with the precise crisis (six ro-ro vessels have been ordered and C-17 aircraft are to be leased pending the availability of the European Future Large Aircraft. Apache Longbow helicopters will shortly be available to become part of JRRF. The Royal Air Force's First Echelon contribution will be a slice across the range of their most capable systems. This is particularly important bearing in mind the need for air that can respond rapidly to provide the Intelligence, Surveillance, Target Acquisition and Reconnaissance (ISTAR) and destructive capability to support light, high readiness land forces. Of special note is the construction of Joint Task Forces from the force elements in the JRRF pool, as this leads to an inevitable, *ad hoc* nature of the deploying force. Whilst this can be mitigated through joint training, there remains a need to develop a sense of teamwork, and a genuine desire to fight as a team.

On a day to day basis, JFHQ is commanded by a brigadier (CJFO) (Army or Royal Marines) who will normally command those JRRF operations which fall within the one-star command level. A larger scale operation would probably see a two-star CJFO appointed to command the operation. There is a group of two-star officers from all three Services whose appointments make them potential Joint Task Force commanders. The 55 staff at JFHQ are broadly organised in the J1-J9 tradition. JFHQ forms the deployable element of PJHQ.

The JRRF concept is still evolving. The Phase 1 development of an initial capability was completed on 1 April 1999. The culmination of the present Phase 2, the development of the full capability, was intended to be Exercise Saif Sareea, currently planned for the Middle East at the end of 2001. The process however has been accelerated due to experience gained in East Timor and Sierra Leone. Meanwhile, as deployments continue, new procedures are continuously being finessed. There is, for example, the

Operational Liaison and Reconnaissance Team (OLRT), one of which is to be ready to move in 24 hours.

Ideally the 6-man team will be commanded by CJFO supported by staff officers drawn from J2, J3, J4 and J6. The immediate impression is that the team is top heavy. That same impression may also have been formed during the course of Operation Langar in East Timor, September-December 1999, where CJFO's presence with an augmented OLRT was evident despite the total British ground contribution only comprising a battalion tac HQ and A Company, 2nd Royal Gurkha Rifles. They were, however, part of the force package which included *HMS Glasgow*, elements of a SAS squadron, 3 C-130s and a VC-10. The justification for the National Contingent Commander (NCC) being of one-star rank is because it is often the lowest rank at which doors can be effectively opened and, if the crisis escalates, he and OLRT form a valuable element in a Forward HQ. The OLRT also contains within its structure individuals with a wealth of experience. They can advise Ambassadors or High Commissioners in or near the hot spots, or, as was the case in Sierra Leone, Heads of Government.

We therefore have this impression of a vibrant, deployable headquarters evolving and refining its procedures over a range of varied operational deployments which, since 1966, have included the operations shown below in Diagram 4-2.

British JFHQ Operational Deployments

Caxton	Montserrat	March 1996
Purposeful	Central Africa	November-December 1996
Determinant	Congo/Zaire	March-June 1997
Alleviate	Albania	June-July 1997
Bolton	Kuwait	February-April 1998
Garrick	Indonesia	May-June 1998
Ladbrook	Congo	August-September 1998
Desert Fox	Middle East	December 1998
Basilica	Sierra Leone	January-February 1999
Agricola	Kosovo	June 1999
Langar	East Timor	September-December 1999
Barwood	Mozambique	February-March 2000
Palliser	Sierra Leone	May-June 2000

Diagram 4.2

UN HQ in New York has none of this sophistication. It is to some degree the victim of circumstances, obliged when considering putting teams together to observe the niceties of gender, ethnic and regional participation, yet ill-at-ease in handling what little intelligence it can access. And yet the answer to many of the problems of the UN's poor responsiveness is provided for in the Charter. The UN's Military Staff Committee has its origins in the 1944 Dumbarton Oaks Conference and was formalised in 1945 at San Francisco with the adoption of Article 47 of the UN Charter. The MSC, comprising the Chiefs of Staff of the Permanent Representatives of the Security Council or their representatives, is vested with the authority and responsibility to enforce peace as directed by the Security Council. It is an unique committee and sole subsidiary body specified by name in the Charter. The disbandment of the Committee would therefore require amendment of the Charter.

The ending of the Cold War meant, in theory at least, that the MSC might at last be resurrected. Russia and France have proposed that be done. There are claims, however, that the MSC is an anachronism and has no place in an international order of a new millennium. But such an argument is equally valid for much of the Charter. Controlled yet creative interpretation of Article 47 could bestow upon the MSC whatever function it is required to undertake. Putting UN forces into East Timor required the *consent* of Indonesia, the responsible state, but, in the meantime, it seems possible that some preventive or anticipatory moves could have been made to ameliorate what was arguably an entirely predictable situation. The UN should become more accustomed to the implementation of preventive deployment. There is no justification for the MSC to be regarded as an exclusive club, even though the three states most consistently involved in world order intervention are members. The Charter specifically permits the co-option of other states with specialisms in dealing with particular problems facing the MSC.

It has been the prospect of collaborating with the MSC and the groundless fear of the dilution of national sovereignty which have caused Washington to steadfastly resist the development of an MSC-oriented, combined planning function in the UN. But international disorder impinges on her interests. President Clinton admitted in February 1999 that Americans should 'embrace the inexorable logic of globalisation' and accept that 'everything, from the strength of our economy to the safety of our cities, to the health of our people, depends on events not only within our borders, but half a world away'.[21] International terrorism affects America, drug trafficking affects her economy (the US has 4 per cent of the world's population consuming 55 per cent of the world's supply of hard drugs) and, since she is likely to be in the forefront of operational planning and operations with principal allies within the MSC, what better place to engage in global contingency planning? The command and control of UN-sponsored operations has invariably been weak. The MSC could provide a valuable buttress.

There is no obligation to turn plans into operations. The open discussion of NATO procedures in New York is becoming a less sensitive issue. States of the Former Soviet Union have operated with NATO in Bosnia and Kosovo. That very specific NATO expertise which became the framework for operations in Bosnia and Kosovo would serve to enhance the MSC as a competent military overview committee with access to quality intelligence and working down to sponsored or sanctioned headquarters. NATO is still likely to operate close to Europe's Central Region and, though only a regional organisation, has a huge military planning staff in relation to what is available to the MSC.[22] The reintroduction of the MSC would promise to reassure those concerned that the Secretariat has too much power by transferring some of that power back to the Security Council where it rightly belongs. The Secretariat is not best placed to decide which military problems should or should not be referred to the Security Council. Ultimately, if any of the Permanent Five is not content with a specific development, there is always recourse to the veto. There were no significant Permanent Five interests associated with East Timor other than the crisis involving the world's fourth most populous state. One of the more negative aspects of the Bosnia crisis was the manner in which the Security Council passed down resolutions which bore no resemblance to what was happening on the ground. The UN does require a competent and credible military authority to provide the Security Council with collective military advice and strategic direction.

That international law is imprecise and open to diverse interpretation is evident from the large number of practising lawyers in this field. Mention has already been made of the two circumstances in which states may legitimately embark upon armed conflict - either by means of a Security Council Resolution or through self-defence in accordance with Article 51 of the UN Charter. It is now apparent that a Third Way has begun to evolve, based upon precedent, to circumvent provisions that some see as too restrictive and outdated. Is this desirable, and can recourse to armed conflict be left to separate understandings of an open-ended international law regime?

UN member states accepted the understanding that the use of force was not the way to settle disputes. But there was no system for arbitration; no international court which could enforce its judgement. The agency of the Security Council could have been engaged to establish peaceful political means to settle disputes yet, today, even responses to intra-state dispute can attract significant international interest. When these interests converge in the Security Council, consideration of the Russian and Chinese veto comes into focus. How frequently we have heard from NATO HQ the assertion that they would not allow Russia or China to set their agenda or recognise the Russian or Chinese veto. The whole basis of the resolution of armed conflict has therefore become undermined. Part of the problem has been the west's failure to appreciate the centrality of the importance of keeping Russia and China engaged and 'on-side'. Giving the states of Central and Eastern Europe (CEE) security guarantees they did not need, through their admission to NATO, exacerbated the isolation of a resentful Russia. It represented the sacrifice of a broad, informed foreign policy to the expediency, in this case, of pay-back time to Polish Democrat voters in the USA and to the then Secretary of State's personal crusade to do good for the Czech Republic. The fact remains, if the leading states do not support established law, no matter how flawed, there will be no law except that of the jungle.

If, therefore, those so inclined can argue that Charter law is no longer appropriate or relevant to today's experience, what is to be said of the right of self-defence? This is an inherent right which predates Charter law. Its *locus classicus* is the 1837 Caroline Incident[23] involving a planned attack from US territory into Canada. The then US Secretary of State conceded that Britain had adopted protective self-defence in frustrating the plotters' intentions. Legitimacy was based on satisfying three conditions: first, it must be a wrongful conflict which poses actual or imminent threat to the *security of the State*; second, there must exist an imperative, immediate necessity to act; and third, action taken must be proportionate to the harm threatened. Since these understandings are couched in the phraseology of inter-state relationships, they have little applicability to today's conflict experiences, the majority of which exist within states.

The Third Way is an opportunistic, pragmatic way of circumventing these admitted difficulties by laying claim to state practice and precedent. Other than humanitarian intervention, military intervention which has been appropriately authorised will be targeted against breaches of international law or acceptable codes of behaviour. If that intervention force then transgresses the law it is, as Michael Howard once remarked, left open to the charge *'tu quoque'*. If the Kosovo example - a clear breach of international law in so far as there was no enabling Security Council Resolution nor an unequivocal case of self-defence - reflects the new wave of thinking it behoves concerned observers to recommend a new way forward. It is no easy matter for, as the Foreign and Commonwealth Office (FCO)[24] admits, there is 'no general doctrine of humanitarian necessity in international law'.[25] Any initiative taken to extend the scope for legitimate intervention through amendment of the UN Charter would require the approval of the Security Council. It may be appropriate to take such an opportunity to make legal provision for implementation-level intervention. There is a beneficial overlap between Chapters VI and VII, as was evident in those resolutions applicable to Northern Iraq and Somalia. Although it can be argued that if legitimacy is in place, that is all that is required, it is a statement open to challenge. The 1975 Helsinki Final Act signed by all participants in the Kosovo conflict (except Albania) debarred any intervention or threat of intervention across the borders of a sovereign state.

There is recognition by a number of senior legal practitioners that the Third Way, the process of change in international law through precedent, is already discernible. In the House of Lords, Lord Milletts cited the Supreme Court of Israel in the 1962 Adolf Eichmann case as a landmark decision. Israel, as did NATO in Kosovo, took international law into its own hands but Israel's recognition of those Security Council Resolutions with which it disagrees has not been a distinguished record. With Eichmann, Israel was on relatively safe ground because, unlike NATO's case for action against Kosovo, there was little question vis-à-vis justification and necessity. Lord Milletts' argument, however, is worth examination:

> The doctrine of state immunity is the product of the classical theory of international law...states were obliged to abstain from interfering in the internal affairs of one another. International law was not concerned with the way in which a sovereign state treated its own nationals in its own territory. It is a cliché of modern international law that the classical theory no longer prevails in its unadulterated form...the way in which a state treated its own borders (has now) become a legitimate concern to the international community.[26]

How does Lord Millets propose that this new, open-ended Third Way can avoid being abused by large powers or powerful organisations using humanitarian intervention as a cloak in the pursuit of naked interests? On the downside in such a reinterpretation of international law, William Rees Mogg wrote:

> It destroys the sanctity of frontiers and the sovereign immunity of nation states. We have gained some legal protection against genocide; we have lost a legal protection against aggression by making every future aggressor a judge in his own cause.[27]

There were arguments in support of the bombing of Serbia to the effect that every care was taken to ensure compliance with Article 57 of the Geneva Convention which prohibits attacks upon civilian targets. British Defence Secretary Robertson, quoting the 'Annan Doctrine' of June 1998,[28] sought legally to justify NATO action in Kosovo. The key component of Kofi Annan's speech was:

> State frontiers, ladies and gentlemen, should no longer be seen as watertight protection for war criminals or mass murderers. The fact that a conflict is 'internal' does not give the parties any right to disregard the most basic rules of human conduct. Besides, most 'internal' conflicts do not stay internal for long. They soon 'spill over' into neighbouring countries.

This is not a new sentiment. Boutros Boutros-Ghali had said the same thing in 1992.[29] Moreover, it does not by itself legitimise military action. Distinguished academicians and lawyers have argued that the bombing of Serbia was legal and morally justifiable.[30] The problem in introducing a sense of flexibility when dealing with the theory of the body of international law, too early to be influenced by precedent, is where to draw the line. Some international lawyers insist that a moral imperative to act may exist when there is no legal justification. This, therefore, is the challenge for the international community; by all means amend the law which relates to armed conflict, define the Third Way, but, in the meantime, obey it.

The maintenance of consensus over the mid to long term will become increasingly difficult to sustain as international organisations expand. This is particularly true of NATO and the EU and so true as to suggest that expansion will render these organisations less effective in the execution of multilateral intervention operations. There is, for example, no common standard vis-à-vis acceptance of casualties. The greater the number of nations involved in the coalition, the less the coalition's chances of surviving, but achieving the politically desirable safety in numbers will tend to reflect a proportional difficulty in achieving military success. It would be wise to examine alternative options. The maintenance of consensus nationally may be no less fraught. *Military Intervention in the 1990s* established the principle that the maintenance of consensus for a successful operation required green lights in three specific areas:

First the need for home support is self-evident. Secondly, but less easy to define (and it would be a mistake to lay down a rule), is what proportion of support is required in the target country. That green light judgement will have to form part of the conflict analysis relating to the target state and consideration of the means available. Lastly, there is the matter of the support of the interventionist forces. The troops that have the requisite mental attitude and military spirit to endure danger and long periods of separation in a war with possibly no national interest present require a special quality. They will need to be convinced that their endeavour is in support of the *bellum justum*, the Just War.[31] The success of the enterprise will be influenced by three factors: the length of time involved in actual fighting; the prospects of success; and (particularly among conscript armies) the casualty rates.[32]

This basic green light theory insists that the three green lights of support have to be maintained in that state. If or when lights flash to yellow, the situation has to be urgently redressed, whereas if the lights switch to red and defy being moved back to green, then disengagement should be investigated.

The green light theory is so self-evident that there is a temptation to apologise for having introduced it. However, if we look at February 1998, Secretary of State Albright, Secretary of Defense Cohen and National Security Adviser Sandy Berger had gone to Ohio State University to lecture on the necessity and justification for launching yet another attack against Iraq. The student body, which had no draft liability to excite them, reacted strongly against the proposal. The three Washingtonians had misread the public mood and its preparedness to cross swords yet again with Saddam Hussein and his suffering people. The fact that there was little domestic support was transmitted to Iraq and around the world by CNN. The Iraqi opposition, the largest in the Arab world, was not effusive in its support for follow-on operations but, more significantly, neither were neighbouring Arab states. Military representatives in London and Washington sought from their political leaders clarification of their concept of operations once Saddam's air defence systems and nbc plants had been hit. The senior commanders had doubts as to the wisdom of the proposed military operation and were clearly unconvinced as to the 'justness' of what their political masters proposed. There were therefore three red lights showing and military action did not, on that occasion, proceed. Not until Saddam Hussein obstructed the work of the UN's weapons inspectors did the international mood change and, as a consequence, military operations were set in train.

NATO's success in maintaining consensus during the Kosovo crisis has been identified as exemplifying a collegial approach to conflict resolution by representative committees. While it is true that consensus was maintained, it would have been a Luddite gesture for any one of NATO's 19 members to challenge the party line. After the bombing of the Chinese embassy, Italy did propose that air attacks on Belgrade should be terminated. But the Italian ambassador realised that there was no prospect of that happening. It was a political initiative taken for domestic consumption. The party line was established by the United States who flew two thirds of the sorties and eighty per cent of the strike missions, selected all but one of 1800 targets and held a monopoly over intelligence gathering.[33] There was only a pretence that this was a NATO campaign. Two other member states, Britain and France, were permitted inputs which were disproportionately high compared with their relative commitments. Lieutenant General Michael Short, commander of the allied air forces over Kosovo, criticised political interference in target selection and singled out France for particular criticism. The general told a Senate Committee that France, which provided less than ten per cent of the air assets, had been permitted to play an overly dominant and restrictive role. It had required the 'personal involvement of General Clark every night to overrule France's determination to withhold a target'.[34] The other 16 member states waited in hopeful expectation of a speedy conclusion to the conflict. The reality is that it is not possible to have 19 individual powers playing meaningful roles.

Neither the North Atlantic Council (NAC) nor the Military Committee found suitable and appropriate roles in NATO's new environment of expeditionary conflict. The NAC became so introspectively focused on the maintenance of consensus that at times they neglected to 'think enemy'. There seems to have been little staff work devoted to addressing Milosevic the person, what was he going to do, what were his options for embarrassing NATO and what would NATO's contingent strategy be for negating the impact of the fast balls coming out of Belgrade? The larger the committee the greater the prospect of it being ponderous. KFOR received its definitive orders to advance into Kosovo a month after it had begun to do precisely that. The main function NATO's committees adopted was to listen to SACEUR and be assured of the acceptability of measures being implemented unilaterally. It is true that the Secretary-General was given the responsibility for approving NATO's targeting plan but this was little more than a fig leaf.

Uppermost in the mind of a democratic superpower intent upon the preservation of its national interest and displaying the product of its power lies in the exercise of control over lesser powers, whether friendly or unfriendly. The machinery through which power is best exercised is the international organisation, of which the two principal organisations in 1993 with which the USA was involved were the UN and NATO. At that time the USA consulted with her allies but it was never more than cosmetic. Power brought in its train a sense of superiority, even of arrogance, which Secretary-General Boutros Boutros-Ghali observed in the fledgling ranking American diplomat in the UN, Madeleine Albright. 'She seemed to assume that her mere assertion of a US policy should be sufficient to achieve the support of other nations.'[35] The increasing expectation of establishing proper, functional internationalism within an egalitarian UN fell foul of a US Congress which complained that UN HQ was threatening the sovereignty of America. The events in Mogadishu on 3 October 1993 created an uncrossable chasm between the UN and Congress. It is easy to rush to judgement to deprecate America's behaviour but this is the nature of power. If the Soviet Union had won the Cold War, who would say they would have been more benevolent in their treatment of the international community? The effective future operation of the UN lies within the gift of the USA.

The Organisation for Security and Cooperation in Europe (OSCE) became a beneficiary of the American coolness towards the UN. However, it was given tasks that could have been performed by other international organisations, arguably with greater efficiency. After the Kosovo crisis reached phase one of its resolution with the establishment of KFOR, the OSCE had two former American ambassadors within its hierarchy. Clinton endeavoured to find tasks for OSCE at the UN's expense. However, the political demise of the UN emphasised the critical importance of America's lead in NATO - a lead which Europe generally conceded as being part of the price of keeping America engaged in Europe. America had a clear understanding of the extent of her leadership role in NATO. On matters which affected her national interest, there would be no compromise. For example when, in 1995, NATO Secretary-General Willy Claes' term came to an unexpectedly premature end, the Europeans nominated as his relief the well-respected former Dutch Prime Minister, Ruud Lubbers. America vetoed that choice for there was no intention of the Secretary-General being a front-line politician. As a compromise, a Spaniard and former pacifist, the unassuming Javier Solana, was appointed. When he became the EU's High

Representative for Foreign Affairs in 1999 he was succeeded by the urbane Briton, George Robertson, who relinquished the proper job of British Secretary of State for Defence with the sweetener of a peerage. As someone unkindly said of Lord Robertson, 'he fully understands what America wants'.[36] Yet he also has strong European credentials and therein lies the potential for a future conflict of interests. It is, however, less of a problem than the lead nation in a defence and security oriented alliance being unprepared to suffer casualties in the execution of the alliance's interests and obligations. That reality renders somewhat suspect the Clinton Doctrine enunciated after the conclusion of the Kosovo conflict:

> I think there's an important principle here that I hope will be now upheld in the future... And that is that while there may well be a great deal of ethnic and religious conflict in the world - some of it might break out into wars - that whether within or beyond the borders of a country, if the world community has the power to stop it, we ought to stop genocide and ethnic cleansing.[37]

An inescapable fundamental is the ubiquity of the media and the immediacy either of their messages or their images. The influence can impact upon the political direction of the conflict, military plans and public opinion. The image of a dead, white American serviceman being pulled through the dust of a Mogadishu suburb by black Somalis had a dramatic and far-reaching effect upon politicians unprepared for such an eventuality. The absence of a contingency plan had, and still has, a profoundly negative influence upon what military action American leaders will countenance in the future. During the Gulf conflict, when both sides watched the same television channel, General Norman Schwarzkopf recollected how:

> One night in early February, we'd turned on CNN to watch a White House press conference. A live report from a pool correspondent in Saudi Arabia preceded it. She said breathlessly, 'There has just been a major artillery duel in my location between the 82nd Airborne and the Iraqis'.

His reaction to this security breach was characteristic 'son of a bitch'.[38] The dramatic images of the battlefield and the state of the defeated Iraqi army had a major impact on the global public, providing justification for the termination of the conflict then and there.

CNN had in Baghdad a television journalist, James Arnett, whose reports, which were subjected to Iraqi reporting restrictions, caused some offence within the United States. This situation was repeated, this time in relation to the BBC's John Simpson (who was also in Baghdad), reporting from Belgrade during the Kosovo conflict. In the privileged environment of the House of Commons, Blair complained that Simpson was reporting under the instruction and guidance of the Serbian authorities.[39] No less excited was General Wesley Clark who 'routinely took time off from the war effort to shout at the television screen in general and CNN in particular'. The press, he said, acted 'under compellence' to 'satisfy the masters in Belgrade'.[40] This case will be more closely examined in the Kosovo chapter but there is no doubt that this type of reporting, apparently as guest of and beholden to the opponent, causes grave resentment among politicians and the military. The fact remains that this is legitimate and invariably honest reporting and as long as producers issue the essential, strong caveat as to the means by which these images were obtained, then there should not be an insurmountable problem. It is something democracy should be sufficiently resilient to stand. It just requires the home political teams to adopt measures to deal with problems which arise from the source of conflict. The Djakovica convoy incident, in which up to 20 refugees died in a NATO air attack, is an example of how NATO's media learnt from the experience. The investigation had been complicated due to the initial identification of the wrong pilot but, after some delay, NATO admitted their error, only for the Pentagon to then deny that there had been any NATO involvement. It was not the most compelling example of unity of command. However, the lesson was learnt and a system of conference calls developed in order to discuss expeditiously and deal with similar problems which were bound to occur. Djakovica also provided the justification for drafting-in spin merchants to assist NATO's media staff with news management. Media operations are an inseparable part of conflict resolution and require strong, plausible messages and resolute action.

Having set out the stall of modern peacekeeping and intervention in this and preceding Chapters, the proof of the pudding lies in its eating. To do this, a number of recent scenarios will be examined, beginning with the Gulf Crisis during which the transition occurred from an inter-state to inter/intra-state conflict, to the intra-state conflicts in Somalia, Rwanda and Kosovo, and concluding with East Timor and Sierra Leone. First, it is necessary to define the new terminology for 'traditional intervention', 'implementation operations' and 'traditional peacekeeping':

> **Military Intervention** is by nature limited war conducted by multinational forces under the authority of a UN Security Council Resolution. It will be regional in nature and involve more comprehensive and more intensive phases of conflict than envisaged for

Implementation Operations Military intervention might see the localised use of WMD (Korea, Vietnam, Gulf Conflict).

An **Implementation Operation** is a multinational military intervention within a state not necessarily with that state's or sub-state's agreement but supported by a UN Security Council Resolution or initially under Article 51 of the UN Charter. The use of armed force is explicit, ranging from proportional response to the adoption of all necessary means (Northern Iraq, Bosnia).

Peacekeeping is conducted impartially by a multinational force comprising the military, police and civilians with the consent of the representative parties involved. Lethal force is only used in self-defence (UNFICYP, Cyprus).

Over ten years ago, the first attempt was made to codify the principles for multilateral military intervention in inter-state conflict. These were: the selection and maintenance of the aim; operate under the auspices and coordination of a valid and supportive international organisation; establish a simple and agreed, united command and control, communications and intelligence organisation; plan the force extraction concurrently with the force insertion; establish an effective *cordon sanitaire* around the target area; maintain consensus; agree and adhere to national contributions; operate within the law; military intervention is the last resort of a collective security machine; utilise the UN's legal mechanism; design a strategy and resource allocation, namely troops to tasks, equipment and finance.[41]

The passage of time and shift of emphasis to intra-state conflict requires some adjustment and some addition to propose revised principles for multilateral military intervention in intra-state conflict, as follows:

- The selection and maintenance of the aim.
- Operate within the law.
- Maintain consensus.
- Plan for the force extraction at the same time as the force insertion - i.e. outline the 'end game'.
- Establish, as required, an effective *cordon sanitaire* around the target area.[42]
- Military Intervention is the last resort of a collective security machine.
- Know your enemy.
- Win the Information War.

5 Operations in Iraq 1990-91 and their Consequences

The 1990-91 Gulf Crisis from the invasion of Kuwait to follow-on operations in Northern Iraq is important but not so much for the conduct of the battle as for the lessons which emerge from its origins and cessation - of sorts. The crisis represented the first occasion since 1945 when the international order engaged in armed conflict against a significant dictator with access to weapons of mass destruction (WMD). At what stage Saddam Hussein decided on a short, victorious war against Kuwait, both to solve his nepotocracy's dramatic economic problems and to resolve the long-standing territorial issues in addition to bonding his disparate tribes, is not clear. It was, however, on 17 July 1990 that the first perceptible move against Kuwait (and the other Gulf states) was made. Saddam Hussein claimed that the Gulf states had used 'a poisoned dagger' to stab Iraq in the back by depressing the price of oil and by exceeding OPEC production quotas. There was some truth in that claim but it hardly amounted to a *casus belli.* The next day, at a meeting of the Arab League, Iraq's Foreign Minister Tariq Aziz claimed that Kuwait had stolen $2.4 billion of Iraqi oil and, furthermore, had laid out defensive positions on Iraq's soil. Kuwait rejected the allegations. Claim and counter-claim continued for four days until 22 July 1990, when Tariq Aziz arrived in Cairo to attend an emergency Arab summit.

Kuwait insisted that the problem should be resolved by the Arabs without foreign involvement. Meanwhile, the Baghdad newspapers claimed that the Kuwaiti foreign minister was an agent of the USA. The tension in the Middle East had already caused oil prices to rise as Iraq had wished. Iraq was still not satisfied, insisting that OPEC should force the price even higher. On 24 July, 100,000 heavily-armed Iraqis deployed on the Kuwaiti border. Western observers determined that the troops' function was to intimidate, not to invade Kuwait. Indeed, Saddam Hussein promised that they would not invade Kuwait. President Hosni Mubarak of Egypt, believing Saddam, indulged in urgent shuttle diplomacy in Baghdad,

Kuwait and Jeddah. OPEC agreed to raise the price of a barrel of oil to $21, but still Iraq was not satisfied.

On 1 August 1990, the talks in Jeddah between Kuwait and Iraq collapsed. Kuwait refused to accede to Iraqi demands for Kuwaiti territory. At 2am local time on 2 August, to the embarrassment of western intelligence analysts,[1] 30,000 Iraqi troops led by the elite Presidential Republican Guard Corps and *coup de main* heli-borne detachments invaded Kuwait. According to Baghdad Radio, their *Anschluss* was in response to a call from young revolutionaries who had mounted a coup attempt. Kuwait's 23,000-strong armed forces were taken completely by surprise and only in some areas was there sporadic fighting. Other than isolated acts of armed resistance, which would continue throughout the early stages of the occupation, Kuwait city had been subdued in just thirty-six hours. The 62 year old Emir escaped to Saudi Arabia in a helicopter, but his younger brother, Sheikh Fahd, was killed fighting on the steps of the Dasman Palace. Kuwait means 'small fortress'; against a large, surprise Iraqi attack, it did prove to be a too small and too unprepared fortress.

A Transitional Free Government announced that the Emir and his 'stooges' had been deposed. Saddam compared the Emir with the fabulously rich, sixth century BC King Croesus. He was the 'Croesus of Kuwait and his aides became the obedient, humiliated and treacherous dependants of foreigners'. It was the thus far unknown new government's intention that:

> the interim free government, after securing necessary stability in the country will hold free and honest elections [which would be a novelty in both Iraq and Kuwait] to elect a new assembly which represents the people and will decide the form of government and other basic issues.

The 'token institutions' established by the al-Sabah family were denounced in a 'pot calling the kettle black' statement which declared the Kuwaiti institutions to be 'nothing but a cover for nepotistic and despotic rule'. It was widely reported at the time that the Iraqi leading the nine-member Transitional Free Government was Colonel Ali Hassan al-Majid. Not only was he prime minister, commander-in-chief and defence and interior minister but exiled Kuwaitis claimed (vehemently denied by Iraq) that he was Saddam's son-in-law. (He was removed from office in November 1990 and re-emerged after the war, in March 1991, as interior minister.) Ali Hassan al-Majid was formerly the Iraqi local government minister. It is also believed that he was responsible for crushing the 1987-88 Kurdish rebellion when he was serving as the senior Baath party member in Kurdistan. 'Brother Arabs in Kuwait', the appeal continued, 'the free interim government of Kuwait greets you and calls on you to support the uprising of your free brothers. You are our relatives. What is ours is yours and our tasks are your tasks'. There were words of reassurance and good intent towards the thousands of resident foreigners, subject to them behaving. If they did not, they would be hit with 'an iron fist'.

Before the thirty-six hours had elapsed it had become apparent to Saddam Hussein that again he had blundered and had made a serious miscalculation in attacking Kuwait. He had gambled on a near-certainty that the world would accept the *fait accompli* of the invasion. Iraq's *Al-Jumhuriya* newspaper advised that 'the imperialist forces should accept the fact and acknowledge it, no matter how bitter it tastes in their stinking mouths'. Not only did the imperialist forces not accept the fact, but far more significantly neither did the Soviet Union who had an in-being treaty of friendship and cooperation with Iraq. Almost as surprising was the condemnation emanating from a majority within the Arab League, which extinguished Saddam Hussein's hopes of a pan-Arab state. All these threads culminated in the Security Council censure of Baghdad by their Resolution 660.

Iraq has enjoyed only two years of peace during Saddam Hussein's presidency. One of the results of the years of war was to limit Saddam's freedom to travel abroad. Besides, autocrats are by nature loath to leave their power base too often and instead surround themselves with minders who limit access to the president. This meant that Iraq's president was the least internationally streetwise of the Arabian leaders for, first, he had totally failed to register the important growth in world interdependence which had coincided with the end of the Cold War and, second, if he had noticed the ending of the Cold War he had failed to grasp its significance in terms of the potential for superpower cooperation. Absolutists are not surrounded by outspoken, impartial advisers who give balanced judgements. His foreign policy representatives had become diplomatic neuters. The consequences of giving Saddam advice he did not want to hear had often proved fatal. Foreign Minister Tariq Aziz was (wrongly) reported to have been executed for opposing the invasion. The then 53 year old politician is a Christian with a degree in English Literature and is well versed in the nuances of western politics. Outwardly, however, he behaved as an obedient party *apparatchik,* aware of both the quality and tone of advice required.

Prior to the conflict, Saddam Hussein drew his military advice from a committee of three generals. The prospect of a military schism existing outside this disparate clique was highly probable, for Iraq's professional officers would have been acutely conscious of their army's capabilities and prospects of military success against the growing Allied forces. The professional military were doubtless aware of the concept of air-land operations developing in the West and the significance that concept had for possible conflict in the Middle East. The thought of a divide between Saddam Hussein and the military, however, was not universally held. A conclusion following the Iran/Iraq war was that:

> Iraq won the war through its own efforts and skill, and a substantial amount of credit for this must go to the Iraqi military. The officers adopted the doctrine needed to take the offensive and then drilled their troops to bring them to a high level of proficiency. Overall, the Iraqi officer corps is professionalized and obviously has pride in its accomplishments. There is virtually no sign that the Iraqi army is estranged from the regime; if anything it appears to be its mainstay.[2]

Saddam's decision to take direct command of Iraq's armed forces against the Allies, as Hitler had done on the Eastern Front, would not have been greeted by his generals with universal approval. The poverty of his strategic prowess did not deter him from interfering in earlier military affairs. In 1986, for example, a series of battlefield disasters obliged a quorum of generals to face up to him and insist that his further meddling in the war would lead to an Iraqi defeat. So parlous had the military situation become that Saddam had to accede and back off but he never forgave, and every member of the group of generals which confronted him disappeared. By drawing together the military and political leadership, Saddam Hussein accentuated the possibility of a military coup. It might at the time have seemed a sensible military appreciation to give up Kuwait in order to save Iraq. But due to his own personal involvement, Saddam Hussein was firmly committed to retaining Kuwait.

It was from 1988 that the 'Ceaucescu-isation' of Saddam Hussein became most apparent. Historically his country had been the centre of world power and the seat of a dozen empires. He harked back to these past glories of Iraq rather than becoming aware of the changes that had occurred around him. In the past, if he had a supply problem with one state he could always rely on finding another state willing to sell him what he wanted. When the former Soviet Union refused to release weaponry for the duration of his occupancy of Iranian territory, he turned instead to France and other western states. Saddam could pick and choose among the western and Warsaw Pact countries so long as he could offer them political, diplomatic and economic benefit. At a stroke, his invasion of Kuwait made him dispensable.

The Soviet newspaper *Rabochaya Tribuna* was unimpressed by Iraq's claim that the intervention had been by invitation. They had, of course, seen it all before: 'We have learned how to send in troops in response to an appeal or in order to block possible foreign interference'. The paper concluded that the 'crime' had been committed because Baghdad 'does not want to pay the bills from the Arab countries which helped it during the conflict with Iran'. The more authoritative Soviet news agency Tass took the view that Iraq's deliberate aggression was 'to resolve at one go all its acute political and economic problems: to boost the price of crude oil, to get from Kuwait $2.4 billion in compensation and to write off its $15 billion debt'. With these strong words had come the suspension of Soviet arms supplies to Iraq. When Moscow was faced with the choice between supporting a wayward friend and damaging her new image as a responsible actor in foreign affairs it was clear that Iraq was expendable. There was also evidence in both Moscow and Washington of a guilt complex for their part in nurturing the monster. All along, however, Moscow attempted to keep a bridge open to Baghdad.

Saddam Hussein enjoyed western support during the struggle with Iran, in which Iraq suffered equally with Iran. Nevertheless, Saddam went on to claim victory, and it was a victory of sorts because, in neutralising Iran, he had opened up the prospect of marching on Kuwait without the fear of intervention by his eastern neighbour. Although Saddam's inability to grasp the finer points of strategy led to his failure to achieve the military objectives against Iran, he enjoyed the support of both superpowers and most of the Arab world. In taking Kuwait, Saddam possessed the strength to achieve his military objectives but this was at the expense of the alienation of both superpowers and most of the Arab world. His political foundation had crumbled. There was to be no political victory and in his dalliance, while the United States and Arab forces reinforced Saudi Arabia, he also let slip the military initiative. This would not herald an immediate collapse for, despite domestic deprivation, cruelty and excesses, the settling of the account with the rich in Kuwait had restored some of the pride of the suffering Iraqi population.

Kuwait was the first domino to tumble in a long-term strategy designed to end in a triumphant final act with a victorious showdown with Israel.

Saddam calculated that such an aim was indeed achievable. Iraq had proved to be a useful sponge for international weaponry, goods and foodstuffs as well as being a beneficial target to divert the attention of what had become an obsessive western phobia of a volatile, virulent and unstable form of Iranian fundamentalism. The western aim had been to neutralise Iran through the willing surrogacy of Iraq. At the time, the USA would have clutched at any straw that promised to assuage the humiliation suffered during the siege of the American Embassy in Tehran. The irony is that Saddam Hussein posed a far greater threat to moderate states in the Gulf, and therefore to Gulf security, than was ever posed by the late Ayatollah Khomeini.

The support of Saddam came at a price. The USA shrugged off the twin Exocet attack by an Iraqi Mirage F1 on the *USS Stark* with the loss of thirty-seven lives in order to preserve a trade agreement and keep Saddam sweet. He was a man who enjoyed a charmed and unrealistic life in international politics. His abysmal record on human rights and acts of ethnic cleansing were overlooked by the West so as not to cause waves at a time when Security Council Resolution 598 was being seriously considered. One US senator, Claiborne Pell, Chairman of the Senate Foreign Relations Committee, attempted to have sanctions imposed on Iraq as a protest against that country's human rights record. The Reagan administration intervened to squeeze the sanction move out. Iraq remained the beneficiary of a kind of deceptive support which was only good for as long as it suited the power brokers. Saddam's sabre-rattling was discernible from a speech in Amman on 24 February 1990 but, as the rhetoric grew both louder and more frequent, governments were warned by their advisers not to overreact. The journalist responsible for a strong, anti-Saddam broadcast on the Voice of America on 15 February 1990 was sacked. Iraq's name was not to appear on the list of the most persistent violators before the UN Commission on Human Rights, even at a time when Amnesty International and the Washington-based Middle East Watch loudly accused Iraq of the most grotesque violations of human rights. The Iraqis also induced a number of developing countries to do a deal so that Baghdad would not be criticised.

With such a record, the judicial murder of the alleged spy and *Observer* reporter, Farzad Bazoft, was already preordained. The execution, in Iraq's eyes, emphasised her superiority. After implementing diplomatic action, the British government worked hard to ensure that the trade links between the two countries had not been irreparably damaged by the justifiable public outcry of protest. In 1982, Iraq became Britain's biggest Middle East customer after Saudi Arabia and, in the two years since the earlier Gulf War, British export credits amounted to £690 million. It was immediately following Saddam's worst chemical attack on the Kurds at Halabja that Britain doubled Iraq's export credit guarantee. The London *Times* of 3 August 1990 commented: 'Observers believe that episode convinced President Saddam that, as long as Iraq had money to spend abroad, all avowed concern for human rights in the world would remain hypocrisy'.

False signals emanated not only from London but also, and more importantly, from Washington. At the time when Iraq mobilised on the border, Congress had enacted a series of unilateral economic measures against Iraq. The Congress initiative was to be opposed both by the State Department and by the White House, who wanted to 'keep the dialogue open'. They saw in sanctions a weakening of the USA's leverage on Saddam Hussein, something which was not in the USA's foreign policy interests. The day after the Under-Secretary of Commerce, Dennis Kloske, testified in the House that he had recommended more stringent controls on the export of US high technology to Iraq, he was dismissed. The immorality of the Iraqi regime had been regularly exposed by the Middle East Watch and openly acknowledged by the most recent State Department review of human rights violations.

Business considerations, however, relegated these widely held moral objections to the giving of unproductive lectures. On 15 June 1990, the State Department's Assistant-Secretary of State for Near Eastern Affairs appeared before the Senate Foreign Relations Committee to justify the administration's appeasement of Saddam Hussein. Trade sanctions against Iraq were not the way forward because, according to the State Department's representative, 'our competitors in Canada, Australia, Europe and Japan would step in quickly to fill the breach'. Iraq was an important US export market, taking US$1 billion of agricultural products each year, including cattle, chickens, eggs, tobacco and 23 per cent of the nation's total rice output. Two months later, during a committee hearing in the House of Representatives, the Democrats blamed the State Department for pursuing a policy which, they felt, might have encouraged Iraq to invade Kuwait. It had been a 'policy premised in fiction and fantasy'. The BBC World Service broadcast a statement by Assistant-Secretary John Kelly to Congress, to the effect that there was no treaty obligation with Kuwait which would require US forces to defend Kuwait.

The State Department's Near East Bureau was not the only source from which Saddam Hussein might have claimed to have misinterpreted signals emanating from the USA. He warned the US Ambassador, April Glaspie, that he would take whatever steps were necessary to halt Kuwait's economic war against Iraq. Allegedly speaking on the instructions of Secretary of State Baker, Ambassador Glaspie said, according to the Iraqi transcript, that the USA had 'no opinion on the Arab-Arab conflicts, like your border disagreement with Kuwait'. The *Washington Post* emphasised the similarities of the presumed diplomatic *faux pas* involving Kuwait and what had happened in Korea. The attack on South Korea by the North was said by some authorities to have been triggered by the State Department's exclusion of Korea from within the USA's defensive perimeter. Similarly, a number of actions by Britain prior to 1982 had led Argentina to the erroneous conclusion that Britain was not prepared to fight for the independence of the Falklands. According to the *Washington Post*:

> The substance of Miss Glaspie's recorded remarks closely parallels official US positions stated in Washington at the same time, in which other state officials publicly disavowed any American security commitments to Kuwait.

Later, the hapless Miss Glaspie explained to the *New York Times*: 'Obviously I didn't think and nobody else did, that the Iraqis were going to take *all* of Kuwait'.[3] What she may have intended to signal to Saddam Hussein was the alleged State Department's official position that there was no fundamental objection to Iraq taking Warba and Bubiyan islands. Interestingly, Secretary Baker did not resign, as Foreign Secretary Lord Carrington did after the Foreign Office misread Argentine intentions towards the Falklands.

April Glaspie made no further public statements after her *New York Times* interview until she appeared before the Senate Foreign Relations Committee in April 1991. The administration had not wished to divert the attention of the anti-Iraq coalition. She told the Committee that the Iraqi transcript had been edited to such a degree that it was 'disinformation'. She said that Saddam had been made aware of Washington's intention to defend its vital interests in the Gulf and of its support for the sovereignty and integrity of the Gulf states. Was this a classic case of plausible deniability? April Glaspie left her critics with a simple choice of 'Saddam's words or mine'.

State Department exasperation over Israeli intransigence sent a false message to Baghdad that the State Department, whose attention was also held by troubles nearer home in Trinidad and Liberia, had adopted a more *laissez-faire* attitude towards a client so despised by Iraq. What these unintentional, small fragments of international body language added up to in Baghdad was the mistaken, cumulative view that indecision and hesitancy were signs of either weakness or lack of interest or both. All that this appeasement had achieved was the feeding of the Thief of Baghdad's megalomaniac appetite. He had come to the conclusion that the West would not be prepared to suffer the quantity of casualties that would be required to stop his ambition. He boasted to April Glaspie that: 'Yours is a society which cannot accept 10,000 dead in one battle'. It would transpire that the shoe was on the other foot when 'the mother of all battles' suffered a severe miscarriage.

But the diplomatic and economic appeasement, which had been a feature up until 2 August 1990, was set aside. The United States, the Soviet Union, Britain and the rest of Europe had all suffered the consequences of the appeasement of Hitler. They remembered their history and determined to stop Saddam Hussein's attempt at Arab hegemony in the 'Rhineland' of Kuwait.

If Saddam's former clients were at fault for what had come to pass, it was the fault of not making their intentions clear. Mention has been made of similar misconceptions arising in the minds of the aggressors in Korea in 1950 and the Falklands in 1982 when they too had misread international body language. The time to have 'drawn the line in the sand' was on 24 July 1990, and the place to have drawn it was the Iraq/Kuwait border in front of the 100,000 massed Iraqi troops. It had been an error of judgement not to have convened a meeting of the Security Council to warn off Iraq and to have backed that warning with the precautionary move of significant force into the Gulf. In such a situation, it would have been possible to initiate the Soviet concept of preventive diplomacy or preventive deployment whereby a force would be established on the Kuwait side of the border with the permission of Kuwait. The force might arguably have forestalled Saddam Hussein, but such an action is more certain to succeed in less cut-and-dried circumstances. Preventive deployment should be seen as a trip-wire deterrent by which violation is linked to certain retaliation. A discreet US 'short notice exercise' was held in the Gulf, 600 miles south of the Iraq/Kuwait border, but it failed to intimidate Saddam. Judith Kipper of the Brookings Institution said: 'I think we have enough experience of the Iraqi approach to protecting what it says are its interests to know that if Hussein puts troops on the border he is not bluffing'. Saddam's *bête noire*, Senator Claiborne Pell, claimed that had President Bush (and presumably

Reagan) responded to previous Iraqi crimes, Saddam Hussein might have got the message that his lawlessness would not be tolerated. Similarly, if the apprehension of declared war criminals post-Bosnia had been energetically pursued, would there have been a Kosovo crisis? Pell likened Saddam to 'the Adolf Hitler of the Middle East. Like Hitler, he is emboldened when there is no reaction to his outrages'. Anthony Eden saw Nasser as an Adolf Hitler, and the US State Department regarded President Milosevic of Yugoslavia in the same light. Linkage such as this provides a rationale for what, in some cases, can be a dangerous obsession. A week after the invasion of Kuwait had occurred, President Bush admitted:

> If history teaches us anything, it is that we must resist aggression or it will destroy our freedoms. Appeasement does not work. As was the case in the 1930s, we see in Saddam Hussein an aggressive dictator threatening his neighbours.

The concern uppermost in the minds of leaders in many state capitals was the influence their own and other forces could exert upon the political and economic life within the ethnic and religious tinderbox of the Middle East.

Saddam Hussein learned an important lesson from the 1967 Six Day War and from the ease of destruction of the Osiraq nuclear reactor. Subsequent builds within Iraq were of special, hardened facilities. In some years, up to 50 per cent of gnp had been allocated to defence. Three hundred super aircraft bunkers were among the protected facilities that this money acquired in a multimillion-pound British contract. The concrete and steel shelters were built on eight new air bases, three of which were in the north of the country. The roofs were made of steel, above which was a four-feet-thick layer of reinforced concrete below a deep sand covering which provided both camouflage and additional protection. The doors, protected by a concrete and sandblast wall, were made of two-feet-thick steel and concrete and weighed 40 tons. The one or more aircraft in each shelter were thought to be virtually immune from damage. Events would prove that they were not.

The interregnum, from the time when the Iraqi army so unwisely marched into Kuwait until the separate Allied operations coalesced into the American-led Operation Desert Storm, had lasted five months and thirteen days. Throughout that period, the search for a diplomatic solution had run parallel with a slow-working and only partially successful embargo. In order to avoid the invocation of the War Powers Act, Washington described the naval blockade as a 'naval interdiction'. Three quite separate sets of positions emerged. First, it became increasingly evident that in no circumstances would Saddam Hussein relinquish his hold on Kuwait. He, as Hitler before him, was prepared to defend his position in his capital from a secure bunker, fighting to the last Iraqi. Secondly, there was a genuinely-held desire for a peaceful settlement based upon Iraq's unconditional withdrawal from Kuwait. This was principally a European goal but Europe had been weakened through being marginalised by Saddam Hussein's dismissive treatment and also through its ill-concealed divisions. It is a truism of international relations that coalition governments rarely respond positively in crises with strong and uncompromising foreign policy. It was during the course of this diplomatic phase that Europe's aspirations to be seen as a political force in the world took a decidedly backward step. 'To be brutally frank', admitted the then EC President Jacques Delors with unusual candour to the European Parliament on 23 January 1991, 'public opinion sensed that Europe was rather ineffectual'. Finally, there were also within the equation others who, while prepared to mouth the utterances of diplomacy, had private hopes that Saddam Hussein would indeed decline to withdraw from Kuwait.

One of the conditions for Iraq's withdrawal leading to 'peace and security in the area' was an Allied guarantee that Iraqi territory would be spared subsequent military action. A number of opposing states took the view that this would be little more than an exercise in papering over cracks, of postponing an inevitable conflict and one which, in time, could but increase the potential of the magnitude of Iraq's destructive force. Among the states to hold such a view were Israel and certain Arab states within the Allied coalition. On Wednesday, 16 January 1991, less than twenty-four hours after the expiry of the United Nations deadline, the air and naval onslaught went ahead.

The intervention proper to liberate Kuwait had begun. Facing each other on the Saudi-Kuwait border were an estimated 1.2 million servicemen from Iraq and the military representatives of seventeen states who had contributed to the coalition land order of battle: at 440,000, the US force level had grown to three-quarters as many as there had ever been in Vietnam. In addition, contributions from other Allied states exceeded 265,000. There were erroneous reports that over half the Iraqi Army - 500,000 - were deployed in or in support of their defence of Kuwait. Subsequent assessments suggest that figure may have been exaggerated. The combined strength of the forty-two divisions facing the Allies probably numbered 350,000. Nevertheless, this conflict was big in every respect. The first air attack was of three hours' duration and, in that one period, aircraft and the $1.3 million Tomahawk Cruise missiles had delivered with great accuracy 18,000 tons of high explosives on pre-selected Iraqi targets. This tonnage was equivalent to that dropped on Hiroshima and was twice that required to destroy the German city of Dresden. Air power made the highly successful hundred-hour land campaign possible.

It might seem curious, therefore, that the facing-up of such powerful forces would not have led to a declaration of war. The legal state or condition of war can only exist where one or more states makes an unequivocal, non-rhetorical war declaration. Saddam Hussein's call for a *jihad* or holy war does not fall within that category. It was the involvement of the United Nations which acted to ensure that a state of war between Iraq and others would not exist. Unlike in Korea, the Allied troops in the Gulf were not put under nominal UN command, but there is no doubt that they had the UN's authority to take enforcement action to oblige Iraq to comply with those UN Resolutions relating to Kuwait. Whether or not war has been declared does not absolve parties of the armed conflict from their freely entered-into obligations under the 1949 Geneva Conventions and the body of international law.

What this crisis demonstrated was the need to investigate the means by which the United Nations would be given positive and credible command functions and an overall higher visibility. That requires the construction of the requisite political and military architecture. Given that the Allied offensive against Iraq and occupied Kuwait was under the UN umbrella, it seems a curious oversight not to have informed the UN Secretary-General when the attack was launched. There was a suspicion among some of the Allies that the UN was being manipulated and used selectively in order to achieve the undeclared aims of the Pax Americana. What irked a number of Europeans was the consistent and unilateral lead taken by the Americans in the decision-making process.

The Gulf Crisis coincided with the end of the Cold War, an event which had served to 'date' some of the Articles in the UN Charter to the degree that, 45 years on, they were no longer relevant or appropriate. Under Article 43, for example, states undertook to make forces available to the Security Council for operations such as that proposed for the Gulf. States did, however, come forward voluntarily to offer military, political and economic support. For the first time, the members of the United Nations had joined together to work in the collegial manner as first envisaged by the drafters of the UN Charter. But this was a states-versus-state conflict, with an identifiable villain, where money was no object, where the legality of the operation was not in doubt, to be fought out in an environment where high technology weaponry could be efficiently used to reduce casualties within defined boundaries. The attraction of the proposed conflict to the remaining superpower was that the end result was not in doubt, success was guaranteed, and therefore putting down Saddam Hussein would be a salutary lesson for other, lesser states considering 'taking-on' the United States. Desert Storm represented the perceived mid-intensity, limited war, fought out not in NATO's Central Region but in the open expanse of Middle Eastern desert, the absolutely ideal environment for the conduct of armoured and high technology manoeuvre warfare.

The Gulf Crisis caused international expectations to be unrealistically raised, for it was an inter-state conflict, something for which the United Nations had been specifically designed. However, by 1990 inter-state conflicts were becoming rare. In 1992, for example, there had been 30 major armed conflicts throughout the world - a major armed conflict being characterised by prolonged combat between the military forces of two or more governments, or of one government and at least one armed group, involving the use of weapons and incurring battle-related deaths of at least 1,000.[4] Only one of those 30 conflicts had been inter-state (India v. Pakistan) and in the following year, when the number of major armed conflicts had fallen to 28, every one was an intra-state conflict. Intra-state conflicts have always been the dominant form of global conflict but intervention by third parties had, until the Iraq Conflict had run its course, been considered taboo.

The Gulf Conflict, of which the intervention into Northern Iraq was a continuation, was a classic Chapter VII enforcement operation. The form the intervention took was as a UN-*sanctioned* operation. A framework state (the United States) commanded and controlled the military operations under the loosest of guidance and authority provided by a UN mandate. What seemed to a number of the more important members of the General Assembly - notably India - to be handing a blank cheque to the Americans, gave rise to adverse comment and criticism which did nothing to raise America's already low opinion of the United Nations. US/UN relations reached a nadir following the Somalia debacle in 1993, to the degree that the superpower virtually dissociated herself from the international body, thereby weakening the organisation. As the then Secretary-General, Javier Pérez de Cuellar confirmed, the operation was firmly in the hands of the United States and her principal supporters:

> The war is not a classic United Nations war in the sense that there is no United Nations control of the operations, no United Nations flag, (blue) helmet, or any engagement of the Military Staff Committee. What we know about the war, which I prefer to call hostilities, is what we hear from the three members of the Security Council which are involved - Britain, France and the United States - which every two or three days report to the Council after the actions have taken place. The Council which has authorised all this (is informed) only after the military activities have taken place.

The launching of the formal Allied ground attack into Kuwait and Iraq at 1am on 24 February 1991 gave rise to the only major test of Security Council collegiality. At the time when President Bush ordered the coalition troops to advance, there had been a Soviet peace plan 'on the table'. The Iraqi response to the plan had been ambiguous, Kuwait's oil wells had been put to the torch, the infrastructure was being systematically destroyed and parts of the population had either been taken north as prisoners or summarily executed. This was the time for the Allied coalition to observe strictly the UN mandate and the twelve resolutions. That is precisely what the Soviet peace plan neglected to do. It had not addressed Iraq's war crimes, nor did it satisfy the UN's requirement that Saddam Hussein should not profit from the invasion and sacking of Kuwait. Certainly there was some vying for regional pre-eminence between the two important powers. What had irked the US administration was that it had been they who had taken the political risks and suffered the slings and arrows of the campaign. At the eleventh hour there appeared to be a risk that they would be upstaged by the Soviets, who had had none of those risks but threatened to capture the political high ground with their own peace initiative. In the event, it did not happen. What the Gulf Crisis so indelibly underlined was the confirmation of the continuing decline of Soviet power and influence. This did not mean that in the future there might not be some Russian political or military display as if to suggest there had been no actual diminution of power. Note, for example, the advance of the Russian detachment in 1999 from Bosnia to Pristina airport.

The arrangements for ultimate peace required that the Soviets remain on-side and for the superpower rapport to be sustained. Beijing regretted the beginning of the offensive and Moscow also regretted that 'the instinct for a military solution won through'. Reading between the lines, it was apparent that the Kremlin, although bitterly disappointed at being marginalised, would keep in step with the Allied coalition as long as the campaign was of short duration. The Soviets had learned that Security

Council Resolutions freely entered into promised to be more difficult to disengage from. One veto from any one of the other four permanent members is sufficient to prevent change coming about.

A long-drawn-out war would have created difficulties for President Mikhail Gorbachev, difficulties emanating from what was then a strengthening conservative lobby. International relations is a series of wheels within wheels. What the Soviets had attempted and failed to achieve with their political initiative in 1991 was what the Americans had succeeded in doing in 1956 at the half-way point of modern Iraq's development. The Americans intervened in 1956 to prevent the Anglo-French coalition from putting down Nasser. President Richard Nixon admitted later that the US intervention had been a mistake: Nasser's survival and the primacy of his will over the former imperialists enhanced his status as an unique pan-Arab leader. His followers went on to murder Iraq's royal family and in 1967 he considered Egypt sufficiently strong to challenge Israel for leadership of the region. There is some speculation that it had become an unspoken Washington aim that Saddam Hussein would not be permitted to emulate Nasser's example or be the trigger to set Israel once more upon the warpath.

This account, beginning with the move to the starting blocks for the military intervention, must obviously be a record of difficulties rather than failure. Militarily, Saddam Hussein was certain to face defeat in the Allied effort to remove his forces from Kuwait. The only circumstances that could be envisaged whereby the putative military intervention could fail would be lack of resolve and substantial erosion of consensus within key sending states. The 1990-1 Gulf Crisis is therefore an illuminating example of a situation fraught with problems and difficulties at a time when the outlook appeared so positive and favourable.

In the Gulf, the UN had shown itself to be an important and effective international organisation and, in view of its comprehensive display of competence, an even more important future role seemed assured. Saddam Hussein's invasion of Kuwait had been almost universally condemned. The international cooperative venture raised to make the point that aggression by one state against another must not be allowed to succeed had the significant benefit of political, military and economic support as well as the all-important aspect of the backing of international law. So how was it that a small, war-weary, virtually landlocked state of 17 million, of whom only 5 million were males over the age of fourteen, which had been the subject of twelve Security Council Resolutions, faced up not only to worldwide condemnation and opprobrium but also to the most sophisticated array of weaponry ever assembled? It is too simplistic to suggest that this was due to Saddam Hussein's stupidity. He had been stupid, but the capabilities of his ground forces were afforded considerable - in time, proved unwarranted - respect. The difficulties that arose are worth enumeration in order to serve as a lesson for the future. There were two distinct paths towards the goal of defeating Saddam Hussein: by laying siege to, or by destroying, his citadel.

There is a rather obvious correlation between allowing time for diplomacy to succeed and the impact which that concession is likely to have upon force structures. There are a number of related threads here. First, there is the recognition that it is in the nature of the autocrat to gamble. In Saddam Hussein's case, he had nothing to lose by gambling. He had made a second, grave military miscalculation during the currency of his leadership. If he had responded to UN Resolution 660 prior to armed conflict and withdrawn from Kuwait, his continuing leadership of Iraq would have been most unlikely. 'I have two options', Saddam Hussein explained to a senior member of the Algerian delegation to Baghdad: 'to be killed by US bombs or by Iraqi officers. In the first case I shall be a martyr, in the second a traitor. If I withdraw unconditionally from Kuwait, I shall certainly have to face the second scenario'. It is also true that some national elements within the Allied consortium would not have been prepared to allow Saddam Hussein the opportunity to withdraw, regroup and attack again as a wiser man with his improving weapons systems of mass destruction still intact. It is for this reason that one of the lessons of intervention - that of offering an opponent who had overreached himself a face-saving exit - was in this case, for some, not applicable.

Secondly, ethnic and national considerations dictated that diplomacy had to be given time to work. The Middle East is a great tinderbox capable of being fuelled from the world's largest reservoir of oil reserves. Damage inflicted upon significant extraction areas - Saudi Arabia as well as Kuwait - might well have driven the cost of oil towards $100 per barrel. Those who would suffer would be not only the economies of the leading powers but also a Third World already crippled by debt. A diplomatic solution offered the additional advantage of not triggering the anticipated worldwide terrorist backlash, some of the groups of which had relocated to Baghdad from Damascus. Among these were Abu Nidal's 300-strong Fatah Revolutionary Council and Abu Abbas's Palestine Liberation Front. Other pro-Saddam groups were the military wing of the Baath Party, the Arab Liberation Front, and a group which had specialised in attacks on aircraft, the Arab Organisation 15th May. In the event, the terrorist backlash did not transpire, for which Syria claimed some of the credit.

A high proportion of states, among them many European, favoured the investigation of those avenues which avoided direct armed conflict, principally through diplomacy and by embargo. It was for this reason that almost four months would elapse by the time, on 29 November 1990, Security Council Resolution 678 authorised:

> member states cooperating with the government of Kuwait, unless Iraq on or before 15 January 1991 fully implements the foregoing resolutions, to use all necessary means to uphold and implement Security Council Resolution 660 and to restore international peace and security in the area; requests all states to provide appropriate support for the actions undertaken in pursuance of this resolution.

It was evident that the main body of those who subscribed to the ultra-cautious approach were those who had not provided ground forces authorised to 'use all necessary means' to force Iraq out of Kuwait. Blood is a more emotive commodity than political support or treasure, and action more fraught than rhetoric. The prospect of bitter recrimination arising between those who had supplied forces and those who had not was avoided due to the short duration of war and the low casualty rate.

During the course of this interregnum the Iraqi Army, which is highly competent in field engineering, built defences of Maginot length if not sophistication, and stationed what was believed to have been half their land forces on Kuwaiti territory. As the defences improved, the size of the opposing Allied force had to be revised upward. It is a lesson of coalition operations that the longer the delay in moving, the greater the response required. There is an association here with available strategic lift and also utilising that lift early. An ideal solution lies in having a force and its equipment close to the problem - a forward presence. Future strategies will develop in a regional context and will attract credibility through having a potential collective security response close at hand. This obviates the problem which acknowledges the shortfall in strategic lift capability by being drawn into a conflict before the decision-making process has been fully exercised and plans fully collaborated. In such a situation, the emphasis falls on the quality of peacetime intelligence and its early sharing between potential coalition states. The problems of Allied strategic mobility have already been highlighted as the Allies prepared for conventional war in an unconventional environment. With the increase in the estimate of the number of Allied troops required to breach the Iraqi

'Maginot' line, so too did the estimates of Allied casualties increase. Rejecting arguments that he should give sanctions more time to work, Bush replied: 'we risk paying a higher price in the most precious currency of all - human life - if we give Saddam more time to prepare for war'.

All this was, of course, bad news in the United States due to the striking similarities being drawn with the Vietnam War. In fact, there were very few similarities. What were perceived as similarities were the result of US domestic ignorance and alarm. Military folklore suggests that the attack is to the defence as three is to one. In effect, the Allied technological advantages, particularly their night-fighting capability, coupled with air superiority would serve as force multipliers, thereby considerably reducing the Allied numbers required.

The Gulf Crisis demanded of the NATO members the consideration of a rethink of their military options and the means available of pursuing those options. Central to the tactical reappraisal was the abandonment of the traditional, defensive concept in favour of a high-intensity, offensive, break-in battle into Kuwait. Light units enjoy a high state of readiness but are lightly armed. 'Low-intensity' conflict had come to be regarded as synonymous with light forces being deployed with light equipment. For the majority of subsequent interventionist circumstances this is still likely to remain the case, but the Gulf became an important exception, the scale of which left the Allies unprepared and slow to respond. It became a large-scale, limited war at the thick end of the intervention spectrum. Significantly, no role was found in the battle *per se* for the traditional British trouble-shooters of the Royal Marine Commandos and the Parachute Brigade. British Gurkha troops, whose Indian counterparts had been the best of the bunch in the Congo, were, however, deployed to the support area.

There were two principal reasons why the Iraqi forces were given an appreciable degree of respect: their sheer size, and the chemical dimension. Reports of the military prowess of Iraq's 950,000-strong Army varied from the very good to the indifferent. Based on their performance against Iran in eight years of desert warfare, a number of truisms had emerged. Demographic factors showed that (in contrast to the Iranians) they were very careful not to suffer heavy casualties. They did not fight with distinction on Iranian territory but were much more tenacious in defending their own land. The defence of Basra in 1987 was conducted with great fortitude and courage. The armour and air wars, however, were not distinguished affairs. Much had been made of the modern Soviet T-72s, but these comprised a small proportion of the total armoured force in a predominantly infantry-heavy Army and too often were kept in the Republican Guard reserve. The more numerous and older models of Soviet tanks were fought as direct-fire artillery. Their ability to be used emphatically to change the balance on the battlefield was severely inhibited by the absence of radios. Such are the precautions that dictators perceive to be necessary. Iraqi air power was not used at all boldly. During the Iran/Iraq War, large elements of the air force were kept on Jordanian airfields beyond the range of Iranian fighters. What the Iraqis were most positive about was their preparedness to use chemical weapons in order to break a stalemate. Iran had not developed deliverable forms of chemical weapons. The Allies could, of course, match anything Saddam Hussein could produce. In January, Prime Minister John Major made it clear that the coalition would have taken a very serious view of the use of any chemical or biological weapon by Iraq, and that forces in the Gulf had a wide range of weapons available but the need to use nuclear weapons was not envisaged.

Deterrence is predicated upon the existence of rational actors on both sides making intelligent, responsible decisions. Saddam Hussein's proven unpredictability and irrationality meant that his capabilities and intentions had to be respected.

In June 1980 the Pentagon wargamed a study designed to investigate the effects of an intervention in which an opponent possessed chemical weapons. The wargame setting was a Saudi Arabia/Iraq environment. The conclusion reached was that US forces would be unable to win without neutralising oil-production facilities, with all the unwelcome, attendant economic implications. The *New York Post* published the findings of the conclusions of a study team set up in 1982 to investigate the feasibility of operations in an intemperate climate under chemical conditions: 'airbase survivability is nil: heat stress reduces our forces to a glob. It would be a sweaty blood bath'. The report strongly supported the thesis that military action in the Gulf environment remains the last resort, particularly where there is the prospect of aims being achieved by non-military means, albeit over a longer period.

A number of reasons have been advanced for the Iraqis apparently not employing their chemical weapons. Central to this was their conceding air superiority to the Allies. Aircraft and missiles were two of only three means available for the delivery of chemical weapons. The fact that so little of the Iraqi air force chose to stay and fight gave the Allied air force complete domination of the battlefields in Kuwait and southern Iraq. Artillery was the other means available for firing chemical weapons, but even in its conventional mode the Iraqi artillery proved to be indifferent. Their Forward Observation Officers (FOOs) were more often than not unable to locate the Allied forces and, when their guns did open up, they faced instant retribution from patrolling taxi-ranked Allied aircraft or from counter-battery fire. In that respect, elements of the Iraqi artillery found the Allied artillery to be more effective than the Allied air forces. The reaction was quicker, more concentrated and not weather-dependent - cogent reasons for no Iraqi first use of chemical weapons. The Iraqis also knew that the Allied nuclear, biological and chemical (nbc) protection was superior to theirs and, in view of the wind and rain blowing in their faces, the use of chemical weapons by Iraq did not make military sense.

The Republican Guard were an important consideration in the war because they provided the backbone of Saddam's regime. Whereas the Guard were kept in reserve until the fourth year of Iraq's war with Iran, they formed part of the spearhead in the attack on Kuwait. After that, they went back into reserve to fulfil their primary function, which has been described as 'the army which watches the army'. For that reason, and for their complete dedication to Saddam, they have been likened to the *Waffen SS*. Certainly they enjoyed privileges not experienced by the mainstream of the Army. For example, prior to the invasion of Kuwait, Saddam Hussein delegated to his Guard commanders the use, without prior clearance, of chemical weapons and missiles. This concession was more widely extended during the course of the war.

There are some striking similarities between Napoleon's Imperial Guard and Saddam Hussein's Republican Guard. When formed in the late 1970s, the Iraqi presidential guard numbered only a few thousand. Napoleon's Imperial Guard was also, originally, a small, personal *corps d'élite*, inactive on the battlefield, enjoying a charmed and safe life until faced with the realities and expediencies of 1812. They were highly dedicated and utterly loyal to Napoleon. The early Iraqi presidential guard was Sunni, like Saddam's tribe, and was commanded by officers from Takrit. Just as 1812 had been an important milestone for the Imperial Guard, the expediencies of the Iran/Iraq War witnessed the expansion of the presidential guard into the Republican Guard.

Napoleon's Guard increased in size. In 1805 it had been 10,000 strong, by 1809 it was 32,000, and it had swelled to 120,000 for the advance into Russia. The Imperial Guard now consisted of the Young, Middle and Old

Guard. It had been in 1809 that Napoleon had created the Young Guard, comprising the very best of the available conscripts. There was a contemporary argument that it was prejudicial to the overall quality of an army to cream off the best talent into an elite corps. From 1814, however, it ceased for the French to be a one-way process. Thirty thousand guardsmen were commissioned and went back to bolster the line regiments, now made up of the very young and the very old.

Saddam Hussein took a leaf from Napoleon's book by recruiting all college student conscripts, irrespective of religion, into the Republican Guard. At the beginning of the war, the Guard had swelled to eight divisions, each of approximately 14,000 men. The three armoured divisions were established for 800 tanks, of which 500 were the most modern Soviet T-72s. There were four infantry divisions and one special operations division which served as a political commissariat spying within the service and maintaining discipline.

The Republican Guard was therefore the best trained, best motivated, best paid, best quality and best equipped group of formations. It was as though the military talent of Iraq had been conveniently gathered in a clutch of baskets. Their destruction became a key Allied war aim, for their survival was regarded as synonymous with Saddam's. What had to be achieved was to crack their resolve in the same way that the cracking of the will of the Middle Guard at Waterloo had signified the end of Napoleon. The Republican Guard did not live up to their reputation in battle. To what degree this was due to the unrelenting attention of B-52 bombers is not known.

Some twenty-eight states supported Resolution 660 by supplying land, sea or air components to the Allied effort. The problems presented by the assemblage of this disparate and unstructured force, not least in command and control, are repeated throughout this book. Absent from the line-up of troop-providing states was the Soviet Union. It is thought to have been an important foreign policy aim for the United States to co-opt the Soviet Union to deploy a token force, apparently to strengthen the Allied multinational credentials. History was again repeating itself for, during the Vietnam War, the US administration had tried very hard to entice a token British battalion into Vietnam. They even went so far as to recommend the Black Watch; the regiment's pipe band had made a most favourable impression whilst playing at John F. Kennedy's funeral service in 1963. The British government, as circumstances were to prove, wisely declined. Soviet Foreign Minister Shevardnadze told Foreign Secretary Baker that the dispatch of Soviet forces to the Gulf was 'not under consideration' and that 'this option is non-existent'.

The legacy of Afghanistan affected the Soviets even more profoundly than the legacy of Vietnam would affect the Americans. It was the mothers of conscripts whose protests had been among the factors conducive to ending the conflict. Here was a case of *déjà vu* because America provided massive support to the Mujahadeen, thereby exacerbating the severity of the Soviet defeat. The Soviets were deprived of the option of some foreign adventure as a means of diverting attention from domestic problems. Both the Russian Federation and Russian Congress of People's Deputies appealed to President Gorbachev to keep Soviet forces out of the Gulf. The deputies went so far as to pass a resolution imploring Gorbachev not to permit the Soviet Union to be 'drawn into a military conflict which could have the most serious consequences for peace and stability on the planet'. Some questions were even raised as to the legality of Soviet support for Security Council Resolution 678.

A token Soviet presence in the Gulf would have been seen through as the transparent gesture that it represented. The Soviet difficulty was not only political but also military. It seems likely that the insertion of even a small-size formation could have posed potentially serious problems for Moscow. Among the conservative officers were many who were pro-Iraq. 'It is not easy for us', said a certain Colonel Valentin Ogurtsov, 'to move from full-fledged relations to zero'. Formations also mean conscripts. Soviet soldiery had become resistant to conscription, and draft-dodging was prevalent in a number of republics. In another unpopular war coming so soon after Afghanistan, the prospect would have existed that the soldiery could have behaved as did their forebears in the Imperial Russian Army of 1917 by voting with their feet or, at least, sitting on their hands. Either way, it would not have made a positive contribution to the broader concept of Allied solidarity. In these circumstances, the political support of the Soviet Union sufficed.

The Gulf Crisis confirmed what had long been suspected; that no one state would wish to bear the burden of the cost of military operations on such a large scale. That the economics of the deployment to the Gulf did not appear to produce insurmountable difficulties was due almost exclusively to the special circumstances relating to that particular environment. There were deep pockets both among the host nations and among those most heavily dependent upon supplies of oil from the Gulf. What had become evident was that the owners of these pockets would need to dig less deep if sanctions succeeded, thereby obviating the need for the perceived, expensive military action. The convergence of so many national interests is such a rare event that, in terms of economic support of a military enterprise, it could not be taken as a new norm in international behaviour. The Gulf Crisis had been the first 'remote control' campaign, the first 'green screen' war. It would be essential that the rather particular environment of the Arabian desert should not be taken as a template for future operations in very different geographical and political environments.

The West had hoped that domestic dissatisfaction would have swept Saddam Hussein away before the situation inside Iraq became too parlous. The benefit of hindsight, however, suggests that this would be an over-optimistic hope. Time was something that the Americans did not have on their side. The real problems in achieving a successful military intervention had again come to the fore. Consensus on the home front was, at the time, on the wane and the keeping of troops indefinitely in the desert could also have affected morale. Time was a most important factor. If intervention is to become the necessary agent of a collective security regime, the ground needs to be prepared politically for a speedy, proportional and legal response. Having said that, the adage 'look very carefully before you leap' is something which needs to be written prominently in all areas where the decision-making process takes place. In this case, the decision to intervene was taken during a fortuitous meeting between George Bush and Margaret Thatcher in Aspen, Colorado, on 2 August 1990. It was here that Thatcher said to the President: 'Don't go wobbly, George'. The position of the United States, and therefore of the Allies, was to a large degree preordained from the time troops deployed into Saudi Arabia with uncertain missions and aims. It was at that point that the clock had started ticking.

The account of the UN-sanctioned conflict versus Iraq has been thoroughly recorded in many worthy books and journals. However, the conflict did have a postscript in the form of an humanitarian operation in Northern Iraq, in support of that country's oppressed Kurdish population, without the consent of the sovereign power. This intervention into Northern Iraq drove a coach and horses through the three and a half century, Westphalian notion that a sovereign state was the supreme arbiter within its own borders. A safe haven was established with an unequivocal intention to defend it. What this follow-on operation signified was a willingness among capable states to intervene in the domestic affairs of a sovereign state in order to alleviate extreme suffering. Of that landmark action, the UN Secretary-General wrote:

> While respect for the fundamental sovereignty and integrity of the state remains central, it is undeniable that the centuries old doctrine of absolute and exclusive sovereignty no longer stands, and was in fact never so absolute as it was conceived in theory.[5]

What was unusual was the fact that Security Council Resolution 688 of 5 April 1991, which authorised the insertion of western forces into Iraq without Iraq's consent, was not framed under Chapter VII despite the verb *demand* being employed in the text. Although many subsequent interventions were framed under Chapter VII for juridical reasons it is apparently not essential (a point upon which there will be disagreement) and therefore, arguably, Implementation Operations require no exceptional, new legal provision.

Out of this action there developed an understanding that UN members have a duty to intervene to stop opprobrious behaviour and atrocities in certain circumstances. What has so far defied definition is what those circumstances are and how expeditiously the avenging forces can be committed to remedial operations. In a world shaped by interests, it is too much to expect understandings for military intervention to be entered into with fairness and consistency. Legitimacy is paramount and although the Security Council might seem anarchic and at times uncooperative it is, short of immediate action taken in self-defence, the authorising body for putative intervention. To that extent it seems incumbent upon the members so to harmonise their foreign and domestic policies as to minimise the possibilities of rift and disagreement within the Security Council.

There is nothing new in the regular images we receive of man's inhumanity to man. What *is* relatively new is the means by which this suffering is brought into people's drawing rooms. The voices to do something or to do nothing are frequently the same. Selective intervention - and choice is an unavoidable factor - will mean that on occasions, Social Darwinism will have to run its course. The west is more likely to intervene in Europe and the Middle East than in Africa. The interventionists, the military, represent a visible manifestation of politics in action; occasionally they might be able to hold the ring sufficiently to enable politicians and humanitarians to help antagonists and sufferers reach accommodation or dialogue. Ultimately, lasting solutions are in the hands of the people themselves.

Again, the timing of military intervention is everything. The UN Charter lays down the concept that armed forces shall not be used save in the common interest, yet 'common interest' is difficult to define. It is further understood that the UN Charter requires the testing of less extreme, coercive measures before recourse to the armed option. The problem in pursuing such a course is that undue delay may result in the problem on the ground becoming so out of control as to defy a military solution - even if there was one. How much different and how much more satisfactory if the intervention in East Timor had proceeded two weeks earlier. The 'glass of water' strategy relates to readiness and signifies the use of a glass of water to douse an infant fire, thus avoiding having to call out multiple fire brigades. The cost benefits in moving early can also be substantial. It has been estimated that the cost of the Rwanda operation to the US government was fifty times more than if forces had been deployed at the earliest opportunity. In addition, tens of thousands of lives might have been saved.[6] The same is true, on a smaller scale, of East Timor.

As was evidenced in the deployment of Apache helicopters in support of operations in Kosovo, 'rapid' is a relative term. The UN has made some attempt to organise a rapid reaction force under the auspices of the DPKO. However its composition, mostly from smaller states with traditional peacekeeping pedigrees, emphasises the reluctance of larger states to put their men under UN or foreign command. The reality is that when moved by interest or conscience, the United States, Britain and France can move more men faster than can the UN's standby brigade known by its acronym SHIRBRIG. SHIRBRIG is a multinational High Readiness Brigade comprising armed forces drawn from Austria, Canada, Denmark, the Netherlands, Norway, Poland and Sweden, aimed at rapid deployment on 'peacekeeping operations'. All these states are closely associated with 'traditional' peacekeeping. Training is a national responsibility but it is the intention that contributing nations should be able to operate in multinational environments and cooperate with contingents from other countries, the UN, ICRC and other inter-governmental and non-governmental organisations. It is intended that the Brigade, which became operational in 1999, should respond to a crisis within 15-30 days.

The consequences following the East Timor referendum could have been forecast by any novice student of the region. It was the place requiring an immediate response to protect the East Timorese from the murderous intentions of the pro-Jakarta militia. Yet the UN's High Readiness Brigade made not so much as a token appearance either in East Timor or Sierra Leone. In response to questions as to what the problem had been, the UN advised that the Canadian battalion component of SHIRBRIG had been placed on standby to operate in East Timor. Why, therefore, did they not make their timely presence felt? Apparently they had not had the recommended inoculations for service in the Far East!

Even with the political will in place, SHIRBRIG's rapid reaction capability is far below that achievable by American, French and British armed forces. It is worth remembering that the British JRRF's Spearhead lead company group is at 24 hours' notice to move, with the land component Brigade Headquarters and the balance of the battalion group at 72 hours' notice. The battalion group is the advance guard of the UK's ground expeditionary capability but, overall, it is a reflection on the political establishments world wide that the ability to sustain and protect expeditionary forces has made little progress over the past ten years.[7] The European Rapid Reaction Corps (ERRC) is essentially a political construction, a military Potemkin village. Urgent investment will have to be made to permit troops thrown into someone else's civil war to fight above their weight. In addition, the political decision-making process requires fine-tuning so that the limited rapid reaction capability is not impaired due to political procrastination.

The United States Army has two quick-reaction mobile brigades - the 3rd Brigade of the 2nd Infantry Division and the 1st Brigade of the 25th Infantry Division - capable of deploying anywhere world wide in 96 hours. The 3000-strong brigades are equipped with 20-ton armoured vehicles, significantly lighter than the 70-ton American main battle tank, the M1-A1 Abrams. The addition of this new initiative should be seen as a belated first step, a model for the future. The Army Chief of Staff, General Eric Shinseki, said: 'I think you will see the entire transformation will go towards capabilities that give those divisional formations the lethality that the heavy forces have and the agility of the lighter forces'.[8]

Central to the United States' capability to move rapidly into a familiar environment is the so-called Unified Command, commanded by a single operational commander answerable to the National Command Authorities. A Unified Command is composed of US combat forces from two or more services. It has a broad and continuing mission and is normally organised on a geographical basis. That means that if a problem arises which requires a military response, the command which will conduct the operation is automatically pre-assigned. For example, Africa falls within the strategic area of interest of US European Command (USEUCOM) and the Middle East is the operational area of US Central Command (USCENTCOM) based at Tampa, Florida. Throughout the structure of Unified Commands are formations at varying levels of notice to move. There will always be elements permanently assigned to rapid response duties. Only the USA has the resources to create a credible and independent standing joint force. In view of USCENTCOM's heavy commitment in the Gulf Conflict, Operation Desert Storm, USEUCOM was nominated to be the lead headquarters in Operation Provide Comfort in Northern Iraq. Britain and France both have quick reaction forces though on a limited scale and with limited strategic lift. France's *Force d'Action Rapide* (FAR) has been replaced by a more general upgrading of the total force's capacity to react quickly to emergency crises. It is significant that the Kosovo operation drew on two per cent of NATO's capability. This proved to be an exercise of enormous difficulty. Each additional percentage point of capability commitment represents an exponential increase in cost and the degree of difficulty to be experienced.

One of the lessons to arise out of the Kuwait crisis is the importance of the maintenance of consensus. There is a political logic in having large numbers involved in coalition operations but it hinders good command and control. Questions are being raised as to the desirability of placing military intervention forces under the auspices of often unwieldy international organisations whose decision-making processes are founded upon concepts of unanimity. As mentioned earlier, crises form their own coalitions and the option of organising a military intervention around a UN-sanctioned US Unified Command or a British or French divisional headquarters are options that should not be neglected.

The emphatic ending of the manoeuvre phase of the Gulf Conflict had an undoubted impact upon parties who might regard western states as potential enemies. The lesson that would-be adversaries should not play to the West's high-technology strengths required no further emphasis. As a result of this conflict, limited war will not disappear but the prospects of its recurrence have lessened. Today, the buzz phrase is 'asymmetric conflict' yet asymmetric conflict is no monolith, having varying levels of commitment and intensity. Korea, Vietnam and the Gulf Conflict were limited wars and also forms of asymmetric conflict. The spectrum involving potential enemies is wide, ranging from the actions of a malevolent sheikh and his adherents to a highly populous state which acknowledges that it will never beat the technologically superior west in a major conflict and therefore chooses different battlefields in which to engage in dirty war. Home cities will feature prominently in strategies which target a state's economy and administration with computer viruses, terrorism, biological and chemical releases and environmental damage.

The threat posed by cyber conflict is recognised in the west but the ability of potential perpetrators to blend into their urban environments and employ unsophisticated means renders defensive mechanisms difficult to design. In 1997, Tamil Tiger guerrillas attacked the Sri Lankan diplomatic computer system intending to swamp Sri Lankan embassies with e-mails. The director of the Central Intelligence Agency, George Tenet, admitted that:

> We face a growing cyber threat from so called weapons of mass disruption. Potential targets are not only governmental computers but the lifelines we all take for granted - our power grids and our water and transportation systems.

Tenet admitted: 'We know of several nations that are working on developing an information warfare capability'.[9]

Terrorism is at the lower end of the spectrum of asymmetric conflict and does not feature as a study *per se* within this book. In a conflict situation, and as during the currency of UNOSOM II in Somalia, the disadvantaged party will configure their small force for the most effective use against a preponderance of force. They will close right up to their enemy in order to neutralise the intervenor's superiority in equipment and technology, rather as the Soviets did against the Germans in the shell of a city that was Stalingrad in the winter of 1942-43. They will organise in such a way as to negate their opponent's strength, to destroy his will rather than his forces. The irregulars will easily identify their opponent's centre of gravity, the vulnerable point or points, against which they will concentrate their limited resources. They will continually be collecting intelligence, engaging in psychological operations both in theatre and in the homeland of the intervenors and they will be prepared to deceive and employ pre-emptive strikes. Above all, they will try to ensure that they always have the initiative, forcing their opponent to adopt reactive tactics. They will therefore engage their opponent with tactics that suit them and their environment. These will not be ignorant tribesmen. General Aideed had a PhD. They will engage in information warfare, will use satellite links and could have access to WMD for use against military and civilian targets. Future enemies are as capable of forming alliances and coalitions, probably an ethnic or religious association, as is the case in the west.

Western policymakers have to understand the several facets of David v Goliath conflict: the advantage which the simple may have over the complex; the advantage of the unscrupulous over the scrupulous; the appeal which the cause of the weak has to world opinion in conflict against the strong; the ability of the weak, by playing it long, to avoid the impact of the ostensibly decisive force of the strong.[10] In terms of size, the United States' experience in Somalia against General Aideed was a David v Goliath situation. Unlike the Gulf Crisis which was an inter-state conflict, Somalia is an example of what promises to be the more prevalent form of conflict: intra-state. In this study to examine why peacekeeping and intervention succeeded or failed, Mogadishu provides salutary lessons.

6 'If you liked Beirut, you will love Somalia' - Ambassador Smith Hempstone

Three distinct 'peacekeeping' operations were conducted in Somalia between 1992-94. UN Security Council Resolution 751 of 24 April 1992 established UNOSOM I to provide humanitarian assistance. That operation was superseded by the authority of UN Security Council Resolution 794 of 3 December 1992, authorising the use of all necessary means to establish a secure environment as soon as possible so that humanitarian operations could proceed without interruption. The resultant US-led intervention, known as the United Task Force (UNITAF) and Operation Restore Hope began over the beaches of Mogadishu on 9 December 1992. In May 1993 the US Marines withdrew, handing over to the UN on Operation Continue Hope or UNOSOM II.

When, over the 1992 Thanksgiving holiday, the news was leaked rather than announced that the Pentagon was preparing plans to send on Operation Restore Hope up to 30,000 troops into Somalia, the situation in that country had become parlous. It had had no central government since the dictator Mohammed Siad Barre was overthrown by rebels in 1991. During the ensuing struggle for power between warlords, 300,000 people died as a result either of that conflict or through the effects of famine. It was estimated that a further 1.5 million were at risk. The food distribution system had broken down, with up to eighty per cent of all food supplies being looted by armed gangs. The port of Mogadishu had been closed from early November 1992 and a UN ship attempting to dock to unload grain was hit by a shell. The UN peacekeepers of United Nations Operations in Somalia (UNOSOM I) seemingly were unable to control the situation. Power in Somalia rested with he who controlled the food supply. Thousands had been left to starve in order to achieve political advantage or profit. Food was being used politically and economically as both a stick and a carrot. The use of resources as a weapon is a particular feature of civil conflict. (As a further example, the Bosnian Serb control of communications into Sarajevo - road, rail and air as well as food, water and electricity - was orchestrated in such a manner as to bring their opponents to their knees.)

The town of Baidoa was central to the humanitarian problem. Siad Barre, the former dictator, occupied Baidoa in September 1991 with a view to advancing on Mogadishu. He remained there until April 1992 with his 8,000 troops and, during that time, they ravaged the grain stores. The population of Baidoa is not nomadic and thus starvation came about as a direct consequence of Barre's occupation of the town. Accounts to the effect that Somalia's problem had been one of anarchy and famine are untrue. This had not been a natural disaster but rather one that was man-made. A number of different clans called upon General Mohammed Farah Aideed, a Mogadishu clan chief, to confront Barre. This he did in a six day war, forcing Barre into Kenya where he was given political asylum prior to moving on to Nigeria. If the Baidoa incident had not taken place, there would have been no need for Operation Restore Hope. Indeed, by January 1993 the situation out in the country was improving. That was evident from the decision to put American Marines ashore in Mogadishu, for the port's capacity became almost totally devoted to the logistic support of the military.

Few could disagree that the UN was slow to react in authorising the deployment of peacekeepers on the original UNOSOM I. What compounded the problem was that once that decision was made, the deployment of five hundred Pakistani troops proved to be ponderous and inadequate. Moreover, when eventually *in situ,* the commanding general was virtually obliged to pursue his military objectives with the approval of the warlords. The UNOSOM I peacekeepers were permitted to take over the barely significant airport, but not the key port of Mogadishu. It was reported that the UN had been spending up to $3m a day on extortion, bribes and payment to gangsters.[1] What was wrong was the failure to grasp or enact the principle of 'forces for courses'. The warlords did not respect the timorous United Nations nor their representative peacekeepers. They respected and understood the principles of the application of power and force. That is why the UN's principal opponent and the only real warlord of consequence, General Mohammed Farah Aideed, had welcomed the US's humanitarian assistance initiative embodied in UNITAF. 'We believe', he said, 'the American move will solve our political, economic and social problems. The United Nations has failed to save the unity of Somalia, the reconciliation process and the recovery programme'.[2] However, there was an informed voice which questioned the wisdom of tackling head-on a xenophobic, heavily-armed, anti-colonial, anti-Christian collection of clans susceptible to fundamentalist influences from the north. Allegedly, Smith Hempstone, America's Ambassador to Kenya, wrote a confidential letter to the State Department: 'If you liked Beirut, you will love Somalia'.[3]

In taking his initiative in setting UNITAF in motion, President Bush did not consult Congress. Bill Clinton, the President-elect, was informed and, though not consulted, was reported by a spokesman to have been 'generally supportive'. He had little option to be otherwise. One of the foremost supporters of the Bush initiative proved to be the African Secretary-General of the United Nations, Dr Boutros Boutros-Ghali. Only a few months previously, the Secretary-General had accused the West of being preoccupied with the Yugoslavian problem at Somalia's expense.

It seems that the original trigger for the Bush initiative was a letter dated 19 November 1992, sent to the administration by a US coalition of aid agencies known as InterAid. The eleven US-based organisations providing relief in Somalia reported that 'humanitarian agencies cannot work effectively in Somalia without greater security', and they asked for increased security under the aegis of the UN.[4]

More significant was a letter sent by the Secretary-General to the Security Council, in which he outlined five wide-ranging options:

- To continue current negotiations with the Somali warlords and endeavour to deploy UN guards with the consent of the parties.
- To abandon the use of international military forces to protect food distribution and withdraw the Pakistani peacekeeping force.
- To mount a military show of force in Mogadishu to guard aid shipments and to deter armed groups from obstructing assistance. This would be achieved by the 4,000 peacekeepers already authorised (but only partially deployed) for duty in Somalia.
- To authorise member states to undertake a country-wide military operation to establish control and provide relief.
- To undertake a country-wide military operation under UN command and control. This is the option preferred by African delegates.

Dr Boutros Boutros-Ghali had already concluded that the Security Council should be encouraged to agree that, under the UN Charter, the anarchy in Somalia represented a 'threat to the peace of the entire region'. In order to stop the violence facing the relief operations, he further concluded that 'a show of force' was the only solution:

> It would be necessary for at least the heavy weapons of the organised factions to be neutralised and brought under international control and for the irregular forces and gangs to be disarmed. This action would help to bring about a ceasefire between the warring factions and this would be a positive factor in the context of national reconciliation.

'If forceful action is taken', continued the Secretary-General, 'it should preferably be under the United Nations Command and Control (Option 5 - a UN-sponsored operation). If this is not feasible, an alternative would be an operation undertaken by member states acting with the authorisation of the Security Council' (Option 4 - a UN-sanctioned operation). Dr Boutros-Ghali concluded, 'I recommend that the Council take a very early decision to adjust its approach to the crisis in Somalia'.

Evidently President Bush required no further prompting. On 27 November 1992, a presidential spokesman announced that the proposal to deploy US forces would only be as part of a UN force. There is a Constitutional requirement and national expectation that US forces will only be commanded by US officers, and therefore ultimately by the president. Washington policy papers consistently declare that the president will never relinquish command of US forces. An editorial in *The Washington Post* explained: 'In circumstances where Americans are supplying the leadership as well as the preponderance of forces, an American president has reason to keep the principal reins'.[5]

There remained elements of residual unease stemming from the Gulf Conflict where some states, notably developing states, believed the USA was given too free a hand by the UN. Accordingly, some African delegates recommended that the multinational force deployed to Somalia should wear blue helmets. Another recommendation aimed at improving presentation was for the Resolution to assign overall responsibility to the Secretary-General who would then delegate military command to the nominated US general. During the course of the drafting phase of Resolution 794, India's representative requested that the humanitarian assistance to Somalia be conducted under United Nations command and control:

> India had noted the Security Council's view that in that case the Secretariat would need to be strengthened for such command and control to be exercised effectively. His delegation believed that given political will, such arrangements could be possible without too much difficulty.

The Marines assigned to Operation Restore Hope, also known as UNITAF, effected their traditional beach landing, fighting their way ashore under cover of darkness between the packed ranks of international media forewarned by a White House media machine with an eye on prime-time television viewing. Forty other countries had originally applied to join the bandwagon but in the final event the American commander, General Robert Johnston, was obliged to take under his wing the representative military from twenty-four states. He did not have so much as the benefit of a strategic plan from New York, the state of training of the military attachments was unknown and many arrived without essential equipment, assuming that they could simply draw from an already overstretched American logistic system. National forces with different standards of training and doctrine, with variable equipment, cannot simply cohere as equal partners on a military operation. But many were there not for military but for political effect. What transpired was an American-led operation with greater accountability than previously to the Secretary-General and the Security Council. The Americans did not wear blue helmets and, although President Bush had said that the troops would be withdrawn by 20 January 1993, they did not withdraw until 4 May 1993, handing over once again to the UN.

Because of pressures on numbers (in 1993, the UN controlled 90,000 troops) and because of the UN tradition of attempting to achieve global representation on its 'peacekeeping operations', some military forces, invariably from the developing states, found themselves in environments to which they were not suited. There were stories of contingents arriving in theatre without footwear, and an expectation to plug-in to western logistics and supplies. Very often they were present because their governments found the $988 per man per month in hard currency to be irresistible. In addition, each soldier received a mission subsistence allowance.

Unsuitability is determined not only through lack of military prowess. It can be due to factors beyond the control of the national military contingents. For example, prior to the American-led 1992 intervention in Somalia, the *in situ* Pakistani peacekeeping force had been so thoroughly restricted by bilateral agreements between the UN and General Aideed that it was holed up at the airport and totally ineffective. To some degree this was also due to a pre-existing attitude within the host state. On the face of it, two Muslim states might be thought to have enjoyed a high degree of empathy. However, Somalis are xenophobic and virulently racist. Curiously, they accepted the Americans but despised the Pakistanis due to their association with the UN. It would seem to have been a good idea to have withdrawn the Pakistani contingent before the main body of Americans had departed Somalia on 4 May 1993. Instead, Islamabad reinforced its contingent in Somalia at the same time as the UN sought to restore its authority. Pakistan's support of the Somalia operation was an important, high profile commitment which Islamabad found impossible to relinquish without sustaining unacceptable political damage. To Aideed and his men, the Pakistani peacekeepers were viewed as an army of occupation and the fact that the UN's Secretary-General was a despised Egyptian and friend of Siad Barre did not augur well for future good relations. The subsequent murder of twenty-four Pakistani soldiers and what appeared to some to be the revenge killing of twenty civilians by the nervous and lightly armed Pakistanis was evidence of the bad blood existing between the two groups. With these episodes and the subsequent bombing of Mogadishu by United States aircraft, the UN once again exposed the uncertainty which exists between peacekeeping and what we propose should be called Implementation Operations. Mohammed Sahnoun, an Algerian diplomat and former UN special envoy to Somalia prior to his removal in October 1992, commented:

> Peacekeepers elsewhere might encounter similar situations (as in Somalia) and they should reassess their methods… it is particularly important for the UN to reassess its role, especially in terms of strategic policy making. At the moment its management is faulty.

Ambassador Sahnoun said that the killing of the Pakistani soldiers pointed to a complete lack of political and military intelligence capabilities. Due to the residual presence of the UN's international Whig[6] traditions, intelligence is viewed with great suspicion. In fact the word is not used. In the few areas where intelligence does exist, it is known euphemistically as information. Episodes such as this may well continue unless the UN is more objective and less dogmatic in its selection of troops to tasks and until those states who do have reserve assets of trained armed forces are prepared to make them more readily available. Politically, the mix and match of armed forces will continue. The more capable should therefore recognise their responsibilities for assisting less able coalition members, but in a discreet manner.

The original UNOSOM I involving the Pakistanis therefore had been a UN-sponsored operation, Operation Restore Hope or United Task Force (UNITAF) a US-led and UN-sanctioned operation, and finally, UNOSOM II was a UN-sponsored operation, but one with a difference. The UN and the US had heeded the undercurrent of international desire to see the US become more accountable to the UN, thereby creating a rod with which to beat the UN. It was agreed by Washington that in appropriate circumstances her logistic troops assigned to UNOSOM II would come under the UN's military commander, the Turkish General Cevik Bir. Bir's *de jure* appointment, approved by the USA, was but a fig leaf. The *de facto* commanders in Somalia were the Secretary-General's Special Representative, retired Admiral Jonathan Howe, a former national security adviser to President Bush's administration, and Bir's deputy, the American Major-General Thomas Montgomery. Bir was not given command of the in-theatre Quick Reaction Force from the US Army's 10th Mountain Division. It was the Americans who called up their armed helicopters in the name of the UN Secretary-General.

What the UNOSOM II operation underlined was a general confusion as to what peacekeeping had become in relation to intervention. The existence of that confusion is still apparent in the higher echelons of the UN as well as throughout the lower levels. It is not as though pointers were not already in place. Ten years previously, in a combined operation in the Lebanon (which was not a UN-approved operation), the United Kingdom and Italy had conducted traditional peacekeeping operations, while the US and France lost their claims to impartiality and were drawn into enforcement activities. The UN has added to the confusion by the excessive application of Chapter VII measures to what were implementation operations. There may be a juridical justification for the linking-up of what is effectively a Chapter VI½ operation with Chapter VII. But Chapter VI½ is not recognised and the majority of the UN's business is conducted in and around this area of operations.

UNOSOM II was therefore officially a Chapter VII operation, but a roll call of its thirty constituent members reveals a majority of states traditionally associated with Chapter VI peacekeeping. Under Chapter VI, it has been standard practice to engage in negotiation to resolve problems. Business is conducted in slow time while national military representatives consult with their capitals before acting. Thus when, on 5 June 1993, twenty-four Pakistani troops were killed in an attempt to close down General Aideed's radio station, the Kuwaiti and Saudi Arabian detachment ordered by UNOSOM II Headquarters to go to their aid, found themselves unable to comply with the desired immediacy. But there was a more philosophical difficulty, and that was between the former colonial power, Italy, and the US.

Italy had remained consistent to the ideal of traditional peacekeeping, attempting to protect humanitarian relief through the process of negotiation and persuasion. Other states - Pakistan, Saudi Arabia and Kuwait -

conducted their business in the time-honoured federal system of peacekeeping by reference to their capitals. But the ground rules were changing from peacekeeping to enforcement. The UN's Special Representative in Somalia, the American Admiral Howe, put a price of $25,000 on General Aideed's head. In the process of the hunt for General Aideed, UN helicopters and tanks killed over one hundred Somalis, as well as causing considerable collateral damage. All that this achieved was the enhancement of Aideed's status. The Italian General Bruno Loi protested at what he saw to be heavy-handed retaliation, referring orders from UN's Mogadishu headquarters to Rome for clearance. His attempted sacking by Kofi Annan, the then UN Under-Secretary General for Peacekeeping, was not unexpected but it created a furious response from Rome. There are questions as to the advice the Secretary-General was being given, and speculation as to exactly who was really in command of the Somalia operation. It seems rather obvious that the UN cannot exercise effective enforcement if the ground forces put into a theatre are only equipped to carry out peacekeeping operations. The conduct of urban warfare requires highly-trained troops. Their absence, or an unwillingness to take casualties, means recourse to use of air power, which can be indiscriminate and at times self-defeating. There was less sensitivity to the increasing number of civilian casualties in Mogadishu, where the hospital had been hit, than was evident in 1999 air operations over European Serbia.

The key question required to be asked in January 1993 of Operation Restore Hope is, what was the mission, and how was the mission to be executed? Originally, the Special Ambassador, Robert Oakley, dealt with Aideed on friendly terms. There was talk of an understanding that the US would make a gesture of confiscating weapons - something which some Americans regarded as imperialist - in exchange for an agreement from the warlords not to target US servicemen. That argument broke down in February 1993. On 4 May 1993, the UN passed what was, in effect, a busted flush. When the main US's UNITAF force withdrew, their achievement had been to anaesthetise the underlying problems, not solve them. By June 1993 another former American client had become identified as a villain. As an example of command and control, UNOSOM II was unfortunate. One military representative in UN Headquarters New York asked the key question:

> The question we are all asking ourselves is whether we can run a peace-enforcement operation, as in Somalia, or whether the Secretary-General should confine himself to peacekeeping as in the old days.[7]

It set out as a compromise but did not work, for it was not allowed to work. The UN was determined to maintain control, managing the concern as a traditional, sponsored, peacekeeping operation. On two occasions, the Security Council authorised the use of all necessary means to protect UN forces and bring about stability. Given that the Americans were in effect in control, such a licence contradicted the ethos of traditional peacekeeping.

What is most surprising of the management of UNOSOM II was the very obvious failure to recognise the political nature of the conflict. The least good plan was to bring down Apocalypse Now on to downtown Mogadishu. Experienced military advisers would have pointed to the similarities of the situation prevailing in Mogadishu to that of a standard Counter-Insurgency Operation. This essentially involves a battle for the minds of the vast majority in the middle ground. Field Marshal Sir William Slim was of the opinion that it only required five per cent of a nation's population to oppose intervention for the intervenors' position to be untenable. Perhaps Aideed had to be punished, but the choice of means was regrettable. All that had been achieved were many civilian deaths and, at the end of the day, the strengthening of Aideed's position. An effective military committee at the UN might have deterred the Security Council from passing Resolutions which were unrelated to the situation on the ground and from demanding that which was militarily impossible to deliver. The intention to kill or capture Aideed was woefully ill-advised for it demonstrated that neither New York nor Washington understood the Somali clan system.

The seeds which would destabilise the Somalia operation were contained in the first enabling Security Council Resolution 794 of 3 December 1992. The Secretary-General had made public his doctrine that the old concept of absolute sovereignty had given way to a concept of universal sovereignty. It is true that Somalia was a shattered society with no functioning government, but the real sovereignty of the clans operating within their own territory should not have been overlooked. The long-standing taboo of recourse to enforcement action in accordance with Chapter VII had been set aside. From its origins, the Charter had provided for military intervention under Article 42 but, due to the Cold War, it had been inoperative. Now, for the first time in such an operation, the manifestation of Article 42 was apparent in the wording of Resolution 794 whereby member states were authorised to 'use all necessary means to establish as soon as possible a secure environment for humanitarian relief operations in Somalia'. 'Secure environment' implied disarmament, yet the restriction of military effort to humanitarian relief operations is said to have fallen short of the wishes of some of those in the UN's hierarchy who were looking towards an overall secure environment in Somalia.

A new Security Council Resolution 814 of 26 March 1993, which was a prelude to the UN taking military control in Somalia on 4 May 1993, widened the mandate. The requirement to establish a secure environment had been retained, but the relative restriction to humanitarian relief operations had been set aside. This was the enabling resolution to cross the 'Mogadishu Line'. The Secretary-General, through his Special Representative, was requested to direct the Force Commander of UNOSOM II to assume responsibility for the consolidation, expansion and maintenance of a secure environment throughout Somalia. It is clear that there were principal decision-makers in the UN who wished to establish a country-wide force to disarm Somalia. The Secretary-General, Boutros Boutros-Ghali, nominated as his Special Representative his friend, Ambassador Lansana Kouyate, the Guinean Permanent Representative at the UN, to be his Special Representative in Somalia. After the appointment had been agreed, the US administration interceded, expressed their dissatisfaction, and insisted Kouyate be replaced by an American. The argument was that the USA was the principal paymaster and therefore earned the right to nominate the Special Representative for UNOSOM II. Kouyate yielded, for he realised that had he not done so, his position would have been undermined.

The United States' nomination for Special Representative was retired Admiral Jonathan Howe. He had no specialist experience of the area of operations nor, as a submariner, could he have been exactly *au fait* with the nuances of air-land operations. Kouyate became Howe's deputy and, in March 1993, was to attend the Addis Ababa Conference which had as its aim the reconciliation of the political factions in Somalia. By most accounts, Kouyate did a good job in encouraging the political leaders to act together and come to agreements which might have led to the establishment of a provisional quasi-central Somalian government. However, at this juncture, the good work became unstuck. American diplomats in Somalia thought the agreements in Addis had gone too far. When, to that, is added what appears to have been an inter-personal problem between key UN appointees, Kouyate took his leave of Somalia.

Ambassador Kouyate had not enjoyed the happiest of working relationships with the Admiral and, for that reason, the State Department sent out a former Ambassador to Iraq as assistant to the UN's Admiral

Howe, to act as an interface between the UN and the USA. Ambassador April Glaspie assumed the by now vacant post created by Kouyate's disappearance, becoming Howe's short-term special political assistant.

Lieutenant-General Cevik Bir of the Turkish Army, the commander of the UNOSOM Force Command, had been nominated by the United States as being a general with whom they could work. The deputy commander of all forces assigned to UNOSOM was the American Major-General Thomas Montgomery, also the commander of US forces in Somalia, reporting to the commander-in-chief US Central Command (USCENTCOM), General Joseph Hoar. In reality, it was General Montgomery who was the *de facto* military commander in Somalia. There is a report that General Bir did not enjoy the best of working relationships with Admiral Howe. In view of the Kouyate experience, this was not at all a propitious beginning.

From March 1993, it had become evident that the US and UNOSOM had become divided within and without as to the future policy towards Somalia. The passive element believed that the UN had no option but to work with the *in situ* leaders and institutions, while the vigorously less passive took the view that Somalia's problems could only be addressed through a fundamental restructuring of the country. Those in-country who appeared to align themselves with this latter position included the American envoy Robert Gosende, April Glaspie and Major-General Montgomery. As far as this somewhat parochial group was concerned, it seemed as though they were subconsciously pursuing American interests on the assumption that these were also UN interests. Observers in the country at the time report how some Americans became increasingly irritated by the apparent impertinence of Aideed in 'taking us on', and how an intention emerged to teach Aideed a lesson. If there was a whiff of vindictiveness in the American camp, that was also true of UN Headquarters in New York. Aideed was not insensitive to the American plan to marginalise him and strengthened his resolve not to be factored out. Professor Tom Farer[8] has noted the undisguised preference April Glaspie was showing towards Aideed's principal political opponent, Mohammed Abshir, 'and was less than discreet about her hostility to Aideed'.[9] Abshir did not benefit from the favour bestowed upon him. It was, said one political observer, 'a kiss of death for Abshir'.

Admiral Howe was by no means in the same camp as his American colleagues. He did take important initiatives without consultation with New York, but he was essentially the Secretary-General's man. When he took over in Mogadishu from Robert Oakley, President Bush's special emissary to Somalia, General Johnston the marine general advised him: 'Look, do not take on Aideed. You have to understand who the guy is in this country. You do not need to make him an enemy'.[10] Both Oakley and Johnston, who admittedly had different mandates, were determined not to suffer unnecessary casualties among their force, and recognised that they had no choice but to deal with Aideed. Not only was he the most powerful of the Somalian warlords, but his own power base lay in Southern Mogadishu, the centre of US/UN operations. Much the same words of caution were given to the Admiral by John Drysdale, political adviser to the Special Representatives of the UN Secretary-General: 'we are not just dealing with Aideed; we are dealing with the whole clan'. Drysdale, a Briton, had served with the Somali battalion in Burma during the Second World War and is a Somalia expert and linguist. He also knew personally many of the warring faction leaders. He found that the Americans were prepared to heed his advice in the early stages of UNOSOM's life but, before long, made their own judgements. It is often the case in foreign affairs that unwelcome, expert, in-country advice can be set aside simply on the assertion that the expert 'has gone native'.

One developing problem in Mogadishu was the sparring going on along the airwaves between the UN's radio and that controlled by Aideed. In his search for a solution, Admiral Howe recommended to Aideed the establishment of a joint committee to control the radios. Although Aideed expressed himself as being in agreement with Howe's proposal, he was extremely dilatory in establishing his side of the committee. For the US hawks who were of the opinion that Aideed had to be politically reduced, the control of his radio station was an essential step towards what they saw as the halting of the undermining of UNOSOM. They did not want another of the Admiral's *ad hoc* committees, and debated amongst themselves how best to take Aideed's radio out. A parallel concern of the Americans was the question of leakage from the dumps of confiscated arms and ammunition put together by General Johnston during the life of UNITAF.

On 3 June 1993, General Montgomery sent a copy of a letter to the Admiral, outlining the establishment of UN surveillance of the dumps and control over Aideed's radio station. The letter was addressed to one of Aideed's minor functionaries and it was proposed that it should be handed over on the afternoon of Friday 4 June, which happened to be a local holiday. Five minutes before she was due to depart for the airport to go on holiday to Nairobi, Glaspie was called into Howe's office. She was asked to give political clearance to the Montgomery plan. It seems that the significance of the plan was misjudged, for there was no attempt to call a meeting of political advisers. 'Ms Glaspie was leaving the country so she glanced rapidly at the piece of paper setting out UN intentions and said: "I approve this".'[11] 'If I had seen the proposal', said John Drysdale, 'I would have acted against it'.

The UN planners were well aware that their intentions would cause turbulence within Aideed's camp. In order to minimise the impact of the UN's action, Aideed was given 14-15 hours' notice. 'Enough time to make the UN appear less aggressive in his eyes but not enough to allow him to move his heavy weapons.'[12] The Pakistani brigadier whose troops were assigned to the mission, had discussed the operation a week earlier and had expressed his reservations as to the political sensitivity of the operation as well as the danger. When the UN's intentions were revealed by two officials to Aideed's head of security, Colonel Qaibdid, he was astonished and said: 'This is unacceptable. This is war'.

> On the morning of 5 June, Pakistani forces were attacked almost simultaneously in places scattered all across southern Mogadishu: at Brigade headquarters in the National Soccer Stadium, at two feeding stations and at several strong points as well as at key points along streets connecting these places. But the principal attack fell on Pakistani troops at Checkpoint 89 on 21 October Road.[13]

Twenty-four Pakistani soldiers were killed and fifty-six wounded, of whom eleven were crippled for life. When the news reached their homes, in a tightly-knit recruiting area in central Punjab, their relatives and friends were dumbfounded. How, they questioned, could such an event come to pass on a peacekeeping operation?

Something had gone wrong. It is at this stage in events that a dotted line will be drawn to assess the situation and its development, and to come to conclusions as to what should be done to avoid a recurrence. If we look back to UNOSOM I, the effectiveness of the Pakistanis had been heavily circumscribed by the understanding by which Chapter VI peacekeeping operations are conducted. Due to the absence of an intermediate mechanism between Chapters VI and VII, the Security Council had increasingly applied inflated, heavy-handed, Chapter VII resolutions to unsuitable environments. For example, between 1945-88, twelve Chapter VII resolutions relating to six disputes were passed by the Security Council. In the next five years, fifty-seven such resolutions were adopted concerning just seven disputes.[14] The implications of this wide though concentrated use of Chapter VII is that out on the ground:

> Blue Helmets go on the military offensive without formal recognition as fully-fledged combatants subject to the laws of war - laws that impose strict limits on the use of force, irrespective of the cause at stake and the conduct of the enemy,

reported Médécins sans Frontières:

> The consequences on the ground are disastrous. In Somalia the UN attacks civilian districts and relief compounds without early warnings or prior evacuation. UN troops prevent civilians from reaching hospital during fighting and prevent aid workers from bringing relief to the wounded. [15]

The situation in Somalia did not need a country-wide mandate. Even UNITAF had only operated in the western quarter of Somalia. The situation in the country was improving to the degree that the only serious problems were in urban central and southern Mogadishu. What the Security Council had therefore done was to authorise the UN military command to use all necessary means within a city environment. This left wide scope for creative interpretation of Rules of Engagement appropriate to the customary use of force employed by national representative forces. There was no group ethos. The UN's intention to control the operation left some contributing states with the distinct impression that this was a UN-sponsored peacekeeping operation in which they operated federally, referring back to their capitals for political clearance. The Americans, however, having sidelined the UN's political nominees, operated as though they were the framework state in a sanctioned enforcement campaign, often resorting to the application of heavy, lethal firepower. The question has to be asked, from where were the Secretary-General, the American Permanent Representative to the UN and the Security Council drawing their military advice?

There is no intention of re-rehearsing the need for structural reform in the UN. However, we have raised the question of military advice available within the UN at New York for the permanent members of the Security Council. The United States is the lead member in that Council and it would therefore be both appropriate and illuminating to examine their military support structure.

The US permanent representative was the inexperienced though ambitious Madeleine Albright, a Democratic political nominee brought in from academe. She had available for regular, on-call, military guidance a Military Adviser's office, the establishment for which was a colonel and two assistants. There has been an incremental increase of two posts. Thus the total military effort available to advise the US Mission to the UN was six out of a total of 75 advisers and support personnel - that is seven per cent. In point of fact it was not quite that because the colonel, being double-hatted, was also the US Representative on the Military Staff Committee. Obviously, with the MSC still moribund, there is not too great a workload in that precise area, but what this linkage does involve is the introduction of the Pentagon to make general demands on the colonel's time which might otherwise be usefully placed at the Ambassador's disposal.

Perhaps it is therefore understandable why it came about that the Security Council overlooked the political nature of the conflict in Somalia, and gave to the military a mission to disarm the factions that was impossible to put into effect. This would not be the first time that the diplomats in New York would draw up a resolution that was at odds with what was achievable out on the ground. They had done the same in Bosnia-Herzegovina. In this instance it was the Pakistanis who suffered. Next time, it would be the Americans.

The performance of the Americans in appearing to concede on the command question had been economic with the truth of the matter. If they had any intention of giving the UN visibility it did not become apparent. The uncoordinated fingers of the Departments of State and Defense, Congress and the White House, all served to add to the difficulties of an operation which became comprehensively hijacked. There can only be one state or organisation ultimately responsible for the command and control of military operations. There are indeed sympathies for both the UN's and the USA's positions, but that is equally true of other troop-contributing states, who have the right to be protected from the effects of the in-fighting which arose between the UN and the USA.

Security Council Resolution 837 (1993) of 6 June 1993, reaffirmed the Secretary-General's authority under Resolution 814 (1993),

> to take all necessary measures against all those responsible for the armed attacks, ...including against those responsible for publicly inciting such attacks, to establish the effective authority of UNOSOM II throughout Somalia, including to secure the investigation of their actions and their arrest and detention for prosecution, trial and punishment.

The killing and maiming on both sides went on apace. The use by the United States of armed helicopters and AC-130 gunships in urban areas was justified nationally both politically and militarily. The President had said in his inaugural address that the USA would use force in circumstances where 'the will and conscience of the international community is defied'. The then Chairman of the Joint Chiefs of Staff supported a policy of going in hard and fast over a short period. The problem with Somalia is that the nature of the conflict did not lend itself to a quick fix settlement. The wrong means were employed to deal with this type of urban conflict.

The conflict was allowed to become protracted because of the political situation in Washington. There was an apparently genuine desire to have the opportunity to use force, to strike out against someone deserving of such action, as a rally event to restore the President's declining fortunes. Elsewhere there had been one clinical strike attack on Baghdad but otherwise, Saddam Hussein maintained a relatively low international profile, while it was extremely difficult to pin anything which would really stick upon Slobodan Milosevic. Besides, the allies had blocked an American plan to bomb the Serbs. The truth is that General Aideed was a convenient baddy for the moment. Even though the end of America's interest in Somalia had seemingly been marked by a ceremony on the White House lawn on 4 May 1993, Somalia provided an antidote to the passivity being displayed in European Bosnia. The US and UN demonstrated a willingness to use lethal force against disorganised clans in Somalia which they were not collectively prepared to use in the politically more sensitive and militarily more difficult environment of the Balkans. It had been without prior consultation with UN headquarters that Admiral Howe had put a price on General Aideed's head.[16] 'I have concluded it is time for General Mohammed Farah Aideed to be detained', the Admiral said on 17 June 1993. 'Wanted' posters appeared in Mogadishu, with a price of $25,000 for the capture of Aideed. 'He will be given all the protection of the law. He will be treated properly, carefully.' So, the hounds were slipped loose from their leashes to search out the fox, and hundreds of people would die as a consequence.

At a mid point between the deaths of the Pakistanis on 5 June and the Americans on 3 October, a small operation took place in Mogadishu which served to suggest that all was not right, and begged important questions as to whether the quest for Aideed was militarily achievable. On 30 August 1993, under the cover of darkness, 50 US Rangers roped themselves down from hovering helicopters to raid a villa in Mogadishu. Information had been received that a number of Aideed's men were in the building. Outside the entrance to the building was a sign declaring it to be the base of the UN Development Programme (UNDP). On the roof of the building was a UN flag. Eight UN officials inside were seized, tied up, and bundled away. An Irishman and a Canadian in the building showed the soldiers their passports, but to no avail.

A study of the Somalia operations does reinforce the point, how the use of high technology is severely constrained in urban environments such as Mogadishu. This fact automatically shifts the burden of intelligence gathering to the field of Human Intelligence (HUMINT). There is little doubt that Aideed's people were intellectually smart and adept at the art of disinformation. The UNDP attack presents all the hallmarks of the presence of a double agent. Information also suggests that the essential intelligence indicators were not assessed and analysed from first principles but were rather conveniently tailored to fit around what was wanted to be believed. Yet what was most revealing was the press conference which followed the débâcle, because it turned the negative into the positive by blurring the issue. The comprehensive intelligence failure was not discussed. Instead, the UN public relations officer described the raid in glowing terms as having been a textbook example as to how these operations should proceed, using lightning speed and overpowering force. The point is that it had been a cock-up. Fortunately no one was killed but, in a similar operation five weeks later, it was apparent that nothing had been remembered, nothing learned and, for the Americans, their luck just simply ran out.

As at 1 October 1993, the American contribution to the 28,000 troops in UNOSOM II comprised 400 Rangers, 1,300 infantry in a Quick Reaction Force (QRF), and 2,800 logisticians. The command of American forces revolved around General Montgomery. However, provision had been made for the non-combatant logistical troops to be placed on occasions under the UN's operational control, albeit through the UNOSOM deputy commander, General Montgomery. The troops in the QRF from the 10th Mountain Division were under the command of General Montgomery. The manner in which the Rangers were employed, however, suggests that the principle of the Unity of Command had been set aside:

> Unity of command means that all the forces are under one responsible commander. It requires having a single commander with the requisite authority to direct all forces employed in pursuit of a unified purpose.[17]

So bad was the coordination between the Rangers and the QRF on 3 October (the latter had barely one hour's notice that an operation was to take place, but were not given advance details) that it seemed obvious that both were not under General Montgomery's command. In fact the Rangers were being commanded from USCENTCOM Headquarters in Tampa, Florida, through an in-theatre, incognito major-general whose headquarters planned seven special operations in and around Mogadishu.

One newspaper reported that General Montgomery was only entitled to be informed of the Rangers' activities. It was said that he had the power to veto their operations but not to direct them. One US military official was quoted as saying:

> Unity of command is one of the (American) principles of war. We complained when other units in the UN force referred orders back to their own headquarters, but when it comes to unity of command, we are the worst.[18]

However, the crucial point that has to be made is that American combat forces were always under US and not UN command.

A review of those critical events is illuminating and the lessons are there to be remembered. An intelligence report advised that a number of Aideed's lieutenants were attending a meeting at the Olympic Hotel, close to the Bakara Market. A Rangers 'capture' mission was immediately set in train. At 14.14 hours on 3 October 1993, the QRF's Tactical Operations Centre was informed by the Rangers that certain sectors of central Mogadishu would be 'off limits to UNOSOM air and ground forces'. The Rangers, led by Lieutenant-Colonel Danny McKnight, then specified the sectors in which they would be operating. At 15.37, the Quick Reaction Company (QRC) located at the university compound adjacent to the former US Embassy compound, responded to the Rangers' notification that they were about a launch their 'capture mission'[19] by reducing their state of readiness and deploying to the airport. Eight minutes later, the QRF were told by the Rangers that the cordon and search elements were in place in the area of the Bakara Market, close to the Olympic Hotel. At 16.10, a Ranger helicopter was shot down. At 16.29, the Quick Reaction Company deployed to the airfield on the orders of their commander, Colonel Lawrence E. Casper. At the same time, a message was received from the Rangers that they were experiencing problems on the objective and that they might need help. States of readiness within the remaining companies of the QRF were shortened. At 16.49, news came through that a second Ranger helicopter had been shot down – a rocket-propelled grenade had removed its tail – while five minutes later, a further aircraft was hit by ground fire but was able to land in a safe area. By 17.00 hours, all the QRF's company commanders had gathered in their Tactical Operations Centre, but remained in the dark as to what was happening. Intelligence and information had not been disseminated down to them. It was not even possible to put aircraft above the area of operations because the Rangers retained airspace control.

At 17.11 hours, the QRC commanded by Lieutenant-Colonel Bill David (Commander 2-14 Infantry Battalion) was put under the 'control' of the Ranger commander. On arrival at the airport, Lieutenant-Colonel David was given his mission and a brief on the situation. He was told of the insertion of approximately 100 Rangers by ground and air close to the

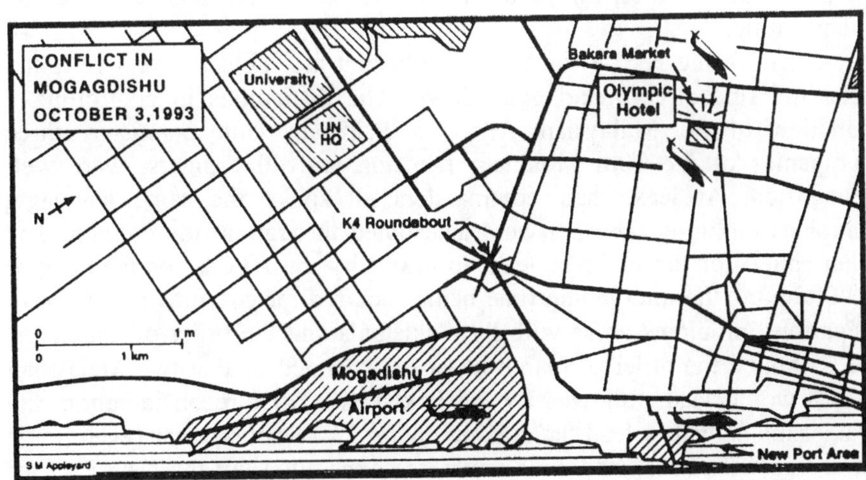

Map 6.1

Bakara Market. The Rangers had succeeded in detaining 24 individuals including three of Aideed's top aides but, once the aircraft were downed, set off on a rescue mission. They converged on the northern crash site to safeguard the crew but, in so doing, became pinned down by heavy fire. David's mission was to deploy to the southern crash site to protect the crew and Rangers in that vicinity. He set off northwards by road, with air cover provided by Ranger aircraft. For half an hour, the QRC was under fire as it moved northwards. David radioed back that he had passed two Ranger vehicles 300-400 metres north of the K4 (kilometer 4) roundabout or traffic circle, that had been hit, disabled, and were burning. At 18.21, the QRC was ordered to break contact and return to the airport as soon as possible. It is approximately at this point that Major-General Montgomery directed that the Malaysian Mechanised Battalion and Pakistani tanks be put at the disposal of the QRF.[20] (General Colin Powell had earlier requested that US tanks be made available for the theatre of operations, but the request was denied by the Secretary for Defense). In addition, the rescue operation was placed under the command of the American Brigadier-General Gile. He and

Colonel Casper planned the follow-on mission between 19.00 and 21.00. At 21.00 the plan was changed. Brigadier-General Gile directed Lieutenant-Colonel David to link up with the Rangers at the northern crash site and, subject to the tactical situation, to then move to the southern crash site to rescue survivors and pick up bodies. Meanwhile, around the Olympic Hotel, the beleaguered Rangers were venting their spleens on 'those bastards' (referring to the UN) who had failed thus far to rescue them. Ironic.

At 21.30, the rescue force was ready and assembled, over five hours after the first aircraft had gone down. The difficulties in controlling a battalion of 32 Malaysian APCs, a Pakistani tank company, three companies of the 10th Mountain Division and 40 Rangers, were well recognised. At least their commanders all spoke the same language. Graphics outlining the plan were distributed throughout the column. The plan called for the tanks to lead, followed by the APCs, commencing at 23.00 hours, the intervening time being required for coordination. Prior to departure, problems arose with the Pakistanis and the order of march. At 22.56 hours, the order of march had been changed so that two Malaysian APCs would lead, followed by the Pakistanis. After reconsideration, the Pakistanis agreed to lead the column and at 23.24 hours, over seven hours after the first aircraft had gone down, the expedition left the New Port for the objectives.

The rescue mission took a further seven hours and was conducted under intense fire and with great difficulty. Eighteen Americans had been killed and seventy-seven wounded. The Malaysians and Pakistanis also suffered casualties. The International Committee of the Red Cross estimated that there had been 200 Somali deaths in the battle, with hundreds wounded. This had not been an operation conducted by national elements that were used to working together as in NATO. It had been a good, honest effort, but the existence of common UN training standards, doctrine and operating procedures as well as a sharing of information, would have served to reduce the response time significantly. Special Force Operations are traditionally conducted in an atmosphere of secrecy. However, the 'can do' Ranger enthusiasm has to be tempered by the consideration of the possibility that things may not go according to plan. The success of any Special Operation depends to a very large degree upon the availability of good quality, unambiguous intelligence. There was no exit strategy that was workable because the elements upon which it depended had not been forewarned. Less secrecy, better coordination and more openness by the

American commanders might have resulted in a less costly operation. However, there would be profound, far-reaching, political and military implications arising from what had been an operation entirely under US command and control.

In a speech made during the evening of Sunday, 3 October, the President said that he regretted the deaths but declared the mission to have been 'very successful'.[21] He had not been fully briefed. It was only the next morning, on returning after his jog to his San Francisco hotel, that the extent of the disaster was revealed to him. When asked by the President how the débâcle came about, Defense Secretary Les Aspin 'put most of the blame on a UN command and control structure that had been unable to rush well-equipped troops to the Rangers' rescue'.[22] The blame undeservedly stuck with the UN. Why did the Secretary-General not remonstrate? 'The UN exists to help member countries solve their problems', he said. If attacking the UN helps President Clinton with Congress, 'I am not going to answer back.'[23]

By now, the pictures were coming in on television. The images of the wounded pilot of the Blackhawk helicopter that had been the QRF's southern objective, Warrant Officer Michael Durant, and worse, that of the corpse of an American soldier being dragged through the Mogadishu streets, were making an immediate impact on the American public. It was these pictures which undermined the US's resolve and confirmed the failure of UNOSOM's mission. Few events post-1945 had such a pivotal impact upon the future direction of US foreign policy. The media, therefore, which had been instrumental in the Bush decision to enter Somalia, had a decisive impact upon Clinton's decision to withdraw. What had happened was not new in warfare; similar images arose in Korea and Vietnam. What is different is the proliferation of cameras to record such gruesome scenes, the speedy means by which to transmit the pictures, and elements within a previously self-regulating medium with no concept of the difference between what is acceptable and what is unacceptable. Faced with an apparent groundswell of public opinion against a continuation of America's presence in Somalia, where no vital interest was perceived to exist, the President decided to withdraw American forces. Thus, a compelling political argument again emerged that the UN was dictating to the US its foreign policy. Many Congressmen had long been ambivalent to the United States' armed forces operating with the UN, and they were content to identify themselves with the myth rather than the truth of the matter.[24] Senator Robert Byrd (D), West Virginia, told senators: 'I do not see in the front of this chamber the UN flag. I salute Old Glory, the American flag'. It was those self same senators who endorsed a presidential recommendation for America to leave Somalia by 31 March 1994, in effect hauling Old Glory down and replacing it with the white flag of surrender. One rule in military intervention is never to impose a sunset clause. Congress may not have known precisely what UN Peacekeeping was but they knew they did not like it. A long, dark shadow was thereby cast upon future American military interventionist operations.[25]

The central question seems to be this: how, in a media war, do states' administrations take the lead in reacting to unwelcome, real-time images transmitted from the seat of conflict? The first requirement is to have a policy. The second requirement is related to the first and it is to de-emphasise the national implications and to emphasise the international nature of a response which had its origins founded upon world order goals. Admittedly, this second requirement is difficult to achieve in those environments where an automatic prejudice exists towards internationalism. However, if there has been no fundamental change to the valid reasons for the armed forces being deployed in the first place, then it is the responsibility of those in positions 'where the buck stops' to hold their ground and to lead their nation.

To recapitulate, what had been the next incremental step to jeopardise future American cooperation with the UN in Peacekeeping and Intervention Operations, had been Security Council Resolution 837. It did not specify General Aideed as the principal object of the UN's military attention. It had no need to. The anti-Aideed stance adopted by Ambassadors Gosende, Glaspie, and General Montgomery could not have been pursued without the Administration's authority. Admiral Howe's 'fingering' of Aideed was also a reflection of the Secretary-General's attitude towards the Somalian leader. To that extent, the UN and US were *d'accord.* In July, the President's interview with Jim Hoagland of *The Washington Post,*

> left no doubt that he was intimately involved in the effort to run Aideed to ground and would not be satisfied until the Somali clan leader is jailed. Decision-making on airstrikes targeting Aideed's lieutenants and the warlord himself has been entirely in American hands.

On 10 August 1993, Madeleine Albright confirmed the trend towards personalising the conflict by attributing the troubles in Somalia to Aideed. She wrote that 'failure to take action (against Aideed) would have signalled to other clan leaders that the UN is not serious', and claimed that those who did not have like views were 'advocates of appeasement'.[26] The implication, therefore, that the Administration was diverted by the UN from its original humanitarian intentions, to engage in conflict against Aideed and his clan, is false. There were cogent political reasons why Washington should be in the forefront of the movement to apprehend Aideed in order to compensate for failure in Bosnia-Herzegovina.

Once again, a UN Resolution set loose the military upon a mission which the armed forces of civilised and accountable states could not achieve. It is not a case of blaming the USA. The United States has particular problems. For example, she is not a complete superpower, her freedom of action being seriously constrained by economic considerations. Operationally, if she works through the UN she is accused of dominance; if she doesn't, she is accused of being unilateralist. There is scope for improving the presentation of actions as well as considering in greater depth the implications of proposed actions. Britain's experience of attempting to track down the 'Mad Mullah' in Somalia at the beginning of the century lasted twenty years, to be ended only by the fugitive's death from influenza in 1919. The questions that have to be asked are, where were the tactics and strategy for dealing with Somalia formulated? Who had 'hands on' at the time?

The Italians, who because of their local knowledge of Somalia and the Somalis were in a strong position to advise on action to be taken on the ground, fell foul of the UN's representatives in Mogadishu. The eleventh hour dawning that Somalia's problem (in fact it was not Somalia's problem but one specific to central and southern Mogadishu) could only be solved politically, matched the thinking that had been in place during the course of UNITAF's life. If the politicians should put the military in a similar position again, firstly the military voice must be heard and secondly, three basic understandings have to be recognised. The first is that the military's moral integrity must be maintained through independent action; secondly, an exit strategy can only be guaranteed to be effective if the mission is restricted to holding the reins while the political process is underway; and finally, if military commitment is unavoidable, then the success being sought through the use of military means has to follow in a short space of time. For example, the inappropriate, extended use of firepower by UN forces between June and October should have been abbreviated. It only served to inflate Aideed's prestige and cause indefensible collateral damage. Yet, in a manner reminiscent of General William C. Westmoreland's regular promises of victory round the corner in Vietnam, so too were the frequent reports from Mogadishu of being 'very close to capturing General Aideed'.

In contexts such as this, the question of command will obviously arise, for it was the attempt to reach a compromise between the UN and the USA which was at the heart of this mission's failure. Nations will invariably retain full command of their own forces through a national commander in theatre. National contingents may well be placed under the tactical control of a multilateral formation headquarters. This state of affairs applies equally to peacekeeping as it does to enforcement operations. The latter command and control arrangements appear more focused and responsive but, as seen in Kosovo, the force Commander could do no more than invite his subordinate national commanders to do as he requested. The reason why Operation Provide Comfort to assist the Kurds in Northern Iraq succeeded and UNOSOM II failed can be attributed to the very different approaches to command and control.

Operation Provide Comfort was a UN-sanctioned operation, while UNOSOM II was a hybrid. UNOSOM II might have worked had it also been a UN-sanctioned, American-led operation, conducted as a unified command model with outline strategic guidelines provided with the benefit of the collective wisdom of the MSC.

As part of the President's damage-limitation exercise after the failed attack, he ordered US forces to become non-operational. Although they were reinforced to provide greater protection, their mission was to sit on their hands in their compounds until March 1994 so as not to appear to have been drummed out of Somalia by Aideed. The need to find further scapegoats continued apace. Clifton Wharton, the Secretary of State's deputy, was sacked, as was the US envoy in Somalia, Robert Gosende. The Secretary for Defense, Les Aspin, was scheduled for a 20 January 1994 retirement, the administration's first anniversary, but that was delayed due to administrative problems. The UN envoy, Admiral Jonathan Howe, could not be touched by the US authorities. Washington placed much of the blame for what had gone wrong in Mogadishu on his shoulders. However, the Admiral had been appointed by Washington. When he visited his capital city on official UN duty, he attended official briefings while his UN colleagues waited in an outer office. Washington's solution to the loss of confidence in Admiral Howe was to call up the special envoy, Robert Oakley, in a unilateral move which by-passed Howe as well as undermined the UN's authority. The Secretary-General said to Albright: 'You have already confused the military situation: now you want to confuse the diplomatic situation too'.[27] Oakley had been the political controller in Somalia in December 1992, just as surely as he was the political commander again in October 1993. His mission was to 'engage Aideed in an effort to make peace'. Madeleine Albright was not sacked but, in January 1997, promoted to Secretary of State.

In his nationally televised speech to the nation after the events in Mogadishu on 3 October, the President announced the sending of the additional 1,700 troops to Mogadishu. He then made the emphasis, unnecessarily and inexcusably, that they would be 'under American command'. It was American command that had been entirely responsible for the original hiatus. Therefore, to perpetuate and pander to Congress's and the public's uninformed xenophobia only served to damage the proper functioning and hopes for the future of UN intervention. The *New York Times* reported how:

> After embracing the UN as the global peace-maker of the future, President Clinton has broken sharply with it over Somalia, signalling the Administration's intense displeasure with Secretary-General Boutros Boutros-Ghali and complicating US participation in peacekeeping operations elsewhere.[28]

Somalia had become a test to see whether there was the international will and stamina to help the oppressed. If there was a fault, it lay in the method used to achieve those ends. Dr Boutros Boutros-Ghali rationalised his obsessive interest in Somalia because it:

> showed the world the terrible consequences of the collapse of a member state. There was no government; there was no law; there was no order. There was death, starvation and war. The UN intervened because it was morally compelled to do so. In Somalia, our common resolve and commitment is being tested. We must ensure that those who have been killed in pursuit of their mission have not died in vain.[29]

The problem is that, noble sentiments aside, by October 1993 the UN had lost direction. Obviously, humanitarian assistance did not have the importance it had earlier. For every UN dollar being spent on humanitarian assistance, ten were being spent on protection.

Harold Wilson once observed that 'a week is a long time in politics'. Ten years would therefore seem a relative eternity. Incumbents in key political and military positions at the beginning of the decade would be unlikely to see it out, being replaced by new, younger people with new ideas and different experiences. If recourse to perpetual improvisation is to be avoided, there is a compelling argument for the establishment of action guidelines in the form of political and military doctrine. It may well have been the case that recollection of the lessons of 1983 Beirut would not have influenced the outcome of America's experience of 1993 Mogadishu but it *should* have influenced decision-makers.

Perhaps the recognition of the importance of *impartiality* in peacekeeping operations might have prevented the development of the obsessive desire to neutralise Aideed. There were individuals who did recognise the power, influence and importance of Aideed in his own territory, people who did *know their enemy* but whose advice was spurned. Similarly, ignoring the concept of *minimum force* drove other, neutral actors into swelling Aideed's ranks. It had all been so amateurish. But among the most reprehensible features of the Somalia experience was the absence of honesty among the ranking American political players. They used the UN as a convenient scapegoat to shield their own inadequacies and keep their ambitions and reputations intact. They found no difficulty in justifying their actions to the domestic body politic which saw in the Somalia experience the confirmation of all their prejudices. It was as a direct result of this failure of moral courage that the long, dark shadow fell over future global crises so that when leadership was anticipated and looked for, it was not there.

Somalia deserves a postscript with reference to its influence in undermining Boutros Boutros-Ghali's aspiration to achieve a second term at the UN. It says a great deal about power and how it can be employed. He became closely identified with, and blamed for, the Somalia fiasco, an operation in which he had worked closely with Madeleine Albright. Albright insisted that Boutros-Ghali use her alone as the point of contact when dealing with American interests. She is alleged to have said: 'I will make Boutros think I am his friend; then I will break his legs'.[30] The right-wing American press lampooned him as the *Secretary-Generalissimo,* running American foreign policy, not that foreign policy was an issue that mobilised many Americans. He was to be the administration's ritual sacrifice to appease Republicans in Congress. As a concession, Washington offered Boutros-Ghali only a one-year extension, which he declined. Among the measures intended to undermine the Secretary-General's credibility was an announcement by one of Madeleine Albright's protégés in New York, James P. Rubin. He announced that *anyone* at the UN working for the re-election of Boutros Boutros-Ghali would be investigated by the US. 'They know who they are', he is alleged to have said. Described as Albright's 'tart tongued janissary',[31] Rubin defended his superior, insisting that Boutros-Ghali only had himself to blame for his demise.

> It was always unfortunate that Boutros-Ghali did not have the skills to successfully manage the most important relationship for any Secretary-General which is smooth cooperation with the United States. It led to his downfall, so it is not surprising that he is bitter.[32]

George Bush announced himself as being 'pro-Boutros' while the Secretary-General believed that the President, his mind occupied elsewhere and fully engaged with the presidential campaign and conventions, appeared 'understandably oblivious to it all'. The 'indications were that Madeleine Albright and the small, secret "task force" remained in charge of eliminating me', wrote the UN Secretary-General'.[33] 'He has lost the confidence of the United States', confirmed Albright. 'It is important, when the most powerful country in the world looks at an international organisation, that we have somebody at the head of it who, we think, is suitable to take it into a new dynamic age'.[34] The United States' nominee, Kofi Annan, was duly elected UN Secretary-General. 'The UN', said Rubin, 'can only do what the US lets it do'.[35] There can be no more telling conclusion to the Somalia chapter.[36]

7 Rwanda – 'Tropical Nazism'

- Boutros Boutros-Ghali

Rwanda is worthy of extended study because it involved three quite separate, concurrent military operations and it was undeniably an humanitarian intervention stimulated by an international desire to 'do something' or, rather, as an outpouring of conscience. The irony of the Rwanda humanitarian intervention was that the majority of the aid and support went to the parties directly responsible for the worst case of genocide since the Holocaust. As events in the later Kosovo crisis unfolded, a number of humanitarian similarities became apparent - not least the massive outflow of refugees into adjoining territories. For convenience, these lessons will be correlated within this text in italics for ease of comparison.

Prior to the Rwanda crisis, there existed an automatic impression that the military and humanitarianism were incompatible entities. The origins of that idea were largely politically and ideologically based. So much so that the twain did not meet, principally because there was rarely a compelling reason why they should. The separation could be maintained in environments where there was either no conflict or where the humanitarian organisations' presence met with the consent of the governments of one or more states. With the increasing involvement of humanitarian organisations in civil wars that distinction has become blurred, particularly where relationships are less with states and rather more with nations and ethnic groups. That reality has the potential to attract a quantum leap in the degree of difficulty in the delivery of humanitarian assistance. 'Humanitarian problems are always the result of some more profound problem and therefore cannot be solved by humanitarian means alone', said EU Deputy, Alain Destexhe. The attendant instability within states means that in a conflict environment, humanitarian organisations will increasingly look to the military, certainly in the early stages, for those capabilities which they themselves do not possess. These capabilities include the provision of security, protection, resources, the capacity to control and information.

Security and protection are obviously linked and that relationship can best be described within a context. A state of security has to exist before a high level of protection can be guaranteed. In Northern Iraq in 1991, the creation of a safe haven enabled Agencies and NGOs to enjoy well nigh complete freedom of operation. This does not mean, however, that there can be no protection in an insecure environment. As will be seen, resolute action by small numbers in dangerous circumstances can achieve results far beyond what might be expected. Protection did not emerge as a major issue in the Kosovo conflict. What the military provided for the agencies and NGOs once they entered the uncertain environment of Kosovo was reassurance. Generally, however, pragmatists within the NGOs are fully aware that the environments in which they have worked in the past have become more dangerous and that in some places they cannot work except under a protective umbrella:

> ...the question of protection is becoming central for NGOs. It is at this point that the tenacious myth concerning their total independence falls down - unable by their very nature to carry arms themselves - the NGOs must of necessity turn, in order to ensure their own protection, to forces to which they are then beholden.[1]

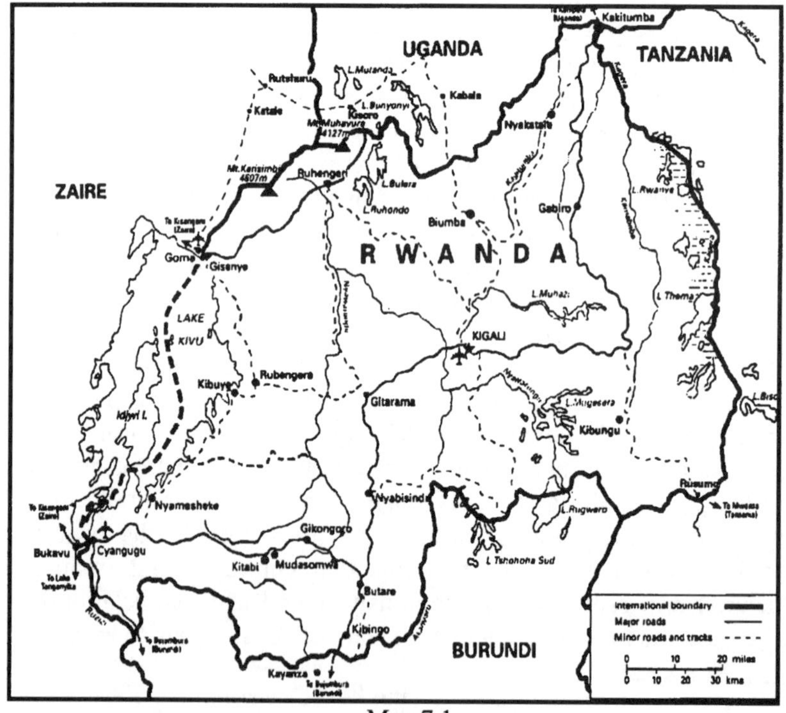

Map 7.1

The resources the military have at their disposal, particularly modern military equipment, will often be in direct proportion to the level of protection that can be offered. Operation Turquoise, the French operation, deployed with a high deterrence capability. Other military resources, engineering and medical, can hold the ring until humanitarian organisations are ready and able to take over. The capacity of the military to control stems from their organisation, available disciplined manpower, administrative skills and communications equipment. Médecins sans Frontières (MSF), Nobel Prize winner and one of the more ideological of the NGOs, used the military to help them with a life-saving programme to immunise 25,000 Rwandans. The military's capability to provide information is self explanatory. However, it is not a one way street. Agencies and NGOs will often be where the military are not and will therefore be in a unique position to pass mutually beneficial information to the military.

Security and Protection were not derived simply from the presence of foreign troops in Rwanda. The Hutu and Tutsi military protected their own, supported by gendarmerie and militia. By creating humanitarian space, the Red Cross, by its presence, saved over 50,000 Rwandans. The presence of NGOs, Agencies and aid workers had a stabilising influence in many of the areas in which they were established. Then, of course, security existed in areas where there was no conflict. The means of protection other than by recourse to arms included a physical presence, witnessing, deterrence, and the reconstitution and training of the gendarmerie.

The tentative convergence of military and humanitarian interests really began in Northern Iraq in 1991 where it was possible to witness British Royal Marines painting a hospital operated by MSF. In Somalia, the level of cooperation appears to have been generally good, yet what has emerged is something of a myth of hostility towards the military from the humanitarians. Hostility did indeed exist, but it was localised. Progress since then has been difficult to quantify. UNPROFOR II and The United Nations Advisory Mission in Rwanda (UNAMIR) were set in totally different environments, one a shooting war and the other a loin cloth conflict principally revolving around the use of the machete. There were also significant differences in NGO and military capabilities, particularly in relation to the conduct of military operations. It bears repeating that the importance of Somalia, however, is the political and military shadow which it cast over Rwanda long before, and continuing well into, the period under review.

For governments and organisations who have had cause to examine the military and their particular capabilities for the first time in terms of Implementation Operations, there are three important points to be made. The first requires no great elaboration. Military forces maintain a variety of capabilities within their structure; the more sophisticated tend to have more capabilities and hence greater flexibility. The training, organisation and equipment of a military unit dictate the environment in which it may best be used, what we have described as 'forces for courses'.

The second point flows from the first. That is, that there are unofficial league tables of military competence and professionalism. Some nations are better than others, some are much better. It is for this reason that he who talks of the 'military' generally, in relation to capabilities, is not best informed. The military is no monolith. There is, however, one extremely important caveat linked to military professionalism and that is, the military will only perform to the level of ability that their government will allow. The third point to be made concerning military intervention is that we have to change an attitude which is far too prevalent, that the use of military force is the ultimate option. This is wrong on two counts. Firstly, there will be rare occasions when military force should be applied early in a conflict without proceeding through the range of other coercive measures. The nub, however, is that so many military interventions which intervening states have justified to themselves in the past have failed, because there was no possibility that they could succeed. As has already been said, justification therefore is insufficient. A reassuring conviction of success is a prerequisite. Not enough effort or investigation has been devoted to making other coercive measures work such as preventive and coercive diplomacy.

Within the coming central discussion there is the proffered sub-division of military support to humanitarian assistance into three phases: intensive, consolidatory and transitional. The reader is invited to note that not all military involvement will necessarily follow this pattern. The French, Chapter VII, Operation Turquoise did fit that model but UNAMIR, constrained by its Chapter VI mandate, began operating from the consolidatory phase, passing into the transitional phase with the support of The United Nations Rwanda Emergency Office (UNREO).

The manner in which this topic is now to be examined is to divide it up into natural compartments and to identify lessons as they emerge in the chronology or sequence. This is the only chapter in the book to be subdivided in this manner. A clear line, 14/15 July, subdivides the period April to December 1994 when the outflow of biblical dimensions took the

Hutus out of the country into refugee camps of which the largest was Goma in Zaire. This therefore conveniently identifies pre-Goma and post-Goma periods. The pre-Goma period also subdivided into: prior to 6 April, and post 6 April, 6 April being the day when the shooting down of the aeroplane carrying the presidents of Rwanda and Burundi triggered the crisis. In the post-Goma phase, there are three parallel activities: the UN's UNAMIR operations under Chapter VI, the French Operation Turquoise under Chapter VII and the United States' Operation Support Hope which we shall describe as Chapter Zero due to the insistence that 'this is not peacekeeping, it is an humanitarian operation'.

PRE GOMA

Events prior to 6 April 1994

The major consequence arising from the Arusha Peace Agreement of 4 August 1993 was to achieve for Rwanda a broad-based transitional government until elections could be held. The agreement promised to bring three years of conflict to a close. The essentially Hutu Government of Rwanda and the Tutsi Rwandese Patriotic Front (RPF) requested that a neutral international force be positioned in Rwanda in order to help implement the agreement. They recommended that its role should be to assist with the maintenance of public security and the delivery of humanitarian aid. As far as specifics were concerned, the reality was not to rise to the aspiration. Both parties requested that the international force should assist in locating arms caches, neutralising armed 'militia', demining, disarmament of civilians and the cessation of hostilities. Further, the international force should oversee the demobilisation of existing armed forces and supervise the formation of a new national army and gendarmerie.

As a consequence of the Arusha Agreement, in August 1993 a UN reconnaissance mission went to Rwanda and reported back to the Secretary-General. On the basis of their report, on 24 September the Secretary-General recommended to the Security Council the creation of a Peace Keeping force with a mandate of 'contributing to the establishment and maintenance of a climate conducive to the secure installation and subsequent operation of the transitional government'.[2] By Security Council Resolution 872 of 5 October 1993, the establishment of UNAMIR was authorised for an initial period of six months[3] under the command of the Canadian, Major-General Romeo A. Dallaire.

The Security Council approved the Secretary-General's plan for a staged entry and withdrawal to and from Rwanda. By their understanding, UNAMIR's mandate would expire after the national elections and the installation of a new government. It was assumed that this would be by October 1995 and certainly no later than December 1995. When the details of Security Council Resolution 872 were released, the Resolution was quite clearly couched in the phraseology of Chapter VI. UNAMIR's principal functions were to contribute to the security of Kigali within a weapon-secure area; to monitor the security situation during the final period of the broad-based transitional government's mandate leading up to elections; to investigate at the request of the parties or on its own initiative instances of non-compliance with the provisions of the Arusha Peace Agreement; to monitor the process of repatriation of Rwandan refugees and resettlement of displaced persons; to assist in the coordination of humanitarian assistance activities; to investigate and report on incidents regarding activities of the gendarmerie and police and, finally, to assist with mine clearance, primarily through training programmes.

UNAMIR's mandate was orientated towards assisting and cooperating with both parties. Its manpower and equipment reflected that role. It meant, however, that if one or both parties became uncooperative, UNAMIR would be unable to react effectively to the changed circumstances. Similarly, in 2000, it was Sierra Leonean rebels' dissociation from aspects of the Lomé Agreement which unsettled the peacekeeping operation in Sierra Leone.

The UNAMIR Force Commander, General Dallaire, arrived in Kigali on 22 October 1993, followed six days later by a small advance party. Two sectors were mapped out, a demilitarised zone (DMZ) sector[4] and Kigali sector. The former became operational on 1 November and the latter in December with the arrival of Belgian and Bangladeshi troops. On 23 November 1994, the Secretary-General's Special Representative, the former Minister of External Relations of Cameroon, Mr Jacques-Roger Booh-Booh, set up his office in Kigali. Gradually, the UN military strength built up towards its authorised establishment of 2,548 military personnel which included 2,217 formed troops and 331 military observers. On 31 March 1994, in the last week before the defining event of 6 April 1994, UNAMIR's strength was 2,539 military, with representatives drawn from: Austria, Bangladesh, Belgium, Canada, Congo, Egypt, Fiji, Ghana,

Malawi, Mali, Netherlands, Nigeria, Poland, Romania, Russian Federation, Senegal, Togo, Tunisia, Uruguay and Zimbabwe (an average representation of less than 130 military per country). There were also 60 civilian police monitors.

On 5 January 1994, the Head of State, the Hutu Major-General Juvénal Habyarimana, had been sworn in as President of Rwanda. This had been agreed during the Arusha Peace Agreement. However, it had also been anticipated that, at the same time, the Transitional Government and the Transitional National Assembly would have been installed, but the parties could not agree on representation in the political bodies. It was from this point that the security situation in Rwanda seriously deteriorated.

On Saturday, 8 January 1994, the first alleged attempt to trigger the civil war occurred. There was also in Kigali a battalion of the Tutsi RPF whose role was to protect the Tutsi members of the opposition. The plan of the Hutu *Interahamwe* (those who attack together), the armed militia of President Habyarimana's party, the MRND, was to hold demonstrations during which the RPF and Belgians were to be provoked to fire into the crowd. Within the crowd were elements of the Hutu 48 Rwandan Government Forces (RGF) Parachute Commando and Gendarmerie in plain clothes as well as a MRND Minister with the *Sous-Préfet* of Kigali. Opposition deputies were to be targeted on entering and leaving parliament and, if the Belgian soldiers were to react, a number of them were to be gunned down in the hope that, *à la* Somalia, the Belgian withdrawal from Rwanda would be guaranteed. It did not happen. Clearly, if the report were true, the opportunity did not present itself.

General Dallaire was not experienced in African affairs but he had in his Kigali sector commander, Colonel Luc Marchal of the Belgian Army, someone who had served for five years in Zaire and who knew the African mentality sufficiently well to advise the commander. On 10 January 1994, a senior figure in the *Interahamwe* militia made contact with Marchal. He sought political asylum because he had received orders from the Hutu leadership to draw up plans for the extermination of the Tutsis. The man said that although he was a Hutu, he could not carry out his orders because it was against his principles. He had also assisted in the training of the *Interahamwe* in an overall programme aimed at teaching the militia to kill with greater efficiency. He believed that in twenty minutes his people could eliminate 1,000 Tutsis. Financial and material help had, he alleged, come from the RGF Chief of Staff and the President of the MRND. At that time there were 1,700 *Interahamwe* scattered throughout Kigali in groups of 40.

The informant told Marchal of the location of a major weapons cache containing at least 135 weapons. Moreover, he had already distributed 110 weapons and could give details as to where they had gone. The man was prepared to go to the arms cache himself that night if he and his family were placed under UN protection.

Marchal told Dallaire of his meeting. Although Dallaire held 'certain reservations on the suddenness of the change of heart of the informant' and 'the possibility of a trap not fully excluded', he informed Major-General Maurice Baril, Military Adviser to the Secretary-General in New York: 'It is our intention to take action (by means of a cordon and search) within the next 36 hours with a possible H Hour of Wednesday (12 January) at dawn (local)'.[5] Dallaire's signal to Baril had told the whole story, a clear picture of a serious escalation around UNAMIR as well as details of a failed plan to kill UNAMIR soldiers. The signal should have received rigorous attention. Parties who saw the copy in New York report having seen it signed off without any indication of action taken. The immediate effect had been to deny Dallaire permission to conduct the proposed cordon and search. 'They refused', said Marchal, 'because UNAMIR was deployed under a Chapter VI mandate, traditional peacekeeping. New York argued that a cordon and search was an offensive operation for which permission would not be granted'.[6] The Secretary-General was out of UN HQ for much of January and was not to learn of the signal and recognise its significance until three years later.[7] The only avenue open to Dallaire was to conduct the cordon and search in cooperation with the local actors, something guaranteed to be unproductive.

Dallaire now recognised that he would either need a very broad interpretation of his mandate, or a change to the mandate to react to the looming crisis. His military judgement told him that he required a light armoured unit of 21 armoured personnel carriers (APC), supported by helicopters, to form a rapid reaction force capable of reaching 'hot spots' quickly. New York was implacably opposed to such an idea. Dallaire had acquired eight APCs from Mozambique but they were Russian (with operation manuals in Russian), they had no spare parts and no mechanics. The Russian APCs proved to be unreliable and the absence of spare parts meant that the small fleet had to be cannibalised to keep the two on the road needed to ferry people between the lines of negotiation.

That something was up had not passed unnoticed by the Tutsis. The radio propaganda from *Radio Télévision Libre des Mille Collines*[8] and *Radio Rwanda*, owned by Habyarimana's associates, had increased the tempo of hatred aimed against them. They looked towards the UN for some prospect of future protection, but all they saw were the open hands of impartiality, as though it is possible to take an impartial position in the prelude to genocide. The situation riled the men at UNAMIR. 'The irony was', said Marchal,

> that we knew exactly what and where the problem was, but our hands had been effectively tied. The consequence of all this was that the population lost confidence in us. They also knew of the existence of arms caches and concluded that the UN was unable to act and to impose its will.[9]

There were two infantry battalions in the key Kigali sector. Until 6 April their humanitarian role had been the provision of escorts to civilian convoys. There were at least two cases where UNAMIR had shown itself to be unprepared and unwilling to intervene to protect NGO expatriate personnel. UNAMIR's primary concern was the political peace process associated with Arusha, not humanitarian support, hence the dramatic change brought about by the events which would occur on 6 April. The humanitarian cell in UNAMIR HQ liaised with the then approximately 25 NGOs in Rwanda and passed on their requests through the UNDP (United Nations Development Programme) representative resident coordinator to Marchal's HQ. The Belgian battalion was a 400-strong parachute battalion which, the year before, had seen service in Somalia. They were perplexed. In Somalia, where they had been operating under a Chapter VII mandate, they had greater latitude in the manner of their response. Now in Rwanda, they sensed a deeper feeling of jeopardy. The other battalion was Bangladeshi. Of it, Dallaire said: 'You have to go to the source rather than the product. Bangladesh was maturing its army through experience'.[10] Marchal was less diplomatic and less generous in his observation that half the soldiers in his command were non-operational.[11]

Marchal suspected there to be an economic rationale for the Bangladeshi presence in Kigali. There were a number of problems which irritated him. Military units serving with the UN are supposed to be self-sufficient for three months but, as soon as the Bangladeshis arrived, 'we had the logistic problem of finding food and water for them'. In an environment where it was usual to send orders by radio, the Belgian Colonel admitted to being nonplussed when told by the Bangladeshi commanding officer: 'I will not carry out your orders unless they are in writing'. However, above and beyond all these problems there is one that stands out, and it is one of the important factors which give western armed forces a qualitative edgc over the armed forces of developing states. It is equipment. Without the right equipment, the military are unable to protect themselves, let alone others. But that equipment also needs its own support:

> In January, I requested more ammunition, anti-tank missiles, mortar rounds and ammunition for the guns on our light recce vehicles. From 16 January I persisted, but got nothing... We approached the Belgian government. Three times I requested ammunition before it was too late. Unfortunately I was proved to be right. I am still convinced the main problem between my country and New York was a problem of comprehension.[12]

The violence which had escalated through January 1994 continued into February when two prominent political leaders, Felicien Gatabazi and Martin Bucyana were assassinated. In addition, a RPF convoy escorted by UNAMIR was ambushed. The government thereupon imposed a curfew in Kigali and other main towns. This measure stabilised the situation for a while and the ceasefire was generally observed. The Secretary-General felt that he could now recommend to the Security Council the extension of UNAMIR's mandate for a further six months, conditional upon the installation of the transitional institutions. On 5 April 1994, UNAMIR's mandate was extended by Security Council Resolution 909, with caveats expressing concern at the delays in forming a broad-based government and the deterioration in security, particularly in Kigali. The next day, 6 April 1994, proved to be a defining moment for the future of Rwanda.

6 April 1994 and its Aftermath

As a French aircraft with the Rwandan President and President Ntaryamira of Burundi on board approached Kigali airport, it was brought down by a surface-to-air missile. All were killed. The bringing down of the presidential aircraft by what were possibly disaffected government troops was the trigger to set in motion a preconceived plan. Before the news of the crash had been released, road blocks had been set up throughout Kigali. The killings then began, with the Presidential Guard in the lead. Their pre-selected victims were Hutu moderates and the Tutsi leaders in the city. The intention to force the Belgian paratroopers, the best foreign troops in Rwanda, to leave Kigali was still extant. Soon after the President had been killed, *Radio Mille Collines* announced: 'It is time to gather in the harvest'.[13] The announcer also speculated that it was the Belgians who had brought the aircraft down. The pregnant Prime Minister Agathe Uwilingiyimana and her ten man Belgian guard proved to be an irresistible target. The Hutus killed the Prime Minister and took the disarmed Belgians off to the barracks of the RGF reconnaissance regiment. Stripped naked, they were brought out in front of the regiment lined up on the square. The commanding officer announced to his men, 'These are the people who killed your President'. He then walked away, leaving the 10 Belgians to be cut down. If the Somalia precedent also applied to Rwanda, then the RGF, *Interahamwe* and *Impuzamugambi*[14] (those with a single purpose) militias could expect the Belgians to be withdrawn in the same way that the Americans had been withdrawn from Mogadishu after the events of 3 October 1993.

The action on 6 April had a dramatic and instant effect upon the Rwandans, expatriates, aid agencies, NGOs and UNAMIR. Whereas, prior to this date, the latter engaged in occasional escorting, there was now a compelling need to provide security and protection for some key groups. The problem was that General Dallaire had little by way of capability and, by the time the month was out, he would have even less.

The Tutsi RPF battalion in Kigali left its camp and engaged the surrounding Hutu RGF. Meanwhile, the Hutu militia, armed in the main with machetes, continued the systematic extermination of their opponents. *Radio Mille Collines* encouraged and coerced ordinary Hutus to join in the spiral of violence: 'The baskets are only half full. They should be filled to the brim'. Death warrants were sent out over the air waves. One targeted the Minister of Labour and Social Affairs, Lando Ndasingura who, with his mother, wife and children, was murdered by the militia.[15] The RPF formed units, which had been within the DMZ, armed themselves and moved rapidly south towards the capital. On 8 April, an interim government was declared. Special Representative Booh-Booh's recognition of a government disowned by the RPF proved to be his undoing and total eclipse. He took refuge in the Meridien Hotel and was eventually replaced by Special Representative Mr Shaharyar Khan, former Permanent Secretary of the Ministry of Foreign Affairs of Pakistan.

On 9 April, unannounced to Dallaire, the French advanced parties of Operation Amaryllis arrived at Kigali airport to evacuate European nationals. The force totalled 1,100 troops of whom 400 were Belgian and 80 Italian. Operating from the RGF side, they conducted the withdrawal of those European[16] expatriates who wished to leave Rwanda. Their mission completed, the French left on 12 April followed by the Amaryllis Belgians on the 13th. By that time the killings had reached a peak of frenzy and ferocity. Was it lack of communication or lack of national will which prevented the Amaryllis troops from being used by Dallaire to attempt to halt the atrocities?[17] By the 12th, the RPF had been in the city outskirts for two days. On the 12th, the 'interim' government fled to Gitarama, 40 kilometres south-west of Kigali, leaving the city open for the RPF to occupy, which they began to do the next day.

The RGF initiative to force the Belgians out of UNAMIR and out of Rwanda worked. On 14 April, Brussels announced the withdrawal and, with almost indecent haste, their troops began to thin out on the 19th. Behind the scenes, the Belgian Foreign Minister, Mark Eyskens, worked hard for a multilateral withdrawal from Rwanda in the hope of lessening the impact of the unilateral Belgian decision to withdraw. The Bangladeshis announced that they had come under pressure to pull out from 'several' countries. Who else would have an interest in a multilateral withdrawal can only be left to conjecture. But that pressure also bore fruit, so that the whole military complement of the Kigali sector decided to quit. This left the UNAMIR planners with the task of drawing the residue of the force back into the city.

At this point, the Secretary-General had not ruled out the prospect of an enforcement mandate but the Security Council was divided. What they were unanimously agreed upon was that the force would not be totally withdrawn,[18] and 'mission creep' towards a Somalia-style operation would not be tolerated. The Security Council's actions being restricted to determining what would not, rather than what might be attempted, underlined the fact that there was precious little collegiality within the Security Council. The Council had been starved of important information by the bureaucracy, and the United States and France refused to allow details of the recovery of their expatriates to pass through the Security Council. However, it was the role of the United States, firmly set against a repetition of the Somalia experience and guided for the first time by a new, thoroughly inflexible doctrine ('a policy of stringent conditionality'),[19] Presidential Decision Directive 25 (PDD 25), which obstructed any progress towards action that might have stemmed the unfolding genocide.[20] 'The new rules were so tightly drawn as to scope, mission, duration, resources and risk that only the easiest, cheapest and safest peacekeeping operations could be approved under them and many current UN operations could not', wrote the Secretary-General. Madeleine Albright sought to impose the Clinton conditions on other countries with varying degrees of success.[21] Britain was content to apply the rubber stamp while France, not unusually, was not. Since the USA stated emphatically that Rwanda was an humanitarian rather than a peacekeeping operation, the application of PDD 25 as a comparator was invalid. The USA was well aware that the killings were continuing on a massive scale. The State Department sent out directives to diplomats in the field to the effect that, whereas the killings they were witnessing might seem to resemble genocide, they were not to be described as genocide but as 'acts of genocide'. (In the event of genocide, there is an unavoidable international responsibility to intervene under the 1949 Convention on Genocide.)

In addition, there had been the budget consciousness of non-involvement. The USA is responsible for almost one third of peacekeeping funding and therefore is understandably wary of entangling commitments. However, it has been assessed that the USA's reluctance to act early resulted in a fifty-fold escalation of the cost when eventually US troops were committed.[22] The circumstances will now be summarised, but the openly telegraphed message, that there would be no western intervention in any circumstances, provided a new momentum to the killings and a reassuring sense of impunity to the killers. Compare that initiative with NATO's 1999 declaration that there would be no ground operations against Serbia and Kosovo.

Attempts were made to negotiate a ceasefire between both Rwandan parties and, although there was greater willingness to talk on the RGF side, the RPF were fundamentally uninterested. Dallaire therefore had to look at his own situation. Troops were leaving UNAMIR by the battalion and all he could secure in exchange was a small number of Senegalese and Ethiopians. His task to protect the overseas aid workers was eased by the evacuation of the majority with the expatriates. The only organisations to remain in Kigali were the Red Cross and Médecins sans Frontières, with a number of others in outstations in the country. The overwhelming need was to protect Rwandans who naturally looked to the UN for help. However, Dallaire's mandate still only allowed him to assist and cooperate with the parties. By 18 April both the RGF and RPF, recognising the UN as non-threatening, allowed them relative freedom of passage. The same was not true of the officious militia, never slow to set up road blocks and interfere with UN relief missions. This behaviour was repeated in 1999 in East Timor. By 19 April, the killings which had begun and continued in Kigali, had moved out and beyond Kigali into the south and west.

What became apparent was the set of circumstances under which UNAMIR could offer protection.[23] The first was the *passive defence* of civilians, which usually related to a fixed site such as the prominent

Amahoro Stadium where UNAMIR could guard the entrances. Protection was provided for 20,000 in this manner. The passive defence initiative was unilateral and, while not conducted in association with either of the parties, was not regarded as being outside the mandate. The second was described as the *active mode.* This was akin to flying pickets or raids conducted with the acquiescence of General Dallaire, when he was aware of them, and implicitly when he was not. For example, on one occasion UNAMIR troops with nothing more than AK47s positioned themselves at the Hotel Mille Collines to protect the Tutsis who had taken refuge there. On another, a Polish officer with other nationals toured the capital in a jeep, plucking Tutsis off the street and to safety under the noses of the *Interahamwe.* Clearly, none of this was done with the coordination and cooperation of the gendarmerie. The active mode stretched the understanding of the mandate as a legitimate act to as far as it could possibly be stretched. Finally, there were *overt operations* where UNAMIR smashed down barricades in order to release victims. UNAMIR rarely had the capacity to conduct overt operations due to lack of troops and equipment. They were certainly never authorised.

Life in Kigali had become very difficult and dangerous. To all intents and purposes UNAMIR was on the defensive. Dallaire's communications had gone with the civilian operators, his food stocks had been exhausted and there was no water. The UN troops were also taking casualties from the sporadic firing going on around them. The General's request for the additional equipment he needed to do the job, and for a change in mandate to allow him greater freedom of movement, was turned down in New York where they were preoccupied with the question of what to do next. Dallaire gave them his recommendations in order of priority. First, to reinforce and to provide proper equipment and a mandate to allow him to act with aggression. Second, to leave things as they were. The third option he had given them he thought was unacceptable but he nevertheless put it forward in the hope that it would strengthen his first and preferred option. He proposed that the troop strength be reduced to a political level of 240-270, which would allow for only the passive protection of civilians. The Secretary-General presented Dallaire's first option to the Security Council as his first option, Dallaire's third option as his second, and, as his third, introduced a new option of total withdrawal. Resolution 912 of 21 April decided to reduce the level of UNAMIR to 270 and rejigged the mandate so that UNAMIR could act as intermediary between the two parties, monitor developments and assist with the delivery of humanitarian aid as far as possible. To the Tutsis, the withdrawal of the UN at their time of need was unforgivable - a view which was repeated by the OAU[24] whose Secretary-General, Salim Ahmed Salim, criticised the decision 'to abandon the people of Rwanda'.

Even from the early days, UNAMIR had attempted to improve both communications and the flow of information. *Radio Mille Collines* was still spewing out its propaganda of hate. There was no 'good guy' radio to combat it by telling the truth to a populace in a state where radios were very widely available:

> Linda Chalker[25] promised radio stations and a jamming facility, as indeed did the Americans and Canadians, but they allowed themselves to be hamstrung on the sovereign state issue even though the Hutu radio was making overt demands that the genocide continue,[26]

said General Dallaire. The General hung on to the media assets he had. UNAMIR fed, accommodated and provided transport to those of the media who had become attached to the HQ in Kigali. 'I guaranteed that they could get their stories out every day', explained Dallaire. 'You see, I knew full well that if the media left, the whole operation would have crumbled.'

UNAMIR was reduced to its new establishment. The killings continued unabated. There were in Kigali three strange bedfellows, the military in UNAMIR including a civilian detachment from UNREO, the meticulously neutral Red Cross, and the independent Médecins sans Frontières. Never, in any of the groups' wide experience, had they witnessed such cruel, bestial inhumanity. They themselves were also at risk. In the southern town of Butare, 13 Red Cross volunteers died whilst attempting to protect 21 Tutsi children, also slain. In Kigali, in one of the largest single losses of life in the history of the Red Cross, many volunteers were murdered.[27] UNAMIR's HQ became the UN actor responsible for and making possible, protection, movement across lines, evacuation and, as the control point for the looming humanitarian catastrophe. This they did in association with the Red Cross. The Red Cross came under real pressure and was prepared to take all the help that it could get. MSF reinforced the Red Cross, being unable to set up by itself. What emerged was a marriage of convenience where past attitudes and perceptions were set aside to address the primary aim of saving lives.

The fellowship which developed among these three disparate agencies went largely without comment among them. The Red Cross did have some residual concern regarding transparency and of being too closely identified with the military, but the emergency was so intense that such thoughts were in the back rather than the front of people's minds. The Red Cross treated Dallaire's casualties in the same way as any others. 'Although our contact was not flaunted', said the General, 'it was used when necessary, for example in stopping firing on hospitals and helping to set up aid stations'.[28] There was also an inevitable association when the RGF began to surrender, sometimes in droves. They gave themselves up, still in uniform, to UNAMIR, from where they passed from the authority of the UN to the Red Cross. 'They were treated as prisoners of war and handed over to the RPF as identified combatants, formally and properly handed over and subsequently monitored by the Red Cross'.[29] The military and remaining humanitarian organisations developed an extraordinary synergy. That there were so few of them made it easier to work together: there was certainly a real need for military protection.

The assessment of this, the initial phase up to 6 April 1994 and its immediate aftermath, reveals the beguiling influence the Somalia experience had upon Washington and New York, to the degree that they resisted effective action. Albright appeared to be working to the letter of the law according to PDD 25. The Clinton Administration could ride out the influences of one Mogadishu but not two. They made their position felt in the Security Council. The Secretary-General and the Secretariat also had their reasons for not repeating the Somalia experience. But both New York and Washington had taken a narrow view of Somalia, emphasising effect rather than analysing cause. If they had learned from Somalia and adopted a different approach to Rwanda, the outcome would not have been the same. It was the Secretary-General, however, who allowed the UN to be tarred with the Somalia brush rather than insist that the blame should reside where it belonged, in Washington. What Dr Boutros Boutros-Ghali understood was the fact that in the USA real power resides in the legislative rather than the executive, as influential senators such as Senate Foreign Affairs Committee Chairman Jesse Helms would go on to demonstrate.

An important difference between Somalia and Rwanda was that the latter had a government of sorts. President Habyarimana, however, had close links with the *Interahamwe* through the MRND and he must therefore have been closely associated with the planned violence. How can the UN offer effective protection to those at risk if it depends upon the continuing consent, implicit in a Chapter VI operation, of one of the principal plotters or his Party? New York would have been validating Dallaire's forecast of impending doom with the Secretary-General's Special Representative, but by all accounts he had taken a position supportive of Habyarimana. The

French decision not to become involved initially meant that it was a closed and fatal loop.

As the RPF progressively gained territory they consolidated their position, putting their gendarmerie in place to provide security before the army continued its movement westward. The RGF offered the RPF no significant opposition, the campaign was fought as a knife cutting through butter but, despite the ease of the RPF advance, they did not move fast enough to overhaul the killings. The Tutsi General Kagame's aim was to clear the country of the militia as he moved forward:

> Defenceless men, women and children were being cut across the neck with machetes and beaten to death with hoes and iron bars. There are several accounts of victims pleading to be shot, rather than face the terror and agony of being cut to death.[30]

For these people, many of whom took refuge in hospital wards and churches, there was no sanctuary, no protection. It was coming, but still over the hills to the east. The tragedy was that many peaceable Hutus, fearing reprisals, were swept forward ahead of the advance. UNAMIR's responsibility for security and protection was progressively eroded as the RPF gained territory, allowing Dallaire and his men to concentrate upon the humanitarian challenge. 'The gendarmerie has sorted out our problems, not UNAMIR', said the Save the Children Fund Manager in Kigali, 'nor have we sought medical help from them'. But he did acknowledge that Rwanda had become the crucible of new possibilities between the NGOs and the military. 'Somalia was something new for which we did not have the opportunity to learn about each other's role', he explained. 'In Rwanda there was more time to get to know one another.' At this stage it was not security and protection which maintained the bond but resources and information. In such a developing, benign environment, the NGOs could function more efficiently and the military, absolved of security tasks, could draw on their capabilities to assist. A Cambridge University team came away from Rwanda with the distinct impression that the experience of the NGOs working with the military had done much to dispel deep-seated prejudices. 'The nature and scale of the operation threw them together. There was some hope that the experience and goodwill engendered might percolate upwards to NGO HQs.'[31]

In the Red Cross HQ in Geneva there was the admission that:

> The military did a good job. There are no better logisticians than military ones, and their resources are enviable. They are disciplined, organised and fast. But it

> is an uneasy marriage since humanitarians and the military have different agendas, different objectives.[32]

A view at the grass roots level is also illuminating:

> We want military we can trust to provide a secure environment as the police do at home, but we do not want them to interfere in our operations. We just want to get on with our job, not have to attend too many meetings and be bogged down in bureaucracy.[33]

The success of this marriage of necessity comes down to the professional skill of the appointed UN commander. 'Our aim', explained General Dallaire,

> was to crack the humanitarian problem in Kigali and help the NGOs in the country, even though we were not so authorised. The NGOs should be self-sufficient, but they were often a burden and under-resourced. We did what we could to help them and made no charge.

Dallaire knew he had to work with the NGOs to keep them on-side. Yet, if the military is not monolithic, the same can be said of the NGOs. Some have a doctrinal reluctance to be associated with the military, some saw the military as competitors, and some were overnight wonders. They each had their own agenda, but their uniting consideration was publicity. Publicity is their oxygen, and the influence that has on their behaviour is but one reason why they have been called 'Non-Governable Organisations'. There has to be some attempt at cooperation because the NGOs have the capacity through their access to the media to destabilise the operation. What the military commander has to achieve is an environment of consensus, creating an atmosphere of a sense of ownership by all parties. But then, the NGOs are not the only organisations to consider. Others include donor governments, UN Agencies and the Red Cross. All these, the NGOs and the military need a common machinery to help them work together for the common good.

The reason why the civilian humanitarian organisations have had difficulties in the past striking either dialogue or understanding with the military is due to their different structures. The military side, in the same way as the political side, works through a hierarchical, vertical structure. It is organised functionally and operationally in a vertical plane. Activities are self-supporting and integrated, while instructions passed down the line are for obligatory action and not the opening shot in a wider debate. The civilian humanitarian organisations operate in unstructured, horizontal planes in which there is no compulsion, merely a frequent desirability to seek consensus among themselves, to cooperate and to coordinate. What is needed between these two distinct disciplines is an intermediary, a simultaneous translator. Out of this necessity, at the height of the crisis, there emerged and evolved what was arguably the most positive, progressive development of the entire Rwandan campaign - the United Nations Rwanda Emergency Office (UNREO). UNREO acted as that intermediary to coordinate humanitarian support.

What UNAMIR, UNREO, the UN agencies and the NGOs agreed upon were rules or understandings as to how the humanitarian crisis in Rwanda was to be addressed. Agreement was reached on:

> the security of relief efforts; joint identification of distribution sites by responsible authorities and UN humanitarian organisations; clear identification of interlocutors to represent the authorities for discussion of humanitarian operations; acceptance by authorities of the monitoring and reporting responsibilities of the UN organisations regarding the distribution and use of relief materials; and an understanding that aid should be provided based on need, regardless of race, ethnic group, religion or political affiliation.[34]

Dallaire found that with some NGOs there was still concern regarding transparency even though Rwandans were still dying. On the other hand, soldiers and representatives of the NGOs would crash through ambushes together to get supplies through. 'When everyone was treated as equal', said Dallaire,

> there was no stigma except from the Ivory Towers. Integration happens rapidly in the field, hence the emergence of autocracy. It has to be remembered that within the NGOs there is a wealth of experience, courage and skill. So, if the military are to coordinate humanitarian aid, they need to respect those NGOs that are so deserving in order to maintain credibility. They should not see their role as a parliamentarian holding conferences galore.[35]

That the trend towards improved cooperation between the agencies, the 120 NGOs and the military was continuing to make progress was evident from the structures which had evolved in 1999 in Pristina, Kosovo. Bernard Kouchner, the UN Special Representative to the UN Mission in Kosovo (UNMIK), customarily held a daily 5pm meeting with the KFOR commander to discuss events and potential problems. There was now even an acronym - CIMIC (Civil Military Cooperation) - as if to confer a blessing upon a marriage of convenience. The fact that more international organisations were involved in what was then a benign Kosovo than had been the case in Rwanda resulted in a more sophisticated humanitarian structure. Kouchner headed a four-pillar organisation, with each pillar's leader constitutionally subordinate to him. The first pillar was provided by the UN and dealt with civil administration; the second was found by the EU, responsible for reconstruction; the third pillar, institution-building, was the responsibility of the OSCE, while the last pillar, humanitarian support, saw the UNHCR given the role of lead agency. There was a sentiment in Pristina that the UNHCR behaved as though it objected to being under control and was reputed to be not the best of team players.

Dallaire did behave autocratically, using external offices to prevent people coming into Rwanda unless he knew about it. The United Nations Observer Mission Uganda-Rwanda (UNOMUR), whose military observers had come under UNAMIR's command, monitored those seeking access at the Rwanda/Uganda border:

> I did not like doing this but I had to because the NGOs could destabilise the security situation. An NGO truck with 4,000 litres of diesel went behind the RPF lines because they had requested the fuel to run the pumps of their 'water supply'. We knew for what real purpose that fuel was used. Security is not simply a physical thing but includes an overall assessment of the humanitarian environment.[36]

Security Council Resolution 918 authorised the expansion of UNAMIR's strength to 5,500 and the formation of UNAMIR II, but the Security Council had failed to ascertain which states would come forward to supply troops. The whole purpose of UNAMIR II was to provide security: 'to assure the security of as many assemblies as possible of civilians who are under threat' and 'provide security, as required, to humanitarian relief operations'. The Secretary-General's plan was for UNAMIR II to fan out from Kigali airport to create safe areas in the interior and along the border with a view to being fully operational by mid June. UNAMIR II would steadfastly remain a Chapter VI operation although the circumstances of self-defence and protection were made clear. Some potential troop contributing nations insisted upon seeing the rules of engagement before agreeing to allocate troops. The Permanent Members of the Security Council, who had the capability, maintained their positions that they had no national interest to be served in becoming involved in Rwanda. Some African states had expressed an interest but did not have the capability to make a rapid response. The Secretary-General ruefully reflected upon the international community's failure to react to Rwanda's genocide, believing it 'demonstrated graphically its extreme inadequacy to respond with prompt and decisive action to humanitarian crises entwined with armed conflict'. Dr Boutros Boutros-Ghali emphasised that the system for obtaining support for UN operations was overdue for review in order to improve its capacity to react to such crises as that in Rwanda. More Security Council Resolutions followed. Resolution 925 of 8 June 1994 endorsed the Secretary-General's recommendation for UNAMIR's expansion. Resolution 935 of 1 July 1994 expressed 'grave concern' at the violation of international law, including genocide, sought funds, and demanded that all parties to the conflict cease fighting. This was not the UN's finest hour. What was emphasised was the reality that the UN's action reflected the wishes of its membership, particularly those of the United States.

The fact was that most of the aid coming into Rwanda in early July was going behind the RPF lines. UNAMIR was therefore placed in a difficult position because of an obligation of even-handedness. Humanitarian aid had to be distributed equally behind the RGF lines as well. The independent NGOs made their own decisions. The majority chose to support the Tutsi RPF and so intense was that support that the RPF soon complained of out-of-control NGOs in their rear areas. For its part, the RGF complained about the RPF and UNAMIR. Dallaire's response was that he was unable to improve the RGF's humanitarian position until a ceasefire had been achieved.

However, the RPF insisted on the killings being halted before implementing the ceasefire demanded by Security Council Resolution 918 of 17 May 1994. 'Thus there was an impasse', said Dallaire. (After 6 April, the beginning of the real military protection phase, when the need for the military was at its height, the Security Council insisted upon a ceasefire as the prerequisite for the maintenance of UNAMIR in place. However, UNAMIR did not have the strength to stop the genocide carving its way out of Kigali westward. The only force capable of doing that was the RPF. A ceasefire at this early stage would have prevented the RPF from stopping the genocide.) 'Humanitarian aid continued to flow with a bias towards the RPF rather than the RGF.'[37] Dallaire, the French national commander, General Lafourcade and Khan did their utmost to persuade the RPF to arrange a ceasefire. The RGF were now well disposed to the formation of a national force and it would have been possible for the RPF commander, General Kagame, to have sought reconciliation. 'General Dallaire knows the Rwandan forces were prepared to sign an unconditional surrender', said the French General Lafourcade, 'but the continuing advance of the RPF westward led to the defeated RGF fleeing into Zaire'.[38]

The movement of the Hutus into Zaire was the last thing the Generals Dallaire and Lafourcade wanted. 'We endeavoured to encourage the Hutus either to remain where they were or to move back home. We knew that once in Zaire, where aid could be delivered, they would stay there and be difficult to shift.'[39]

To General Lafourcade's intense frustration, the UNHCR was encouraging Hutus to leave Rwanda. Whilst in Rwanda the Hutus were categorised as Internally Displaced. Only in the Congo could they be described as refugees and thereby fall within the responsibility of UNHCR. This demarcation had also been evident in 1991 in Northern Iraq. There, UNHCR declined to help prepare indigenous Kurds for winter on the grounds that that was the responsibility of 'Development'. Such an interpretation was by no means universal. For example, in 1992 the UNHCR was criticised for ethnic cleansing in Bosnia by facilitating the expulsion of Croats and Muslims from Serb areas. UNHCR officials maintained their action was justified on humanitarian grounds but other observers claimed UNHCR was helping the Serb war effort. Similarly, in 1999, UNHCR was fully engaged in moving Serbs out of Kosovo to the intense annoyance of the UN Secretary-General's representative, M. Kouchner, and also NATO. The latter organisation had entered Kosovo to stop the ethnic cleansing of Kosovo Albanians. It had no wish to be accused of acquiescing in the ethnic cleansing of Kosovo's Serbs. It is a difficult ethical issue. If people at risk are not moved to safety, their lives may be endangered.

General Lafourcade recognised that the RPF did not know how to manage the crisis. When they were implored to arrange a ceasefire, they did not and the chance went begging. The General accepted that it would have been difficult for the Tutsis to have accepted the recent genocide, but he believes Kagame should have made a gesture:

> Kagame's strategy should have been to concentrate upon punishing the principals rather than individuals. The RPF had a list of 30,000. The Hutus were aware of the existence of this list and, suspecting they might be on it, none was prepared to move.[40]

The lesson the General drew from this was the world community's slowness to respond in establishing a War Crimes Tribunal. Had the machinery been in place, he believed a reconciliation with the Kigali government might have been possible. Fearing that a mass exodus of Hutus would destabilise the region, on 1 July 1994 the Secretary-General called for an end to hostilities. Again on 14 July 1994, the President of the

Security Council expressed his alarm at the continued fighting, but the movement all had feared, the 'nightmare scenario', took place. Over a two week period, 1.5 million Hutus sought refuge in Zaire. On 18 July, the RPF unilaterally declared a ceasefire and, on 19 July, a Tutsi-dominated government of national unity was formed in Kigali.

POST-GOMA

To include the French Operation Turquoise under this post-Goma heading is not entirely accurate since the French deployment preceded the outflow into Zaire. It does serve our purposes, however, to examine the three distinct military operations side by side. They were: the UN's UNAMIR and UNAMIR II Operations, Chapter VI operations; the French Operation Turquoise launched under a Chapter VII mandate; and the American Operation Support Hope which, since it was specifically declared to be 'humanitarian not peacekeeping' (Secretary of Defense Perry had said 'the United States does not have combat forces here, therefore we are not providing peacekeeping')[41] we shall describe as Chapter Zero. Obviously, operating with different missions and mandates under differing circumstances in different places, the lessons arising will vary according to where and when they occurred.

UNAMIR

The transition which occurred at the end of July from the pre- to post-Goma phase proved to be dramatic.[42] (Media gurus and Africa specialists who had been preoccupied with events in South Africa, switched their point of focus upon Rwanda.) The media images of the terrible conditions in which the former Hutu government had placed their own followers had an immediate impact. Aid support moved from the RPF to the RPG and the military support from the West, which until now had been denied, became available. The response was to the needs of the Hutu people suffering malnutrition and sickness - the principal of which was cholera. A great influx of NGOs followed, resulting in the direct support of the Hutus in the camps to which prior planning had directed them. The RGF and militia controlled the camps and were not averse to selling-on humanitarian aid to rebuild their defeated army. For the medium and long term this was of course undesirable and unhelpful. When the Hutus fled Rwanda, they emptied the national banks. Now, in late July through into August 1994, three quarters of the aid funds entering the bankrupt state of Rwanda flowed out again into the Hutu camps. Of the balance that was spent in Rwanda, almost all of it was targeted upon the displaced, the majority of whom were Hutu. Some sympathy has to go out to the Tutsis who had responded militarily to a Hutu plan of genocide aimed against them and which had accounted for approximately one million of their people. Their army had not been paid for months.

To those agencies and NGOs that had been in Rwanda from the beginning of the troubles, the new Klondikers in the newly-arrived NGOs were true participants in a gold rush. 'It was convenient and rewarding for some people to be there', wrote Geoff Loane, the Red Cross's deputy head in Nairobi, 'and they did not necessarily bring the best resources'. (There was no great interest in being involved in low-profile activities such as sanitation and the provision of water.) 'Everyone rushes for the pot at the end of the rainbow but, having participated, they wonder what to do with their piece of it. It's all a bit donor-driven. People run for the emergency. It's where the money and the glory are.'[43] Significantly, the newly-arrived NGOs brought with them attitudes of the military which had been largely dispelled earlier, in the heat of the crisis.

Of the military, 'the first on the ground were the ABCA countries (America, Britain, Canada and Australia)', recalled General Dallaire.[44] What is truly amazing of the western military is the well nigh total absence of contingency planning for such operations. As we shall see with the American operation, the suddenness of its launching affected its efficiency. The designated British logistic contingent was away on manoeuvres at the time it was nominated for Rwanda, and its reconnaissance group left without having been given a defined mission. Bearing in mind that the United Kingdom had no military experience of Rwanda, the reconnaissance programme is revealing. The team was briefed at the Ministry of Defence on 26 July, flew from the United Kingdom on 27 July, arrived in Kigali on 28 July, departed Kigali on 29 July, returning to the United Kingdom on 30 July.

It is usual for military in support of humanitarian operations to comprise logistic troops supported (or protected) by a number of infantry. In the case of military intervention (as reflected in Turquoise, although this was something of a hybrid operation) the reverse is true. Four hundred British soldiers were declared available for the British Operation Gabriel, later to be increased to 600. The aim of the British contingent was, for three months, to help with the repair of roads, buildings, bridges and electrical installations as well as to provide medical support for aid agencies. The then Minister for Defence said: 'They have soldiers (he meant infantry) with them to protect them, and of course they have the right to self-defence if they are themselves in danger'.[45] The British, Canadian and Australian[46] uniformed reinforcements, as with the military forces from other states, were placed under UNAMIR operational control by their governments. There were also Dutch and Irish military working in plain clothes in Goma in support of NGOs.

By the end of July, UNAMIR was no longer playing the lead role. The need for protection had passed. Instead, the emphasis was upon the establishment of security and stability in western Rwanda and upon the provision of humanitarian assistance. UNAMIR's continuing function remained crucial to the success of the humanitarian intervention but there is a principle of a civilian lead because it is the civilians who provide the continuity and development strategies in war-torn environments. As mentioned, it seems that there are three basic phases to an humanitarian operation which involves a military response: the first intensive, the second consolidatory, and finally a transitional phase. As a general rule, in the intensive phase there is the requirement or preference for highly-trained armed forces who have at their disposal the sophisticated equipment, resources and materiel with which to simply gain control, to calm. The NGOs and agencies may be present but their capabilities remain to be developed. In the consolidatory phase, military and civilians will be working together to stabilise the situation before transition, at which stage the military handover to the professional humanitarian is complete.

The 1999 Kosovo experience followed the same pattern of intensive, consolidatory and transitional phases. The UN had forecast the outflow of almost a million Kosovar Albanian refugees into the adjoining territories but was unable to react in a timely manner. The crisis became apparent mid week and, by the Sunday, NATO had set up an air bridge of up to 40 aircraft a day providing humanitarian aid. Military aircraft have the benefit of using military airfields and are not confined to civilian air traffic lanes. The military were already deployed in Macedonia, ostensibly as the extraction force for the OSCE's observers. A local contractor was engaged to build refugee camps but this proved beyond the contractor's capability. Ninety-five per cent of the camps were built by the military and 60-70 per cent were run by them for four weeks. From the commander down, most of the military effort was involved in humanitarian support operations.

As the need for offensive operations became apparent, the military had to step away from providing dedicated support to the refugee camps. UNHCR was accordingly advised that they would have to assume full responsibility for the management of camps in two weeks time. 'It came as a shock', said a KFOR logistician. According to the House of Commons' Lessons of Kosovo *Report: 'one of the key failings in respect of the humanitarian crisis was the disorganisation of the UNHCR itself'.*[47] *With the exception of a few minor functions, transition was achieved over a three week period so that by mid May, the full cycle to the transition of responsibilities had been run.*

Now, within the framework of the three phases there has to be an understanding as to where the line is drawn between what the military and civilians do. The military has to understand that the environment into which it is arriving has, by tradition, been sub-divided into areas of interest and specialisation by the larger of the NGOs. At the outset there is scope for friction - thus the importance of building bridges before they need to be crossed, and the development of an educational programme and understanding between future participants in humanitarian crises. The provision of medical support is probably the one function where there is the greatest scope for friction. A general criticism of the military in Rwanda was that they raised levels of expectation and had no plan or programme for handover on their departure. The military medical representatives are generally used to supporting the fit, not mother and child feeding. In addition, their medical strategies differ, the military curative, the NGO preventive. There is also a third party consideration. That is to bring local people into the process from the beginning. The end state must include an end date so that the timing of the final transition is known in advance and does not come as a surprise to those who remain and who will invariably be unable to respond to the vacuum being created. In all fields of endeavour, there has to be a complete and collaborated strategy between the military and the humanitarian organisations, and that depends upon a willingness on the part of both parties to achieve a dialogue at the outset.

'The British military deployment was very effective because it was light', said General Dallaire. 'The Canadians brought a large hospital, so big it was "tied down", whereas the British medical facilities were nimble,[48] moving quickly from north to south. The British, Canadians and Australians were all free with the resources at their disposal.'[49] A senior UN official remarked how he 'preferred the Canadians because they stayed on when life was very difficult. The British were excellent, but why did they not arrive sooner and why did they not stay longer?'. The British did a great deal while they were there, building, as someone said, 'not just bridges but diplomatic bridges'. A principal task was to maintain the Main Supply Route from Uganda. 'They were impressively reticent', said one observer:

> They did not try to gazump the locals, seek publicity, they demonstrated a great capacity for humanitarian consideration and listened to the wishes of the people. They were quick to learn. The Field Ambulance was set up *after* consultation with the NGOs. This pulled in the local population and they also conducted outreach visits to the surrounding villages. This work was taken in the stride of the self-contained contingents who did what they do best - using their military intuition, ability and resources to resolve local difficulties.[50]

When the military was asked who was going to continue the good work, there would be an embarrassed silence. Contractorisation was part of the answer, politically neutral but not without problems.

On 19 August 1994, Major-General Guy Tousignant (Canada) took over command of UNAMIR from General Dallaire. By the beginning of September, UNAMIR II, its strength at 4,167, was approaching its permitted strength of 5,500. A large number of African states had come forward with small numbers of troops to address an African problem, (meaning a problem in Africa). Troop-contributing nations were Chad, Congo, Guinea Bissau, Malawi, Niger, Nigeria, Tunisia and Zambia. There was, however, strong African representation among the larger contributors: Ghana (819), Ethiopia (800), United Kingdom (606), Canada (394), Australia (312) and Senegal (214). The strong African presence remained heavily dependent upon the West's high technology, communications, medical and engineering support. An Oxfam spokeswoman said of the situation approaching the year's end:

> The African battalions adjust to doing nothing very easily but when employed and properly led, one felt proud of them - the Ethiopians were particularly brave and knew how to deal with the rebels. UNAMIR II was a success because the 'big brass' was not here. They wanted to know what to do and where; their attitude was, 'let's start now'. The military set out the strategy and we collectively became more resilient as the relationship between us improved. Then, as we entered 1995, the big boys came in, turf protection was to the fore, the quality of the NGOs' work deteriorated and this naturally impacted upon UNAMIR's effectiveness. They found it difficult to deliver in an environment

> so changed by the new arrivals that the relationship between the outsiders and the government became irreparably damaged.[51]

UN Security Council Resolution 965 of 30 November 1994 extended UNAMIR II's mandate until 9 June 1995. Out on the ground there was no consciousness of a difference between UNAMIR and UNAMIR II. The original aspiration had drifted for too long. Now that the condition of the Hutus in the camps both inside and outside Rwanda had improved, UNAMIR's primary function became assistance with their repatriation. Resolution 965 also authorised the creation of a second 'peacekeeping' force to be deployed principally in Zaire with a separate mandate and budget from that of UNAMIR II. The plan was that both UN forces would cooperate to implement Operation Retour, the return of 3.5 million Hutu refugees and the internally displaced. The new 'peacekeeping' force did not materialise and, while Operation Retour did have some initial success, it was unable to separate the refugees from the former RPG military and militias whose own survival depended upon the refugees remaining *in situ*. The case for the Hutu refugees staying where they were was compelling. To move, threatened retribution from the Hutus, and arrival in their former homes held out the possibility of retaliation by Tutsis. The situation in December 1994 was therefore an impasse but, with the support of refugees and the internally displaced costing $1 million a day, it had become unsustainable.

Operation Turquoise

Security Council Resolution 929 of 22 June 1994 authorised France to mount a unilateral humanitarian intervention into Rwanda until UNAMIR II could be brought up to strength but restricted the intervention to a duration of two months. The international cynicism was immediate. There is a very neat summation as to why that should have been so:

> The French had facilitated Egyptian arms sales to Rwanda, the French had equipped and trained the RGF, the French had advised and reportedly fought alongside the RGF against the RPF, and the French had acted as apologists for RG (Rwandan Government) sanctioned or RGF-led massacres of Tutsis.[52]

Concurrently, French emissaries went to Marshal Mobutu with sweeteners in exchange for the use of the airfields at Goma, Bukavu and Kisangi and to Kigali to assess RPF reaction to the French military crossing into

Rwanda. The order to the French forces to prepare to move was given on 17 June, five days before authorised by the UN and nine days before the Rwanda/Zaire border was crossed (23 June).

The majority of France's Turquoise troops were routinely deployed in Africa as part of the *Force d'Action Rapide.* They were reinforced by an unusually high proportion of Special Forces. The African foot on the ground was of considerable importance for it facilitated rapid deployment on the continent. As a result of 28 defence treaties and 25 technical cooperation agreements there were seven pre-positioned African bases, which put France in a favourable position during the course of no less than 18 African interventions undertaken between 1960 and 1994.

French reconnaissance was supposed to probe 15 km into the south-west corner of Rwanda. As is so often in such cases, the amount of human intelligence is inadequate for the formulation of sensible military decisions. The intelligence gathering pushed on in the direction of Kigali. The RPF, fearing the French intervention would disrupt their victory, told the French to keep out of their way, but the French had neither desire nor mandate to interpose themselves between the RPF and RGF. The latter withdrew over the Zaire border in the hope that the RPF would engage the French in a one-on-one conflict, as had occurred in 1990. However, General Lafourcade had held discussions with the RPF's General Kagame through the offices of UNAMIR[53] and persuaded Kagame of the French humanitarian intentions. On 5 July, the RPF gave the French a guarantee that their limited incursion into the south-west would not be interfered with.

The foundation upon which General Lafourcade took his force into Rwanda was not at all politically propitious. There was political division in Paris. In the planning stage, many of the military firmly believed that they were going into Kigali to confront and defeat the Tutsis, 'the Khmer Noir', and return Rwanda to the *status quo ante.* President Mitterand represented a groundswell of humanitarian opinion which had seized itself with the notion of hundreds of orphans to rescue and care for. The Foreign and Defence Ministries viewed Turquoise as the opportunity for them to recapture foreign policy from the President. It was also hoped that in the process of conducting Operation Turquoise, an example would be established to denote a clear improvement on the UNOSOM humanitarian intervention fiasco.

The size of the force and its equipment were limited due to the distance of Rwanda from France, but it was sufficient to guarantee, as far as was possible, the avoidance of facing difficulties on the ground. The French did not use US C-5 Galaxies (to have done so would have delayed the force insertion by 4-5 days), nor did they, according to General Lafourcade, commandeer Air France 747 aircraft, due to their not having a tail-loading facility or the ability to land at Goma. The government hired Russian Antonov heavy-lift aircraft which went into Goma and Bukavu. Of the options, a direct insertion into Kigali was dismissed as being too problematical, the north-west too sensitive politically and, moreover, there were few Tutsi survivors there. Bukavu presented logistical problems necessitating trans-shipment into the short take off-landing STOL Transall. Bujumbura, used by the Americans to evacuate their expatriates, was not considered a viable alternative due to the fragility of the humanitarian situation and the fierce opposition of some political parties.

General Lafourcade's force reached 2,555 French and 350 Francophone troops from seven different countries but principally from Senegal. The force structure emphasised the role being combat-related although the strategy was to show a capability but to avoid the use of force. The French had within their deterrent force 12 Jaguar and F-1 jet aircraft and equipment, which 'brought with them their own unspoken message', artillery and light armour. Of the total force of almost 3,000, only half were ever in Rwanda, sending a political message that this was a short-term occupation. Turquoise's logistic base was over the border in Zaire and all their logistic units, with one exception, were related to their combat support. The exception was a military hospital which was intended to be placed at the disposal of the civilians as part of the 'bio force' - essentially inoculations.

With him in his Headquarters in Zaire, Lafourcade had a political adviser, an equal-ranking diplomat of ambassador rank over whom the General took precedence. All French diplomatic representation in the area was devoted to Turquoise liaison. The Ambassador became head of the in-country Diplomatic and Humanitarian Cell within the inter-ministerial *Cellule de Crise*. The cell was responsible for the centralisation of information, as a point of contact with Goma, to maintain contact with Bukavu, and to chair military-humanitarian meetings.[54]

General Lafourcade's goals were: to end the massacres in Rwanda, facilitate humanitarian operations, protect the population, and to hand over to UNAMIR II in due course. Operation Turquoise can be divided into four phases:

Phase 1 : Becoming Established and Preliminary Action (23 June - 7 July).
Phase 2 : Establishment of the Safe Humanitarian Zone (4-20 July).

Phase 3 : Dominating the Area and Humanitarian Action (7 July-8 August).
Phase 4 : Withdrawal and Handover to UNAMIR II (8-22 August).

Phase 1

The General's first major problem was that of neutrality, particularly given France's earlier role in Rwanda:

> The Hutus thought the French had come to their aid. That accounted for the warmth of our welcome, but we had to make it clear that this was a misappreciation on their part. Very soon we began to disarm the Hutu militia. Ensuring from the outset the security of the Tutsi camps provided evidence of French neutrality.[55]

The General emphasised how desperately short of information he was. All the time, throughout this preliminary phase, Special Force recce groups plunged further eastward into Rwanda in heavily armed columns. These columns were a sign of what could follow. 'The concept', explained Lafourcade, was:

> to use our power immediately to emphasise our principal aim of stopping the slaughter and making a safe area. It was essential that we demonstrated a determination to intervene quickly and not be distracted by other factors, as had been the case in Yugoslavia. There were two different aspects. I wanted the necessary power to face the problems and yet avoid the difficulties which arose in Somalia. I also wanted to guarantee the security of my soldiers.[56]

By the end of June, UNREO had established regular coordination meetings in Bujumbura. They discovered that the only agencies operating in what was still a lawless south-west sector were: ICRC, CRS, Caritas, Trocaire, Care and Solidarités. There was a list of some 20 NGOs expressing an interest in becoming involved, subject to greater freedom of movement and without the obligation of going through genocidal local authorities. Suspicion of the French was not easy to set aside. The NGOs asked UNREO to coordinate the operations rather than the Turquoise humanitarian cell located at Cyangugu. Cyangugu was one of three Task Force areas within what would become the French protected zone. The others were at Kibuye and Gikongoro.

On 29 June, a high level meeting was held to discuss the coordination of Turquoise, UNAMIR and humanitarian aid. Among those present were the French Chief of Staff, Admiral Lanxade, General Lafourcade, General Dallaire, and a representative of UNHCR. Lafourcade offered to make available the spare capacity of his logistic support. Although the Turquoise area was yet to be defined, there were within the approximate area, two million Hutus and a further one million displaced persons from the east. These people were gathered in Hutu and Tutsi camps, some totalling 100,000. In addition, there were 30,000 Tutsis hiding in caves and in the Nyungwe forest - potential victims of the militia. Already uppermost in the minds of those responsible for the coordination of humanitarian support was the probability of the flight of displaced persons into Zaire after the French withdrawal. The delivery of assistance became the linchpin of a plan to contain that movement.

Lafourcade admitted that when he arrived, there was no specific plan vis-à-vis what would become their area. They were guided by their mandate:

> We came across military checkpoints and refugee camps. As soon as we came across a road block, we removed it and disarmed the militia. We protected the refugee camps, particularly from night attacks. We displayed our capability and an intention to use it. Every time we met the militia, we disarmed them.[57]

The militia were not an organised group: everyone with a weapon was described as militia. They engaged themselves in controlling road blocks and villages, and by threatening and killing the population. They were more akin to bandits than an organised force. On Sunday 3 July, while a French reconnaissance column in Butare was evacuating 700 Hutu orphans and 50 civilians, they stumbled into an RPF blockade. There was a short but intense fire fight.

The philosophy relating to the manner of French military conduct revolved around the rules of engagement and what were described as 'behaviour guidelines'. The general rules of engagement identified the security of French forces to be the priority. In their concept of 'wider self defence'[58] the use of force was approved in circumstances where there was: a threat to own forces, a threat against the protected population, obstruction of the mission and, in a conflict situation with refugees, weapons were to be used only as a last resort. The basis of 'behaviour guidelines' was recognition that the mission was under political and media constraints and its legitimacy questionable. The rules were fashioned on these understandings. One golden rule was that the French were not to wear helmets or anti-shrapnel jackets except when engaged or in immediate danger.

Phase 2

Butare was the extent of the French reconnaissance. Lafourcade had hoped to establish a hospital there but, intent on not engaging the RPF, he withdrew to an area 70 km x 70 km, the boundaries of which were identified by geographical features. The negotiations regarding boundaries involving the French, Kagame and Khan took 4-5 days. Conscious of the fact that, if the RPF continued its advance there would be a further one million refugees, Lafourcade recalls: 'I explained to Kagame my intention of not allowing any military into the Safe Humanitarian Zone. When we did have clashes with the RPF and other groups not under control, we solved these problems through the established channels'.[59] Throughout this period, efforts were made to stabilise the Safe Humanitarian Zone. At this stage, the French military had three aims: to deny any infiltration of the RPF, to disarm and neutralise the Hutu and RFG-associated militias, and to protect the refugee camps and to provide them with emergency assistance.

On 5 July, the Safe Humanitarian Zone was formalised on the basis of the Security Council Resolution. By this date, all old Rwanda hands in Turquoise who by their thoughts or actions were found to be incompatible with the spirit of the Resolution, were purged and removed from the theatre of operations. The most pressing of problems for the French were matters legal, administrative and policing. The absence of UN police was sorely felt. When the French disarmed the militia, they could not put them in jail. The rule of thumb which they established was to jail only those whom the French had witnessed as being involved in the killing. In the absence of police, the French established an organisation comprising former gendarmerie and volunteers to organise administration and policing in the villages. The crucial question was, since so many had been involved in the massacres, how could an untainted and effective gendarmerie be established? Those who came forward as volunteers were made to swear in public that they had no blood on their hands. Since, ultimately, the new gendarmerie would have to work with the RPF, this was the only safety measure that had any prospect of working.

The UN has to have a professional police backup waiting in the wings to accompany or follow the army into such operations. To be really progressive, it must be an ultimate aim for future military intervention for the military to be the majority stakeholders in a wider coalition which will include police, lawyers, representatives from Government Organisations (GOs) and NGOs.

It became evident from the example of June 1999 Kosovo that none of these lessons had been assimilated. It was all so predictable, almost banal, the lack of centralised planning for a serious civilian presence of administrators to restart the process towards normalisation. International Organisations were vying one with another for visibility and states manoeuvred to have their own national representatives placed in positions of authority. Initially, there was no law, no police with which to enforce order: the British were applying English common law as a temporary expedient and when judges were eventually appointed in Pristina, they were four Albanians and one Serb. Little prospect therefore of unfettered and unbiased exercise of the law. Writing of French military operations in Mitrovica, Kosovo, June 1999, the International Herald Tribune *observed:*

> *It will be the job of the United Nations to form a police force and to run everything from garbage collection to prisons. For the moment, it is up to the French troops to keep order. But since they have no prisons, courts or police, when they rounded up a group of looters Wednesday, they searched them for weapons and let them go.*[60]

This is not exactly progress. The first UN-sponsored civil police course did not begin in Kosovo until 6 September 1999.

The French had no authority to work on Zairean territory. The mission was to assist the suffering population in Rwanda, not Zaire. The responsibility for refugees over the border rested with the Governor, the GOC of the area and the UNHCR representative. The Zairean government was the host state for French logistical support - nothing more. The French did help UNHCR logistically, planned with them the work to be done, essentially that which UNHCR could not do by themselves. That included the collection and burial of bodies, providing transportation, some water and the provision of medical aid. Even hard-bitten special forces were adversely affected by what they saw in Rwanda. One of the lessons to arise from Operation Turquoise was to provide counselling and be prepared for psychological damage among their own troops.

By the middle of July, the French became aware of the unwelcome influence of *Radio Mille Collines*. 'This was a real failure of the French', admitted Lafourcade,

> and an important lesson for the future. To be frank, we were not conscious of the problem soon enough. Our attention had been largely held by operational and logistical problems, that is, priorities of air movement, fuel, food, and the military hospital.

The necessary electronic means arrived soon after, and the broadcasting was stopped on the 17th. The French did not have the capability to jam a radio from aircraft, but the need to do so by other means has been learnt. 'I also requested the means to spread positive information', said Lafourcade, 'but, be assured, we are now very much aware of the importance of a counter-radio situation'. There is a view that if 'friendly' radio had been established for the duration of the genocide that would have been acceptable, but the new government had an expectation of maintaining control within borders. It is a subject that requires discussion with, and the consent of, the government. The only way to sidestep the sovereignty issue in the interest of ongoing military operations is either to carry on regardless or to establish a continuous test broadcast.[61]

Phase 3

The RGF had now been defeated and, on 19 July, the RPF declared a belated unilateral ceasefire. The French estimated that they had saved 80-100,000 Tutsis and prevented a large number of Hutus from being killed. With the military situation stabilised, the Turquoise mission shifted from the operational to the humanitarian, identifying Phase 3 with two particular problems. The first was concerned with the repercussions arising from the flight of the Hutus into Goma, with the associated food and health problems, and the second, the increase in disorder in the towns. Therefore, in addition to controlling the Humanitarian Zone, the Turquoise forces had to participate in humanitarian assistance outside the Zone and also deal with public order issues.

The French military were well aware of the NGOs' wariness of them. The initial diffidence was overcome to some degree by the civilian humanitarian cell acting separately from the military operations cell. One unexpected spin-off was the good quality information arising as to what was going on in Rwanda. The general organisation of the humanitarian effort was overseen by UNHCR. The coordination between UNHCR and the military people, with the capabilities they lacked, went particularly well. For example, the French claim to have collected 8,000 corpses and buried 20,500. Whereas the humanitarian cell divided its interests between the UN agencies and NGOs,[62] the military cell undertook the coordination and control of those activities beyond their capabilities. That included air delivery, assistance with water supply, provision of vehicles, helicopters and aircraft. 'We did four parachute drops of supplies', said Lafourcade, 'but this system requires a great deal of preparation'. There was some criticism of US airdrops, suggesting that their reluctance to go out on the ground meant that neither their information nor their organisation was adequate.

Phase 4

Despite requests from some humanitarian organisations, and even the RPF, for the French to stay, they were quite clearly going to honour the letter of their mandate. The existence of the French sunset clause meant that the UN was obliged to replace them and had time to do that. The level of security within their Zone had improved and the capabilities of the humanitarian organisations had also much improved. 'In order to plan our break-clean', explained Lafourcade,

> I met Dallaire in Kigali to prepare for the relief of the French forces. We had good liaison with UNAMIR and I was also in touch with Khan. The existence of these channels permitted the French to explain the situation to the RPF while planning the withdrawal. It was essential to tell Dallaire and Khan that the RPF should not enter the Security Zone once we had left because the population was afraid of them.

The great fear was another massive exodus of refugees into Zaire. The displaced people feared Tutsi reprisals once the French had gone and had no great confidence in their African successors. One refugee explained why he was not impressed by his fellow Africans:

> If American or English troops were deployed, many people would stay. African soldiers do not reassure people. We judge the strength of an army by its materiel; that is why the French have been so effective.[63]

The French did have problems during their handover to UNAMIR II. Their concept of operations in what had become a policing action was decidedly different from those who followed. Their *modus operandi* had been to deploy small units, not less than platoon strength, out on the ground to show the flag and provide protection, but all the while having the capability, if necessary, to concentrate forces and firepower at a given point. When the French discovered that the Ghanaians arriving in Gikongoro had the intention at night of concentrating their wherewithal, including APCs, within guarded compounds, they did their utmost to change that intention. The handover/takeover period lasted for ten days, during which General Lafourcade tried to persuade his Ghanaian counterpart to adopt the tactics which the French had found to be so successful. 'I impressed upon him the necessity of scattering units so as to cover the ground, and to conduct night patrols, but I believe that as soon as we left, they crept back into their shells.' By now, the Ghanaians had taken possession of the American-leased M-113 APCs.[64] The French were never in favour of introducing tracked APCs into their tactical area of operations because of the attendant conflicting signals. 'Either the UN is to fight a war', said Lafourcade, 'or its representatives are afraid. It was entirely contrary to our concept of operations. My men had no helmets, no flak jackets, and kept their weapons out of sight'. By 22 August, all French forces were clear of Rwanda, having made their exit through Zaire.

Unlike UNAMIR II and the American Operation Support Hope, Operation Turquoise was more positive and direct in confronting the problems out on the ground. It was the precise geographical delineation between Turquoise and the other, less robust, operation which facilitated the management of different regimes of rules of engagement. Under normal circumstances it would not be possible to have 'Chapter VI' and 'Chapter VII' operations co-existing in the same theatre. The change of direction seen in Bosnia in June 1995 with the injection of quick reaction forces also reflected the more 'hands on' approach rehearsed in Rwanda.[65]

Assessment

Few military interventions have been launched under such a dark cloud of doom, gloom and an anticipation of inevitable failure. That it did not fail, and that it succeeded so well, is in no small part due to the command and control qualities of General Lafourcade. If we consider that a sizeable proportion of the French intervention force had been involved in earlier anti-Tutsi operations, then Turquoise represents a worthy leadership study. The threat posed by Lafourcade's men to the Rwandan bandits and elements of the RGF was the sum of their capability and a telegraphed intention to use it. The 1994 Rwandan experience proved again the value of professional soldiers, but it also tipped the balance somewhat in identifying equipment as being no less a consideration.

Turquoise was a UN-sanctioned operation with a Chapter VII mandate. It became a Chapter VII operation because it was certainly not Chapter VI. Nor was it a traditional Chapter VII, but it was launched with that association because there was no other option. For Turquoise to have been a traditional Chapter VI operation, it would have needed the consent of both belligerent parties and would have required a mission to achieve the peaceful settlement of the conflict. In a true Chapter VII operation it is difficult to see in what military circumstances it would be possible to define quite so precisely the intended date of withdrawal. Moreover, the French were required to be neutral and act impartially towards Hutu and Tutsi. France has moved towards the recognition of the existence of other types of operations: 'France distinguishes peace keeping or peace enforcement operations from those of which the purpose is to give assistance to civilian populations affected by conflicts, natural or technological disasters'. The residual issue is the level of force used, or available to be used, in a conflict. It is that consideration which places Turquoise in the grey area of implementation-style operations, between VI and VII.

Turquoise was an entirely *Francophonie* operation. France was the framework state and gathered round her a small number of troops from her former colonies - to the prejudice of UNAMIR. There is no doubt that the USA's role in Rwanda disappointed, a fact recognised by President Clinton who apologised to the people when he made his first visit to Rwanda. The United Kingdom and France have already strengthened their bilateral air and land associations and it may well be through the instruments of *La Francophonie* and the Commonwealth that new collective security possibilities might arise. Each separate grouping has a common language, common operating procedures, similar staffing arrangements and both cut across the First/Third World divide to forestall any allegation of neo-colonialism.

When the French arrived, there was little humanitarian representation in their area of operations. That which existed was initially hostile. The French organisation had been well thought through and the antipathy recognised in advance, so that their humanitarian cell was civilian-run and separate from the military. As the security situation came under control, so did the protection level for the humanitarian organisations increase, drawing more and more into the vacuum. Admittedly the French did pre-place food stocks to the east of the centres of the displaced, but the prevention of a second Goma was due to the harmony and confidence which had developed between the civilian and the soldier. The political will within the displaced camps vis-à-vis the militia was also supportive.

Operation Support Hope

Operation Support Hope was a two-phase operation, with the phases falling before and after the 5 August declaration that the corner had been turned in Goma. The nature of this operation lends itself to continuous assessment.

As a result of their interpretation of the Somalia episode, the US Congress adopted a view that it did not like UN Peacekeeping. In April 1994, when effective action might have achieved something in Rwanda, both the executive and the legislative agreed that there was no US national interest in Rwanda. However, the unfolding TV tragedy of the post-Goma period had a political impact which was not evident pre-Goma when the worst incidents had occurred. What the Americans and the rest of the world had seen were the negative results of a manoeuvre operation by the defeated Hutu government to move its power base - i.e. the people - out of Rwanda to regroup, refurbish and return. 'The displacement of the Rwandan Hutu population at Goma and Bukavu should be seen as an operational-level manoeuvre by the former government.'[66]

It was a concept that the former Rwandan government had not thought through. The scale of the disaster very soon overwhelmed the relief agencies. People died of starvation, exhaustion and a massive cholera epidemic which swept through the camp at Goma. There was a clear public message and pressure from the Africa lobbies to Washington to do something, and this was something the executive could no longer avoid. It was not *interest* therefore that mobilised the USA, but *conscience*. The Administration determined that in salving the conscience of the American people it would do just enough to avoid potential risks and to be able to claim that they had tried. Congress's reservations vis-à-vis peacekeeping were circumvented by the insistence that the planned Operation Support Hope was not peacekeeping but humanitarian assistance.

On 22 July 1994, President Clinton ordered General George Joulwan, the Commander-in-Chief United States European Command, to assist with humanitarian relief in Rwanda. There were no pre-existing plans. General Joulwan nominated his deputy, Lieutenant-General Daniel Schroeder, to command a Joint Task Force, designated Operation Support Hope.[67] Also on 22 July, public speeches were made by the President, his National

Security Adviser, the Deputy Secretary for Defense, the Chairman of the Joint Chiefs of Staff and the Director of USAID. In their individual speeches they referred to the proposed military assistance for the Rwandan refugees. The national policy towards Rwanda arose as either specified or implied tasks through the process of distilling the key points in those speeches. On top of all this, the US Senate placed a time limitation on the operation, requiring all US forces to be out of Rwanda by 1 October 1994 unless the restriction was set aside by Congress. The Joint Task Force's mission was to provide assistance to humanitarian agencies and third nations' forces conducting relief operations in theatre to alleviate the immediate suffering of Rwandan refugees, to include:

- The establishment and operation of water distribution and purification systems in Goma.
- The establishment of an airhead and cargo distribution capability at Entebbe.
- The provision of round-the-clock airfield services at Goma, Kigali and other sites.
- The establishment of logistics management in support of UN and other nations.
- The protection of the force.

There were also succinct essential tasks:

- 'Stop the Dying'
- The Return of the Refugees to Rwanda.
- Support Stability.
- Hand over to UN Agencies.
- Redeployment.

The mission had a multiplicity of aims which were rather more a checklist than a mission. The initial confusion with the mission was therefore not surprising, but it was the precision of the checklist which effectively deprived the commander of any flexibility of manoeuvre. Politically, that may well have been the aim. But since General Schroeder, unlike General Lafourcade, had no in-country political support to weigh the risks and convey recommendations to Washington, what happened was that if new eventualities arose which were not on the list, they were not entertained. In the Operation's *After Action Review*, there is constant reference to 'clear mission guidance' which 'permitted the commander considerable freedom of action in determining his operational objectives and end state, and was key in avoiding the additional taskings to deployed forces that has been known as "mission creep"'.[68]

The strong guidance in PDD 25 regarding command status was meticulously observed. There was no prospect of third parties leading US soldiers in directions which ran contrary to political and military aims. It may seem that efforts to maintain purity went too far:

> ...the JTF, on a humanitarian assistance mission, could not appear to be taking sides, or cooperating with the United Nations Assistance Mission in Rwanda (UNAMIR), a UN military command with a peacekeeping mission...Given such a volatile environment, the safety of our soldiers was a constant concern, and maintaining mission focus became a major building block of force protection.[69]

The Americans' rules of engagement included self-defence, the defence of other relief workers and the protection of 'mission essential' property. However, the reality was that the Americans' priority for protection was not the Rwandans, not the aid workers, but their own soldiers. The security concerns resulted in additional soldiers being shipped in, thereby increasing the logistical load to sustain them. Domestic political logic had been turned upside down so that the situation had been reached where the death of a civilian aid worker would barely cause a stir but the death of a soldier on operations was likely to cause a hiatus.

A US military survey team arrived in Goma on the day of the key political speeches. Here the team leader found a refugee population of approximately 850,000 with approximately 6,500 dying each day - mostly from cholera. As a result of the survey officer's report, Goma became the US military's centre of gravity. After liaison with UN personnel, the priority requirement was clean water. What the US military do really well is related to their strategic lift capability. The first water purification units in the task force left Germany on 23 July and were in Goma by the 25th. On the morning of 26 July (10.47) the first clean water began to flow from the US Army installations.

Before the 3,000 Americans arrived in theatre, the work in Goma had already been divided by the NGOs into spheres of responsibility: CARE (non-food items), ICRC (food supplies), MSF (health), Oxfam (water supplies) and the World Food Programme (transportation). There were problems of coordination on the ground. The Germans assumed they were to be in charge of water and were designated by UNHCR as being responsible for the water 'service' package.

Oxfam recorded their attempts to work with the American officer in charge of the military water installation: 'I take my orders from

Mannheim', he is said to have told them, leaving the reporter to observe: 'he appears to have no interest in, or understanding of, the word "coordination".[70] The water purification men had arrived in advance of the Civil-Military Operations Centres (CMOCs) which, compared with the ongoing US military activity, were slow to become operational. 'Turf wars' were not uncommon, as is the truth in the observation that agencies and NGOs rarely have good words to say of groups they see as competitors. Oxfam criticised the American water purification equipment as 'inappropriate to the task. The equipment they flew in was designed to provide high quality water for small numbers of people; whereas what was actually needed was safe water for hundreds of thousands of people'.[71] Such criticism is unworthy. How can you criticise equipment for what it was designed to do, or the operators for getting it there early to alleviate the suffering? In time, improved methods were employed and tankers became available for water distribution. On 12 August, once supply exceeded demand, use of the American purification system was discontinued and the manpower redeployed to other engineering tasks.

General Schroeder established the Joint Task Force Headquarters at Entebbe, Uganda - neutral, English-speaking territory, Joint Task Force-A in Goma, and Joint Task Force-B in Kigali. Civil-Military Operations Centres (CMOCs), which were national facilities operating in parallel with the UN, opened in Entebbe and Kigali and a two-man CMOC was established at Goma. The CMOC is a US military focal point where the UN agencies and NGOs exchanged information, identified support requirements and coordinated activities with the JTF. Collocated with them were civilian Disaster Assistance Response Teams (DART) who liaised between the military and the humanitarian organisations.[72] Unlike the French, the Americans had no predetermined period to remain in Eastern-Central Africa.[73] General Schroeder had his fixed list of tasks. Once those objectives that were attainable had been ticked off as accomplished, he could recommend to General Joulwan the withdrawal of the force. Due to the volatility of the situation in Zaire and Rwanda and the fear of wider commitment, the sooner the better. The humanitarian organisations were largely unaware of the limitations and constraints under which General Schroeder was working. They anticipated more help than they would get, although that expectation was encouraged initially by the US military. There was a failure in communications, and the need for a clear public relations policy became self-evident.

The USA undertook to repair the water system in Kigali and the establishment of a radio station, but did not follow through. Mission creep was fast becoming mission shrink. When General Schroeder first met General Dallaire (whom he outranked) he told the UNAMIR commander that he was in support of the UNAMIR mission. General Dallaire has described how he gave General Schroeder the UNAMIR draft Operations Order and requests for support with water, medical facilities, transport, APCs and helicopter lift:

> Schroeder took the shopping list off, but all that was achieved was 300 US servicemen sitting on the Kigali airfield for which Canada was doing the air traffic control. There were far too many people to do the job. They turned the airport into a white elephant. I simply could not get the stuff out of the airfield to the NGOs.[74]

The Americans were confined to the airport by their military orders. Concerns for their security had led to limits being placed on their freedom of movement, not only in Kigali but also in Goma. Given the freedom enjoyed by other national forces, the agencies and NGOs could not comprehend the American restrictions placed on their own people. In the evolving US military doctrine, the leadership had no problems with this situation because, in humanitarian assistance, they had a clear understanding that the US role was akin to the wholesaler while the agencies and NGOs were the retailers moving goods on to the people. In this context, therefore, the wholesaler's depot was the airport, from which there was no requirement for the wholesaler to venture further. It could be argued that such a clear distinction does not compromise the neutrality and impartiality of the aid workers.

Presentationally there are two problems here. Firstly, there will be occasions when the wholesaler will have to undertake retailing duties. In Rwanda, the US trialled a new concept of 'adopt a battalion'. In this case it was a Ghanaian battalion that undertook the retail functions (shorthand for risks) while the US picked up the bills. The trial was not a success, not least because the other African states represented by military in Rwanda asked, 'what about us?' Second, wholesaling is synonymous with timidity. It is entirely inappropriate for the soldiers of the world's most powerful nation to be put in such a belittling position. There is no doubt that military morale suffered because thinking soldiers believed that the restrictions placed on them were excessive.

The Kigali CMOC was collocated in the Embassy building, working separately from the UNAMIR/UNREO coordinated humanitarian arrangements. Caution and fear of transgressing the limits of the Department of Defense's mandate occasionally stultified the decision-making process. US representatives found themselves pulled between an inclination to say 'yes' and 'no'. What this often led to was a pedestrian response time. On 16 August 1994, UNHCR urgently requested information on US intentions. The reply took three weeks. As a result of this hesitation, the agencies could not forward plan or rely on the Americans for the provision of equipment which in many cases was readily available. General Schroeder's policy was not to release equipment if there was an adequate supply elsewhere. At a time when water distribution was a major problem, General Dallaire was unable to persuade the Americans to release the water tankers parked up at the airport.[75]

The Americans, UNREO and the RPF fully expected the refugees to return to Rwanda once the fighting had stopped and the new government had been installed. There was the quite reasonable belief that the people had left Rwanda to escape the fighting and would return home when the fighting ended. It was not considered that the exodus was to do with a broader plan orchestrated by the former government to take its supporting population with it. Much of the American planning and liaison with NGOs and agencies was devoted to determining how they could help prepare 'way stations' along the road from Gysenia to Ruhengeri to support the returning population. Then, how to distribute equitably aid and assistance within the prefectures once the majority of the refugees had returned. One of the Kigali CMOC's principal concerns was how to prevent returning Goma refugees infected with cholera from entering the capital. The RPF insisted that the UN should not provide transport. They wanted the returnees to walk. The walk would have taken them five days, during which time the cholera victims would have been identified.

When it became clear that the refugees were not returning in numbers of any consequence, it did, in the short term, make the American and UN task simpler. Concentrated in their great Hutu camps, it was much easier to support the refugees logistically. It was also worryingly self-evident to the American military that the Rwanda problem was going to be long drawn out. What they had seen were the initial stages of what would be a protracted civil conflict. All this served to reinforce, first, the American view that they should not undertake any tasks that would tie them down for any length of time and, second, that they should extricate themselves as soon as possible, before they could be identified and related to long-term solutions.

General Schroeder had felt obliged to revise downwards the original criterion for success, which had been: 'the effective establishment of humanitarian support by international agencies to the citizens of Rwanda and their home districts', redefining success as 'a drop in refugee camp death rates to a level determined by the UN to be commensurate with "normal" camp operations'. The speed with which the operation had been mounted had resulted in an over-optimistic view of the criterion for success. There had been insufficient time for the Americans to achieve a realistic understanding of the situation on the ground. The only way the mission could be declared a success was to move the goalposts.

On 30 July, JTF-A was established in Goma. On 5 August, a consensus among the NGO relief agencies reported that the corner had been turned in Goma. On 10 August 1994, General Schroeder wrote:

> After three weeks of intense effort, the crisis in the Goma refugee area is over. The mortality rate has fallen dramatically, from over 3,000 per day to less than 500. Soon the camps will no longer qualify as crises under the UN definition of the term (2 deaths/10,000/day).[76]

On 14 August, UNHCR requested all agencies to stop airlifting food into Goma. On 15 August, American water purification equipment was removed from Goma while on the same day, in the Secure Area, the relief of French forces began. On 25 August, JTF-A withdrew from Goma to Entebbe. On 27 August, JTF-B left Kigali for Entebbe. The operation proper had lasted barely four weeks. The Americans' precipitate and surprising departure left NGOs floundering.

The two principal assets the Americans had brought into the theatre were airlift and organisation. US air crews flew an impressive 380 strategic and 996 tactical missions, and delivered 15,331 tons of supplies.[77] The UNHCR formally requested a six months extension of US military support. On 8 September 1994, General Schroeder sent a Memorandum to General Joulwan. Schroeder said of the tasks UNHCR asked the USA to tackle: 'I do not assert they are invalid'. However, at the end of his memorandum, he recommended to his chief:

> The political decision on how to answer the UNHCR request for sustainment operations is, in my view, best met by empowering the agencies already in existence to do that work. *The US military's function is to fight and win the nation's wars.* We leveraged those capabilities to mitigate the crisis of July as we were directed. Now is the time to declare an end to the *unilateral*[78] US military effort.

The American forces left Rwanda, having been seen to be there, and having made a contribution, according to General Schroeder, 'with no loss of US military personnel and no residual US military obligations'.[79] Despite all the rhetoric, it must be said that they achieved much less than they were capable of achieving. The US government was not alone in having no intention of seeing the problem through. Operation Support Hope had been an exercise in visibility, not in creating any impact of long-term significance. 'The cost of failure in Rwanda', observed General Dallaire,

> has been nearly one million people killed and half a million injured; one million people are still displaced; and two million are refugees in neighbouring countries sowing the seeds for the next conflict and human disaster. This is a high human price to pay for inaction and apathy, even though many countries have tried to smother their guilt by throwing hundreds of millions of dollars in aid at the problem.

The Administration now seriously considered General Schroeder for command of the upcoming intervention into Haiti.[80]

The General's emphasis that the military's function is to fight and win the nation's wars is valid, but exactly *who* are America's military going to fight? The Humanitarian Operation such as that conducted in Northern Iraq in 1991 is as close as military units are going to get to train for war. Simulated training can go just so far. Yet, politically, Support Hope was a highly constrained operation. It stands as a reflection of the confusion in Washington as to what means to employ to achieve what ends. The first step is to set aside procedures and methodologies which are inappropriate to modern environments. It cannot be acceptable for the world's superpower to be so demonstrably 'timid and tentative'.[81] It is not the American Way.

To a large degree, the future use of America's (and other states') available armed forces in support of humanitarian endeavours will be budget driven. This is not to consider the wider question as to whether America's national budget can support what is an already reduced military force but whether there are not cheaper options for the provision of humanitarian assistance. Certainly, the Department of Defense's and Ministry of Defence's treasurers are those departments' worst enemies, for they are pricing military support out of the market.[82] In recent, pre-budget years, the job was done and the tab picked up. However, in 1994 Washington faced an annual bill for 'peacekeeping' in the order of $3.5 billion. Congress asked whether the US share was not excessive and how the US might successfully budget for operations such as Support Hope (which, Secretary of Defense Perry said, had come in 'under budget and ahead of schedule'). How can you budget for such an operation without the total removal of flexibility? Did this contribute to the rigidity in the USA's participation in Rwanda's disaster? We must, however, move away from hypothesis to fact. Paris did not formally publish the cost of Operation Turquoise but it is rumoured to have been one billion francs. Now that these operations are being costed-out and becoming subject to budgetary pressures, the indicators of wider military assistance in humanitarian affairs is not at all propitious. To which Departments should these additional costs be apportioned? As the Red Cross said: 'today's immensely costly use of soldiers to carry out and support humanitarian operations is a transformation which neither government nor troops have fully understood or mastered'.[83]

Humanitarian Assistance is one component which fits within an interventionist spectrum but it is the predominant component. The ideal course to steer to avoid the political and military risks involved in humanitarian intervention is to tackle the broad humanitarian problem at its source. Humanitarian intervention is not a solution, merely a palliative. The richest twenty per cent of states have eighty-six per cent of the world's gnp, while the twenty poorest countries have only one per cent. The vastness of the differential that exists between rich and poor is often most apparent within the state that is the recipient of humanitarian aid. Among the worst offenders at flaunting wealth in the faces of the deprived and underprivileged is the United Nations. There are stunning recollections of UN mandarins chauffeured in sleek, top-of-the-range, air-conditioned, flag-bearing Mercedes along the miserable, dusty streets of Kigali. It seemed that every lowly UN and NGO official had his or her white 4x4 jeep while the people had nothing but their own, personal, horrifying memories. It is just so insensitive, so apparently gratuitous. Nevertheless, it seems to be a common and unreformable practice. When KFOR entered Pristina in June 1999 it resembled a ghost town. The centre was virtually dead and there was little traffic. By September, however, central Pristina had, to all intents and purposes, been taken over by the UN. The trappings of privilege, power and the huge amount of individual transportation and tax-free wealth caused understandable resentment among decent Kosovar Albanians.

The lesson of Rwanda supports a consistent view, not only that the methodology is inappropriate to today's environment but also that the UN is neither able nor structured to deal with complex humanitarian crises. In addition, where the military are to be involved, the command and control structure should ideally reflect sanctioned rather than sponsored operations.

It is often said that the UN can only do what its membership allows. That is largely true, but the assertion must not go totally unchallenged. During the course of this study there was incontrovertible evidence that the Secretariat was not conveying important information to the Security Council. This may not have affected the eventual outcome of the crisis but it is important, as part of this learning process, that the Secretariat's files are opened to reveal exactly what details of crucial developments were passed to the Security Council. There is no question of a witch hunt but, if decision-making is over-centralised, or the Secretariat is overwhelmed by activity, then it is essential that this becomes known.

Similarly, the existence of the grey area, Chapter VI½ or an environment for Implementation Operations, was incontrovertible. How long does the Secretariat propose that this situation should continue before it is addressed? Cynics report that the UN is both unwilling and incapable of anything other than cosmetic reform. Here is an important matter requiring urgent attention, to demonstrate that these widely held views of the UN as a status quo organisation are misplaced. We have proposed that the concept and requirement for the recognition of Implementation Operations be accepted and it is desirable that an affirmative decision be taken without further prevarication.

Rwanda demonstrated the USA's capability of hobbling the UN. Part of that problem had been the ambiguity and confusion surrounding her then foreign policy. For example, there was the unequivocal statement that Rwanda was an humanitarian operation, not 'peacekeeping', yet the State Department determined its responses according to criteria specifically developed for 'peacekeeping'. Washington's interests are as much to do with superpower sovereignty as budgets. Somalia has influenced US political opinion far more than it deserves, but America's initial, negative position cannot be argued away simply as being Somalia-orientated or casualty-averse. The events in Bosnia had a concurrent impact because what Bosnia did, for the first time, was to demonstrate that in the field of foreign policy America would not always have her own way. The USA's willingness to support the UN and pay one third of the 'peacekeeping' budget has always been conditional upon the USA leading and controlling the UN. If the USA is to continue along the neo-isolationist path, then there are two emerging problems relevant to this study.

The first is budgets. With the UN severely in debt, further reductions in US contributions will reduce the UN's capacity to become involved in collective security and supporting its agencies. America's continuation within the world order remains pivotal. There is, admittedly, the possibility of the United Kingdom and France forming new coalitions around themselves but, as the deployment of rapid reaction forces into Bosnia in June 1995 revealed, someone still has to pick up the bill. It could be that the USA will become content to be the treasurer and/or wholesaler.

What President Clinton said, to the effect that if America is to say 'yes', the UN must learn to say 'no', is undoubtedly right. What was wrong was to apply that understanding to Rwanda. The UN already had a presence in Rwanda, similar to a preventive deployment. The military advice from Kigali was not for massive reinforcement but for a deterrent, reinforced presence, with suitable equipment and a mandate which could convey an unequivocal message to the two parties. But the Security Council said 'no'. It is difficult to comprehend how international diplomats could not anticipate the impact such a transparent declaration would have upon a Rwandan powder keg where the presence of planned genocide had already been conveyed to New York and presumably to Washington through its intelligence means. There may be other Rwandas. The results of such blatant, public hand-washing can be guaranteed unless procedures are changed. The international community must never publicly say 'never' to military intervention. Then, on top of a declared position of non-intervention, the UN reduced its manpower to that of a political presence. The Hutus were thereby given two very explicit signals that their programme of genocide could commence without suffering international interference. And then, before Rwanda had had time to slip from people's memories, in 1999 NATO told Milosevic that a ground campaign would not be considered.

The item for which the military and the humanitarians had an insatiable appetite was good quality, current information. There are various forms in which information can be categorised. There is that which exists between the intervening actors[84] and information passed from those actors to the indigenous people. Information is a vital fuel which permits the soldier and the humanitarian to function efficiently. It does not come on a plate; it has to be fought for, sought out and offered up. Rwanda demonstrated how the exchange of available information between the two sides proved to be so beneficial. At UNREO, the convergence of accurate and timely information permitted the formulation of collaborated plans. The exchange also occurred at a local, bilateral level. The case for a non-propagandist, friendly radio and a 'friendly' radio policy is self-evident. Moreover, there has to be an implicit understanding that those who use the airwaves (and newspapers) to foment riot and murder, seemingly with impunity, will be brought to account before an international court. There are few deterrent measures more effective than assured accountability.

During the course of this period there were few protection opportunities for UN forces. What opportunities there were, were mostly policing in secure environments. The UN's protection duties came after 6 April for a few weeks in and around Kigali, and two phases of Operation Turquoise. Most of the genocide was perpetrated beyond the reach of UNAMIR and the RPF. One important lesson to be derived from Rwanda is how the application of force, even the most modest of means, bore results out of proportion to the effort made. Hence the error of judgement in persevering with an inappropriate mandate. Observers might suggest that the application of force by the UN in Mogadishu was unproductive. It is true that what we are discussing here are not rules for future action, but trends. Each case has to be separately evaluated and assessed according to circumstances and environment. In the case of Mogadishu, the UN sought an *active* role in taking on a powerful warlord in his own domain. What General Dallaire sought, and what General Lafourcade achieved, was to act as a deterrent so that, armed with the requisite capabilities, he could *react*, if need be, to the crises he knew had been planned for Kigali.

The lesson Rwanda provides for military planners is that, in circumstances where their own government may declare an intention of not intervening, there is no reason why contingency planning should not proceed. We have to comprehend the switch away from *interest* to *conscience*, and the speed with which the media can influence that change coming about. As it was, the American deployment went ahead on the basis of a verbal mission and the British reconnaissance did not have the benefit of a mission statement at all. It is the function of Joint Planning Staff to ensure that these nonsenses do not occur. The move towards coalition operations is undeniable. However, the UN maintains a mere skeleton of a military staff compared with NATO, despite the reorientation of the nature of conflict. The UN does require a Combined Planning Cell and the Charter does specifically provide for one in the form of the MSC.

Rwanda witnessed a quantum leap in understanding and harmony developing between the humanitarian organisations and the military. Neither is monolithic: the constituents all have their foibles and differences.

What Rwanda revealed to the humanitarians were the resources, organisation and levels of protection the military can introduce in order to facilitate their work. It was by no means a total conversion. There is still much work to be done through education to overcome pre-existing attitudes. Education of the parties in terms of capabilities, organisations and functions has emerged as a key requirement. It is not just the humanitarians who need to adapt, the majority of the West's military establishment still reflects a Cold War rationale. There are far too few civil affairs experts in the military headquarters. All this can be overcome by a process of education and the conduct of joint exercises. Ultimately, an humanitarian deployment should reflect a coordinated coalition of military, GOs, NGOs, civil police and lawyers. There is the ultimate conclusion of a pressing need to develop more effective mechanisms for the provision of security and military support to humanitarian operations.

The reality must remain that the military presence in an humanitarian operation will be of shorter duration than the civilian presence, particularly in the later development phase. Military effectiveness will be in proportion to its speed of movement, because it will be at its most effective in the early stages when the humanitarian organisation is building up its infrastructure. Who does what, where, and for how long are vital pieces of information for the design of an humanitarian strategy. We emphasise the importance of an UNREO-type organisation to act as coordinator and instrument for exchange of information in an overarching strategy. What UNREO provided was a potential model for the organisation and coordination of civil-military relations. Civilian control is explicit but it has to be informed civilian control, looser at the beginning than at the end of the mission.

Rwanda begs the question, were the military necessary? They were necessary in the protection phase post-6 April 1994, but the focus of attention is the post-Goma phase, when the corner had been turned, as early as 5 August, before a number of national military teams could create an effective impact. The military costs are horrendous, although, to a large degree, these costs are the creatures of creative accounting. The conduct of the US forces also underlines the strong political overtones which come to bear when men in uniform are put out on the ground. For the humanitarian organisations there is the lesson that they need to be better structured to 'dock' into those national and international organisations which will arise as a result of the crisis. They are also likely to learn from the military example and become better organised and thus more independent. In Rwanda they could, in time, have managed the operation. What they could not provide initially were the organisation, communications, structure and resources of the military. It matters not greatly whether the man in uniform is infantry or a logistician. As long as they all behave professionally, take a leaf out of the Turquoise book, they will all exude an impression of being able to provide a level of security and protection with which the humanitarian organisations cannot compete.

The bottom line is that third parties can not make Hutus and Tutsis like one another. Third parties can help them reach accommodation or dialogue, they can feed them and protect them pending a political solution, but, what is true of Rwanda is universally true; lasting solutions to people's problems are in the hands of those people themselves. Towards the end of his tour of duty in Kosovo, General Sir Mike Jackson gave an interview in which he said that the creation of a multi-ethnic society in Kosovo - NATO's reason for going to war - would take many years but was not a military task. 'You cannot expect soldiers to change people's minds', he said. 'That has to be done in other ways',[85] which thought provides an appropriate entrée to the wider topic of Kosovo.

8 Kosovo – 'Only a bunch of bad options'

- Bill Clinton

As an example of military intervention, Kosovo proved to be unlike any other experience. There were, for example, significant differences between the American-led, UN-sanctioned Gulf Conflict and the Kosovo intervention, not least because the latter was conducted through the instrument of an international security organisation without the benefit of a legitimising UN mandate. Moreover, a consequence of the Kosovo conflict was to consign existing national military doctrine to the melting pot.

Slobodan Milosevic's suppression and curtailing of the self-governing rights previously enjoyed by Kosovo's ninety per cent Albanian population preceded the Bosnian armed conflict 1992-95.[1] It had been by chance that Slobodan Milosevic visited Kosovo Polje on 24 April 1987. Previously he had shown no interest in Kosovo but had gone there to listen to the complaints of the minority Serbs, principally because the Serbian President Stambolic refused to enter a hostile 'bear pit'. Nervously, Milosevic confronted the crowd and uttered words, on camera, that would be immortalised by Serbs: 'No one should dare to beat you'. It was precisely through the exploitation of the Kosovo issue that Milosevic became a national leader.[2] The effectiveness of the controls imposed by Serbs determined to maintain the integrity of their sovereign territory served to anaesthetise the problems of Kosovo until after the ink had dried on the Dayton agreement. This chapter is not dedicated to the muddled experience of the Bosnian conflict because there are many other admirable sources of reference. Yet it is not possible to discuss the fate of Kosovo outside the context of the experience of the Former Yugoslavia's six socialist federal republics. In this examination of the Kosovo crisis, discussion of the Bosnian conflict will be confined to a preliminary thumbnail sketch supported by comparative references throughout the text of the chapter.

At the end of 1991, we find the international community still imbued with the heady 'can-do' enthusiasm redolent of what was assumed to have been the successful defeat of Iraq by the forces of good, operating under the auspices of the UN. The Iraq experience, however, had been an inter-state conflict of the type which the UN had been specifically designed to combat. The bubbling problem in the Balkans was an entirely different matter, being addressed by the interested parties as an intra-state problem by virtue of the intention of preserving established borders. However, Yugoslavia was an artificial state created at the end of the First World War and held together after the Second World War by one man, Josip Broz Tito. He restored the Bosnian borders which had existed in the late Ottoman and Austro-Hungarian periods.[3] The essential bonding influence of Tito did not survive after his death in 1980.

The UN, NATO, EC (later EU), and CSCE (Committee for Security and Cooperation in Europe, the forerunner of the OSCE) all aspired to find roles in the resolution of Yugoslavia's problems. One significant development had been the unification of Germany and the emergence of a Germany intent upon playing a more committed foreign policy role under Foreign Minister Hans Dietrich Genscher than had previously been the case. The EC, keen to put behind it the organisation's past diplomatic failures, planned to resolve what was, after all, an emerging European problem. America was accordingly requested to allow Europe a free hand to address the Balkan problem. 'The US complied, some hoping and others fearing that the Europeans would be unable to cope and would have to acknowledge US leadership eventually.'[4]

In examining the respective cases of the former constituent members of Yugoslavia to be recognised as independent states, the EC established three principles: no unilateral change of borders; protection of the rights of all minorities; and full respect for all legitimate interests and aspirations.[5] The principles were not fully implemented. However, in support of these principles, the Europeans established an Arbitration Commission under a French constitutional lawyer, Robert Badinter. Part of the Badinter formula was the examination of the aspirant states' human rights record. Ethnically pure Slovenia passed, as did Macedonia but whose forward progress was blocked by Greece. It was the examination of Croatia's credentials which proved crucial. Croatia had a population of 4½ million of whom 600,000 were Serbs. It was the Croat treatment of the minority Serbs which resulted in Croatia failing the Badinter test. Genscher stepped in to intercede on behalf of Germany's wartime Balkan ally, threatening unilateral recognition if the EC failed to recognise Croatia. Not one EC state interceded to stop the Germans having their way. The consequences of the resultant recognition of Croatia in January 1992 put the possibility of an international, political and military solution to the emerging Bosnia problem out of reach. 'When the German government announced on 15 December, 1991, that it would recognise Croatia a month later, it effectively signed the death warrant for Bosnia-Herzegovina.'[6]

Bosnia-Herzegovina was settled principally by Serbs, Croats and Muslims, yet the Serbs disproportionately possessed seventy per cent of the former republic. Britain's Lord Owen replaced Lord Carrington as the EC's Bosnia representative and formed a good working relationship with the UN's Balkan representative, the American Cyrus Vance. Eventually, the UN took over from the uncertain EC as lead organisation in the Balkans because Europe had demonstrated how easily it could be divided by its history; it had insufficient experience and had forfeited any claim or pretence to impartiality.

By January 1993, however, the UN found itself out of its depth, having allowed the concept of peacekeeping to become embroiled in a nasty Balkan shooting war. In America, there had been a change of administration which brought Clinton to the White House and Albright to the UN. The London Conference of 26 August 1992 confirmed the international community's intention that Bosnia-Herzegovina was to remain a State. It was on that basis that Vance and Owen developed a canton concept, giving each ethnic group three cantons, with Sarajevo shared by all three. In territorial terms, forty-three per cent would go to the Serbs and the remainder to the Croats and Muslims. There were no illusions that this was not the best of plans, but it was the best available. Lord Owen described it as 'a peace from Hell'.[7]

Implementation of the plan would have required the Serbs to forfeit sixty per cent of the territory they had seized through force of arms. The Muslims who were receiving some arms and equipment from sympathetic Muslim states called for a lifting of the 1991 arms embargo. Not wishing to become involved in an ever greater shooting war, states providing ground forces to the UN Protection Force (UNPROFOR) threatened to pull out if the arms embargo was lifted. The Europeans supported the Vance Owen plan which required the placing of 30,000 troops on the ground to police the agreement. Half of those troops were planned to be American. This was the point of departure of Clinton from the Vance Owen plan. Clinton was resolutely opposed to putting American ground forces into Bosnia and wanted instead to develop the Vance Owen plan under American leadership. The starting point was to reduce the 43 per cent of territory intended to be given to the Serbs. As Boutros Boutros-Ghali sadly observed: 'It would take two and a half more years of bloody war and war crimes before the United States, at Dayton, would give the Serbs 49 per cent'. Lord Owen considered that 'if George Bush had won the American elections...then the war in Bosnia would have been over long ago'.[8]

Not unnaturally, as America became more actively involved, so too did NATO. What followed was an uncertain relationship between the UN in its forlorn hope of maintaining a peacekeeping operation in a conflict environment and NATO, with political directions emanating from Washington, which strove to 'lift and strike', that is lift the arms embargo and bomb Bosnian Serb targets. The vital humanitarian assistance provided by UNPROFOR is often overlooked but it continued distribution among the three warring parties and involved troops from non-NATO and NATO states, not least the United Kingdom and France. The troop-providing nations were rightly concerned for the security of their troops on the ground, not simply being casualty averse but also fearful of the 'h' word, hostages. It was they who originally opposed American air intervention. America had resolutely resisted putting troops into Bosnia but gave an undertaking that if it became necessary to extract UNPROFOR, then American forces would be committed to their rescue.

There being no consensus within NATO, America pursued an independent line aimed at establishing a Muslim-Croat Federation to defeat and balance out the Bosnian Serb presence. Analysts seeking to explain such an initiative, championed by Madeleine Albright in the UN and supported by Vice-President Al Gore, might have sought justification in a strategic rationale and the negative influence the Balkan crisis could have upon NATO members Greece and Turkey. Whereas that might well have been a consideration, as perhaps was the hope of appeasing Muslim fundamentalist tendencies, the rationale for American intervention was simply as a moral crusade against perceived evil Serb aggression in general and the hated Hitler/Stalin figure of Slobodan Milosevic in particular. It was Albright who championed the safe areas concept once the Vance Owen plan had been discredited and rejected. It is one thing to chastise an inexperienced Ambassador for championing the safe areas policy, 'a disaster waiting to happen', but where were the essential checks and balances against putting in place a policy that became 'the fatal fault line in the UN mandate in Bosnia'?[9]

NATO had become a fractured alliance, the Europeans on one side and the self-determined Americans on the other. America's proactive line was almost entirely politically inspired because the American military (the air forces had been operating in the Balkans from the outset) and the CIA warned Washington of the folly of taking a partial and preferential line in support of the Muslims and Croats. The White House and State Department preferred to form their opinions or have their prejudices confirmed by news stories emanating from beleaguered Washington and New York press reporters with heads down in Sarajevo rather than from the Pentagon or from the CIA. The possibility of the decision-making process becoming skewed and hostage to routine and established attitudes was first postulated by Graham Allison in his examination of the Cuban Missile Crisis.[10]

Albright was born Marie Korbelova in Prague in 1937 of Czech parents of Jewish extraction and had thus been subjected to the evil influences of both Hitler's and Stalin's regimes. Milosevic, however, had neither of these men's intentions or capabilities. Albright's prejudice against dictatorial figures is understandable but, in that prejudice she was inconsistent. The Serbs were undoubtedly more sinning than sinned against and Milosevic was not an idle spectator of what was happening in Bosnia-Herzegovina. And yet Washington and Bonn supported an almost equally odious dictator, Croatia's late President Franjo Tudjman. 'Tudjman', wrote Misha Glenny, 'almost certainly did not care that he was a monster because, unlike Milosevic, he was our monster'.[11] This was a case of undiluted *realpolitik* because America needed Croatia to join the Muslims in a new Federation to confront the Bosnian Serbs. Such an inconsistency was excusable in what Washington saw in simple terms as a good versus evil conflict - the assumption being that the Muslims were the 'good guys'. Muslims, however, had shown themselves not averse to creating situations aimed at generating a response in support of their position. Boutros Boutros-Ghali wrote of the mortar attack on Sarajevo market, which killed sixty-eight civilians. 'I told (Warren) Christopher that Akashi (Yasushi) reported that the mortar round that had exploded in the Sarajevo market on Saturday night might have been fired by Bosnian Muslims in order to induce a NATO intervention.'[12] Of that event, Albright told Boutros-Ghali: 'Something has to be done'.[13] Former Swedish Prime Minister and new EU envoy Carl Bildt observed that there would be no peace in Washington until there was war in the Balkans.

Factions within the National Security Council and the State Department operated outside NATO to reach an accommodation with the Croats and Muslims in order to defeat Bosnia's Serbs. The American Ambassador in Zagreb apparently turned a blind eye to the shipment of Iranian arms through Croatia into Muslim hands in Bosnia. There were also secret arms flights into Tuzla. Far more extreme was the State Department's action in licensing an Alexandria, Virginia, mercenary organisation, Military Professional Resources Inc (MPRI) to provide military assistance to Croatia's armed forces. MPRI provided the military direction which forced the Serb population out of the Krajina. That action was no less extreme than the MPRI's Military Stabilisation Program, also known as Train and Equip (T&E) which trained and armed Muslim forces in Bosnia. One British colonel observed:

> Sadly, despite the best political intentions of the US and its predominantly Islamic T&E partners and the practical efforts of its American contractors in theatre, MPRI, the programme has delivered a great deal of capable equipment and individual and collective training without managing to transform the mindsets of the two VF (Federation Army) partners.

He then added: 'Bosnian Serbs have seen the T&E programme of continuing US bias against the RS (Serb Republic)...the Alliance has never bombed any party other than the Serbs'.[14] Voices were raised against such bias, duplicity and deceit within a supposed alliance. American General Charles G. Boyd, the deputy commander of EUCOM and an airman, wrote how:

> The United States watched approvingly as Muslim offensives began, even though these attacks destroyed a ceasefire Washington has supported. This duplicity, so crude and obvious to all in Europe, has weakened America's moral authority to provide any effective kind of leadership. Worse, because of this, the impact of US action has been to prolong the conflict while bringing it no closer to resolution.[15]

Boyd's opinion finds resonance in an observation by Nik Gowing, the BBC television news presenter:

> Not only did diplomats and political leaders often allow themselves to be misled about their own level of knowledge and understanding of Balkan intentions and motivations. They then went on to deceive and manipulate both allies and colleagues with whom they were meant to be working harmoniously.[16]

The political and diplomatic breakthrough in Bosnia was achieved by the American Richard Holbrooke with the eighth peace plan drawn up for Bosnia. For three weeks in November 1995, incarcerated in an air force base at Dayton, Ohio, Holbrooke brokered a peace for a ravaged and war weary Bosnia-Herzegovina. Dayton did produce a political settlement but it only anaesthetised the situation in the country in so far as the only commitment to it is by the internationalists involved. Significantly, there was no UN presence, the Organisation being ignominiously muscled out by the USA in the name of NATO. The UN did not deserve the dismissive treatment it was subjected to, but what Dayton did was to conclude an era of misplaced expectation on behalf of the UN which, as an organisation, had peaked at the end of the Gulf Conflict. The UN had now lost direction and failed in Bosnia just as it had suffered reverses in Angola, Cambodia, El Salvador, Mozambique and Somalia. Was the *Pax Americana* buttressed by NATO to be the way forward in multilateral military intervention? The answer must be 'no' because the ghost of Mogadishu still haunted Washington's corridors of power. As General Rose wrote: 'For if NATO is not prepared to accept a risk to its soldiers in either support operations or war, then it is militarily useless'.[17]

What the Department of State did, however, to overcome this high hurdle was to interpret the victory of Dayton as having been achieved through the use of air power. This was to suggest, therefore, that future humanitarian crises might be resolved through the use of air power alone. Such an erroneous interpretation was not shared by the Pentagon but parties in the State Department embraced the air option, claiming that if it had been introduced earlier, lives would have been saved. Air power targeted against the Serbs had been a contributory factor, as was the overwhelming sense of war weariness arising out of a conflict in which 150,000 had died. The Bosnian Serbs recognised that the time had come to formalise the temporary borders around the smaller area of Bosnia-Herzegovina they now possessed than had originally been intended. The State Department's misreading of the role of air power in achieving a peaceful settlement could present difficulties in the future but, what reassurance there was lay in the knowledge that it is the Joint Chiefs of Staff who have the constitutional authority to advise the Commander-in-Chief, the President, on military matters.

Holbrooke's achievement in bringing peace to Bosnia had particular significance for the United States. Had he failed, the USA might have had to deploy troops to Bosnia to assist with what could have been a fighting withdrawal. In October 1998, Holbrooke brokered a deal with Milosevic to defuse the conflict in Serbia's southern province of Kosovo. A formal ceasefire was established between Serbs represented by policemen and soldiers, and the KLA, the Kosovo Liberation Army or UCK, *Ushtria Çlirimtare e Kosovës*. Moreover, the reinforced Serb military were obliged to withdraw the additional manpower which had arrived in Kosovo after

February 1998. The withdrawal of this increment of the Yugoslav Army has been the subject of undue emphasis because it masks the influence of the still *in situ* Serb extremists cultivated and militarised by Milosevic from the 1980s. Milosevic was concurrently given his first NATO warning of bombing, reflecting a new interpretation of international law to the effect that opprobrious behaviour and barbarity within a state, in certain circumstances, would not be tolerated. UN Security Council Resolutions called upon Milosevic to behave but did not contain threats of force.

The subsequent request to the OSCE to monitor the ceasefire arrangements brokered between Holbrooke and Milosevic came like a bolt out of the blue. They did not know they were 'in the frame' for consideration to undertake the verification of the peace agreement in Kosovo, the Kosovo Verification Mission (KVM). Their Secretariat is kept deliberately small[18] and the only military planners they had at the time was a team of ten working on Nagorno Karabakh.[19] The scale had been hugely greater than anything experienced before, a requirement for 2,000 men rather than 300 which had been the previous, largest commitment. The 'one at a time' method of selection, a Russian budgetary veto[20] and the fact that 300 individuals called upon failed to arrive, meant that by late February the total rose to only 1,379. The OSCE put together four-man teams as soon as they were able to marry-up individuals, equipment, vehicles and communications (all of which had to be procured from scratch). They were assisted by NATO's Verification Mission which was intended to help OSCE with the production of aerial photographs. The extraordinary situation arose whereby OSCE requested NATO to take photographs of particular areas and, on asking for delivery of the imagery, were refused on the grounds that the photographs were NATO SECRET. As one OSCE observer noted, 'NATO is incapable of producing anything that is not automatically classified'. But why no UN representation in this process? The best answer appears to be that, at this juncture, Milosevic would not accept their presence, whereas in not so many weeks he would be insisting on a UN presence.

One of the lessons of Bosnia was to try to avoid using separate agencies to run six aspects of support. On 14 October, the American component arrived to join OSCE, complete with a plan in the hands of one Bob Beecroft. The other 53 national representatives declined to accept the American plan and spent the best part of two weeks producing something similar. In the equitable allocation of representative posts, each deputy head provided from the Contact Group of the OSCE's Kosovo Verification

Mission (KVM) was given a dedicated function. Civil police, for example, were the responsibility of Italy's nominated representative. That particular individual wanted to work with the Serbs to reach an accommodation. At that time, the Yugoslav Army was viewed as a good and reliable organisation in contrast to the police and paramilitaries. In November, the Italians were invited to remove their representative. After an acrimonious debate, the individual was allocated another, equally prestigious job in December and his original job was given to a judge who arrived in late January, two weeks after the Racak massacres. What this spat caused was the freezing of any attempt by OSCE to make progress in the critically important area of the future policing of Kosovo. It became impossible to progress with the overseeing of Serb police activities to the same degree as progress being made on the military side, for fear of offending the Italians.

Eventually, Ambassador William Walker, American, was appointed to head the KVM. Walker, who was Albright's nominee, had been American Ambassador to El Salvador when the USA was supporting the government against left wing rebels. A colleague of his, Christopher Hill, American Ambassador in Macedonia, had spent the best part of a year attempting to put together a peace plan which, in Holbrooke's words, would provide the Kosovar Muslims with 'autonomy and self determination', but not the independence they demanded. Washington opposed any deal which would break up the Serbian state. It would be a bad example to Europe's many other potentially fractious states and would not generate support from either Russia or China who both had their own particular interests to protect in this field.

The Holbrooke-Milosevic peace agreement between Serbia and the OSCE (it was not a KLA or Kosovar Albanian agreement) was consistently broken by the pro-independence KLA intent upon forcing Milosevic to renege on his deal with Holbrooke. It is important to realise that the KLA had not signed up for anything in October 1998. There was an undoubted procedural difficulty: who would have signed, and on whose behalf? Ambassador Hill remained until mid December in the hope of brokering some sort of agreement. In the ensuing low intensity civil war, the KLA fought small scale engagements with the Serbs. The KLA was no Salvation Army: there were casualties on both sides including non-combatants. A pattern developed whereby KLA action would invariably lead to Serb reprisals and overreaction. A gradual increase in the level of attacks on Serbs took place up until early January. In one particular ambush of Serb police by the KLA, four Serb policemen died. Representatives from the local Yugoslav army brigade at Uresovac, supported by Serb police, struck at what they believed to be the base of the perpetrators of this and similar attacks, the village of Racak. In this disproportionate reprisal on 16 January 1999, dozens of Kosovar Albanians were murdered by the Serbs. That the Serbs had indeed been responsible for the crime could not have been known at the time by William Walker, supposedly impartial, when, in front of the cameras of the international media he laid the blame squarely on the Serbs. 'Sometimes', he admitted, 'you step off too fast'.[21] Walker was heavily criticised,[22] particularly by the French who, with others, suspected a Muslim act of provocation similar to the Sarajevo market incident.[23] But Walker had been right in terms of apportioning blame. The Muslims would not have shot their own old men. OSCE invited the Serbs to produce evidence of non-involvement but they refused to cooperate.

A subsequent enquiry by a Finnish forensic science team produced two reports. The first, and the one formally released, proved a touch circumspect. In what was described as 'a crime against humanity' the Finns refused to call the killings a massacre, to blame Serbian security forces or to divulge how the Albanians had died. But the second report was more damning, giving scientific post-mortem evidence that the Racak victims had been shot where they were found. This second report was allegedly suppressed by Germany which then held the EU presidency.[24] The Racak massacre had the same impact in America as the Sarajevo Market massacre in so far as it increased the political determination to do something short of putting troops on the ground in Kosovo. 'Spring has come early', Madeleine Albright is said to have declared. She worked quickly to capitalise on the tactical advantage presented by Walker. In that respect, the KLA had achieved its aim of provoking a US-led reaction. Three days after the massacre, Albright persuaded Clinton to make ground forces available to Kosovo if a political settlement was forthcoming. NATO arranged for up to 10,000 troops to be deployed to Macedonia as an extraction force to ensure the OSCE monitors were not taken as hostages or human shields. Conceptually, this role is difficult to envisage since NATO had no helicopters. The five companies of OSCE monitors were big enough to worry the Serbs but too small to do anything. Their presence, however, served to raise the temperature.

In direct response to the Racak massacre, the six nation Contact Group on Yugoslavia (America, Britain, Russia, France, Germany and Italy) acceded to America's proposal that the warring parties in Kosovo attend a peace conference on 6 February at the fourteenth-century French chateau at

Rambouillet, 48 km south-west of Paris. The implication was that if the parties either failed to attend the conference or come to a diplomatic agreement within 21 days, NATO air power would be turned loose. Such a threat could only have applied to Serbia since it was an impossibility to target the KLA.[25] What Washington did instead was to threaten to declare the KLA a terrorist organisation. This was no insignificant threat because, if implemented, it would have provided Serbia with a *carte blanche* with which to deal with the KLA insurgents.

Rambouillet would be significantly different from Dayton. The lead was taken by Albright supported by British Foreign Secretary Cook and French Foreign Minister Hubert Védrine. There was therefore no major role for Germany which, in view of what was to unfold in Kosovo, is a situation unlikely to be repeated. It took place not at the end of an exhausting conflict but in the initial sparring phase of what could become a major conflict but as yet had not reached the severity of other, concurrent conflicts around the globe - Sierra Leone being one particular example. Milosevic did not attend but was represented by Ratko Markovic and other delegation individuals who played virtually no active role. The secessionist interests were expressed through four separate Kosovo Albanian delegates, all of whom were free to come and go as they chose. At Dayton, the parties had been of a like mind to endorse an agreement that would end four years of suffering. What the Kosovo Contact Group, through three international mediators led by Christopher Hill, were offering the Serbs and Kosovo-Albanians was autonomy for Kosovo within the Yugoslav Federation, something which neither party wanted. The entire Rambouillet process was cloaked in coercive NATO threats which had not been the subject of an enabling UN Security Council mandate. As peace brokers, therefore, NATO had compromised itself, unable or indifferent to presenting the organisation as impartial.

It was never going to be easy to find an acceptable and enduring political compromise. So much depended on the ability, subtlety, strength and experience of the designated power broker. For an ambitious politician, however, opportunities such as this, to establish a permanent legacy and reputation, are few and far between. Albright was already in line for a public relations coup in the upcoming April celebrations of NATO's 50th Birthday but, what NATO proposed to do with its New Strategic Concept[26] and culmination of the Secretary of State's plans for expansion represented initiatives that could, in time, seriously backfire. The experienced Holbrooke was sidelined as Madeleine Albright took it upon herself to manoeuvre to resolve the problem of ethnic Albanians living in the Serb province of Kosovo.[27] Clinton conceded the right to Albright to take centre stage and attract the heady publicity which she enjoyed if not craved. Earlier, in the Lewinsky saga, Albright humiliated herself by supporting the President in his less than honest assertions vis-à-vis his relationship with the intern. Giving her the requisite authority to close deals could be interpreted as a reward for her loyalty, no matter how misplaced or naïve. Senator Bob Dole, who had been a negotiator with the Serbs in the early stages of shuttle diplomacy, remarked how 'Kosovo was the first casualty of the Lewinsky affair'.

Albright, however, had already held the position of Secretary of State for two years and it had become apparent that the Democrats might have problems being re-elected. At the time of Rambouillet it was difficult to identify any success of substance during the currency of her appointment. Rambouillet was therefore an ideal if not essential opportunity for the first female Secretary of State to have her name written into the history books. Her approach was to be fashioned by her belief. 'I am', she said, 'a great believer in American power and the importance of making it clear we can use it'.[28] The State Department saw no apparent need to have either an American or NATO military adviser present at Rambouillet. Whereas soldiers can be diplomats and politicians, diplomats and politicians cannot be soldiers.

Albright was convinced that Milosevic only understood brute force and it was this understanding which fashioned her 'negotiations' with Milosevic. It was not subtle, nor was Milosevic's obvious unwillingness to accept Albright as anything other than a dilettante likely to create a fertile diplomatic atmosphere. The other delegates called to Rambouillet were the fractious Kosovo Albanian quartet, all with intentions of independence: Ibrahim Rugova, Hashim Thaci, Reschep Qosja and Veton Surroi. The pacifist-inclined intellectual, Ibrahim Rugova, representing the Democratic League of Kosovo, was in theory the ranking delegate since he had been unofficially elected president of the Albanian Kosovars in March 1998. The Serb violence of that year, however, had served to radicalise the KLA whose demand for full independence had begun to marginalise the moderate position of Rugova. Hashim Thaci was the KLA's commander-in-chief and had been identified prior to the Rambouillet process, along with others, as someone with whom Washington could do business. There was talk of James Rubin having been involved in the preliminary discussions with Thaci. The 29 year old Kosovar leader was a clean-cut, personable, suit-wearing man cast in the image of a Clinton or a Blair and known by his detractors as 'the snake'.[29] If Kosovo had truly been about a new world order founded upon universal human rights, then Albright must surely have supported Rugova rather than Thaci.[30] Given the failure of previous endorsements of doubtful characters such as Saddam Hussein, Noriega and Bin Laden, this was surely an opportunity to pass Thaci by. But it was not to be. Qosja was president of the United Democratic Movement, more radical than Rugova and a supporter of the concept of a Greater Albania. Finally, there was Surroi, an independent, formerly editor of *Koha Ditore* which remained his mouthpiece. He was considered by many to be Kosovo's only politician of substance.

An intelligence report, apparently having come from German sources, revealed a Serbian plan - Operation Horseshoe - allegedly intent upon the systematic ethnic cleansing of Kosovo. The Germans had apparently taken the Horseshoe information from an uncorroborated report emanating from Bulgaria. There are many such reports which have no substance but this one had the potential to be used to political advantage. The horseshoe analogy comes from the image of placing a ring of steel around Kosovo's borders but leaving the open face up against Albania's border in order to facilitate the flow of refugees out of Kosovo. The State Department used the supposed intention of Milosevic to rid Kosovo of its Muslim population as a rationale to persevere in achieving Washington's aims at the Conference. General Wesley Clark, however, told a BBC reporter that he had never heard of Operation Horseshoe. Was it therefore a ploy, similar to the disinformation doing the rounds at that time that 260,000 internally displaced Albanians had already been ethnically cleansed? If that were the case, then where were the refugees? Few were readily apparent prior to the bombing. Perhaps ten per cent of that figure had been displaced and absorbed within the community but there had been a significant, voluntary outflow of Kosovar Albanians into greater Europe, many young men of military age seeking to avoid service with the KLA.

The source of the erroneous information on the internally displaced and refugees had been the UNHCR which, throughout this conflict, proved lackadaisical and casual in its production of crucial statistics. An OSCE representative told how they tried not to contradict UNHCR figures. 'They do it to justify themselves', he said. 'If they don't exaggerate their figures, they don't get their funding'. In September 1999, when UNHCR claimed the Serb population in Kosovo had been reduced to approximately 20-30,000, statisticians from the UK's Defence and Evaluation Research

Agency (DERA) showed the true figure to be at least 97,000. No less doubtful was Foreign Secretary Cook's taking as a *casus belli* the 400,000 people in Kosovo 'driven' from their homes since March 1998 and the fact that Milosevic 'has comprehensively shattered that (Holbrooke-Milosevic) ceasefire'.[31]

One of the senior OSCE representatives suggested that if indeed there had been an Operation Horseshoe, it may not have originated in Belgrade:

> I do not believe the ethnic cleansing was planned in Belgrade. I think one thing led to another. Agreed, Belgrade did have operational plans which targeted the KLA but the reason the Yugoslav Army took to the villages and factories was to escape NATO air forces' imagery.

Over 60 per cent of Kosovo's population lived in villages. Although there are expanses of woodland, the trees are stunted, approximately four feet high and with little foliage. The woods are mostly transparent when viewed from above. Living cheek by jowl, the Albanians proved for the Serbs to be impossible neighbours. 'The Serb military suspected the KLA of passing on information with regard to their dispositions and therefore as the bombing campaign began, they threw the Albanians out.'

When the OSCE wanted to be less than gentle with the KLA - which was often between December and March because, for example, there was a general view among the OSCE in Kosovo that the February meeting at Rambouillet had been inequitable - the KLA appealed directly to other parties. KLA representatives went from agency to agency to secure the best answer. Western diplomatic agents were operating in Kosovo from mid November to the end of December 1998, until they could be absorbed by OSCE. The Kosovo Diplomatic Observer Missions (KDOMs) were intended as an interim measure and were sponsored by their embassies in Belgrade. The EU and US KDOM, which had lives of their own, were in Kosovo in the summer of 1998 and allowed access by Milosevic as an interim measure. The teams varied in size from 10-60 and all except the EU and US representation were absorbed once the national teams arrived. A large proportion of the American component was provided by the CIA. 'It's their job', admitted Walker. This development caused problems with other OSCE representatives. 'The American agenda consisted of their diplomatic observers, aka the CIA, operating on completely different terms to the rest of Europe and the OSCE', said a European envoy.[32] By the New Year, OSCE had cover over the west of Kosovo but not the east. The worst of the fighting had occurred in the west which saw the worst of the damage and the worst excesses of the Serb police and paramilitaries.

In the east, the Serbs comprised up to 30 per cent of the population and there had been little fighting or damage. From New Year 1999, it was in the east that most of the national KDOMs were to be found. In addition to those KDOMs there was the OSCE under Ambassador Walker and his Liaison Staff, the US KDOM under Sean Byrnes (the deputy Chargé d' Affaires in the US Embassy, Rome, attached to the US Embassy, Belgrade) and the EU KDOM headed by the EU ambassador. Over and above this representation were all the other visiting ambassadors who could and would interfere to varying degrees. The French Ambassador to Macedonia had the worst reputation. It is easy to see how the KLA were able to play one interest off against another. That the OSCE had no formal agreement with the KLA now began to tell. After mid December, the Serbs asserted their right of self-defence which was contained in the agreement. 'It appeared', said an OSCE monitor,

> that every time the Serbs did something wrong, the press jumped on it. When the Albanians did something wrong, the press did not jump on it with the same alacrity. I am not surprised the Serbs were dismayed by their treatment. Rambouillet was a crucial event for us. We felt the diplomats there had not tried hard enough. The Albanian side was courted and feted assiduously for 2½ weeks until they deigned to sign. As soon as that had been done, the Serbs were told 'sign now or be bombed'. A great deal of diplomatic effort had been invested in the Albanians but the diplomats deliberately overlooked the sensitivities of Serbs.

Washington's terms adopted by NATO for the Kosovo settlement had all the hallmarks of the uncompromising anti-Serb bias so reminiscent of Bosnia. There were five initial aims with a further two added as afterthoughts. First, that all refugees should be allowed to return safely home. This condition rankled with the Serbs who saw in it explicit favouritism. Why, they asked, was there not similar enthusiasm among the international community for Serb refugees to return to their homes in Krajina and Sarajevo? Second, that all Serb forces should withdraw from Kosovo. Third, that an international military force, specifically NATO, should oversee peace in Kosovo and also have the right of passage to operate in Serbia proper. The 'right of passage' clause was inserted in order to get US troops from Europe into Kosovo through their staging base in Hungary. This logistic constraint became a major stumbling block. Serbia had already declared that 'No foreign troops can be stationed on the territory of the Federal Republic of Yugoslavia under any circumstances and that is beyond question'.[33] Fourth, that Kosovo should be granted extensive measures of autonomy with a view to there being a referendum after three years to determine Kosovo's future, and finally, that a multi-ethnic democracy must be established. The follow-on two codicils were mutually unsupportable: that Milosevic was to be overthrown and that military victory was to be achieved without the necessity of introducing allied ground forces into the conflict.[34] Blair told an American audience: 'We will not negotiate on these aims. Milosevic must accept them'.[35] What Blair was saying was that NATO's adjudication between what had become the apparently incompatible, internationalist notions of the protection of human rights and state sovereignty, had come down emphatically in favour of the former understanding.

The Balkans is the cradle of conspiracy and conspiracy theories but western conspiracies have also existed; it's just that Washington, London and Paris are rather more secretive and circumspect about decisions taken within and outside the margins of international diplomacy. Arguably, it was personal animosity, vindictiveness and obsession which influenced Anthony Eden and his approach to the 1956 Suez Crisis and President Abdel Gamal Nasser, Eden's Hitler figure substitute. Intervention is often associated with conspiracy because international law relating to armed conflict is restrictive; so much so that states either sail very close to the wind or, as was the case with Kosovo, take a calculated decision to break the law. Presentationally, states do desire to be seen to be operating within international law, even if, as happened at Sèvres, the UK, France and Israel colluded in military intervention against Egypt. There is some similarity between the Suez crisis and Kosovo in so far as the *bona fide* leaders of targeted sovereign states sought to exercise sovereignty over their legitimate national territory.[36] As was the case with Suez, it is possible to adduce a plausible argument of conspiracy in connection with the Kosovo intervention.

The starting point must be the end game, the elimination of the last of the Soviet-style dinosaurs, Slobodan Milosevic. The reason why Kosovo became un-negotiable for him was because his continuing hold on power was perceived as being dependent upon keeping hold of Kosovo. The entire history of his behaviour related to his preoccupation with staying in power. Washington's motive was undoubtedly highly laudable despite setting a dangerous precedent in so far as the removal of the democratically elected President of Serbia promised a new beginning for that tortured country. Among those most prominently associated with ridding the international community of that particular tyrant were Secretary of State Madeleine Albright and General Wesley Clark.

How, therefore, was Milosevic to be winkled out? The only certain course of action was at the point of a NATO bayonet. But with NATO beset by sentiments of casualty aversion, the ground option had been publicly discounted. However, there was within the United States a tension between the President's reluctance to commit ground forces and a determination that NATO would not, must not, be beaten. The latter was the stronger condition of the two which ultimately would clear the way for a ground offensive to be launched and in fact, plans would be set in place for a ground offensive, Operation B-Minus, to commence on 13 September 1999.[37]

But the risky and unpopular ground option would only be implemented if the far less risky air option was on the brink of failure. Initially, it was by no means certain there would be a consensus within NATO for the initiation of offensive air operations although, progressively, air operations became the highest common denominator for offensive action to find consensus within NATO. Milosevic was banking on NATO being unable to sustain support for a prolonged bombing campaign against Serbia. A catalyst was required to facilitate the next step. The adoption by NATO of a bombing campaign against Serbia might be possible if successive public warnings to Milosevic were ignored, the supposition being that NATO must not be seen to lose face. What concerned commentators were witnessing, an organisation apparently painting itself into a corner by persistently warning Serbia to sign-up or be bombed, may therefore not have been as dumb as it appeared. It was all so reminiscent of Bosnia, with America straining to bomb the Serbs but the difference this time being that there was not the restraining influence of European allies deployed out on the ground once the KVM left on 20 March - only four days before bombing began.

It therefore became essential, if this rolling circumstantial logic was to be set on its way, for Milosevic to reject NATO's entreaties. It could quite possibly have been by design that Rambouillet presented Milosevic with ultimata and conditions which no elected representative of a sovereign state could accept. Rubin admitted, 'obviously, publicly, we had to make clear that we were seeking an agreement but privately, we knew the chances of the Serbs agreeing were quite small'.[38] Thus it came about, to use Henry Kissinger's words, that 'the Rambouillet text...was a provocation, an excuse to start bombing'. As the Rambouillet process drew to a close, a tension developed among the continental Europeans opposed to the direction being taken by the insufficiently experienced Albright and Cook. Cook seemed disinclined to oppose Albright, despite her telling one of the Albanian negotiators, Hashim Thaci, that he should adopt Gerry Adams, the Sinn Fein leader, as a role model. British support was essential if America's aspiration to bomb Serbia was to proceed. 'Quite honestly', said an EU negotiator of Madeleine Albright, 'she's been unimpressive on the details. It's clear that she hasn't grasped the full deal under discussion but having said that, she has massive clout - she's the one who can say to the Serbs "sign this or we'll bomb the hell out of you"'.[39] The Kosovar Albanians caused an unanticipated complication by initially declining to sign the Rambouillet proposals.

The deadline passed and the conference reconvened in Paris on 15 March. Eventually, the Kosovar Albanians did do what was expected of them, leaving the way open for the bombing of Serbia to commence on 24 March 1999:

> It is as if the nineteenth century Concert of Europe had forced President Lincoln to accept southern independence and European troops on American soil, and had threatened to intervene militarily in support of the Confederate Army if Lincoln refused.[40]

Or, put another way, 'in Bosnia, the air power and Croatian and Muslim ground forces were working as a hammer and anvil. Right now (in Kosovo) there is only a hammer'.[41] Politically, Rambouillet had been a disaster. 'Some students of the Rambouillet talks say Madeleine Albright was just hopelessly out of her depth'.[42] It had been during her first visit as Secretary of State to Belgrade in 1997 that Milosevic told her she was a neophyte in Balkan politics. She replied angrily, 'Don't tell me I'm uninformed. I've lived here'.[43] 'This war', concluded a Cambridge academic, 'by comparison with Suez which was an operation of Metternichian cunning, is the most culpably reckless, half-witted adventure that this country has embarked upon in my lifetime'.[44]

Conventional wisdom buttressed by military experience in Vietnam, the Gulf and Bosnia presented conclusive evidence that air power was not an autonomous system. Milosevic undoubtedly found reassurance in Saddam Hussein's continuing resistance to the best efforts of allied air power. This chapter is not intended as a polemic against individuals in the American and British governments or of the Kosovo intervention *per se*. It does however question a number of the actions of individuals and the course the intervention took. How was it, therefore, that the politicians resurrected the

Bosnia air option and applied it to an environment which was historically and politically different from Bosnia? It had been a *political* decision because, as had been the case in Bosnia, the Joint Chiefs and significant intelligence sources again advised against the coercive bombing-only option:

> The Chairman and the Joint Chiefs of Staff complained that US security interests in the Kosovo crisis were insufficient to justify going to war and warned their civilian superiors that bombing would not likely achieve its political aims. The bombing campaign in Bosnia had been targeted against one of three ethnic groups within a fractured state, not as was the case of Serbia proper against a sovereign state whose response would be predictably different. Indeed JCS Chairman General Henry Shelton reportedly stunned Secretary of State Albright with his prediction that air strikes would encourage a humanitarian disaster in Kosovo.[45]

'In February, CIA Director George Tenet publicly testified that Milosevic would indeed attempt to cleanse Kosovo of all its Albanian inhabitants.'[46] Comprehensive ethnic cleansing was something that did not occur until after the NATO bombing began.

Albright, supported by Secretary of Defense Cohen and National Security Adviser Sandy Berger, set aside the professional advice of the military and intelligence communities. On the day bombing began she said, confidently, that she did not see Operation Allied Force as a 'long term operation' but something that could be achieved within 'a relatively short period of time'. Ninety-one targets were selected to be bombed over a period of three days. Some analysts suspected that the State Department had struck a deal with Milosevic whereby NATO indulged in some token bombing, after which Milosevic would claim Serbia's inability and unwillingness to accept further damage and, as a consequence, would accept the Rambouillet terms. That impression was dispelled in less than a fortnight when Albright said: 'We never expected this to be over quickly… We are in there for a long time'.[47] There was no evidence, from logistic provision to the numbers of aircraft initially deployed, that this was the case. Rarely has a military operation been so inadequately prepared. It was not a convincing advertisement for NATO. What was being seen in Kosovo was the reappearance of the 'he's taking us on syndrome' which had been so evident in the USA/Aideed relationship in Somalia. To some representatives of the world's only democratic superpower, any challenge to that power has to be robustly addressed. Moreover, NATO's 50th birthday was only a month away from the commencement of the coercive bombing campaign. Was Kosovo not the ideal opportunity to show to those in Congress who took the view that NATO had 'to go out of area or out of business' that NATO had continuing relevance and utility into the new millennium? To take on a minor state over a matter of peripheral interest should not have presented NATO with a challenge. The timing was apposite and the prospects appeared fruitful to intervene in Kosovo whereas it had not been apposite or appeared fruitful to have intervened in Turkey, Kashmir, Sudan, Rwanda, Croatia, Sierra Leone, Eritrea and the Democratic Republic of the Congo.

It is unlikely that British professional military and intelligence advice was any different to that given by American professionals to their politicians. In London, advice given to Ministers is classified and subject to the thirty year rule. What Chief of Defence Staff (CDS) General Sir Charles Guthrie advised Blair will not be revealed by the then CDS despite it being one of the more interesting of many unanswered questions. 'Tony Blair and I have many intimate chats and I regard his confidence as a privilege', said Guthrie. 'If he thought I was going to write an insider best-seller, there would be no trust between us'.[48] One observer commented upon 'the warmest relationship between a CDS and No.10 that anyone can remember (that) has coincided with a period of unprecedented government neglect of and contempt for the armed services… it is debatable whether he (Guthrie) is better at representing the military position to the government or the government position to the military'.[49] It takes little military experience or intelligence, however, to comprehend that if a powerful air force is allowed to become the *de facto* air force of secessionists, then the effect of the introduction of this new dimension to the conflict will be taken out on those parties which are the most accessible. The Pentagon's spokesman had said publicly that not to recognise such a reality was a form of 'historical amnesia'. A senior British military lawyer said: 'Not for one moment did I believe NATO would bomb Serbia'.

As mentioned earlier, the historian Correlli Barnett once referred to Britain as 'America's warrior satellite'. Hitting out at the British government's refusal to allow Parliament to debate the conflict, he wrote: 'First, it is nothing short of moral cowardice for the Government to hide from criticism behind our Armed Forces. Second, the aggression against Yugoslavia is in any case not the British nation's war but a Blair-Clinton war'.[50] It is apparent that the novice ministers Cook and Robertson followed the American line rather than what has occasionally been the case in the past, to ask Washington to reflect upon its military intentions.

Clinton had gone on television to tell 'my fellow Americans' that 'I do not intend to put our troops into Kosovo to fight a war'. Thus the green lights were prematurely given to Milosevic to begin the concurrent ethnic cleansing and selective killings of the Kosovar Albanians. Reassured by NATO's declared policy that there would be no ground offensive, Milosevic was able to deploy his ground forces to best effect to support the clearing of Kosovar Albanians from their homes. Precisely the same procedure had taken place in Rwanda in 1994 when a decision not to intervene with ground forces had been publicly announced. In 1994, Clinton was President and Albright was at the UN. The whole desperate experience can be attributed to having politicians in high places who are not of the requisite quality.

'It is one thing to urge a ground war on leaders simply incompetent to carry it out', wrote Charles Krauthammer. 'It is another to urge it on leaders unwilling to carry it out'.[51] It is no exaggeration to say that many of the estimated 10,000 Kosovar Albanians who were killed between March and June 1999[52] died as a consequence of this folly. The bombing initiated what the politicians intended it should prevent. Ironically, it was the presence of elements of NATO's military in Macedonia under the ACE Rapid Reaction Corps (KFOR) which absorbed and neutralised the impact of Kosovo's humanitarian disaster, stabilised the situation and deprived Milosevic of a lasting victory. Macedonia had been stunned by the influx of Kosovar Albanian refugees. KFOR had the strategic task of keeping quiescent a Macedonia which already had a thirty per cent Albanian population. It was essential to keep this state which aspired to become the Switzerland of the Balkans on side for use as the launch pad into Kosovo. Of equal importance was Greece's support. Ninety-five per cent of the population opposed the NATO intervention but the government steered a canny course enabling NATO access to the strategically important port of Thessaloniki. In that respect, the military saved their political masters from a political backlash. In London, Clare Short, the International Development Secretary, defended the lack of government preparation by insisting that no one could have predicted the scale of ethnic cleansing. Was that not the explicit message of Operation Horseshoe? Intelligence communities on both sides of the Atlantic forecast this very outcome following NATO bombing. UNHCR did, and anyone remotely connected with the 1994 Rwandan genocide could also have hazarded an accurate guess.

On 12 March 1999 an immensely proud-looking Madeleine Albright stood on the stage at the Harry S. Truman Library in Truman's home town of Independence, Missouri, symbolically near to Westminster College, Fulton, Missouri where Churchill delivered his 'iron curtain speech'. With her were three beaming men in dark suits. For their photo call, the Foreign Minister of the Czech Republic put his arm over her shoulder while the Foreign Ministers of Hungary and Poland beamed on. Massive additional funding was still required from the existing as well as the new NATO member states if the armed forces of the newly joined states were to be adequately equipped and operationally upgraded so as to be interoperable with the armed forces of the established NATO states. However, this, the first tranche of NATO's new expansion, came at a time when there was virtually a universal downward pressure on defence budgets rather than the essential increase. The expansion of NATO to include these three former Soviet satellite states, taking NATO's Article 5 boundary 1,000 km eastward, was in part an American solution to defining a new mission for NATO and to justify to Congress a rationale for a continuing American presence in Europe. Central to the new perception or new Strategic Concept was a restatement of the principal role of NATO to defend members' borders but also to adopt the capacity to reach out and thump with weapons of mass destruction (WMD) parties who threatened world order and stability. 'NATO must be prepared to cope with the very real threat to our people, our territory and our military forces posed by weapons of mass destruction and their means of delivery' said the US Chairman of the Joint Chiefs of Staff, General Henry Shelton. 'This is arguably the most significant Article 5 threat we collectively face, and one we must address seriously...together and soon. We must do more than just acknowledge WMD as a priority challenge; we must turn rhetoric into reality.'[53]

This rationale, however, did not apply to NATO's first ever attack upon a sovereign state, which can be argued away in part by French Foreign Minister Hubert Védrine's view that Bosnia and Kosovo were 'on the immediate periphery of NATO and not clearly out-of-area'. Nevertheless, NATO action in Kosovo was bound to agitate relations within the Slavic brotherhood, namely Russia. Yeltsin warned that the conflict could lead to a 'great tragedy'. The expansion of NATO served to further isolate Russia and was in breach of guarantees given to Gorbachev when the Berlin Wall came down. 'Were I a Russian anarchist bent on causing the maximum amount of trouble', wrote Michael Howard, 'I could not have come up with a better idea than NATO expansion. It plays into the hands of Russian xenophobia and paranoia. It divides the allies, and it can only weaken such military effectiveness as the alliance retains'. NATO expansion was, he said, 'a bad idea whose time has come'.[54] It was a move unlikely to enhance cooperation between NATO and Russia, or to facilitate the production of legal, legitimate resolutions within the Security Council. As one Russian Defence Ministry spokesman said: 'The enlargement of NATO is a dangerous and historic mistake. European history convincingly shows that as soon as the balance of forces is upset on the Continent, the result is instability in political processes, conflicts and wars'.[55]

Kosovo presented itself as a convenient cause upon which to test NATO's new future. It proved to be a leap of faith into the dark, the assumption being that Milosevic would roll over. When he did not, the Alliance was acutely embarrassed through having no contingency plans to engage in a lengthy campaign, nor to deal with the humanitarian crisis which arose as a result of NATO bombing and Serb ethnic cleansing, nor was there a long-term strategy other than to increase the rate at which Serbia was to be bombed. It was self-evident as early as March 1999 that the KLA could not defeat the Yugoslav Army, nor could Serbia fully defeat the Kosovo Albanian secessionist guerrillas. Not only was NATO creating a dangerous precedent in supporting the KLA, formerly a Marxist-inclined terrorist organisation, partly funded by organised crime, which had re-roled as freedom fighters, but NATO's military action threatened to agitate minority aspirations among the Balkan states contiguous with Serbia. On 22 March, Holbrooke was back in Belgrade in a final attempt to get Milosevic to climb down. 'If I leave here without agreement today, bombing will start. Are you clear what will happen when we leave?' asked Holbrooke. 'Yes', replied Milosevic, 'you will bomb us'.

The nature of the insurrection within Kosovo did not lend itself to the planned, three-phase bombing campaign, politically constrained to the extent that pilots were obliged to fly above the ceiling of Serbian air defence cover - 15,000 feet. At this height, target identification is imprecise and collateral damage was to be expected in so far as the risk was shared among the parties on the ground. Even when pilots identified military targets, there could be no absolute certainty that they were attacking live targets. The reality of the situation on the ground, therefore, was at odds on two counts with what George Robertson on 24 March 1999 declared the military objective to be: 'to reduce the Serbs' capacity to repress the Albanian population and thus to avert a humanitarian disaster'.[56] The Yugoslav Army was proficient at camouflage and building dummy vehicles, guns and bridges. They created two types of dummy military equipment, the obvious dummies and the plausible equipment. The latter was tactically sited and primed to 'brew-up' when hit. It is partly for this reason that initial NATO claims of Serb equipment destroyed far exceeded the actuality. After 78 days of bombing, the Yugoslav Army was over 85 per cent intact. Given the limited scope within Kosovo, the attacks upon static economic and infrastructure targets within Serbia were of greater significance. However, attacks such as these, including upon the electricity supply - illegal under international law - rather than turn the people against Slobodan Milosevic had the opposite effect of rallying them in support of his defiant line. What the west had not fully comprehended was the genuinely-held belief of the majority of Serbs that they had done nothing wrong. A strategy founded upon the economic destruction of Serbia was seriously flawed since it passed the initiative to Milosevic in so far as it left the decision as to when he had had enough in his hands - a strategy which had failed against Saddam Hussein. As will be revealed, the reason the allied plan worked was not ultimately down to NATO's aerial skill and persistence but rather to Milosevic's poor judgement.

On 26 March 1999, Russia sponsored a Security Council draft Resolution which called for 'an immediate cessation of the use of force against the Federal Republic of Yugoslavia'. Only China and Namibia supported the Russian initiative and it failed by 12 votes to 3. There was no serious attempt to claim that the Security Council's rejection of Russia's draft resolution legitimised NATO's bombing of Serbia but there is no doubt the politicians felt reassured. The impact of the bombing was slow to develop. This was not only due to the initial presence of a token air strike capability but also to poor weather conditions (only 23 of the 78 days were absolutely clear) and the non-American allies not having adequate means to put bombs accurately on targets. Gradually the air capability was ratcheted up, more than doubling from 400 to 912 the number of aircraft involved in the 78 days of the air campaign. The air plan was divided into three sequential phases of concentration, firstly upon Serbia's air defences, secondly upon Kosovo and thirdly upon Serbia generally. NATO moved from the phase 1 state to the third state in the first week. At this early stage, a sense of frustration was already discernible. SACEUR admitted, 'we cannot stop paramilitary operations on the ground'. If NATO could not defeat third rate opponents, inevitable questions would arise as to its value. There is a body of opinion, mostly silent in March 1999, that a massive use of air power should have been applied from day 1, yet since the action was technically illegal, the unintended gradual response which developed was undoubtedly a less contentious approach to the Kosovo conflict.

Pentagon planners estimated the loss of up to ten aircraft in First Phase attacks upon Yugoslav air defence systems. In the event, and to Serbia's huge elation, the first of only two aircraft to be lost was a Stealth fighter, F-117A. That aircraft was lost because its arrival was said to have been anticipated by virtue of a security breach within NATO. The BBC's correspondent in Belgrade commented how the BBC's sources 'are categorical - and there is the evidence on the ground; someone was telling the Yugoslavs where each night's attacks would take place'.[57] After the first two weeks, when the 'need to know' procedure was implemented, the leak was plugged. However, claims that the Stealth fighter had been lost due to a security breach appear unlikely. The conventional fighter effort was controlled by NATO HQ. Bomber operations, B-52 bombers from Fairford, Gloucestershire and B-2s from Missouri, and Stealth fighter operations were not made available for NATO tasking but tasked directly from the Pentagon. The Department of Defense's unclassified Report to Congress admitted that 'parallel US and NATO command and control structures complicated operational planning and unity of command'.[58] The attack on 7 May upon the Chinese Embassy by a B-2 bomber was therefore not the responsibility of NATO.[59] What that attack achieved, in killing three Chinese intelligence operatives, was to antagonise a second member of the UN Security Council. Moreover it deflected the Chinese public's attention away from the tenth anniversary of the Tienanmen Square troubles. Every cloud is said to have a silver lining and it is believed that as a *quid pro quo*, America agreed to waive its objections to China joining the World Trade Organisation (WTO). After the attack on the Chinese Embassy, Russia and China agreed to put troops into Kosovo once a ground intervention became possible. In the event, Russia did, China did not.

If Racak was the pivotal event, the catalyst which triggered the bombing campaign, there was a second, equally significant event which appeared to provide further justification for the bombing. That event was the mass expulsion by train, now under way, of Kosovar Albanians from Pristina in the days leading up to Easter; the weekend 27-28 March 1999. It was partly the use of trains to transport refugees *en masse* which had resonance and memories of another time and another place but also the images of 50,000 people, destitute and carrying nothing but small bundles of personal belongings. It was a harrowing experience for the aid people involved as they watched individuals systematically deprived of their identities. Macedonia, fearful of the destabilising influence likely to be caused by the influx of Albanians, refused to allow them access. The majority of the members of the international organisations who had responded to the crisis had been in Kosovo the week previously. Unlike those in East Timor who felt guilty at their precipitate departure, this was not the experience of the members of agencies now assembling on Kosovo's borders who felt only anger and frustration. They too believed the United States had come to an understanding with Milosevic that he would toe the international line after a period of token, light bombing, at which time they would return to resume their work inside Kosovo.

By mid April, the Alliance suffered from not having thought through its strategy. One senior employee observed how 'there was no strategy: plans were made on a day to day basis'.[60] Now it found itself 'caught between an air war that doesn't quite work and a land war it dare not unleash'.[61] While there were few striking similarities between the Vietnam experience and Kosovo, the war was being run from Washington by people for whom the Vietnam war had been part of their formative political upbringing. The political and military hierarchies persisted in the belief that one key lesson from Vietnam was that the public would not tolerate casualties and therefore operations should be planned in such a way as to avoid casualties. It proved to be a convenient cop-out for a leadership loath to make the kind of operational decisions necessary for successful mission completion, which would inevitably imply the acceptance of casualties. Their dislike for the land option was, however, out of kilter with the public view. In a *Newsweek* poll, 54 per cent of Americans interviewed favoured the employment of ground troops 'to force Milosevic to agree to a NATO peace plan'.[62] A University of Maryland poll proved the *Newsweek* poll to be an accurate reflection of public attitudes. Sixty per cent favoured the despatch of troops, even at the cost of 250 lives.[63] In a less than honest gesture, Clinton implied that the decision to send in ground forces rested not with him but with NATO's Secretary-General, Javier Solana.[64] It is true that, with the exception of Prime Minister Blair who may not have fully grasped the military implications of a ground campaign into Kosovo, NATO's leaders were unanimously opposed to putting troops on the ground. German Chancellor Gerhard Schröder declared such an option to be 'unthinkable'.

Intent on securing higher profile in the Kosovo conflict for the UN through a new diplomatic initiative, Secretary-General Kofi Annan visited NATO Headquarters, Brussels on 14 April. Annan empathised with the primacy of NATO's Five Points but sought to 'intensify the search for a political solution'. NATO, however, was not prepared to concede a leadership role to Annan until the problem with Milosevic had been resolved. Washington's memory was not so short as to have forgotten Annan's diplomatic initiative into Iraq where he appeared to have achieved a diplomatic coup by brokering peace with Saddam Hussein. Others intended to be the beneficiaries of bouquets arising from the satisfactory resolution of the Kosovo conflict. The central problem, however, was Slobodan Milosevic's determination not to accommodate NATO, now preferring instead to deal with the UN. It was NATO's inability to remove Milosevic which ensured the UN's eventual leading role in Kosovo and in history.

The problem was that NATO had already been launched on its roller-coaster ride. People such as Henry Kissinger who opposed involvement recognised that the process now had to be seen through to a satisfactory conclusion. But the ground option was fraught with difficulty. The defence of Serbia was what the Yugoslav Army was trained for. Kosovo, the size of Wales or Maryland, has a central plain surrounded by high mountains, with few points of entry, and is susceptible to flooding and uncompromising winters with attendant poor visibility. Getting the estimated 175,000-200,000 troops there, sustaining them and getting them out under 'non-permissive' circumstances were all problems recognised by ambitious, cautious politicians in the majority of NATO's capitals. There was also the consideration of the refugees in their tented camps and the question how were they to survive winter. In late May, and under the guise of strengthening the road to support the flow of refugees, NATO military engineers strengthened the intended invasion route through Albania from Tirana to Kukes. Clark's enthusiasm to develop a ground invasion plan was not reciprocated by Defense Secretary Cohen or Joint Chiefs Chairman, General Shelton. What encouragement he did receive from Washington now came from the White House National Security Team.

Heady idealism transcends none of these military realities and Blair must have known that the military option was a non-starter without American troops being alongside their British cousins. The French might have been persuaded to go along also but that was the sum of the potential contribution. The rest of NATO did not want to know. But Blair is no Thatcher and Clinton no Reagan or Bush. Nonetheless, Blair recognised the need to maintain contact with a President becoming increasingly annoyed at the antics of a lesser partner endeavouring to take America to a place he had no intention of going. Clinton was not likely to be impressed by Blair's eulogies: 'In Kosovo but on many other occasions', Blair said, 'I have had occasion to be truly thankful that the United States has a President with his vision and steadfastness'.[65] Blair's ground force plan began to find support within the United States to the extent that the President told him in effect to wind his neck in. The President told Blair that what Herr Schröder described as 'this specifically British debate' was giving an unwanted appearance of disunity within the alliance. The eminent military historian, Sir John Keegan, said that Blair's populist brand of politics was no way to fight a war:

> He has no experience of conducting the diplomatic or military side of war. He is running terrible risks. Polls show that he has a majority of public support, but it is the support of the tabloid readers. The well informed feel uninformed, are anxious and racked by doubt.[66]

Blair responded to the Djakovica convoy incident by sending his own personal Rasputin, a former political editor for a London tabloid, from his Party Headquarters into NATO Headquarters. There he assembled kindred spin-merchants from the United States, Germany and France. In helping to win the information war, NATO admits to these increments having assisted with the organisation and presentation of news. For their part, NATO tried to keep the visitors honest. For example, when one wanted to report the pulverisation of a Yugoslav Division in an air offensive on Mount Pastrik on 7 June, NATO said, 'not without evidence'. Such controls were clearly not consistently employed. After a civilian train had been struck by NATO missiles, NATO produced a video to support its argument that the train had appeared so quickly, there was no time to abort the missiles. The video was played to the press at three times the correct speed.[67]

However, with the benefit of an element of foresight, the attachment of spin-doctors to NATO should have been seen as both nugatory and undesirable. There was short-term benefit to be gained but, in the mid to long term, NATO will have been irreparably damaged and its information flow become a source of automatic distrust. Spinners regard truth purely in terms of its political ramifications and will present a form of truth in the way that is best calculated to achieve a desired political objective. They can, for example, control the timing of news releases to coincide with the most politically opportune, or least prejudicial, moment. Such people who are routinely conditioned to mental self-abuse eventually find that they are blind to the importance and primacy of truth. In British domestic politics, economy with the truth had become an unashamed feature, a political tool of the government. It was in the domestic context that the observation was made: 'You cannot fool all of the people all of the time. Some day they will find you out. The overblown announcements, tweakings with the truth and clever doublespeak of today is storing up trouble for tomorrow'.[68] But the western military have a higher code of ethical and moral behaviour than their political masters; so much so that Kosovo became a remarkable armed conflict in so far as a tension developed between the politicians and their own military vis-à-vis means and ends. Rarely have armed forces been so beset by doubt and guilt about what their political leaders were asking of them. 'I don't know of any military people who are supporting this other than the national command figures and appointees... what we're hearing is this force was established over the objections of most of our senior leaders in the military',[69] said an American retired officer. Described in some quarters as a cowardly way to conduct armed conflict, the air campaign was certainly anti-heroic and, in the light of widespread international condemnation, will be difficult to repeat in the form which applied to Kosovo. Even within the alliance, targeting and the imposition of oil sanctions were always subordinated to the desire to maintain consensus.

Originally there may have been up to 500 KLA fighters in seven operational zones (of which one was on paper). The overall strength ebbed and flowed. The majority of the population may have been sympathetic but they were having to do timeshare on the available rifles. By early April 1999 there was only a ragtag representation of no more than 4,000 KLA men in Kosovo. The remainder had either been killed, had withdrawn into Albania or joined their families among the 800,000 refugees in the camps in the contiguous states. The KLA had suffered serious reverses against the better-organised, trained and equipped Yugoslav Army and Serbian Interior Ministry paramilitaries. But, from this point, a remarkable transformation occurred to the KLA. Reinforcements joined them from around the globe and their training and equipment showed signs of perceptible improvement. Yet NATO consistently maintained its refusal to arm the KLA.

Part of the catalyst for change was organisational. As often happens during the course of armed conflict, peacetime commanders or political appointees are removed or moved into less important posts. That happened to the KLA's commander, Sylejman Selimi, who was appointed to the National Guard and replaced by Brigadier Agim Ceku. Ceku is a man of more than passing interest. An ethnic Kosovar Albanian, he was formerly a gunner captain in the Yugoslav Army and attended Belgrade's Military Academy. In 1991, he left the Yugoslav Army to join the newly-formed Croatian Army and, for the next four years, was engaged in planning and participating in operations to sweep 300,000 Serbs from Croatia. It is possible that Ceku could be indicted for war crimes committed against the Serbs in Croatia 1993-1995. An American military consultant who joined MPRI in the pivotally important year of 1995, spoke of Ceku's competence: 'We were impressed by his overview of the battleground and the ability to always predict his enemy's next move'.[70] It was Ceku's involvement in an attack on three Serb villages in Croatia in September 1993 and the subsequent massacre of civilians there which has left Ceku vulnerable to indictment.

Arms and equipment for the KLA flowed over the porous Albanian border and down through Croatia. There were also unconfirmed reports of supplies disguised as humanitarian aid entering Kosovo by way of Skopje airport. NATO had no need to break the UN arms embargo to equip the KLA, some other agency was doing it for them. For example, every self-respecting secessionist army will have its own satellite communications yet somehow the KLA were trained and equipped with specialist ground-to-air communication systems which enabled them to act as NATO's eyes and ears on the ground, fulfilling the function of Forward Air Controllers to NATO and US strike aircraft. Moreover, in the border town of Kukes, NATO established a Special Forces operations centre manned by the CIA. This liaison between NATO and the KLA had begun in late April. Ever sensitive about being seen to be dealing directly with people who the President's special envoy to the Balkans, Robert S. Gelbard, had as recently as February 1998 described as 'terrorists', the US Special Forces worked through the Albanian 2nd Army as intermediaries to pass on and receive intelligence.

Meanwhile, in the corridors of power, urgent diplomatic efforts were being sought to broker peace in Kosovo. The most frenetic political activity was not in Belgrade, however, but among NATO's coalition partners, a partnership that threatened to burst at the seams - Germany's Green Party, part of the ruling coalition, had called for a limited halt to the bombing. *The Economist* summed up NATO's predicament: 'The trouble was that they had never intended to do more than drop a few bombs. Then, when a few bombs proved inadequate, they found they had stumbled into a war they did not mean to fight, had not prepared to fight and were not willing to fight, at least with men who might get killed'.[71] Peace feelers were also discernible in Belgrade where Milosevic, under pressure from reservists who were withdrawing from Kosovo of their own volition, made a public show of formally withdrawing some troops from Kosovo. He insisted, however, that details had to be 'negotiated with the United Nations'.

The former Russian Prime Minister, Viktor Chernomyrdin, had been appointed Boris Yeltsin's Kosovo envoy and was already engaged in shuttle diplomacy between Moscow and Belgrade supported by the State Department's Deputy Secretary of State, Strobe Talbott. The duo became a trio in response to UN Secretary-General Kofi Annan's recommendation that a further independent broker be appointed. The State Department concurred but, instead of taking a UN nominee, chose as an EU mediator, the Finnish President Martti Ahtissari. However, there can be little doubt that diplomatically what swayed Milosevic towards a peace deal was Chernomyrdin's withdrawal of Russian support and endorsement of NATO's demands. Operationally, more than 400 NATO sorties a day against Serbia provided Milosevic with a point of focus, particularly since an increasing number of sorties were being targeted against his, his family's and cronies' economic interests. Shortly after peace was signed on 9 June, the IMF announced a massive loan to Russia. Claims, therefore, which originated in the Dailies, of *mea culpa*, ascribing Milosevic's capitulation to the influence of air power were overstated. Air power played a part, but so too did Russia's abandonment of Serbia and the belated signs that NATO was seriously reconsidering the ground option. Clinton had said, 'all options are on the table'. On 25 May, NATO decided to reinforce Macedonia to bring the strength there up to 50,000.

The release by American and British intelligence of evidence which enabled Milosevic to be indicted on 27 May as a war criminal[72] (the first indictment of an incumbent head of state for violations of international law) served to justify the prosecution of the air war and to tie America more closely to the ground option. What it also did was to remove any claim of impartiality a future War Crimes Tribunal might attempt to make. There was now no prospect of a negotiated settlement with NATO which would be fully acceptable to Milosevic. 'A Munich-style agreement was not politically compatible with a Nuremberg-style charge sheet.'[73] What is remarkable is quite how well Milosevic did.

NATO Secretary-General Javier Solana argued that the eventual Kosovo peace deal should not be seen as a reverse for NATO. Yet Milosevic had prevailed in so far as NATO came under the aegis of the UN and NATO was denied the free access to Kosovo and Serbia which had been a key component of the Rambouillet diktat. For the KLA, Rambouillet had not lived up to its earlier promise. They had signed up in the assumption that a referendum after three years would deliver into their hands the independence which they demanded. The referendum proposal had been conveniently dropped, not least because NATO was opposed to Kosovar independence. Rambouillet had resembled the Vietnam experience in so far as it offered no compromises. If the compromises offered at the end of the conflict had been on the table at the outset, it should not have been necessary to unleash NATO's mighty conventional power. Up to 3,000 Kosovars may have been killed prior to the bombing campaign - some in conflict with the Serbs and 'quite a few at the hands of Kosovar guerrillas'.[74] As early as 13 November 1998, one NATO source had observed that the KLA was 'the main initiator of the violence which is threatening the ceasefire arrangements'.[75] Thousands of Serbs and Kosovars died once the bombing began, over 500 killed by NATO bombs.[76] This was the irony of a poorly thought through, double-edged strategy. The aim of the war had been to halt ethnic cleansing when in fact it not only intensified it but also, after the Kosovo peace agreement, threw the process into reverse in so far as the majority Albanians, understandably, exacted revenge upon the minority Serbs. Politically, it had been a disaster. The sovereignty issue had been left up in the air:

> The Albanians had fought for independence based on the right to national self determination. The Serbs had fought to keep Kosovo part of Yugoslavia in the name of the inviolability of existing borders. While insisting that Kosovo be granted autonomy, NATO asserted that it must remain part of Yugoslavia. The alliance had therefore intervened in a civil war and defeated one side, but embraced the position of the party it had defeated on the issue over which the war had been fought.[77]

In the Kumanovo Military Technical Agreement (MTA) drawn up between NATO and the Yugoslavs (it was called an agreement because technically no one had been defeated), the Yugoslav Army had 11 days in which to leave Kosovo. The MTA and UN Security Council Resolution 1244 provided for the return of a small number of Yugoslav military personnel to guard Serb cultural monuments and maintain a presence at the border.

The KLA offered a unilateral 'undertaking' which was received by KFOR. As in the case of MTA, there was no agreement *per se*. What the KLA accepted was to disarm and disband by K+90, but paragraph 25 of the Undertaking acknowledged the KLA's aspiration to be 'transformed' into a police force (paragraph 25a) and an Army or National Guard. The international community agreed to give this aspiration 'due consideration'. At the outset, that was the extent of any agreement. The next 90 days were spent in intensive negotiations haggling over what to do with the KLA after they had officially ceased to exist on K+90. The original answer to the KLA was that, having given their aspiration due consideration, the international community agreed their men could apply to join the Kosovo Police Service (KPS) as individuals; there would be no Army or National Guard. If the situation had been left like that, the KLA might well have gone underground and popped up later, or, more awkwardly for KFOR, manifested themselves earlier.

With minutes to go and various forms of extensions to deadlines after K+90, a formula was agreed whereby all sides accepted the establishment of the Kosovo Protection Corps (KPC), the TMK, under UNMIK authority but under KFOR's day to day supervision. The force's primary role was to be civil defence, with no armed or coercive missions and no security or policing duties. The KLA's weapons - all, in theory, handed in - would remain under KFOR's physical control. The authority for setting up the KPC was the UN but only after three months of hectic negotiation with national governments and NATO. The title, KPC, was one of the last decisions to be made. The man appointed to command the organisation was General Agim Ceku. 'Our aim', he said, 'is to build a democratic Kosovo and it has to be multinational…our strategic decision was to wage a "clean" war, in accordance with Albanian moral values'.[78]

Kosovo's five counties were assigned as Multi-National Brigade (MNB) areas, each commanded by a framework state: France in the north, the British in the centre, America in the east, Germany in the south and Italy in the west. That there was no high profile brigade area made available to Russia would be the source of future political anxiety. The military plan, which had been well rehearsed and war-gamed, was for General Jackson's Rapid Reaction Corps or KFOR to enter Kosovo as the Yugoslav Army withdrew, thereby systematically occupying the vacuum created. This had formed part of the agreement because the Yugoslavs feared that the KLA would occupy their abandoned territory and massacre the Kosovo Serbs unless NATO was close behind. Coordination proved almost impossible as only belatedly did brigades come under the Corps' tactical control. On 12 June there were only nine battalions in KFOR, of which four were British (two of which had arrived in the previous 4-5 days). By 14 June, two further battalions had arrived, one British, one French. Although British politicians have been deservedly criticised, their resolution in resourcing the Kosovo intervention cannot be faulted. The American contingent did not arrive until the day after the advance into Kosovo should have begun. The unusual feature of this operation was that a Corps Headquarters was dealing directly in detail with five brigades, with no intervening divisional headquarters to facilitate command and control. A further complication was that after Pristina had been occupied, the brigades were not pure - i.e. not being from one nation they had not previously trained and worked together. Twenty-nine different countries provided forces - politically beneficial but not militarily efficient. There were, for example, Slovenian platoons in an Austrian unit in a German brigade whose brigadier in Prizren had a major-general as national commander, from whom the German brigade commander had to request half his assets. It is possible for a Corps on peacekeeping operations to exercise command and control over five multi-national brigades, but this was an Implementation Operation where the Corps units might have fully expected having to fight the Yugoslav Army. When the entry into Kosovo began, there was one journalist for every five soldiers.

KFOR, however, had good reason to feel confident that their entry into Kosovo would be a *relief* in place of the Serbs, not an *advance to contact.* Exceptionally good professional and personal relations between KFOR and the Serb military forces existed throughout. There was always going to be a possibility of individuals or small groups sniping at KFOR, but General Jackson was conscious of the reality that he had brokered a cooperative venture with the Serbs and had good cause not to anticipate hostilities against them. If, on the off-chance, that optimism proved to be misplaced, KFOR would have withdrawn at any early sign of trouble because the force was not configured to fight in anything larger than a small tactical engagement. In such an eventuality, KFOR would have waited until they had the proper force structure to do the job which was the next stage in the escalation.

The Serbs deeply regretted abandoning their own people to the Albanians at KFOR's insistence and demanded that KFOR guarantee the safety and security of their own people they were leaving behind. They claimed that General Jackson's signature on the MTA was in effect a guarantee given on behalf of NATO, hence their dismay at KFOR's perceived failure to protect the Kosovo Serbs in the months that followed.

There is more than the usual amount of political and military obfuscation as to the events commencing Friday, 11 June 1999. On 12 June, when the Stabilisation Force (SFOR) reported that a Russian convoy had left Bosnia for Kosovo via Belgrade, the 200-strong Russian detachment from SFOR in Bosnia arrived in Kosovo and occupied Pristina airport with a view, so KFOR believed, to making rendezvous there with

5,000 Russian paratroopers.[79] NATO's Combined Air Operations Centre in Vicenza, Italy had issued what were later described as spurious reports that the Russian paratroopers were airborne for Kosovo. The arrival of the Russians in their battered APCs caused much jubilation and jingoism in Russia. 'For them, it was a moment to savour, a rare act of one upmanship by a faded power against a military that once viewed them with fear and awe'.[80] But, in view of the closure of national airspace of the contiguous countries to Russian aircraft, Russia's flying column had driven itself into an unsustainable, operational cul-de-sac. When news of the Russian intentions became manifest, SACEUR, General Wesley Clark, ordered General Jackson to stop the Russian advance. Jackson allegedly declined, saying: 'I have no intention of starting the Third World War'. Obviously, if a clash had occurred, the only beneficiary would have been Milosevic. Besides, Jackson had personally negotiated the MTA with the Serbs. The strategic pre-emption required by General Clark would have undermined the MTA before it even got underway and would have called into question General Jackson's honour and integrity.

The ramifications of an alleged disinclination to obey a superior's orders rumbled on into the following weeks but the requirement was politically rather than militarily oriented and Jackson put his objection to London through the BRITFOR national commander, Major-General Richard Dannatt. Lines were opened between London and Washington with the upshot that political support publicly favoured Jackson's action. SACEUR's desire to raise the profile of the conflict had not sat easily with Secretary William Cohen's and General Henry Shelton's concepts of operations for Kosovo. General Clark was short-toured in favour of General Joseph W. Ralston USAF - only the second air force officer ever to be appointed by Washington to command NATO. John Warner, the Republican chairman of the Senate Armed Services Committee, announced his intention of investigating General Jackson's 'insubordination' in refusing to accept SACEUR's orders.

It is a feature of coalition operations that national commanders will always have the right to blow the whistle and raise the red card when military action proposed by a non-national appears contrary to the military and political interests of the designated state. In Korea, on no fewer than five occasions in the first three months did Major-General A.J.H. Cassels advise his American Corps Commander, Lieutenant-General J.W. O'Daniel that he believed he had been tasked to undertake military operations which, to his mind, were militarily unsound.

Air power had not succeeded in 'degrading' Serbian land forces; a fact which led Adam Roberts to observe that:

> if this view is correct, then the disturbing lesson of the air campaign may be that its most effective aspect involved hurting Serbia proper (including its population and government) rather than directly attacking Serb forces in Kosovo and protecting the Kosovars.[81]

As Figure 8.1 indicates, attacking civilian targets and therefore, by implication, civilians rather than the military, is a trend already evident during the twentieth century.

Wars and Armed Conflict	Dead	Servicemen %	Civilians
First World War	10m	95	5
Second World War	50m	52	48
1945-98	35m	17	83

Figure 8.1

Observers of video conferences between General Clark and his air commander, Lieutenant General Michael C. Short, soon became aware of the tension and philosophical differences which existed between the two generals. Clark wanted NATO's air power to hunt down and destroy tactical targets in Kosovo - 'are you bombing those ground forces yet, Mike?' - while Short preferred to strike at strategic targets in Serbia proper. Strategic targets included predictably empty Kosovo Yugoslav barracks whose destruction denied their use to incoming NATO forces. That Short's view triumphed is more a reflection upon the impossibility of what Clark sought to achieve from aircraft flying 3 miles high which could locate targets but not consistently identify them. Clark was, of course, responding to the initial, political, moral imperative to be seen to be striking those responsible for the turmoil in Kosovo, Serbia's Third Army. 'I don't wish to be impertinent', said Short, 'but I don't think most of our civilian leadership generally understands air power and how it should be used. Their exposure to it has been films of the Gulf War, which looked like a video game'.[82]

Much has been made of General Short's underlying objection to the use of strategic assets upon tactical targets and rather less upon the reasoning for the refusal to release or provide appropriate tactical assets to strike at tactical targets. Once again we are reminded of the unacceptable reaction given to casualty aversion and the consequential adoption of inappropriate military means. In eventually approving Short's targets, his political masters, committed supporters of the Bosnia International War Crimes Tribunal, exposed themselves to charges of inconsistency and hypocrisy. Parties who go forward to address a criminal act as perpetrated by Milosevic yet who also engage in criminal means to counter the original crimes do attract the charge of *tu quoque*. Attacks on Serb Television and Radio in Belgrade, power stations and seven bridges, which led to civilian deaths, were not *bona fide* military targets. In the future, military commanders will have to be far more wary of the orders they carry out or initiatives they undertake.

Post-conflict analysts have examined the role of video conferencing during the Kosovo conflict to assess its value as a command and control tool. Used properly, teleconferencing eliminates the need for commanders to be collocated, provides the means for the transmission of clear, unambiguous orders[83] and can reduce the amount of time required to come to a decision. Those not involved in the process, however, would have been unable to assess their commanders' intentions by virtue of the absence of any form of body language and rarely would there be call for reassuring, written orders. Teleconferencing takes many strides beyond the Nixon era tapes in terms of self-incrimination. Archivists collected 94 high command tapes from NATO which include images of Generals Clark's and Short's internal conflict. As the implications for the use of such visual records dawn on future commanders, they may well become more circumspect in the use of teleconferencing systems.

It does seem, however, that General Jackson prepared plans for the forward deployment of the British 5 Airborne Brigade to pre-empt possible Russian intentions to occupy Pristina airport. (The airport was the intended location for HQ KFOR. Film City, an alternative location on the fringes of Pristina, had previously been occupied by OSCE. The ending of their active participation meant Film City became available to KFOR and is where they moved to after being blocked by the Russians at the airport.) Warning and confirmatory orders were passed to Brigadier Adrian Freer, Commander 5 Airborne Brigade. Elements of 5 Airborne Brigade were soon aboard RAF Chinook helicopters in anticipation of an air landing on Pristina airport.

It is at this juncture that the report of 5,000 airborne Russian paratroopers arrived at HQ KFOR. The atmosphere in the HQ was likened to that in the film *Ice Station Zebra*. 'We could have been at war with Russia in minutes.' In an ensuing video conference the American and

British generals decided to refer the matter back for political clearance. The British Airborne Brigade was still awaiting the final order to lift off. Clark is said to have wished Jackson good luck 'in his bayonet fighting with the Russians'. By late evening on 11th it became apparent that the report of Russian paratroopers being en route was a myth. Jackson then ordered UK Special Forces and the Airborne Brigade's Pathfinder platoon to seize the airport under the cover of darkness. Unfortunately, a poorly secured, heavily armed landrover in a C-130 carrying a SAS platoon shifted on take-off. The plane crashed on the airstrip at Kukes, Albania.

Although KFOR had a planned strength of 50,000, only a small proportion of that number began the tentative advance into Kosovo on 12 June 1999. Jackson's strength was half that of the largely intact, withdrawing, Yugoslav Army - a force considerably more intact and undamaged than NATO's creative accounting led them to believe. In June 1999, NATO announced that 120 Yugoslav tanks had been destroyed - a figure which was revised downward in September to 93. These figures compared with the Yugoslav Army's declared loss of only 13 tanks - a figure which a senior KFOR representative was inclined to support. KFOR found evidence of fewer than a dozen heavy armoured vehicles having been destroyed. From Brussels' point of view therefore, the placing of a British airborne brigade miles in advance of its nearest ground support, in the heart of strong, armoured, enemy forces, with orders to attack the Russian allies of the Yugoslav Army, may have appeared less dotty than it did to KFOR's planners.

At 5am 12 June, the Pathfinders eventually arrived at Pristina airport accompanied by elements of G Squadron, SAS. Their arrival coincided with that of the Russians. A 'Mexican stand-off' occurred as the outnumbered British advanced troops had inadequate Rules of Engagement (ROE) and firepower with which to prevent the APC-borne Russians from securing the airport. Brigadier Freer requested of General Jackson permission to upgrade his ROE. Jackson is said to have refused and ordered Freer to await the arrival of 4th (UK) Armoured Brigade.

The Armoured Brigade, however, was delayed in a traffic jam at the Kacanik defile. At mid-morning, Jackson ordered Freer to move by road to the airport to make rendezvous with the Pathfinders. Freer arrived at mid-day and was warmly welcomed by the Russians who apparently agreed to UK forces entering the airport. The 1st Battalion the Parachute Regiment (1 Para) at Kacanik was accordingly given a warning order to heli-lift to Pristina airport. Meanwhile, General Jackson was instructed by Downing

Street to hold a Press Conference at Pristina airport. General Jackson and his command group arrived at Pristina airport to hold the requisite press conference. The Russians, oblivious to General Jackson's intentions, withdrew their original offer to Freer for British troops to occupy the airport. Accordingly, 1 Para were stood down.

It is evident that whatever the military intentions were intended to achieve, this was a highly charged political environment. The impression of order, counter order and disorder is nevertheless accurate. It does seem that Jackson may have found his military superior in Brussels to have been excitable but both appeared to have been in agreement to permit the Russians to enter Kosovo only on NATO's terms. In that respect they both failed but, turning the other cheek, playing down the impact of the Russian coup, being patient and supportive of the Russians in their predicament, did prove to be the proper, pragmatic course of action.

NATO persisted in the production of unbelievable figures, thereby serving to further undermine the organisation's credibility. Ninety-nine point six per cent of bombs apparently found their targets, and this was an organisation which unintentionally also bombed Albania, Bosnia, Bulgaria and Hungary. NATO would later admit 'that its estimates of the numbers of tanks and artillery pieces destroyed were, to put it politely, optimistic...by the time the truth came out, it no longer mattered'.[84] The Serbs would have known NATO's claims to be nonsense, which leads to an interesting conclusion and a re-visitation of the Vietnam era's 'body count'. Winning the Information War is domestically orientated - i.e. it is NATO's membership that is being targeted and conned - part of the spinners' technique, through the means of reassurance, to maintain consensus within the coalition. Exaggerating the success of NATO bombing helped a majority of politicians argue against the necessity of a ground option. Quite apart from the real-time operational dangers of such a deception, who will believe NATO in the future? 'The perception that spin-doctors were more interested in the message than accuracy and were running our information activities was damaging and remains a stereotype impression', admitted NATO's information spokesman, Jamie Shea. If, as a matter of policy, truth does become an intentional victim of war, such a decision should not be accompanied by a fanfare of trumpets drawing attention to that fact.

British post-operations reports indicate that KFOR's advance into Kosovo was not the complete success it has been painted. Brigadier Adrian Freer, commander of 5 Airborne Brigade, told how he had found that 'the gap between corps and brigade was too great'. Something had apparently gone awry with the concept of mission-oriented orders, for the brigadier felt he needed more detail.[85] 'Commander KFOR's intent was not always transmitted with sufficient detail and coordinating instructions. Even when detail was subsequently requested from KFOR it was not always forthcoming.' A staff officer serving at HQ KFOR commented how: 'Adrian (Freer) never quite understood the "force profile" required even though General Jackson had spent numerous O Groups and briefings explaining the concept'. Bearing in mind the political baggage the Corps headquarters had to carry, lapses in attention to detail are understandable, hence the importance of mission-oriented orders which give commanders the bare tapestry of the requirement, leaving them free to proceed with the embroidery. On reflection, this is easier said than done when trying to coordinate five national brigades. Freer reported how the breakdown in communications had 'led to improvisation at brigade level and a consequently asymmetric effect within KFOR as different brigades made their own interpretations'.[86] In fairness, it was observed how each differently configured brigade continued to make its own interpretations and responses well into the period of deployment in Kosovo. Molly Moore of the *Washington Post* saw the first 900 US Marines enter south-eastern Kosovo:

> in a high alert, high caution wartime stance that contrasted sharply with the demeanor of British armored troops who led the peacekeeping contingent into Kosovo two days earlier. Whereas the British revelled in the outpouring of emotion by the crowds of ethnic Albanians who greeted them with tears, chants and bouquets of flowers, the Marines saw danger.[87]

In a separate report, one of the Brigadier's COs criticised the performance of some radios and personal weapons. General Jackson responded to these criticisms:[88]

> The force I commanded that went into Kosovo on June 12 was structured as a *peace implementation* force. It made no pretension to be anything else. Had we had to take offensive ground action to force entry, that would have been an entirely different scenario.[89]

The reason the British force that entered Kosovo included armour and self-propelled guns of the 4th Armoured Brigade was because KFOR's superior headquarters believed that a benign passage could not be guaranteed. In these circumstances, although organisational change could have been effected, the failure of personal weapons and radios would have been of inestimable concern and not susceptible to a quick-fix solution. The point to be made here is what the General meant by *peace implementation* since it is a contradiction in terms. By our definition, Implementation Operations assume armed conflict may take place. General Jackson was responsible for the development of British Army doctrine before he assumed command of NATO's Rapid Reaction Corps. What General Jackson did by his action, however, was to provide one of the most illuminating examples in modern conflict of the principle 'know your enemy'. The operation had begun as virtually all air and ended as virtually all ground.

It is not pedantry which raises objections to the proliferation of mumbo-jumbo doctrinal definitions. Their very imprecision carries real dangers, as is apparent from this extract from a newspaper article published prior to the peace agreement:

> NATO believes that an 'entry' into Kosovo can be made on terms that, while not combat-free (or casualty free) do not amount to full scale war. This would be described as *peace establishing* or *peace enforcing,* and current thinking is that even NATO members opposed to a ground *intervention* would be willing to go along with this.[90]

In Bosnia, the Serbs, Muslims and Croats accepted a political decision to partition the country, thus providing IFOR/SFOR with universal consent upon which to build their military plans. In Kosovo, however, KFOR had been obliged to evolve a military plan without there being consensus between Serbs and Kosovo Albanians. The thin spread of Serbs throughout Kosovo also meant that Kosovo could not be effectively divided into ethnic areas or enclaves. One important lesson from Bosnia was how partition polarised ethnicity in so far as it placed ethnic groups on their own side of a line. Each ethnic group's place, therefore, was defined in relation to that internal border. It left ethnic outposts, unwisely described as safe areas, as hostages to fortune. Milosevic's aspiration that the Russians control the northern sector would have involved *de facto* partition and is why such an aspiration met determined opposition from Washington. After the flying column had given Moscow a victory of sorts and suitable political gestures had been made in advance of the December Duma elections, the Helsinki agreement allowed for Russian representation within the American, French and German MNB areas. KFOR's multiple mission based on UN Security Council Resolution 1244, which the staff stoutly defended amidst a sea of cynicism, was to monitor, verify and, when necessary, enforce compliance with the conditions of the Military Technical Agreement (MTA); provide humanitarian assistance in support of UNHCR; establish initial basic law and order enforcement and core civil functions in order to facilitate peace and stability within Kosovo. The 'end game' was to see Kosovo become a multi-ethnic, democratic and substantially autonomous region of Serbia. The Security Council Resolution was neither an end game nor an end state but an unsatisfactory halfway house requiring an answer as to how much autonomy Kosovo should be granted if it is to remain part of Serbia.

Shortly after KFOR occupied Pristina, I flew by helicopter from Skopje to Pristina. Accustomed to the considerable damage wrought upon Bosnia, I was immediately struck by the sense of normality and absence of damage in the unfolding panorama below me. There had been damage but it was largely to the west of the country where the fighting had taken place. A UN study indicated that 35 per cent of homes had been damaged and 'only a small percentage have been totally destroyed'. The north, east and area around the southern city of Prizren were noted as having suffered little damage.[91] I scanned the stunted forests for evidence of the 600,000 internally displaced but saw none. They did not and had not existed but were a figment of NATO's and UNHCR's imagination.

Waiting in Macedonia and Albania for their cue to assist KFOR with the civil aspects of its mission were the remnants of the OSCE preparing to re-designate from having been the Kosovo Verification Mission (KVM) to the Kosovo Implementation Mission (KIM). During February 1999, the OSCE had dedicated 1,000 hours to a concept of operations enunciating how the OSCE would administer prisons, the legal system, medical support, power supplies, sewerage, general administration, border controls, customs and excise, airports, military activities in the border zone and distribution of scarce commodities. The plan envisaged establishing operational hubs in each of Kosovo's five counties. It was during April and May 1999 that what had been a simmering turf war broke out, with the EU more opposed to OSCE taking a lead role than the UN. Up to late April 1999, OSCE believed it would be running the show but appreciated, post-Rambouillet, that plans had to be adapted in the light of the subsequent agreements. The police in Kosovo had been Serb. (Indeed, following Milosevic's initial interest in Kosovo, the infrastructure, utilities, health, and law and order were reserved for the minority Serbs.) At the end of the year, that ratio would have to swing to the Kosovar Albanian advantage to the order 80:20. Then the UN intervened, wanting to know whether the police were to be armed, and trained to whose standard? The USA volunteered to undertake the training of the police and to provide trainers.

By June 1999, the number of in-country OSCE experts had fallen to 200 but included the commanders and skeleton cadres familiar with each of the county/MNB areas. The experienced Brazilian peacekeeper and locum senior UN representative, Sergio di Mello, arrived with a competent staff plucked out of UN HQ in New York. The OSCE simply did not have this operational capability. The OSCE discerned an apparent UN unwillingness to take on individuals capable of running their regions, recruiting just one of the five OSCE regional commanders then available. Had the UN had the wisdom to take the OSCE experts under their wing, the rehabilitation of Kosovo could have been advanced by many weeks.

Slobodan Milosevic had made two strategic errors which let NATO off the hook. By virtue of the ethnic cleansing of the Kosovar Albanians, for whatever reason, he made the same mistake as Saddam Hussein before him, that was to justify rather than legitimise NATO's attacks upon Serbia. This was the consensual cement which would hold the coalition together. Secondly, he capitulated too soon. The American Deputy Secretary of State, Strobe Talbott, admitted that if Milosevic had not capitulated on 3 June, 'there would have been increasing difficulty within the Alliance in preserving the solidarity and resolve of the Alliance'.[92] Fortunately for NATO they did not have to implement the ground option scheduled for September 1999 when the roads of Kosovo were already choked with men on tractors searching out timber in preparation for the drawing-in of the usually harsh Balkan winter. NATO would have required an active force structure of up to 200,000 prepared for the long haul and the prospect of possibly not achieving military success before domestic consensus brought the armed conflict to an inconclusive end. Meanwhile the KLA set about the business of consolidation, firmly of the opinion that they had won the war.

As KFOR advanced into Kosovo, NATO's politicians, guided by their media gurus, sometimes accompanied by wives and children, held their last grandstanding tours of the refugee camps, whose occupants were already mentally prepared and in their starting blocks for their return home. It was not going to be a controlled exercise. One politician who had not assimilated the message, chose to take his photo opportunity at a mass grave. But what had the politicians to celebrate? Early estimates suggest up to 10,000 Kosovars had been murdered and up to 500 Serb non-combatants killed by NATO bombs. They had consigned their armed forces into an even deeper quagmire than Bosnia which at least had the benefit of a political settlement. In terms of the mechanics of a military operation, the ground forces had done a good job.[93] However, as the extension of a political arm that was weak and unreliable, there was a finite limit to what the military could achieve in Kosovo. The military were to remain, in theory, until a truly multi-ethnic society had been created in Kosovo. Yet if Montenegro declared its independence then so too would Kosovo. Accommodation for the Serbs might be found by the ceding of Kosovo territory in the north and east as extensions of the Serb border but this would represent a point of separation from their friends the Russians and Chinese. Enclaves would be an impossibility. But such territorial compromise would be prejudicial to the economic integrity and viability of Kosovo whose ethnic Albanian population is disinclined to seek unity with Albania. Whatever the outcome, the only certainty will be uncertainty.

In defending the Kosovo intervention, Blair described the situation in Kosovo as having been 'the closest thing to racial genocide seen in Europe since the Second World War'. 'Genocide' is not a word to be used loosely. It refers to a calculated attempt to exterminate totally a specific ethnic group or groups. In the Second World War period, the Germans targeted Jews and Romanies. In Rwanda, the American diplomats there had been instructed by the State Department that the genocide they were witnessing was not to be described as genocide but 'resembling genocide'. A proven case of genocide requires an obligatory international intervention under the 1949 Convention on Genocide, something America did not wish to do in Rwanda despite the best efforts of western politicians. Kosovo had not come close to being an example of genocide but the application of the term could be interpreted as a devious justification for military intervention. It would not be the first time that an intervention had been conducted ostensibly as a matter of *conscience* when in reality it camouflaged an underlying *interest*.

It was Richard Holbrooke who said: 'The UN's future in international crises is going to be determined in very large part by what it achieves in Kosovo'. Kosovo was therefore for the UN an opportunity to restore its credibility with the USA. The UN has consistently shown that it cannot conduct operations which contain a conflict element, and that includes humanitarian intervention. What it can do lies in the field of international politics and in the provision of legitimacy to military action. Of interventionist operations, two observers commented: 'The UN is not equipped to handle these types of operations; indeed, Kosovo shows that it is not even well prepared to handle the post conflict side of interventions'.[94] By September 1999, the UN's presence in Kosovo was more apparent than its achievements. UN and NGO 4x4s caused traffic jams in Pristina, accommodation was taken and restaurants filled with humanitarians with money to burn.

Meanwhile, the Kosovar Albanians were routinely engaged in the intimidation and murder of Serbs living in Kosovo while the Albanian mafia tightened its grip on the province. On the international stage, China and Russia examined the feasibility of developing an anti-NATO alliance and Russia accepted the precedent of NATO's freedom of action against Serbia as the green light to confront alleged Chechen terrorism. The Kosovo intervention ended as it had begun - a political morass. Claims of a just war, a model humanitarian intervention, were bogus. The aim of the exercise had been a White House and State Department demonstration to a Republican Congress that NATO at 50 could aspire to address new, out of area, challenges. Since 1993, America had been involved militarily in Somalia, Haiti, Rwanda and Bosnia. None of those performances had been distinguished. The Clinton administration 'had promised order in Somalia and left chaos. It had gone to Haiti to restore democracy and had left anarchy. It had bombed in Bosnia for the sake of national unity but presided over a *de facto* partition'.[95] The British government had acquiesced in putting its long-suffering armed forces into a situation the soldiers' grandfathers would have recognised as a re-run of post-war Palestine, from where they suffered the ignominy of precipitate withdrawal. Kosovo has been described as Madeleine's war. Speaking to GIs about to enter the unknown in Kosovo, she reassured them, saying: 'This is what America is good at, helping people'. Kosovo, she said, was 'simply the most important thing we have done in the world'.[96] NATO is the agent of its political masters, yet its military component can feel justifiably aggrieved that NATO's power and prestige had been abused for the sake of parochial political advantage.

NATO presented the conduct of the Kosovo operation as having been smooth, having 'run on rails'. Nothing could be further from the truth and in terms of keeping the NATO coalition together it was, to use Wellington's phrase, 'a damned close run thing'. The Kosovo experience highlighted for NATO four generic problem areas: casualty aversion, legitimacy, the airpower myth and relationships (external and internal).

Casualty aversion is not a problem peculiar to the United States. However, the fact that it is so deeply embedded in the psyche of NATO's leading framework state accentuates the fact that it exists and it is a profoundly serious problem. How can a potential opponent take seriously an Organisation that appears unprepared for its soldiers to take casualties? All that this undesirable transparency reveals is a soft underbelly of a centre of gravity for an opponent to attack. It is an area which requires urgent political attention and certainly would benefit, by means of clarification, from a Presidential Decision Directive (PDD) from Washington.

There were two *legitimacy* aspects which gave rise to concern within the Organisation. The first was the fact that the Kosovo operation did not have the benefit of an authorising UN mandate. The second concern arose during the course of the operation and involved the legitimacy of attacking non-military targets. There was a dichotomy which the UN Secretary-General, Kofi Annan, sought to adjudicate:

> Defenders of traditional interpretations of international law stressed the inviolability of state sovereignty; others stressed the moral imperative to act forcefully in the face of gross violations of human rights… Only the Charter provides a universally accepted basis for the use of force.[97]

After the Bosnia operation, politicians in Washington talked-up the success of the bombing missions there, partly to justify their decision not to make ground forces available. Thus the *myth of air power* was fostered. Air Force generals do not need encouragement to exaggerate the effects and influence of air power. They have massive budgetary aspirations fuelled by a requirement for expensive, high-tech equipment. Unlike the army which equips men, the air force mans equipment. The air power hype emanating from Kosovo was not discouraged or questioned by politicians content that the inflated claims of the merchants of air power justified their own collective decisions not to put ground forces into Kosovo. The danger is that politicians who erroneously believed that Bosnia's problems were resolved through the use of air power will be perfectly amenable to accept that was also the case in Kosovo. The truth is that air power is not an autonomous system but synonymous with being one of a number of clubs in a golf bag. The appointment of only the second air force General as SACEUR in NATO's history to replace the out-of-favour General Wesley Clark may well be a coincidence, yet it is an ominous coincidence.

In June 1999, a NATO team went into Kosovo to conduct a battle damage assessment. The Munitions Effectiveness Assessment Team (MEAT) conducted what at first was essentially an aerial audit of the damage. They were taken aback by the Yugoslavs' skill at deception. MEAT was able to verify 14 tanks, 18 APCs and 20 artillery pieces had been destroyed by NATO air forces. When General Clark was presented with these figures he is believed to have ordered the 30-man team to get out of their helicopters and be more systematic. The statistics did not change. However, of the 744 confirmed NATO air strikes, MEAT found evidence of only 58 strikes on the ground.[98] The figures were suppressed and Brigadier-General John Corley was tasked to conduct an independent repeat assessment. This Corley did, producing, through a process of creative accounting, figures which were more in line with NATO's original, discredited claims.

The Kosovo air campaign was trumpeted as a great success. Success had been achieved at the strategic level by attacking fixed targets such as communication centres, bridges and power supply - contrary to international law. When taking action that is justified by an opponent's breach of international law, presentational difficulties do arise when the intervening organisation itself pays scant attention to the law. It was those strategic attacks along with other factors which contributed to the Milosevic capitulation. Needless to say, after the conclusion of the conflict he was still in power, only to be removed by the democratic process. The air attacks at the operational and tactical level achieved what might reasonably be expected in an unheroic campaign where pinpoint targets were attacked from an altitude of three miles. It is too simplistic to assert that the politicians are dumb enough to accept the Generals' inflated claims. On the contrary, politicians are adept at turning the negative to the positive to prove that they were right all along. In playing into the politicians' hands, the generals are putting future operations and servicemen at risk.

The risk is that policymakers and politicians will become even more wedded to myths like 'surgical strikes'. The lesson of Kosovo is that civilian bombing works, though it raises moral qualms and may not suffice to oust tyrants like Milosevic. Against military targets, high altitude bombing is overrated. Any commander-in-chief who does not face up to those hard realities will be fooling himself.[99]

If, with the benefit of hindsight, legitimacy is deemed by NATO to be a factor to be more heavily weighted, then the consequence of that decision is to *improve relations* with Russia and China in general, and the former in particular. NATO's failure to discuss Kosovo in detail with Russia was a breach of the 1997 NATO Russia Founding Act. Relations with Russia were severely strained over the matter of NATO enlargement but this subject no longer has the driving force it once had. The new NATO states of the Czech Republic, Hungary and Poland have not achieved the requisite standard of training, equipment or doctrine to be interoperable with the rump of NATO's forces. The problem is compounded by the fact that these three newly joined NATO states were reluctant supporters of the Kosovo conflict and, domestically, their support for NATO has substantially declined. The situation in the states waiting to be invited to join is no better. There is a general conclusion in NATO Headquarters that the Partnership for Peace programme more than adequately satisfies the needs and aspirations of states seeking a closer affiliation with NATO. There is the reality that a Congress beguiled by Clinton and Albright's rhetoric into agreeing to the admission of the Czech Republic, Hungary and Poland into NATO is unlikely to repeat that mistake.

Whereas the Kosovo experience did emphasise the military and political weakness of Russia and China, it also emphasised their capacity to generate problems. Kosovo provided a green light for Russia to intervene in Chechnya II and, what is more, demonstrated that she is not casualty averse. Moscow had a new President determined to restore the pride and prestige of Russia. How President Putin would respond to a tranche of NATO enlargement, which might include the Baltic states, is not worth second guessing. The need for NATO to rebuild its relations with Russia was one unequivocal lesson to emerge from the Kosovo experience. There were others: for example the relationship between the NATO members' political and military representation was so hesitant and out of harmony as to have an adverse effect upon the decision-making processes, the coordination of intelligence and the drawing up of collaborated plans.

There is then the question of America's leadership of NATO. In an attempt to justify NATO's continuing *raison d'être* post-Cold War, Washington seized upon the opportunity of an humanitarian problem and turned the problem into a crisis. The resultant juggling act in keeping 19 disparate states on-side owed its success to the team members' determination that NATO must not be seen to fail rather than upon the merits of the Kosovo situation. Few of the participants saw a national *interest* in their involvement in Kosovo or had their national *consciences* profoundly stimulated. Almost without exception, however, NATO member states regarded the preservation of NATO to be a national interest. It was a case, therefore, of bureaucratic politics rather than a politico-military strategic objective. With such a skewed point of focus, it is not surprising that America experienced many and various difficulties which, in relation to the conduct of the conflict, were not universally interest driven.

It would be unwise to take the Kosovo example as a precedent because invariably the presence of a national interest in a conflict in which nationals will be put in a position of jeopardy is a *sine qua non.* Compare, for example, the Gulf Conflict's successful *ad hoc* coalition with NATO's brittle and often dysfunctional alliance. There is now a broadly held view in Washington that the UN mandate and the legitimacy it affords is valuable; so valuable as to require a review of relations with Russia and China - both UN Security Council permanent members. The act of by-passing Russia's and China's veto in the Security Council represented a highly visual degradation of their power and was hardly conducive to winning over and influencing those states. It is as well to remember the adage that it is the crisis which creates the coalition.

9 East Timor and Sierra Leone – A Coming of Age

UN Operations in East Timor and Sierra Leone are worthy of comparison for, despite the contrast in scale, they demonstrate the essential difference between UN-sanctioned and UN-sponsored operations.

Indonesia's necklace of 13,677 islands stretches from Thailand's southern border to Irian Jaya, linking the continents of Asia and Australia and canalising sea traffic passing to and from the Indian and Pacific oceans. It is the world's fourth most populous state, 200 million people of whom 80 per cent are Muslim, mostly Sunni. Eighty-seven per cent of the population lives on the fifth largest island, Java.[1]

President Suharto's departure in 1998 after 32 years of authoritative rule led to widespread forecasts of doom and disaster within this fractious state. Suharto had been to Indonesia what Tito had been to the Balkans. His demise gave rise to the same fears of decoupling which afflicted the Balkans. The Association of South East Asian Nations (ASEAN) was founded in 1967, the year after President Suharto seized power. A core purpose had been to bond Indonesia into a political alliance in order to foster regional harmony. ASEAN was not and is not a security organisation. The concept of non-intervention remains paramount among a group of states whose principal security concerns are internal rather than external.

East Timor was a former Portuguese colony, predominantly Christian. Its population is over eighty per cent Roman Catholic - the Muslim minority are, for the most part, *transmigrassi*, those who were given land to settle in East Timor by Suharto. In 1975, Indonesia invaded and seized East Timor with the tacit support of the USA and Australia. This was an action which posed problems in the lead-up to and during the 1999 intervention but the USA's and Australia's decision was not at all surprising since both states had been actively involved in campaigning in Indo-China. Therefore, at the time, it had been a pragmatic gesture set against a backdrop of the sight and sound of tumbling dominoes throughout South East Asia.

Independence aspirations were not confined to East Timor but were also apparent among other communities in Aceh, Irian Jaya, Maluccu and Riau although East Timor had the loosest ties to Indonesia proper. As *The Economist* pointed out, 'legally, historically and morally, East Timor is a different nation'.[2] The general consensus was that the new President, Bacharuddin Jusuf (B.J.) Habibie, would be unable to contain the many aspirations for independence, which in turn would give rise to the appearance of the forces of the status quo - the military. The military view was that to appease one independence group would set in train an unstoppable process which would disconnect and destroy the state of Indonesia. Provocatively, the departure of Suharto saw a rising demand for independence, particularly in East Timor.

The East Timor relationship with the parent state was different from that which existed between Kosovo and Belgrade. The Christian/Muslim antipathy in terms of oppressor and oppressed was the reverse and, whereas Belgrade was the *de jure* capital of Kosovo, Jakarta was only a *de facto* capital of East Timor.

East Timor is on the eastern half of the island of Timor: the western part belongs unarguably to Indonesia. East Timor has a population of approximately 800,000. It is therefore a small territory, half the size of Kosovo and more rugged - a difficult area in which to exercise operational control. Its capital, Dili, is 392 nautical miles from Darwin. Australia's attitude and willingness to take action in East Timor were of inestimable importance. She was the indispensable actor, not out of a sense of altruism but strategic pragmatism. Every country needs an enemy to keep its armed forces up to the mark and, whereas Indonesia was not an enemy *per se,* any threat to Australia's security would almost certainly come through the Indonesian islands to the north. Serious problems in East Timor would therefore impinge upon Australia's strategic interest since a stable and peaceful Indonesia was essential to Australia's peace of mind. Not surprisingly, therefore, Canberra keeps a watchful eye on developments in Indonesia. A contributory factor in the political decision-making process was the presence of a significant body of people of East Timorese origin domiciled in Australia.

Officials close to B.J. Habibie have recounted how he decided at 1.30 one morning to allow a referendum for East Timor to decide its future. This allegedly followed a telephone call from Australian Prime Minister John Howard who is said to have inspired the decision. Moreover, few members of the government were aware of the decision before it was announced and there was no internal support for this unilateral whim of the President. Habibie's announcement also surprised the East Timorese political leadership who admitted that the country was not ready for independence. If Habibie had attempted to build a consensus in Jakarta for the East Timor referendum he would have failed. Making his decision a *fait accompli* proved to be the most effective, probably the only, course of action. The armed forces in particular were furious with the President and repeatedly insisted that most East Timorese wanted to remain part of Indonesia. The President replied that that was precisely the purpose of the referendum. A majority of Indonesia's population believed that the East Timorese would vote to remain part of Indonesia.

The United Nations monitored the 30 August 1999 referendum. The presence of the United Nations Mission in East Timor (UNAMET) was heavily circumscribed by Indonesian conditions. The small UN force had no authority to be armed, their protection being the responsibility of the Indonesians. The UN was fully aware of the implicit dangers but was obliged to acquiesce and accept the risk, for failure to do so would have meant no referendum. One observer noted how the UN mission in East Timor 'is now fully staffed with about 900 personnel, yet it does not manage to make a show of force robust enough to intimidate possible assailants so that its real job - monitoring the referendum - can go ahead'.[3] In fact the referendum passed off quietly. It was only after the result had been announced that UNAMET was found unequal to the task. Eighty per cent of the electorate (of whom ninety-eight per cent voted) voted for independence. After the election results were released, serious and sustained outbreaks of violent disorder broke out throughout East Timor. The UN had no contingency plans. The scale of the disorder was predicted by a number of sources but unanticipated by the UN.

There had been an agreement in May 1999 between Indonesia and Portugal (recognised by the UN as the administering power of East Timor) that law and order duties in the former colony were to be undertaken by the civilian police and not by the 20,000-strong Indonesian Army. There were reports during May of rampaging pro-integration militia factions, with the support of the Army, terrorising the East Timorese. 'Indonesia's civilian government promises the Timorese due process, but its military arm appears ready to pre-empt the offer by force. Whether the inconsistency proceeds from artificial or from real internal conflict is uncertain.'[4] The problem was that the indigenous police force was incapable of maintaining law and order and the Indonesian Army was content to point out - in the face of serious, ongoing rioting, looting and arson - that they had no mandate to intervene. It was soon very apparent that the militia was continuing to play a leading role in provoking and carrying out violent protest. In the face of this anarchy and violence the UN hurriedly withdrew, leaving Secretary-General Kofi Annan to admit that 'many people believe the UN has abandoned the people of East Timor in their greatest hour of need'.

An estimated 400,000 East Timorese fled the towns and villages while their homes and property were set on fire by militia members in an orgy of destruction. The international community seemed disinclined to take action which, coming so soon after the breakthrough in Kosovo, gave rise to claims of double standards. Kosovo had appeared to indicate that when two key principles of international order - state sovereignty and protecting human rights - conflicted, then the latter would take precedence. During this interregnum in East Timor, it seemed that the concept of state sovereignty was being favoured because the capable powers were unprepared to move without Indonesia's consent. 'Behaving as if we need Indonesia's consent to protect the East Timorese discredits the United Nations and its leading member nations, whose commitment to human rights now looks scandalously selective', wrote Professor Stanley Hoffman.[5] The UN can only do what its membership empowers it to do, as was evident when Kofi Annan wrote:

> The tragedy of East Timor, coming so soon after that of Kosovo, has focused attention once again on the need for timely intervention by the international community when death and suffering are being inflicted on large numbers of people, and when the state nominally in charge is unable or unwilling to stop it.[6]

Consent therefore once again loomed large but, this time, as a factor in putative interventionist operations. But such an operation in East Timor against murderous bands of militia would not be phrased in terms of Chapter VI but under the strongest terms of a Chapter VII mandate. The issue here was a case of *realpolitik.* Australia was fully prepared to lead an intervention into East Timor. It was an Antipodean form of manifest destiny. Contingency plans had been discussed with likely partners months previously, including the United Kingdom which has considerable business interests in Indonesia. But Canberra was fully aware that whereas such coalition partners could come and go, Australia was an immovable regional component. Australia's relationship with Indonesia is an important bilateral relationship but whereas Indonesia is of considerable strategic importance to Australia, the reverse is not the case. There were also going to be other regional sensitivities from other Muslim states, notably Malaysia. Prime Minister John Howard recognised something had to be done and that Australia would have to take the lead, but not without Indonesia's consent. Moreover, Canberra was keen, for strategic and political reasons, that a UK presence was on the ground in East Timor from Day 1. This was a beneficial learning experience for the UK's interventionist machinery which would soon be called upon to make a significantly larger commitment to Sierra Leone.

The civilian pro-integration militia groups resembled Rwanda's *Interahamwe* Hutu militia. Their attacks had little semblance of military order but were more to do with mob engagements in which the men were characteristically armed with machetes, knives, spears and axes. Some home-made weapons were seen and, on occasions, the mob was loaned army rifles for the duration of specific short engagements. These militia groups were originally formed by the Indonesian army in order to foster the deceptive impression that there was wider public support for integration than was the case. In fact, so sparse was the level of support that recruits had to be moved in from West Timor. These civilian pro-integration groups, which had been active since September 1998, were not part of the formal security system. The militia that is an integral part of the formal security apparatus is the WANRA or People's Resistance and Security units. WANRA stands for *Pahlawanan Rakyat* (People's Heroes) and is a constituent part of the nationwide Trained Populace programme, a form of territorial army comprising trained civilians used to augment the Indonesian army on security, policing, intelligence and counter-insurgency duties. WANRA, joined by KAMRA (*Keamanan Rakyat* or People's Security), was legally armed by the army and, unlike the civilian mob, was reasonably well trained. As immigrants from West Timor, they were passionate stakeholders in the maintenance of the status quo in East Timor.

The political impasse was broken on 15 September 1999 when Indonesia eventually conceded to the UN permission to select peacekeepers for the East Timor mission. The decision gave rise to widespread rioting throughout Indonesia. A sitting defence parliamentary committee in Jakarta urged the government to blackball America, Australia, New Zealand and Portugal on the grounds that they were not impartial. But the enabling UN Resolution 1264 of 15 September 1999, calling on the UN force 'to restore peace and security', was framed under Chapter VII. The UN had approved a military intervention into East Timor, not a peacekeeping operation, authorising the members of the International Force East Timor (INTERFET) to shoot guerrillas on sight rather than only in self-defence. Australian Prime Minister John Howard threatened that attacks on INTERFET by Indonesians would be met by 'a much stronger level of intervention and retaliation'.[7] Australia had the presentational difficulty of persuading the Indonesians that the assembling coalition was not an invasion force. INTERFET represented the first occasion Australia had assembled and deployed an intervention force as a sanctioned operation of the UN. The action was a visible manifestation of Australia's coming of age. Canberra knew that their bilateral relationship with Indonesia would suffer as a result. In that respect, for Australia, INTERFET was also an exercise in damage limitation.

Some commentators have suggested that the UN Security Council agreed to the East Timor mission because, cognisant of the Kosovo model, an intervention could and would proceed even without their authorisation. That is an over-simplification. The United States was never opposed to an East Timor intervention, just against American ground forces being involved. Russia and China, whose opposition to the Kosovo intervention undermined its legitimacy, supported the East Timor intervention. China went so far as to make police available. Russia no doubt remembered Jakarta's hostility to the Indonesian Communist Party and China would have recalled the numerous attacks upon the Overseas Chinese by resentful Indonesians.

Australia nominated as the UN commander Major-General Peter Cosgrove who, at the age of 21, won a Military Cross in Vietnam. General Cosgrove was the commander of Australia's First Division and Deployable Force Headquarters based in Brisbane, Queensland. An authorised manning level of 9,500 international troops was set, significantly fewer than KFOR. Numbers of troops drawn from contributing states and deployed in East Timor, off-shore aboard ships or playing a direct support role in Darwin[8] were: Australia 5,570, New Zealand 1,053, Thailand 656, France 544, Korea 419, USA 399, Canada 306, UK 285, Singapore 270, Philippines 246, Italy 69, Brazil 51, Southern Ireland 34, Malaysia 30, Germany 5 and Norway 4. Major-General Songkitti Jaggabatra was nominated second-in-command. He and General Cosgrove flew into Dili on 19 September for consultation with the Indonesian army and the next day the first troops began to arrive in Dili. The Indonesian army was officially cooperating with INTERFET which was in East Timor by invitation of the Indonesian government. The well-trained Indonesian army posed no direct threat to

INTERFET. Any covert assistance provided to the militias would be denied and the loan of weapons was effectively discouraged due to the risk of those weapons being identified as having links with Indonesia.

While General Cosgrove's Brisbane Division honed up on the specialist skills that would be required in East Timor, representatives of the humanitarian agencies assembled in Darwin to the north. There was therefore *ab initio* a considerable geographical division between the two disciplines and the resultant conflict of interests was unsurprising. General Cosgrove's plan was: first, to restore peace and security; second, to protect and support UNAMET which still had a presence in East Timor; and third, to facilitate humanitarian assistance within the force's capability. When the Indonesian army withdrew they left a law and order vacuum which INTERFET and UNAMET were obliged to fill. The General's concept of operations was heavily influenced by his Vietnam experience. He intended to establish a security zone, build up his base and logistics and establish a patrolling programme thereby dominating territory sequentially. The General's cautious approach was influenced by reports of significant numbers of militia in camps in West Timor forming-up to attack INTERFET. There was no such threat, which serves to underline the importance of good quality intelligence on such missions. According to one regional expert, the General's 'fear of casualties and lack of decision and vision restricted everyone. He should have prevented more killings. As it was, over ninety per cent of all habitable dwellings were destroyed'. Commanders, however, have to deal with situations as they appear at the time and are conditioned by their own training and experience.

There was a view among the military that their force structure was not adequate to allow them to provide immediate assistance to the humanitarian agencies. For their part, the restless agencies believed the priority to be the avoidance of an epidemic among the internally displaced. The humanitarian agencies were particularly aggrieved to observe that in terms of priorities, the media preceded humanitarian aid in order of importance. The truth is more to do with the reality that the media, who travel light, are easier to accommodate than humanitarians and their support baggage. Reporters were flown into Dili while humanitarian agency people impatiently bided their time in Darwin.

The media were critical of the emphasis General Cosgrove placed upon force protection because it appeared to isolate the military from the East Timorese. There was no shortage of media representatives to pass such impressions back to their editors. At one time there were 250 UK media representatives in East Timor - as many as the number of Gurkha troops deployed there. (Although the Gurkha presence was confined to one company flown in from Brunei, they arrived acclimatised and highly trained, particularly in jungle warfare. Moreover, their mere presence put the fear of God into the militias. It is becoming a recurring feature how quality can often be more profitable than quantity.) The consensus among the press was that the military should have managed the risk rather than have attempted so single-mindedly to eliminate it. Protection was not provided for unaccredited journalists.

When General Cosgrove sat down to work out with the Indonesian army the plan for their withdrawal, he was involved in the same process General Jackson had initiated with the Yugoslav army, with the resultant production of the Military Technical Agreement (MTA). Concurrently, the combat arms slowly and surely eradicated the militia threat, leaving the way clear for the UN to reinforce UNAMET. Once the Indonesian army had been withdrawn, the militia disarmed and, peace and security restored, the way was clear for the East Timorese themselves politically to consider and plan for their future. One of the most urgent problems to tackle was the eighty per cent unemployment in the country. In order to help them, a new Security Council Resolution 1272 of 25 October 1999, framed under Chapter VII of the UN Charter, established a United Nations Transitional Administration in East Timor (UNTAET). UNTAET had a wide-ranging, protective mandate: to provide security and maintain law and order throughout the territory of East Timor, to establish an effective administration, to assist in the development of civil and social services, to ensure the coordination and delivery of humanitarian assistance, to support capacity-building for self-government and to assist in the establishment of conditions for sustainable development. UNTAET's Charter looks very much as though a UN Protectorate had been established but UNTAET has a short mandate. Perhaps ASEAN will admit East Timor to its ranks, thus bringing the country into the South and East Asian family of nations.

INTERFET had been described as a 'peacekeeping' mission. It was not. It was a conflict operation in which the warring militias were effectively engaged. It was therefore an Implementation Operation which only became a peacekeeping mission once the security situation permitted, thus showing how these missions can move up and down the spectrum of military options. It has been estimated that 700 East Timorese lost their lives post-referendum. To put that tragedy into perspective, that is approximately one tenth of the loss of life in protests in Ambon where, of course, there was no significant coverage by the international media. Religious conflict had increased substantially in Maluccu and Sulawesi where there was evidence of direct intervention of *Laskar Jihad*, the militant Islamic movement of Indonesia. A cabinet minister drew attention to how well armed the militants were, adding: 'The only source of guns in Indonesia is the Army'. During the East Timor campaign, the British trialled many of their rapid deployment and command and control techniques. The same commander and Headquarters that had cut their teeth in East Timor ran the much larger commitment in Sierra Leone. Conceptually, the PJHQ had come of age.

When the West African state of Sierra Leone achieved its independence from Britain in 1961 after 174 years of colonial rule, its future looked rosy. One of the smallest countries in Africa - smaller than Scotland - it has significant mineral resources which, in theory, should have provided a good life for its 4.5 million population. As is the case with Angola, not only does the country have a great wealth of diamonds in the north and east but also extensive reserves of bauxite and iron ore. 'Sierra Leone', said *The Economist*,

> manifests all the continent's worst characteristics. It is an extreme, but not untypical example of a state with all the epiphenomena and none of the institutions of government... It is unusual only in its brutality: rape, cannibalism and amputation have been common, with children often among the victims.[9]

The life expectancy of the Sierra Leone population is 49 years; it is among the poorest of the world's states and has the world's worst healthcare.

A major contributory factor towards the Sierra Leoneans now being among the poorest in the world is down to one man, Foday Sankoh. Sankoh became leader of the Revolutionary United Front (RUF) in January 1991. He had come to prominence earlier when, as a corporal photographer, he accused the government of neglecting the army. As an unreformable barrack-room lawyer he spoke up in the name of other ranks and received a jail sentence of seven years for his trouble. After serving five he went to Libya, returning in 1991 embittered by prison and airing wide-ranging grievances that the government was corrupt, tribal and not running the country in a democratic manner. In that respect he was correct in so far as the government had victimised its opponents who were liable for arbitrary arrest and occasional disappearance. The RUF was originally part of Liberian President Charles Taylor's National Patriotic Front. For eight years, Sankoh led a war against all-comers in Sierra Leone. It was not an ideologically-driven crusade but one based upon a settling of scores by taking control of the country's diamond resources. Sankoh argued that the gap between the rich and poor was too large, having in mind the 'fat cats' on the Peninsula. The conflict in Sierra Leone had begun in March 1991 when the RUF launched an attack into Sierra Leone from the east, close to the Liberian border, aimed at overthrowing the government.

In 1996, Ahmed Tejan Kabbah,[10] leader of Sierra Leone's People's Party, became the democratically elected President of Sierra Leone, only to be deposed the next year in another military coup engineered by an officer sympathetic to the RUF. The army joined with the RUF to form a ruling junta, the Armed Forces Revolutionary Council (AFRC). The Commonwealth suspended Sierra Leone from the organisation and the UN imposed sanctions upon the country. However, a British-based mercenary organisation, Sandline International, with the knowledge of Britain's Foreign and Commonwealth Office was supplying arms to the government of Sierra Leone in contravention of the UN embargo. The laudable outcome had been a contribution to the return of the democratically-elected President Kabbah on 10 March 1998. When Sandline's involvement became known, it caused considerable embarrassment to the architect of Britain's ethically flavoured foreign policy, Robin Cook. Cook entered a plea of plausible deniability; he had not been told what his subordinates were doing. Sankoh, who was responsible for thousands of deaths and mutilations, was first captured in 1998 and sent into exile in neighbouring Togo by the Nigerians who were then leading the military operation in Sierra Leone, the Ecowas Monitoring Group (ECOMOG). A Freedom Court sentenced Sankoh to death *in absentia.*

In June 1998, the Security Council established the United Nations Observer Mission in Sierra Leone (UNOMSIL). UNOMSIL's observers were unarmed, being dependent upon ECOMOG for their protection. ECOMOG's presence in Sierra Leone was vital for on 6 January 1999 the RUF again invaded Freetown. UNOMSIL personnel were evacuated, leaving ECOMOG to clear the city and reinstate President Kabbah.

The death sentence against Sankoh was never carried out. On the contrary, the British government persuaded President Kabbah to rehabilitate Sankoh. Cook is said to have recommended that Sankoh, far more barbarous and extreme than Milosevic, should be pardoned and receive immunity from prosecution for his crimes against humanity. Moreover, it was proposed that he should be appointed vice-president and given a Cabinet position - unbelievably, Minister for Natural Resources, thereby making him responsible for the diamond resources. Allegedly the mines provided Sankoh with $90 million (£60 million) with which to pay his adherents. The political arrangements were formalised in the Lomé Peace Agreement of 7 July 1999, and UN Security Council Resolution 1270 of 22 October 1999 provided for the creation of the United Nations Mission in Sierra Leone (UNAMSIL) to monitor the process of the agreement and disarmament. UNOMSIL was terminated by the Security Council. UNAMSIL took over its duties. Sankoh flattered the optimists in London and New York with a token, partial disarmament, but retained sufficient arms and weapons with which to continue to terrorise and intimidate those outside his group. The RUF received support from Charles Taylor, the President of Liberia whither Sierra Leone's diamonds were being smuggled. Sankoh supported President Taylor's seizure of power in Liberia and it was the diamonds coming from Sierra Leone which helped Taylor to maintain his position.

UN Security Council Resolution 1270 was framed under Chapter VII and attracted for its policing essentially African and Asian troops of a standard required to monitor a peacekeeping agreement where the consent of both parties was in place. The better trained Indians and Nigerians were exceptions to this rule. It was not long before the parties to the Lomé agreement disputed its terms and conditions, thus completely undermining Resolution 1270 upon which it was based. The withdrawal of consent of one party and the support the UN provided to the other made a nonsense of two of the essential criteria of peacekeeping, namely *consent* and *impartiality*. Although mandated by reference to Chapter VII, the conditions of Resolution 1270 were pacific and what might be expected of a peacekeeping force. UNAMSIL was not authorised to 'use all necessary means' but:

> UNAMSIL may take the necessary action to ensure the security and freedom of movement of its personnel and, within its capabilities and areas of deployment, to afford protection to civilians under imminent threat of physical violence, taking into account the responsibilities of the Government of Sierra Leone and ECOMOG.

'If the UN Security Council hesitates in changing the mandate, ECOWAS countries may be forced to go on their own in Sierra Leone with a peace enforcement mandate', said the head of ECOWAS, Lansasa Kouyate. UNAMSIL's mandate in effect was restricted to using force in self-defence, to defending the capital, to protecting civilians and to aiding operations. Only the last proviso could be interpreted as permitting offensive operations against the RUF. However, UNAMSIL chose not to interpret Resolution 1270 in the manner intended. In the Chapter VI rather than Chapter VII tradition, the UN would only use lethal force if attacked. 'The Lomé Agreement cannot bring peace to Sierra Leone', said a senior UN official. 'Certain parts cannot be implemented, they need to be rewritten by the Sierra Leone government and the RUF'. Another added, 'the RUF understood fully what they were doing when they signed up to Lomé but they do not have the people to guide them with the due processes. Too much emphasis is being placed upon the military aspects of the agreement and insufficient upon the political'.

The emphatic withdrawal of the RUF's consent to parts of the Lomé agreement and the discovery of a number of murdered peacekeepers implied that no longer could the 'peacekeepers' act impartially. UNAMSIL was a peacekeeping operation in name only. Sankoh, however, had a separate agenda to keep the diamond wealth to himself and to take over the country. It was in May 2000 that the last vestige of a personal political fig leaf was removed. Sankoh knew his cohorts had once ruled Sierra Leone and he intended to be President. The RUF had no political organisation in so far as it could not claim to have been a shadow government. It was a collection of bush chiefs who had lost political interest. The weak 8,300-strong UN force did not have the presence or capabilities to intimidate the RUF who systematically seized a large number of UN men and disarmed them. 'The United Nations is not very good at using force', said a Freetown businessman, 'and, believe me, the RUF knows that. That's why the UN can't win'.[11] The RUF had soon captured 500 UN peacekeepers, thereby hugely embarrassing the UN and bringing into question once again the viability of peacekeeping in Africa and elsewhere. Sankoh's 'seizure of the UN battalions that were operating the demobilisation camps follows directly from their success in providing a way out for boy soldiers and other villagers conscripted by the RUF', reported a *Times* editorial. 'His commanders saw their private armies melting away; his fellow smugglers suspected that the UN operation would eventually cut off their supply of diamonds.'[12]

The irony of these developments is that they could possibly have been avoided if Sandline and the South African-based mercenary organisation Executive Outcomes had been permitted to act on behalf of the Sierra Leone government. A military solution might have been achievable at a cost of $20-30 million whereas by December 2000 the cost to the UK alone exceeded $150 million. Some serious thought must now be turned to the circumstances in which mercenary forces might be supported in the interest of a desirable outcome, particularly when states are reluctant to put supporting troops on the ground.

UN Secretary-General Kofi Annan realised that if Sankoh was permitted to force upon the UN the kind of humiliating withdrawal seen in Mogadishu in 1993, the UN's credibility would count for nothing. He appealed to the United States, the United Kingdom and France to send rapid reaction forces into Sierra Leone. 'We know that the international community and the western countries were not ready to go to Rwanda', said Annan, 'and after Sierra Leone I think there's going to be very little encouragement for any of them to get involved in Africa'. The United States, the United Kingdom and France, the three states with plausible rapid reaction capabilities, declined Annan's initial invitation to put combat troops into Sierra Leone. On Friday 5 May, British Foreign Secretary Cook said that the UK would only be providing technical and logistical support to the UN.

The news of the RUF's advance on Freetown placed the British Government in a difficult position. This was a crisis partly of their own making. Already an initial £60m ($90m) had been injected into this Commonwealth country to prop it up. Whereas the Commonwealth continued to underperform as a serious international organisation, Britain, as the former colonial power, had a residual obligation to act. The same was also true of the concurrent Zimbabwe crisis. There were additional, compelling reasons for the British Government to take rapid action in Sierra Leone. The support given to the Sandline mercenaries[13] provided the party's left-wing element with a stick with which to beat New Labour, a government which in February 2000 had been the subject of valid criticism for having been slow to respond to the humanitarian flood crisis in Mozambique. Nevertheless, anticipatory contingency action was put in hand.

At 10am on 5 May 2000, Britain's Joint Task Force Headquarters' (JTFHQ's) commander, Brigadier David Richards, was ordered to deploy to Freetown to be prepared to oversee the evacuation of British, Commonwealth and EU nationals from the country, which in military parlance is known as Non-Combatant Evacuation Operations (NEO). The Brigadier's Operational Liaison and Reconnaissance Team (OLRT) is, as its name suggests, as much a reconnaissance as an operations organisation. Reviews are constantly being made of emerging hot spots. A NEO had been practised in Sierra Leone over Christmas 1998 and two operations were conducted there in 1999.

Kofi Annan's linkage of rapid reaction to the Rwanda situation had been apposite. As a concept, rapid reaction is in vogue, as is evidenced by the movement in Europe towards a rapid reaction capability. Rapid, however, is a relative term. During the lead-up to the Rwanda crisis, the UN had also attempted to have forces on standby in order to move rapidly to implement the Glass of Water strategy. The UN Standby Arrangement System (UNSAS) was introduced in 1993 with a view to increasing the speed with which troops could deploy on UN operations. UNSAS was a database containing details of military units of member states available in principle to the UN for short-notice missions. In April 1994 the details of the armed forces of 19 member states were on the database, available provisionally to the UN. When called to help Rwanda they all declined. What the database did achieve was a swifter than usual, negative response. After the failure of UNSAS it was decided to establish the High Readiness Brigade (SHIRBRIG), to be made available to the UN in appropriate circumstances. There were to be designated components from what are essentially those states normally associated with traditional Chapter VI Peacekeeping. Provision was made for command and control, standardised training and the adoption of Standard Operating Procedures (SOPs).

SHIRBRIG made no move towards East Timor or Sierra Leone. When M. Bernard Miyet,[14] Head of the UN's Department of Peacekeeping Operations (DPKO), was asked to account for this inaction, his Military Adviser, Lieutenant General Giulio Fraticelli, replied:

> There are two issues related to the employment of SHIRBRIG. Firstly, it is not an entity that is currently under the control of the UN. Each deployment needs the approval of the individual contributors. Secondly, the current advice we have from SHIRBRIG is that it will only be made available for operations mandated under Chapter VI of the UN Charter, although we believe the SHIRBRIG nations are reviewing this policy. The mission in Sierra Leone, UNAMSIL, is mandated under Chapter VII of the Charter (enforcement).[15]

Since Chapter VI peacekeeping is initiated after the due diplomatic process and with the consent of the parties involved, it is arguably the precise circumstance when there is no requirement for rapid reaction.

The British government's positive initial response to the Sierra Leone crisis stood out in stark comparison to the zero response of SHIRBRIG. A number of JTFHQ officers moved alongside the planners of the Operations Team (OT) in PJHQ to enhance the understanding between PJHQ and its subordinate HQ. Eight hours after being given orders to deploy 3,500 miles to the south, the OLRT comprising eight key officers was in the air, arriving at Lungi International Airport midday Saturday 6 May. Lungi Airport is separated from the capital Freetown by a five mile wide strip of water. The two are connected by a strategic, 75 mile long, horseshoe-shaped road, two thirds of which, in May, were susceptible to RUF interference. On reviewing the situation where the Nigerians had stopped the RUF advance at Waterloo, Brigadier Richards requested PJHQ to release immediately the lead Company of the Spearhead Land Element followed by the remainder of the Group. NEO could not be properly effected without helicopter support. Four CH-47 Chinooks were ordered to Sierra Leone via Gibraltar, Tenerife, Mauritania and Dakar. The first pair arrived during the evening of Sunday 7 May to support NEO, only 30 hours after being tasked. 'We are sending British troops to sort out a mess that is largely created by British politicians', argued *The Spectator*'s Boris Johnson, 'as was the case in Kosovo, which was a disaster at least partly caused by Cook and Albright'.[16]

Meanwhile, the concurrent political and military activity upon which a successful rapid reaction to a crisis is founded moved on apace. On 7 May, orders were sent from London to re-deploy Royal Navy assets to ensure ships were 'going in the right direction' if circumstances should prove necessary. The Amphibious Ready Group (ARG) led by the helicopter carrier *HMS Ocean* received orders to sail from Marseilles, to make for Gibraltar and thence south, down the West African coast. The ARG spends up to six months of the year at sea in the Mediterranean. In addition to *HMS Ocean*, the group comprised the Type 22 frigate *HMS Chatham*, no stranger to Sierra Leone waters, two Royal Fleet Auxiliary (RFA) landing ships and a replenishment ship. Embarked in *HMS Ocean* was the 600-strong 42 Royal Marine Commando Group with heavier weapon support than was available to the Spearhead Battalion, the 1st Battalion the Parachute Regiment.[17] In the event of close air support being required, the carrier *HMS Illustrious* with seven Sea Harriers and six GR7 Harriers aboard and accompanied by a RFA ship were ordered to make for the West African coast from Lisbon.[18]

On Monday 8 May, Lungi Airport had been secured. 1 Para Group, together with B Squadron SAS which was operating further forward under a separate SF component commander answerable directly to the JTFC, set about the domination of their tactical areas of responsibility. Rapid reaction becomes progressively less relevant and effective the longer it takes ground forces to dominate the territory into which they have been inserted. Within 36 hours, the paras were on operations in the unbenign environment of Sierra Leone. They faced a drugged-up, well armed guerrilla force intent upon inflicting casualties upon the newly arrived troops in order to stimulate the kind of withdrawal seen in Mogadishu in 1993 and Kigali in 1994. The principal difference between Sierra Leone's militias and those seen in Rwanda and East Timor was that the former had large numbers of rifles, many in the hands of unwilling children. In addition, the British were not acclimatised. Moreover, they could never be fully protected against malaria which is endemic in Sierra Leone. But military success can rarely be seized without the taking of calculated risks. Troops were trained to recognise the symptoms and to take action accordingly. Of the 4,500 deployed, approximately 80 men contracted mild forms of malaria.

Two hundred and ninety-nine expatriates were evacuated from Sierra Leone in the first 48 hours but the calming influence brought about by the force's arrival stemmed the flow of civilians seeking repatriation. By now, the OLRT had become JTFHQ and Brigadier Richards, the JTFC, faced up to the reality that his NEO mission had been completed. Loath to offend his political masters by entering freely into a whole new regime of mission creep, the Brigadier nevertheless had to face the reality that his withdrawal would undermine the UN mission and possibly see the fall of the democratically elected government of Sierra Leone. The adoption of a new, twin-track approach to a revised mission, in the best tradition of mission-oriented orders, was endorsed by the British government a number of days after it was unavoidably implemented in Sierra Leone. 'We must not allow a few thousand rebels to prevent an end to violence', declared Foreign Secretary Cook. 'His judgement', said *The Times*, 'may be unduly influenced by his earlier bruising over Sierra Leone'.[19] In fact, it was the unfolding situation on the ground which dictated his course of action but one that could have a beneficial outcome. 'Robin Cook must be presumed', opined *The Times*, 'if only to reverse his earlier humiliation in Sierra Leone and his frustration at not being able to stop the rot in Zimbabwe, to be the Cabinet member nearest to score a "success" in Sierra Leone'.[20]

The success of the British Operation Palliser was largely due to respective commanders at the tactical and operational levels being entirely focused upon their own responsibilities. At the tactical level, the paras pressed on, keen to engage in the business for which they had been trained, until relieved in place by the Commandos on 26 May 2000. 42 Commando withdrew on 15 June 2000, leaving behind a profoundly more confident

UN, a bolstered President and a modest training team to expedite the training of the Sierra Leone Army.

The JFHQ staff are used to working routinely at the Operational level. The daily police-military (polmil) coordinating meeting established in Freetown had its roots in intervention doctrine prior to the Malaya Emergency. The aim is to penetrate the rebels' decision cycle. Key considerations toward satisfying that aim are: media; legal; tasking of Special Forces; Information Operations; liaison with coalition partners, political and civil agencies; campaign planning and force level logistics. As ever, success depends so much upon the quality of the commander. He has to be a natural leader, the ultimate professional, schooled in combined and joint operations, politically aware (nationally and internationally) and an astute manager of the media.

In this post-Cold War era when, in theory and occasionally in practice, military force can increasingly be utilised in pursuit of foreign policy goals, the number of political actors with their various reasons to wish to influence military operations has increased significantly. There remains the risk at the strategic level therefore, that the JTFC will be bombarded by ministerial questions emanating from Downing Street, the Cabinet Office, Foreign Affairs, Defence and Development. Conceptually it is the Chief of the Defence Staff (CDS) who should absorb such aspirations, interests and concerns and often divergent opinions of the broad political leadership, leaving PJHQ and its JFHQ free to focus upon operations.

Within a few days of arrival, the Joint Task Force Commander, observing the UN's impotence, took upon himself the training and disciplining of the three Sierra Leone battalions with a view to reversing the RUF's advance. In this they were substantially successful in so far as they regained much of the strategic Horseshoe route connecting Freetown to the airport. The role of the 250 trainers and approximately 70 advisers was to maintain momentum and to build an army of nine battalions in three brigades with supporting arms and logistics. The intention was that this national force would eventually take the battle to the RUF, defeating it in its heartland to the east. During the training period, trained elements would maintain the military initiative and, in the event that the UN should go wobbly, secure key terrain. A principal component of the UK exit strategy, especially in information operations terms, was to keep Operation Palliser in being until the UN had been brought up to what was then its mandated strength and capable of deployment into key terrain on the Horseshoe.

There is a very close connection between the methodology developed in Sierra Leone and the immediately post-independence Zimbabwe. The British Government was keen to display a total disconnection between Operation Palliser and the subsequent, substantial training effort. Politically, therefore, the British government had gone full circle in its intention to arm and train Sierra Leone's army. On 19 May, the UN Security Council unanimously approved raising UNAMSIL's ceiling from 11,100 to 13,000 troops, including 260 military observers. Eventually, quantity attracts its own form of quality. Sankoh was captured for a second time but, on this occasion, there was no prospect of immunity being on offer. He had overseen sufficient human rights abuses post-Lomé to qualify for a long term in jail.

Britain's experiment in turning around the poorly-trained Sierra Leone Army is being watched with great interest in the event that it provides a solution to the accumulating problems of the suffering continent of Africa. The international community is used to coming freely to Africa's aid when constituent states are ravaged by climatic disasters which require urgent humanitarian relief. What the international community is far less good at is providing military support in conflict situations. In the year 2000, almost forty per cent of the membership of the Organisation of African Unity (OAU) were engaged in armed conflict. The author vividly recalls a discussion held in Kigali with a Rwandan senior official. 'There's one thing that will sort out this country's problems', he said. 'What's that?' I asked. 'The return of the Belgians.' Brigadier David Richards, commander of British forces in Sierra Leone is on record as having said: 'I am constantly surprised by the number of people who come up to me and ask that Britain recolonises Sierra Leone'.[21] Operation Palliser marked the British PJHQ's coming of age. No longer would the concept of rapid reaction be just an impossible dream. According to Brigadier Richards:

> The real key to success was and will remain the quality and motivation of personnel at every level; a willingness to encourage and use individual and collective initiative; a determination not to be thwarted by inevitable setbacks, matched by a corresponding preparedness to innovate; an inability to accept anything other than excellence in pursuit of assigned tasks; and, as ever, an irrepressible humour that ensures high morale.[22]

The organisation of UNAMSIL followed an established, convoluted UN pattern. First there was the civilian bureaucracy set up in the Mammy Yoko Hotel, Freetown, with an established strength of 230 international and 104 national civilians, to which should be added the locally employed. Second, there were the armed Force Troops,[23] generally formed units at battalion strength. An exception was the Russians who flew the helicopters. Third were 260 unarmed Military Observers[24] and 60 civilian police[25] included in the authorised military strength of 13,000 projected to rise to 20,000.

The first impression of UNAMSIL was that they had settled-in for the duration; there was a sense of inertia, no sense of urgency or incentive to finish the job. There were the trappings of excess. The daily cost rose to $2.1 million (£1.5 million).[26] Everyone appeared to have a personal vehicle and the parks in the front and to the rear of the large hotel were permanently crammed with white four wheel drive vehicles and staff cars. Staff lived very comfortably and yet this was one of the world's poorest countries. If this had been an international company it must surely have gone under. That is not to say that the staff were not dedicated but rather that the direction or coherence seemed not to be there, there was no apparent concept of the end game.

Of the formed units, some were operationally challenged and unable to carry out the mandate. Six years after Rwanda there were still problems with the quality of troops sent on UN operations. 'You must understand', said a UN African official, 'that some states struggle to find the resources to provide just one battalion. That is why we have been pushing for a western presence and resources and why we are so distressed at the poverty of the response'. Jordan cited as the reason for withdrawing her two battalions from UNAMSIL the absence of NATO troops. The UK had a presence in Sierra Leone and a quick reaction capability but no troops were assigned to the UN Force. This was undoubtedly a military rather than a political decision, a matter of lack of confidence in the command and control arrangements. 'It has taken us six months to get everyone on the same radio frequency and speaking English' claimed one UN military officer.

Although the United Kingdom did not form part of UNAMSIL it performed an essential function of buttressing the UN operation and providing effective leverage against the RUF. Within UNAMSIL there was divided opinion as to precisely what the mandate permitted or meant. The undeniable inclination transmitted throughout Sierra Leone was one of disengagement. The attitude of the United Kingdom and her forces was the antithesis of UNAMSIL's passivity. The majority population under Government control applauded Operation Palliser and then again in September 2000 when special forces and paras conducted an audacious raid on a bandit camp to free a number of British soldiers taken hostage. What this action told the RUF was that the UK was not going to allow casualty aversion to inhibit its freedom of operation.[27]

The Sierra Leoneans had mixed opinions as to the value of UNAMSIL. 'Ten weeks have passed and nothing has happened militarily', said one. They respected rather than liked the Nigerians and they valued the Indian contribution which was operationally sound and included a balanced and effective hearts and minds programme. India withdrew her 3,000-strong force after dissent within the UN hierarchy. There was a view that too high a proportion of the military was deployed in Freetown rather than up country where the RUF were. One highly qualified teacher who had not been paid for months said: 'There is something wrong, that here am I with this crucial role of educating the new generation of this reborn country who gets nothing, yet each state whose private soldiers are manning the myriad of road blocks throughout the city receives $145 a day per man'. One UN official described this payment of hard currency as 'a form of foreign aid'.

A conflict of ideas was apparent between Force Troops and Observers in the same way that a lack of harmony was discerned in UNAMSIL HQ between the civilian executive and the military. That is not to say that the Observers were the *crème de la crème* but that they suffered, as is so often the case, from the UN having to find a role for all-comers. Thirty-two countries produced 260 observers and civilian police. When asked how many among that 260 could be considered effective, the answer was 80-90. At Port Loko, 48 miles northwest of Freetown, the centre for Disarmament, Demobilisation and Reintegration (DDR), twenty-five per cent of observers could neither speak English nor drive.

The problem within the hierarchy deserves amplification because it involved representatives of the two most capable UNAMSIL forces and dealt a blow to UNAMSIL's morale, credibility and viability. The general principle has already been established that the major shareholder votes the majority of the stock. It is for this reason that establishing a permanent staff to direct UN-sponsored operations is unworkable, because the Force composition will not be known in advance of the crisis.

When the Indian Major-General Vijay Kumar Jetley was appointed Force Commander, the Indians were the major troop-contributing country, a situation which changed when Nigeria reinforced her UNAMSIL presence. This should not have created a difficulty in this sensitive area of who gets the important jobs because the Special Representative of the Secretary-General (SRSG) and Chief of Mission was a Nigerian, Ambassador Oluyemi Adeniji. Command of Peacekeeping Missions is about creating a coalition consensus so that national commanders comply with the wishes of the Force Commander for the common good, knowing full well that the Force Commander has no full command authority over them. It was not long before General Jetley complained that the Nigerians consistently refused to do what he wished – an oft-repeated complaint from other national commanders throughout UNAMSIL's chain of command.

In May 2000, General Jetley sent a memorandum to UN Headquarters in New York claiming that the SRSG and his Nigerian deputy, Brigadier M.A. Garba, had conspired to force him out with a view to Nigeria controlling UNAMSIL's political and military operations. Moreover, Jetley accused the Nigerians of colluding with the RUF over the illicit diamond trade. Nigerians do have a reputation of accruing additional bonuses from their peacekeeping missions. One Freetown diplomat said of the Nigerians: 'They fight well and they plunder well. They consider it their payment for defeating the rebels'.

The SRSG would obviously have been appraised of the Force Commander's complaint and yet they appear to have worked convivially together until the Jetley memorandum was leaked to a London newspaper in September 2000. By that time Jetley, who had contracted malaria, was convalescing in India. The Nigerian Army Chief of Staff, General Victor Malu, threatened to withdraw his country's troops if Jetley were to continue as Force Commander. The Nigerian presence in Sierra Leone was more important than Jetley's and, in anticipation of UNAMSIL's strength rising to 20,000, the Force and Deputy Force Commanders' ranks were upgraded. The UN was adamant that the Force Commander was not to be a Nigerian and, unusually, appointed a Kenyan as Force Commander, Lieutenant-General Daniel Ishmael Opande, whose deputy, in the rank of Major-General, was a Nigerian and, unusually again since UK had no troops within the Force, the Chief of Staff's post was allocated to a British officer.

A line has been drawn under the ongoing Sierra Leone situation in November 2000. Unilateral peace proposals were being delivered separately to the UN by RUF units notoriously unpredictable and unreliable. By this time Issa Sessay, who had taken over from Sankoh as one of the three warlords involved, had a genuine desire for peace. It was not a desire that was completely shared by his peers who feared a loss of revenue through forfeiting the mines and a loss of liberty through the offices of the War Crimes Tribunal. Nigeria exerted the greatest pressure upon Charles Taylor, President of Liberia, to cease his interference and interest in Sierra Leone. Neighbouring states saw him as a destabilising influence in West Africa, and Nigeria threatened to let loose her army into Liberia. Taylor knew what that involved. The USA placed visa restrictions upon Taylor and his allies. The Sierra Leone Army had two brigades available to take the offensive and the UK's *HMS Ocean* maritime task force was on the horizon off Freetown. These sticks were available in association with any carrots dangled in front of the RUF at the peace conference held in Nigeria on Thursday, 10 November 2000.

Concurrent with the peace conference, Britain conducted a show of military strength, cleared in advance with the UN mission in Sierra Leone. The arrival of warships, attack helicopters and 600 Royal Marines immediately followed the signing of a ceasefire agreement between the Sierra Leonean Government and the RUF. Liberia's Charles Taylor said Britain should leave Sierra Leone and the sabre-rattling was criticised by the UN's acting military commander, Nigerian Brigadier-General Mohammed Garba. Brigadier Garba, who had spoken up for the RUF in the past, told the BBC that the RUF had reason to fear they were being 'tricked into signing a ceasefire while there is another plan'.[28]

There had been so many past failures of UN peacekeeping operations and Secretary-General Kofi Annan staked his reputation on UNAMSIL's success. In an article in *Time* magazine,[29] the Secretary-General espoused his idea of a new moral order where states automatically intervened to help states suffering in humanitarian disasters or armed conflict. These are noble, idealistic sentiments but, as aspirations, they will be rarely deliverable in the real world. Conscience does indeed play a part in the decision-making process whether or not to assist a disadvantaged state but, politically, conscience eventually becomes an interest to be weighed alongside other factors whether help should or should not be given and in what form. The prerequisites for a successful UN mission are confidence, high morale, professionalism, and the various parts of the machinery working in harmony in accordance with an unambiguous mandate. That this was not the case in Sierra Leone indicates that decision-making time has come. Past experience indicates that generally, intervention is likely to have better prospects for success where the UN sanctions another state or organisation to provide the overall framework for the operation. What UNAMSIL reminds us is that it may not always be politically desirable for, say, a regional hegemony to play the role of the framework state. But the UN can be more effective in the prosecution of both sponsored and sanctioned operations by paying due attention to factors which have been closely associated with past failure. Why has the UN failed so consistently in its peacekeeping objectives?

There are a number of reasons why UN missions fail and among those are:

- At the outset, the principal question to ask is not whether the operation is justified but can it succeed? This comes down to a fine judgement but, since the concept of operations should include a statement as to what can be considered to denote the success of the mission, it is not insurmountably difficult. The UN must avoid commencing military operations as though past experience counts for nothing.
- It is essential that the limitations of traditional peacekeeping are fully recognised and that the UN does not habitually drift into areas never intended and for which it is unqualified. Traditional peacekeeping is about policing ceasefire lines, not intervening in other states' civil wars. If there is no peace to be kept, it is not peacekeeping. It is not possible to maintain a position of impartiality in an environment where one party is clearly blameworthy or to adopt a neutral stance in order to avoid confrontation.
- Casualty aversion among contributing states. This reservation would normally preclude states' commitment before the start of the mission but unacceptable casualty levels during an operation can lead to withdrawal. Opponents may well play upon the sensitivity of some states' attitudes to casualties to force their withdrawal from UN operations.
- Weariness of contributors. Weariness or evaporation of will can be generated through a mission lasting longer than imagined, a sense of inequity or through exasperation at not being paid for services rendered.
- The emphasis can be disproportionately focused upon military aspects to the detriment of proper consideration of social, political and economic factors.
- The drafting process of a Resolution within the Security Council can be adversely affected by compromise, with the result that the mandate leaves too much room for creative interpretation.

- Resolutions can set out goals which are unachievable on the ground due to a crisis of comprehension.
- Resolutions can be founded upon peace agreements. If any party to that agreement subsequently reneges, the opportunity for the UN to continue to operate with consent and impartiality will evaporate.
- The Forces for Courses issue manifested in a mismatch of quantity and quality of armed forces to achieve the mission.
- Peacekeeping missions are managed and not commanded in the true sense of the word. National politicians or military representatives of troop-contributing nations have the right to use the red card, to blow the whistle. It is for that reason that the Force Commander needs to be adept at coalition management so that national component commanders trust him and his competence and are prepared to carry out his wishes. If the management of operations is conducted effectively, other aspects have a habit of falling into place.
- The lack of competence among the political and military leadership.
- The political and military leadership being adversely influenced by personal or national considerations.

What both East Timor and Sierra Leone confirm is the absolutely clear distinction between peacekeeping and the conflict environment which we describe as Implementation Operations. Implementation Operations must not be described as peacekeeping because to do so ignores 'forces for courses' ramifications which include due recognition of the balance to be drawn between quality and quantity as well as the additional manning and logistical implications of being able to move up a gear in the level of involvement. Matters such as these will need to be included in a long overdue, relevant new doctrine – not one that exists as a doctrinal colostomy bag but one within the main body of military doctrine. Attention must be paid to the principles of multilateral military intervention in intra-state conflict. There was no United States ground force presence in either conflict. As her contribution towards restoring order in Sierra Leone, the United States instituted a training programme in Nigeria. The Nigerians doubted the Americans could teach them anything but were attracted by the promised $20 million package of equipment. Casualty aversion is a serious problem with which the new administration will have to come to terms. General Morillon pointed out the curiosity of having armed forces that can kill but not be killed, to be 'a globocop without a posse'.

Resolving problems through the use of air power alone will continue to give rise to problems of legitimacy which in part will be due to the calculated avoidance of a Russian or Chinese veto in the Security Council. But as the USA as NATO's hegemonic power discovered, the absence of a UN mandate for Kosovo presented a myriad of command and control difficulties not experienced in the Gulf Conflict which was properly authorised by the UN. Improving relations with both Russia and China seems to be a sensible foreign policy objective. The core reality is that without the active support of the USA, and to a lesser extent that of the United Kingdom and France, the UN is impotent in terms of military operations. The UN represents a community that does not work as a community, hence the prerequisite of the Security Council supporting and being engaged in UN activities. Governments have shamelessly used the UN as a dumping ground for hot potatoes and problems they have to face but do not wish to confront. We have now reached the situation where the scapegoat role, though valuable to governments, has been overdone to the point that it has gravely damaged the UN's reputation, its future effectiveness and its ability to solicit essential support.

Of the USA/UN relationship, one observer wrote:

> Moving the United States and the United Nations back to a place where they can at least coexist in mutual respect will, in the words of one UN official wise in the ways of Washington, require 'a piece of almost Dayton-like shuttle diplomacy'.[30]

There are grounds for optimism. Congress has agreed to pay $926 million of the $1.8 billion due to the UN and the principal parties on both sides involved in the October 1993 Somalia fiasco have disappeared from the scene. Pessimists claim that President Bush the Younger has neither the experience nor interest to set a new standard in international affairs. These claims have been made before in respect of a number of his predecessors. What people do or say whilst in the process of being elected often differs from their behaviour once in office. If the UN can more consistently deal on a day-to-day basis with such a degree of obvious realism and the USA introduce one essential ingredient so long absent from its foreign affairs, then both entities could find the new relationship beneficial. That which has been absent on the American side is political leadership.

The problem we face at the end of this book is twofold. Firstly, it set out as a Realist study of international collective security but ends with a heady dose of Idealism. Second, it identifies the associated urgent need for suitable leadership within the international security system. The most effective source of usable power lies in the USA yet the international community has almost no say in the direction in which that leadership and power are to be channelled. American Domestic and Foreign policies are tightly linked. Is a new Administration which came to power on the promise of lower taxation going to want or be able to embark upon overseas missions where there may be no obvious American interest? The answer is probably not. That is reality.

Select Bibliography

Adams, Guy Vassal. *Rwanda, An Agenda for International Action* (Oxford, 1994).
Allison, Graham T. *Essence of Decision. Explaining the Cuban Missile Crisis* (New York, 1971).
Archer, Clive. *International Organisations* (London, 1983).
Bell, Coral. *The Conventions of Crisis: A Study in Diplomatic Management* (London, 1971).
Boutros-Ghali, Boutros. *Unvanquished* (London and New York, 1999).
British Joint Warfare Publication 3-50. *Peace Support Operations* (PSO).
British Maritime Doctrine. Second edition. BR 1806 (London, 1999).
Buchanan, Pat. *A Republic, not an Empire* (Washington DC, 1999).
Carr, E.H. *The Twenty Years' Crisis* (London, 1939).
Claude Jr, Inis L. *Swords into Plowshares* (New York, 1956).
Connaughton, Richard. *Military Intervention in the 1990s – A New Logic of War* (London and New York, 1992).
Connaughton, Richard. *Military Support and Protection for Humanitarian Assistance. Rwanda, April-December 1994*. SCSI *Occasional* No.18 (HMSO, 1996).
Connaughton, Richard. *The Nature of Future Conflict* (London, 1995).
Defence Committee. *Lessons of Kosovo*. House of Commons. Vols I & II. HC 347 (1999-2000).
Department of Defense. *Kosovo Operation Allied Force After Action Report*. Report to Congress. Unclassified (31 January 2000).
Design for Military Operations. The British Military Doctrine (1989).
Fuller, J.F.C. *The Generalship of Ulysses S. Grant* (London, 1929).
Goodrich, Leland M. *The United Nations* (New York, 1959).
Gow, James and Smith, James D.D. *Peacemaking and Peacekeeping. European Security and the Yugoslav Wars* (London, 1992).
Hackett, General Sir John. *The Profession of Arms* (London, 1983).
Hastings, Max. *The Korean War* (London, 1987).
Henig, Jan Willom and Both, Norbert. *Srebrenica. Record of a War Crime* (London, 1996).
Henkin, L. *How Nations Behave* (London, 1968).
Hinsley, F.H. *Power and the Pursuit of Peace. Theory and Practice in the History of Relations Between States* (Cambridge, 1963).
James, Alan. *The Politics of Peacekeeping* (London, 1969).
James, D. Clayton. *Refighting the Last War. Command and Crisis in Korea 1950-53* (New York, 1993).
Malcolm, Noel. *Kosovo. A Short History* (London, 1998).
Nutting, Anthony. *No End of a Lesson: The Story of Suez* (London, 1967).
Ripley, Tim. *Operation Deliberate Force. The UN and NATO Campaign in Bosnia 1995* (Lancaster, 1999).
Rose, General Sir Michael. *Fighting for Peace. Lessons from Bosnia* (London, 1998).
Rufin, Jean-Christophe. *Life, Death and Aid*. MSF Report on World Crisis (London, 1993).

Russell, R. and Muther, J.E. *A History of the United Nations Charter. The Role of the United States, 1940-1945* (Washington DC, 1958).

Seiple, Chris. *The US Military/NGO Relationship in Humanitarian Interventions* (Carlisle, 1996).

Thompson, Robert. *Make for the Hills. Memories of Far Eastern Wars* (London, 1989)

Ullman, Richard H. *Anglo Soviet Relations 1917-1921.* Vol II. 'Britain and the Russian Civil War' (Princeton, 1968).

Urquhart, Brian. *A Life in Peace and War* (London, 1987).

World Disasters Report. *Special Focus of the Rwanda Refugee Crisis 1994.*

Notes

1

1 Vladimir Kulagin. *Contemporary Security Policy,* Vol.20, No.2 (August 1999) pp 116-126.
2 Ibid.
3 Inis L. Claude Jr. *Swords into Plowshares* (New York, 1956) 233.
4 The view that the peace settlement was vindictive is not a unanimous view. See, for example, Manfred F. Boemeke et al, *The Treaty of Versailles : A Reassessment After 75 Years* (German Historical Institute/CUP, 1998). The counter view is that Germany refused to accept that they had been defeated or accept the consequence of that defeat. The Anglo-Saxon Allies wanted - what they got in 1945 - an admission by the vanquished that the allied cause had been 'just'.
5 R. Russell and J.E. Muther. *A History of the United Nations Charter. The Role of the United States, 1940-1945* (Washington DC, 1958) 939. Clive Archer. *International Organisations* (London, 1983) 25.
6 United Nations Charter, Article 42.
7 E.H. Carr. *The Twenty Years' Crisis.* (London, 1939) 8. The 'how' and 'why' questions were taken as the formal structure of *Military Intervention in the 1990s - A New Logic of War.* Those same questions permeate this work although in a less formal manner.
8 Robert Rothstein. 'On the Costs of Realism'. *Science Quarterly* 87(3) (1972) pp 347-62.
9 Leland M. Goodrich. *The United Nations* (New York, 1959) pp 164-65.
10 UN Letter S/956 dated 9 August 1948.
11 Brian Urquhart. *A Life in Peace and War* (London, 1987) 93.

2

1 Richard H. Ullman. *Anglo Soviet Relations 1917-1921,* Vol.II. 'Britain and the Russian Civil War' (Princeton, 1968) pp 353-4.
2 Alan James. *The Politics of Peacekeeping* (London, 1969) 1.
3 *Peacekeepers Handbook* (New York, 1984) 22.
4 James. 3.
5 India's takeover of Goa and Ethiopia's of Eritrea.
6 Jeffrey L. Sands. *Blue Hulls : Multinational Naval Cooperation and the United Nations* (1993).
7 Minutes of British COS meetings, uncatalogued records and quoted in Max Hastings, *The Korean War* (London, 1987) 240.
8 D. Clayton James. *Refighting the Last War. Command and Crisis in Korea 1950-1953* (New York, 1993) 150.
9 Anthony Nutting. *No End of a Lesson : The Story of Suez* (London, 1967) 95.
10 CAB 128/3Q Part 2, 625 (CM.74(56)).

11 Coral Bell. *The Conventions of Crisis : A Study in Diplomatic Management* (London, 1971) 120.

12 The National Security Council was formed to minimise the impact of bureaucratic politics by bringing advice directly to the White House. Arguably all it did was add another player to the game. It did not replace Realism as a paradigm and, as is evident from the Kosovo conflict, had little influence in controlling the activities of the Department of State.

13 Robert Thompson. *Make for the Hills. Memories of Far Eastern Wars* (London, 1989) 138.

14 L. Henkin. *How Nations Behave* (London, 1968) 266.

15 Ibid.

16 Oscar Schachter. 'The Right of States to Use Armed Force'. *Michigan Law Review 82* (Apr/May 1984) 1623.

17 Henkin. 219.

18 Approximately 185,000 died fighting for the South Vietnamese Government and 1.5 million for the North Vietnamese Army and southern Vietcong, of which 300,000 were missing in action.

19 Including Roosevelt here might seem a contradiction. He did lead America into the Second World War at a time when a substantial majority of Americans were opposed but, nevertheless, he remained extremely sensitive to public attitudes.

20 Brewer. *Dictionary of Phrase and Fable.* 1147.

3

1 General Sir John Hackett, *The Profession of Arms* (London, 1983), 104.

2 Fuller to Liddell Hart. Liddell Hart Papers, 1/302/61.

3 J.F.C. Fuller, *The Generalship of Ulysses S. Grant* (London, 1929), ix.

4 There are three levels of doctrine: tactical, operational and military which is the highest level.

5 Design for Military Operation. The British Military Doctrine (1989).

6 Don M. Snider, John A. Nagl and Tony Pfaff. Army Professionalism, the Military Ethic, and Officers in the Twenty-First Century. US Army War College Strategic Studies Institute. Figure 3. p.18 (Carlisle, PA, December 1999).

7 Reginald Brett. 'Journal' in James Lees Milnes *The Enigmatic Edwardian* (London, 29 August 1879) 85.

8 Snider et al. Figure 4. p.26.

9 Dana Priest. 'Risks and Restraint: Why the Apaches Never Flew in Kosovo', *Washington Post*, 29 December 1999.

10 Conclusions drawn from the related West Point studies.

11 Richard Cohen. *The Washington Post.* 1 December 1992.

12 Chris Seiple. *The US Military/NGO Relationship in Humanitarian Interventions* (Peacekeeping Institute, Center for Strategic Leadership, US Army War College, 1996) 163.

13 *Americans in UN Peacekeeping. A Study of US Public Attitudes.* Program on International Policy Attitudes (Maryland, 27 April 1995).

14 Eric V. Larson. *Casualties and Consensus. The Historical Role of Casualties in Domestic Support for US Military Operation.* RAND Corporation.
15 Michael Williams. *Sunday Times,* 18 August 1996.
16 Brian Urquhart in an address to New Dimensions of United Nations Peace-Keeping Operations Symposium (Tokyo, 19-20 January 1995).
17 Interview with the author, The Hague, Netherlands (22 March 1995).
18 Quoted in R.M. Connaughton, 'Military Support and Protection for Humanitarian Assistance. Rwanda, April-December 1994'. SCSI *Occasional*, No 18 (1996), 11.
19 Tim Ripley. *Operation Deliberate Force. The UN and NATO Campaign in Bosnia 1995* (Lancaster, 1999).
20 Jan Willem Henig and Norbert Both, *Srebrenica. Record of a War Crime* (London, 1996), pp 118-119.
21 Martin Bell, *The Times,* 2 November 1996.
22 Interview author and Colonel Luc Marchal, Brussels, 30 March 1995.
23 Bell, *The Times,* 2 November 1996.
24 *The Times,* 31 July 1996.
25 *Daily Telegraph,* 16 November 1999.
26 Henig and Both, 181.
27 *Sunday Telegraph,* 19 September 1999.
28 Ibid.
29 *The Times,* 16 September 1999.
30 *British Maritime Doctrine,* Second Edition. BR 1806 (London, 1999) pp 226-7.
31 Author's italics.
32 Author's italics.
33 *Peace Support Operations.* Joint Warfare Publication 3-50. 1-1.
34 Australia for example would not intervene in East Timor without the consent of Indonesia.
35 'Wider Peacekeeping - How Wide of the Mark?' *British Army Review,* No.111 (December 1995).
36 General Sir Michael Rose. *Fighting for Peace. Lessons from Bosnia* (London, 1998) 271.
37 Might normally be associated with intra-state conflict.
38 Might normally be associated with inter-state conflict.

4

1 Sandy Berger subsequently apologised.
2 *Time,* 11 October 1999.
3 Rose, 82.
4 Peter Riddell. 'Former Peacenik Cook Warms to Heat of Battle'. *The Times,* 30 March 1999.
5 *The Times,* 22 September 1999.
6 Kofi Annan. UN Press Release SG/SM/7134SC/6729.
7 Minutes of evidence taken before the Foreign Affairs Committee, 4 April 1984, Question 263,53.
8 Ibid., Question 280,57.

9 *International Herald Tribune,* 11 October 1999.

10 *Time,* 18 October 1999.

11 *Daily Telegraph,* 9 November 1999.

12 Michael Lind. 'Civil Wars by Other Means', *Foreign Affairs,* September/October 1999, pp 123-142.

13 Lord Carrington. 'Our Great Mistake in the Balkans'. *Saga Magazine* (September, 1999).

14 France pulled out of the proposed £3 billion ($4.5 billion) multi-role armoured vehicle programme with the UK and Germany. France wanted a more heavily armoured vehicle - not a battlefield taxi. Swingeing defence cuts in Berlin could lead to Germany pulling out also.

15 House of Commons All-Party Defence Select Committee. 8th Report. Session 1998-1999. HC 544.

16 Edward Luttwak '...and the Pentagon thinks it's a Joke'. *Sunday Telegraph,* 26 November 2000.

17 Strobe Talbott. Chatham House. 8 October 1999.

18 Caspar Weinberger. 'American NATO commitment will be weakened by Euro force'. *Daily Telegraph,* 23 November 2000.

19 John Batten. 'Foreign Office' Minister. Letters. *Daily Telegraph*, 30 December 2000.

20 The French system is broadly similar but their planning staff divides: some remain in the headquarters, whilst others take their experiences of the developing crisis with them to augment the field headquarters.

21 *The Times,* 22 September 1999.

22 'The total professional and support line organisation at NATO, not including a number of the administrative staff, totals some 92 of which the Defence Adviser's Office constitutes 47 or 51 per cent of the US Ambassador's assets. Whereas the US Mission to NATO has a Defence Adviser's Office of some 30 professionals and 17 support staff, the US Mission in the UN Military Adviser's Office comprises just three professionals and three support staff - 51 per cent versus 8 per cent of the respective Ambassadors' assets. The ability to deliver quality "Defence" advice undoubtedly reflects this allocation of resources.' John O.B. Sewall. 'Peacekeeping Implications for the US Military : Supporting the United Nations' in Dennis J. Quinn (ed) *Peace Support Operations and the US Military.* NDU Press. (Washington, 1994) 36.

23 *Caroline* was a ship involved in the incident in which a US citizen was killed.

24 Yet in a note of 7 October 1998 sent to NATO allies, *FRY/Kosovo : The Way Ahead : UK View on Legal Base for Use of Force,* the FCO said: 'as matters now stand and if action through the Security Council is not possible, military intervention by NATO is lawful on the grounds of overwhelming humanitarian necessity'. In a follow-on memorandum of 22 January 1999 the FCO also suggested to the House of Commons Select Committee on Foreign Affairs that the use of force over Kosovo would be justified under Article 51 of the UN Charter in terms of individual or collective self defence. See Adam Roberts, 'NATO's "Humanitarian War" over Kosovo', *Survival,* Vol.41, No.3, Autumn 1999, pp 102-23. Ironically, at the time of Suez, when the FCO gave Anthony Eden categorical advice that the planned Suez intervention was illegal, he

dismissed the advice on the grounds that 'this is a political matter'. Have our diplomats and military not become seriously politicised?

25 *RUSI Journal*. October 1999. v.

26 William Rees Mogg. 'Where's the Justice?', *The Times,* 29 March 1999.

27 Ibid.

28 Part of a lecture given at Ditchley Park.

29 Boutros Boutros-Ghali. 'Empowering the United Nations'. *Foreign Affairs,* Winter 1992/93, pp 98-99: 'the centuries old doctrine of absolute and exclusive sovereignty no longer stands, and was in fact never so absolute as it was contrived to be in theory'.

30 In 'NATO's "Humanitarian War" over Kosovo', Adam Roberts wrote in *Survival,* Vol.41, No.3, Autumn 1997, p.105 that:

> Although NATO's decision to use armed force in the form of air-power did not have as clear a legal endorsement as its governments might have wished, it was far from being an unambiguous violation of international law. Two main legal arguments were used in support, the first based on UN Security Council resolutions, the second on general international law.

Professor Roberts does, however, make the telling observation on p.104 that the reason NATO did not seek to secure legitimacy from the Security Council for its military action in Kosovo was because:

> it could have been more difficult to get public support for a military action which had actually been vetoed in the UN, and the whole process might expose divisions in the alliance.

Another distinguished legal commentator, Marc Weller, wrote:

> The connection of the legal justification of humanitarian action with the aim of achieving FRY (Federal Republic of Yugoslavia)/Serb acceptance of the Rambouillet package in its entirety, if it is maintained, would represent an innovative but justifiable extension of international law.

International Affairs, April 1999, Vol.75, No.2.

31 Jamie Shea suggests there are four guiding principles of Just War:

- Armed conflict is an act of last resort.
- Means employed should be proportional to the ends pursued.
- Collateral damage is unacceptable.
- The good that arises as a result of intervention must exceed the cost - in lives and treasure - at the conclusion of the total process.

Based on Jamie Shea. *The Kosovo Crisis and the Media : Reflections of a NATO Spokesman.* Reform Club, London. 15 July 1999.

32 *Military Intervention in the 1990s - A New Logic of War.* (London and New York, 1992) pp 58-59.

33 Source: NATO HQ.

34 *Daily Telegraph,* 22 October 1999.

35 Boutros Boutros-Ghali. *Unvanquished.* (London, New York, 1999) 68.

36 Clinton and Albright requested Blair to provide a senior British politician for the job and asked for Cook or Robertson. It would have been an opportune moment to provide a career move for the Foreign Secretary and, although Blair regarded the left-winger Cook as 'dispensable', Cook requested that he remain in-post and Blair agreed. Robertson,

'who was eventually subjected to strong persuasion' to take the lucrative job was believed by Blair to be 'the more likely candidate'. *The Times,* 11 December 1999.

37 Ivo H. Daalder and Michael E.O. Hanlon. *Foreign Policy.* Fall 1999.

38 General H. Norman Schwarzkopf. *It Doesn't Take a Hero.* (London, 1992) pp 339-340.

39 John Simpson. *Strange Places, Questionable People.* (London, 1999).

40 Edward Stourton. 'Spinning for Victory', *Daily Telegraph,* 16 October 1999.

41 *Military Intervention in the 1990s* pp 120-176.

42 This measure (embargo, sanctions, quarantine) will not always be necessary - e.g. East Timor. It needs to be carefully applied if the innocent population of the target state is not to suffer unjustly. An embargo also impacts upon neighbouring states.

5

1 A CIA spokesman made the defensive comment that: 'We provided policymakers with very useful and timely information on these events. There were no surprises'. Not everyone agreed that to be the case. In May 1991, CIA director, William Webster, resigned.

2 Stephen C. Palletiere, Douglas V. Johnson II and Leif R. Rosenberger. *Iraqi Power and US Security in the Middle East* (Carlisle, Pennsylvania, 1990) 74.

3 My italics.

4 Department of Peace and Conflict Research. *SIPRI Yearbook of World Armament and Disarmament*, 1993.

5 Boutros Boutros-Ghali. 'Empowering the United Nations'. *Foreign Affairs,* Winter 1992/93. pp 98-99.

6 Holly Burkhaiter. 'US might have avoided Rwanda Tragedy'. *Christian Science Monitor,* 9 August 1994.

7 Unacclimatised troops are at their most vulnerable during the first five days of their deployment. The problem with finding suitable equipment is that most nations' procurement is locked into a long and arduous production cycle. In general, the types of new weapons and equipment required for expeditionary conflict might include a direct fire anti-armour weapon effective up to 2km, a grenade launcher with a range up to 1.5km, off-the-shelf back-up communications equipment, improvements to body and vehicle protection and smart logistics.

8 *Daily Telegraph,* 14 October 1999.

9 *The Times,* 20 November 1999.

10 Some aspects within this Chapter have appeared in an earlier book, *Military Intervention in the 1990s - A New Logic for War* (London, 1992).

6

1 *The Washington Times,* 1 December 1992.

2 *The Independent,* 28 November 1992.

3 *Independent,* 30 June 1993.

4 InterAid supported the proposed military option but it was by no means a universal view. After the BBC World Service gave the news of the administration's plan on 26 November 1992, the aid agency leaders held a meeting in Mogadishu. *The Independent* of 27 November 1992 reported: 'Aid agencies in Somalia said that imposing troops on

the country would be a disaster. A spokesman for the Save the Children Fund said it would have to leave if food aid were militarised'.

5 *The Washington Post,* 2 December 1992.

6 Whig is an old term to describe those of Liberal persuasion.

7 *Independent on Sunday,* 18 July 1993.

8 He prepared a report for the Secretary-General on the killing of the Pakistani peacekeepers on 5 June 1993.

9 Reported in *The Independent,* 22 September 1993.

10 T.W. Lippman and B. Gellman, 'A humanitarian gesture turns deadly', *Washington Post,* 10 October 1993.

11 *The Independent,* 22 September 1993.

12 Ibid.

13 Report Pursuant to para 5 of the Security Council Resolution 837 (1993) on the investigation into the 5 June 1993 attack on UN forces in Somalia conducted on behalf of the Secretary-General. S/26351, 24 August 1993.

14 Dr Jim Whitman and Commander Ian Bartholomew, *Collective Control of UN Peace Support Operations : A Policy Proposal,* Cambridge, November 1993.

15 Françoise Bouchet-Saulnier, *Life, Death and Aid,* the Médécins sans Frontiéres Report on World Crisis Intervention (22 November 1993).

16 Hella Pick, *The Guardian,* 16 October 1993.

17 Final Draft FM 100-5, *Operations,* 19 January 1993, 2-9.

18 *Independent on Sunday,* 17 October 1993.

19 The Rangers were inserted by helicopter and road convoys.

20 There are varying accounts as to how that order was received.

21 *Time International,* 18 October 1993.

22 Ibid.

23 Hella Pick, *The Guardian,* 16 October 1993.

24 Many members of Congress are ambivalent about America's leaning towards consolidating its Empire, preferring instead to support the introspective notion of the American Republic. This attitude is summarised in Pat Buchanan's *A Republic, not an Empire* (Washington DC, 1999) in which he deplores the last decade's imperialist drift of US Foreign Policy.

25 *The Nature of Future Conflict,* pp 195-196.

26 *Time International,* 16 October 1993.

27 Boutros Boutros-Ghali. *Unvanquished* (London, 1999) 105.

28 Boutros Boutros-Ghali. 106.

29 *The Guardian,* 16 October 1993.

30 Remark attributed to Joseph Verner Reed. *Unvanquished.* 304. *International Herald Tribune,* 25 May 1999.

31 Cassell's *Concise English Dictionary* defines 'janissary' as 'a soldier of the old Turkish infantry forming the Sultan's bodyguard (originally young prisoners trained to arms), disbanded in 1826. In 'Bonkers in the Balkans' (*Spectator,* 14 August 1999) Tom Walker ironically refers to 'the Serb view on fair Madeleine, which derides her as a traitor or 'janissary', a descendant of one of the Balkan subjects carted off to Constantinople by the Ottomans, only later to return and inflict misery on their countrymen'.

32 *International Herald Tribune,* 25 May 1999.

33 Boutros Boutros-Ghali. pp 287-288. Other than Somalia there were at least two incidents during the Secretary-General's tenure of office which gave rise to anger within US diplomatic circles. At the end of 1995, Rubin had made a critical comment of Boutros Boutros-Ghali's reluctance to put UN peacekeepers into eastern Slavonia. The Secretary-General expressed himself as being 'shocked by its (the comment's) vulgarity'. Albright sprang to Rubin's defence, complaining that vulgarity was not a term to be applied to a superpower. According to Boutros-Ghali, she could talk tough but was unable to accept tough talk directed at her. The second incident arose out of the Israeli shelling in April 1996 of the UN observation post at Qana. The Secretary-General investigated the attack and submitted a report to the Security Council. On 13 May, Warren Christopher told Boutros Boutros-Ghali that the United States had decided to remove him from the UN.

34 *The Times,* 25 July 1996.

35 Democratic National Convention. August 1996.

36 The content of this Chapter was also largely featured in Chapter 9 of *The Nature of Future Conflict* (London, 1995).

7

1 Jean-Christophe Rufin, *Life, Death and Aid,* MSF Report on World Crisis (London, 1993), 113.

2 United Nations Peacekeeping. Information Notes (May 1994), 158.

3 UNAMIR's further extension was dependent upon substantive progress having been made towards peace.

4 The DMZ had been monitored by troops from the OAU from June 1993.

5 Most Immediate signal from Dallaire to Baril at DPKO dated 11 Jan 94.

6 Interview author and Marchal, Brussels, 30 March 1995.

7 Boutros Boutros-Ghali. 130. (The author was one of the technical specialists involved in a Joint Evaluation of Emergency Assistance to Rwanda - *The International Response to Conflict and Genocide : lessons from the Rwanda Experience* - and had been critical of the handling of the Dallaire communiqué. At a meeting at Southampton, Under-Secretary-General Marrack Goulding said to the author: 'That communiqué never existed. We had a thorough search in New York and did not find it. It was Hutu disinformation - they do that sort of thing'. When I told him I had a copy of the Dallaire communiqué [courtesy of Geneva] he appeared concerned. 'But we had an internal inquiry, did not anyone from New York contact you?' I replied in the negative. The next day I faxed to Marrack Goulding a copy of Dallaire's signal to DPKO, New York. The mystery is why General Dallaire was not asked for confirmation or a copy from his war diary. I decided it was probably due to Canadian military sensitivity - the Secretary-General's military adviser being a Canadian.

8 Mille Collines (Fr.) - a thousand hills.

9 Interview author and Marchal, Brussels, 30 March 1995.

10 Interview author and Dallaire, The Hague, Netherlands, 22 March 1995.

11 Interview author and Marchal, Brussels, 30 March 1995.

12 Ibid. There is a report that the Czech representative on the Security Council stated that the Security Council had not been apprised by the UN Secretariat of the intelligence coming from Kigali prior to 6 April. (Paul La Rose-Edwards, *The Rwandan Crisis of April 1994. The Lessons Learned* (Ottawa, 30 November 1994), 4.

13 World Disasters Report. Special Focus on the Rwandan Crisis, 13.

14 The *impuzamugambi* were the militia of the Hutu CRD party.

15 World Disaster Report. Special Focus on the Rwandan Crisis, 13.

16 US expatriates were escorted by UNAMIR troops to the Rwanda-Burundi border to be evacuated through Bujumbura.

17 The UN was particularly concerned at the presence of Belgian troops working to two masters. The RPF ordered the Belgians and French out of the country, but that situation might have changed if the Amaryllis troops had come under UNAMIR command and demonstrated their intention to save Tutsi lives.

18 Between 12-15 April the USA had pushed for total withdrawal, this stance being encouraged by Belgian political activities behind the scenes. Washington's hard line had softened by 21 April (allegedly through the intervention of their New York delegation) so that the way was clear for the passage of Resolution 912.

19 Milton Leitenberg, 'Rwanda, 1994 : International Incompetence (PRD 50) Produces Genocide', *Peacekeeping and International Relations,* November/December 1994.

20 Presidential Decision Directive 25. (PDD 25) The Clinton Administration's Policy on Reforming Multilateral Peace Operations, May 1994. The subject of Emergency Humanitarian Relief was reviewed as a result of the Rwanda experience under Presidential Review Directive/NSC 50 (PRD 50) of 10 January 1995.

21 Boutros Boutros-Ghali, pp 134-135.

22 Holly Burkhalter, 'US Might Have Avoided Rwanda Tragedy', *Christian Science Monitor,* 9 August 1994.

23 As enunciated by Professor Howard Adelman.

24 The nature of Rwanda's neighbouring states would have made a sub-regional intervention unlikely. The OAU was content for the UN to take the role of lead organisation.

25 British Minister for Development.

26 Interview author and General Dallaire, The Hague, Netherlands, 22 March 1995.

27 World Disasters Special Report on the Rwandan Refugee Crisis, 9.

28 Interview author and Dallaire, The Hague, Netherlands, 22 March 1995.

29 Ibid.

30 Guy Vassall Adams, *Rwanda, An Agenda for International Action* (Oxford, 1994), 37.

31 Dr Jim Whitman. UN Project. Global Security Programme. University of Cambridge, 16 March 1995. It was not just a number of NGO HQs and their representatives whose views appeared out of kilter with what was happening out on the ground. A DHA Report prepared by Antonio Donini and Norah Nilana, *Rwanda : Lessons Learned. A Coordination of Humanitarian Activities,* examined the interaction with UNAMIR. Despite admissions that the authors had neither time nor mandate to investigate this area in any detail, and despite evidence to the contrary that there had been valuable information sharing between the humanitarian organisations and the military, their report said: 'too close an association, or worse, with the military will definitely not facilitate information gathering'.

32 World Disasters Report. Special Focus on the Rwandan Refugee Crisis. 1994. 31.
33 Source: Whitman.
34 United Nations Peacekeeping, *Update,* December 1994, 217.
35 Interview author and General Dallaire, The Hague, Netherlands, 22 March 1995.
36 Ibid.
37 Ibid.
38 Interview author and General Lafourcade, Toulouse, 28 March 1995.
39 Ibid. The French assessment differed from that of the Americans.
40 Ibid.
41 National Public Radio, 31 July 1994.
42 UNAMIR's strength on 25 July numbered fewer than 500 men.
43 World Disasters Report, *Special Focus on the Rwandan Refugee Crisis,* 20.
44 Other states to provide troops were Ethiopia and Zimbabwe. Interview author and Dallaire, The Hague, Netherlands, 22 March 1995.
45 The London *Times,* 1 August 1994.
46 The Australian military developed a close association with Care Australia.
47 House of Commons Defence Committee, *Lessons of Kosovo.* HC 347- (1999-2000) pp 87-88 & 126.
48 23 Parachute Field Ambulance.
49 Interview author and Dallaire, The Hague, Netherlands, 22 March 1995.
50 The British deployment into Rwanda was completed on 20 August 1994, 15 days after the UN announced 'the corner had been turned' in Goma and 5 days before the American Task Force withdrew from Goma.
51 Discussion with the author, Kigali, 27 April 1995.
52 Paul La Rose-Edwards, *The Rwandan Crisis of April 1994. The Lesson Learned.* 30 November 1994.
53 Kagame had a RPF liaison cell in Dallaire's HQ.
54 UNREO took over the humanitarian linkage responsibility in early July until it was taken over by UNHCR after 20 July.
55 Interview author and General Lafourcade, HQ 11th Parachute Division, Toulouse, 28 March 1995.
56 Ibid.
57 Interview author and General Lafourcade, HQ 11th Parachute Division, Toulouse, 28 March 1995.
58 Discussed later.
59 Interview author and General Lafourcade, HQ 11th Parachute Division, Toulouse, 28 March 1995.
60 *International Herald Tribune,* 25 June 1999.
61 View provided by Global Security Programme, Cambridge.
62 On 28 July, the French Embassy in Bujumbura issued an 'advice and directives' document for the NGOs to inform Turquoise of all movements. Dallaire imposed a similar control regime within his area of responsibility.
63 London *Times,* 16 August 1994.
64 Which cost the UN US$10 million.
65 Bosnia also showed 'quick' to be a relative statement.

66 Operation Support Hope. US Military Brief, 23 August 1994.

67 This was precisely the same manner in which the Joint Task Force was sent into Northern Iraq.

68 Operation Support Hope 1994. After Action Review, 26.

69 Lt-Gen Daniel R. Schroeder. Operation Support Hope 1994. After Action Review, 4.

70 Oxfam SITREP from Goma, 28 July 1994.

71 Guy Vassall-Adams, *Rwanda. Oxfam Insight. An Agenda for International Action,* (Oxford, 1994), 50.

72 DART has been developed by the US Agency for International Development (USAID) and the Office of Foreign Disaster Assistance (OFDA) as a method of providing a rapid response to international disasters. Each DART comprises specialists trained in a number of disaster skills.

73 Other than the Senate's imposed limitation of up to 1 October 1994 which could be set aside by Congress.

74 Interview author and Major-General Dallaire, The Hague, Netherlands, 22 March 1995.

75 Very often such problems were procedural.

76 JTF Support Hope Operational Concept Update Number 3.

77 38% of this total was UN relief, 24% for UNAMIR, and 38% was own and own operation support.

78 Our italics.

79 Lieutenant-General Daniel Schroeder: Lessons of Rwanda, *Armed Forces Journal,* December 1994.

80 When the proposal was 'floated' to Congress, there was opposition. Not wanting to fight Congress, the Administration nominated instead a two-star general. Three-star generals such as Schroeder require Congressional approval for such appointments. Two-star officers do not.

81 Yasushi Akashi, the *Economist,* 30 April 1994.

82 A Save the Children Fund representative quoted the occasion the organisation required priority items to be flown into Kigali: 'The Ministry of Defence pricing system was unhelpful', he said. 'I was quoted £7.00 a kilo for freight via the Royal Air Force yet Sabena were asking £1.60 a kilo.'

83 World Disasters Report, *Special Focus on the Rwandan Refugee Crisis,* 1994, 31.

84 More precisely, this means what *should* exist between the intervening actors, most notably the military informing the humanitarians as to their intentions.

85 *International Herald Tribune,* 14 September 1999.

8

1 Kosovo's population in 1991 had been just below two million but, since that date, approximately one quarter of the Kosovo Albanians had resettled elsewhere in Europe. A KFOR-sponsored census of August 1999 found 1,394,200 Albanians (176% of 1998 estimation), 97,100 Serbs (51% of 1998 estimation) and 73,000 Croats, Romas and other ethnic minorities (43% of 1998 estimation).

2 Noel Malcolm. *Kosovo. A Short History* (London, 1998) pp 341-342.

3 Ibid. xxii.

[4] Jane M.O. Sharp. *Bankrupt in the Balkans - British Policy in Bosnia.* Institute for Public Policy Research. (London, 1993) 11.

[5] James Gow and James D.D. Smith. *Peacemaking and Peacekeeping. European Security and the Yugoslav Wars* (London, 1992) 27.

[6] Misha Glenny. *New York Review of Books,* 27 May 1993.

[7] Boutros Boutros-Ghali. 50.

[8] Ibid. 71.

[9] Ripley. 89.

[10] Graham T. Allison. *Essence of Decision. Explaining the Cuban Missile Crisis* (New York, 1971).

[11] Misha Glenny. *Sunday Telegraph,* 12 December 1999.

[12] Boutros Boutros-Ghali. pp 144-145.

[13] Ibid.

[14] P.G. Williams. 'From Coercion back to Consent. SFOR's Endgame'. *British Army Review,* No.122. Autumn 1999.

[15] Charles G. Boyd. 'Making Peace with the Guilty'. *Foreign Affairs,* September/October 1995. 23. Ripley. 93.

[16] Ripley. 6.

[17] Rose. xxi.

[18] The OSCE ethos was to select and appoint individuals rather than groups.

[19] If they had switched their attention to Kosovo after the organisation's appointment, the planning process would have been greatly speeded up.

[20] KVM worked on an initial/interim spending authority pending the presentation of a full budget. This budget went before the OSCE Permanent Council in late March when it was vetoed by Russia.

[21] *Time,* 1 February 1999.

[22] Milosevic, mimicking Saddam Hussein's ordering of Richard Butler, the UN Chief Arms Inspector, out of Iraq, ordered Walker out of Kosovo in 72 hours but the international community resisted and he stayed.

[23] The supposition being that the dead had been killed singly or in pairs in conflict elsewhere and their bodies assembled to achieve maximum impact.

[24] *The Times,* 18 March 1999.

[25] *The Times,* 30 January 1999.

[26] A concept which 'expresses NATO's enduring purpose and nature and its fundamental security tasks, identifies the central features of the new security environment, specifies the elements of the Alliance's broad approach to security, and provides guidelines for the further adaptation of its military forces'. NAC-S(99)65 dated 24 April 1999.

[27] Holbrooke was sent on a mission of last resort to Belgrade to try to persuade Milosevic to accept the peace deal. He failed. 'Will I ever see you again?' asked Milosevic. 'That's up to you, Mr President', said Holbrooke as he left.

[28] *Time,* 1 March 1999.

[29] *The Spectator,* 14 August 1999.

[30] In municipal elections held in Kosovo in October 2000, elections widely regarded as a preliminary move towards ultimate Kosovar independence, Rugova's Democratic League of Kosovo trounced Thaci, achieving 60 per cent of the vote.

31 Robin Cook. Debate in the House of Commons. 25 March 1999. If 400,000 had been 'driven' from their homes, the vast majority must, at some stage prior to 24 March 1999, have returned to their homes.

32 Tom Walker and Aidan Laverty. 'CIA Aided Kosovo Guerrilla Army', *Sunday Times,* 12 March 2000. When the OSCE withdrew from Kosovo, the CIA handed over to the KLA many of its satellite telephone and global positioning systems so that the KLA could keep in touch with Washington and NATO. According to this source, 'several KLA leaders had the mobile phone number of General Wesley Clark, the NATO commander'.

33 *Time,* 9 February 1999.

34 *The Economist,* 8 May 1999.

35 Blair's speech to Economic Club of Chicago, 23 April 1999.

36 The Suez Canal Company was established under Egyptian law with its Head Office in Egypt. The company had a *concession* to run from 1869-1968. Nasser gave notice of termination of that concession by virtue of nationalisation of the Suez Canal. Compensation was to be paid at the prevailing value of shares on the stock market.

37 Source: NATO HQ, Brussels.

38 Allan Little. 'How Albright Manoeuvred NATO into War'. *Sunday Telegraph,* 27 February 2000.

39 *The Times,* 16 February 1999.

40 Benjamin Schwarz and Christopher Layne. 'The Case Against Intervention in Kosovo', *Nation,* 19 April 1999. Jeffrey Record. 'Serbia and Vietnam. A Preliminary Comparison of US Decision to Use Force'. *Occasional Paper* No.8. Center for Strategy and Technology, Air War College, Maxwell Air Force Base. May 1999. 8.

41 The KLA did become progressively involved in support of NATO's action in Kosovo but it was never more than a limited form of assistance. David Rhode quoting Robert Pape in 'Tactics of '95 Bosnia Crisis May Not fit Kosovo Case', *New York Times,* 3 April 1999. Record 6.

42 *The Spectator,* 14 August 1999.

43 Which she did, living in Belgrade for three years, where her father was the Ambassador of Czechoslovakia. *Time,* 1 March 1999.

44 John Casey. '"Big Lie" Behind a Reckless and Half-Witted Adventure', *Daily Telegraph,* 29 April 1999.

45 Michael Hirsch and John Barry. 'How We Stumbled Into War'. *Newsweek*, 12 April 1999.

46 Record. 5.

47 John F. Harris. 'Reassuring Rhetoric, Reality in Conflict'. *Washington Post*, 8 April 1999.

48 *Daily Telegraph,* 19 April 2000.

49 Peter Oborne. 'An Officer and a Politician'. *The Spectator,* 27 May 2000.

50 *The Times,* 13 May 1999.

51 *Time,* 31 May 1999.

52 US State Department estimate. An unknown number will have been combatants. *The Times,* 11 December 1999.

53 *Jane's Defence Weekly,* Vol.31, Issue No.15, 14 April 1999.

54 Professor Sir Michael Howard, *Evening Standard,* 8 July 1997.

55 *Time*, 22 March 1999.

56 Question 356, House of Commons Select Committee on Defence. 24 March 1999.

57 *Sunday Telegraph*, 12 March 2000.

58 Department of Defense. *Kosovo Operation Allied Force After Action Report*. Report to Congress. Unclassified - 31 January 2000.

59 The erroneous attack upon the Chinese Embassy was the only target selected by the CIA throughout the campaign. Most of the other 900 targets struck during 78 days of bombing were chosen by NATO, EUCOM or the Pentagon. Following so soon after the attack on a Sudanese pharmaceutical factory, this further gaffe proved hugely embarrassing for the CIA.

60 The official also advised: 'If you really want to know what went on in NATO during the conflict you will need to interview widely. In that way you will come across those prepared to talk, almost all of whom were sickened by what we had done'.

61 Josef Joffe. 'Down to Earth in the Balkans', *Time*, 31 May 1999.

62 39 per cent opposed. *Newsweek*, 19 April 1999.

63 1206 Americans were surveyed. *Time*, 31 May 1999.

64 Press Conference. NATO's 50th Anniversary. Washington, 23 April 1999. Clinton also implied that the decision to move from Phase 1 to Phase 2 of the air campaign was the Secretary-General's.

65 Blair's speech to Economic Club of Chicago. 23 April 1999.

66 *International Herald Tribune*, 25 May 1999. This was an early judgement of Sir John's. He would later become a supporter of armed conflict in Kosovo.

67 *Frankfurter Rundschau*, 6 January 2000. *Daily Telegraph*, 7 January 2000.

68 Joe Murphy. 'Lies, damn lies and Government Statements', *Sunday Telegraph*, 24 October 1999.

69 *Washington Times*, 10 May 1999.

70 *Jane's Defence Weekly*, 12 May 1999.

71 *The Economist*, 12 June 1999.

72 Indictments are not normally declared in public but kept sealed.

73 François Heisbourg. 'Airpower Alone Didn't Force Milosevic's Capitulation', *International Herald Tribune*, 26-27 June 1999.

74 *The Economist*, 12 June 1999.

75 Little. *Sunday Telegraph*. 27 February 2000.

76 Report of Human Rights Watch (New York, February 2000).

77 Michael Mandelbaum. 'A Perfect Failure. NATO's War Against Yugoslavia', *Foreign Affairs*, September/October 1999. 5.

78 Said apparently with sincerity.

79 The parachute threat never materialised.

80 *International Herald Tribune*, 17 June 1999.

81 Adam Roberts. 'NATO's "Humanitarian War" over Kosovo', *Survival*, Vol.41, No.3, Autumn 1999. 118.

82 *Daily Telegraph*, 5 March 2000.

83 That many vague and imprecise orders and instructions were generated attests to the fact that the system was not always used properly.

84 Edward Stourton. 'Spinning for Victory', *Daily Telegraph*, 16 October 1999.

85 Mission oriented orders or *auftragstaktik* relate to when a commander gives his subordinate commander(s) his concept of operations and leaves him/them freedom to operate within the given operational framework.

86 *Daily Telegraph,* 4 January 2000.

87 *International Herald Tribune,* 16 June 1999. The key to a balanced NATO force structure in the future lies in possessing the requisite equipment, an improvement in strategic mobility capabilities and in preventive deployment.

88 *Daily Telegraph,* 5 January 2000.

89 The General's mission also included 'when necessary, enforce compliance with the conditions of the Military Technical Agreement (MTA)'.

90 William Pfaff. 'All Milosevic Can Negotiate is Terms of His Surrender'. *International Herald Tribune/Los Angeles Times Syndicate.*

91 *International Herald Tribune,* 10-11 July 1999.

92 BBC TV, *Newsnight Special,* 20 August 1999.

93 General Jackson and his staff of the ACE Rapid Reaction Corps withdrew from Kosovo in October 1999, to be replaced by the German general, General Klaus Reinhardt, commanding NATO's Central European Land Forces in Heidelberg. Reinhardt is a scholarly soldier, a student of Bismarck, with a PhD. It was Bismarck who said that 'the Balkans are not worth the healthy bones of one Pomeranian Grenadier'. According to Günther M. Wiedemann in 'General vor Schwieriger Mission' in *Kölner-Anzeiger* of 12 August 1999, Reinhardt 'counts as a shop-window intellectual among Germany's generals rather than as a Bundeswehr swashbuckler'. The Euro-Corps took over from Reinhardt's command.

94 Ivo H. Daalder and Michael E. O'Hanlon. 'Unlearning the Lessons of Kosovo'. *Foreign Policy* (Fall, 1999).

95 Michael Mandelbaum. *Foreign Affairs,* September/October 1999.

96 Ibid.

97 Report of the UN Secretary-General, 31 August 1999.

98 'The Kosovo Cover Up'. *Newsweek.* 8 May 2000.

99 Ibid.

9

1 Kalimantan (539,460 sq km), Sumatra (473,606 sq km), Irian Jaya (421,981 sq km), Sulawesi (189,216 sq km), Java (132,187 sq km).

2 *The Economist*, 20 June 1998.

3 Anna Husarska. 'Empower the UN to Prevent Renewed Violence in East Timor'. *International Herald Tribune,* 17-18 July 1999.

4 *International Herald Tribune,* 20 May 1999.

5 Professor Stanley Hoffmann. 'Principles in the Balkans, but not in East Timor', *New York Times,* 11 September 1999.

6 Kofi Annan. 'Two Concepts of State Sovereignty', *The Economist,* 18 September 1999.

7 *Daily Telegraph,* 18 September 1999.

8 As at 26 October 1999 (total was 9,941). Source: *Australian Army Magazine*, December 1999.

9 *The Economist*, 13 May 2000.

[10] Kabbah had worked for the UN for 22 years before returning to Sierra Leone in 1992.

[11] *Daily Telegraph,* 8 May 2000.

[12] 'Somalia Revisited. *The Times,* 9 May 2000.

[13] These were the mercenaries who had restored Kabbah to power - a result which could not be deplored with conviction.

[14] By chance, M. Miyet was in Freetown when the British arrived. There is no doubt that his presence and pragmatism eased the way for what potentially could have been a very difficult relationship between the UN and UK forces. 'The arrival of the British is good for us', said a UN spokesman, but there were initial problems, particularly with the Nigerians.

[15] Fraticelli to Connaughton. 6 June 2000.

[16] Boris Johnson. 'Yet Again the Paras Sort Out a Cookie Cock-up'. *Daily Telegraph,* 18 May 2000.

[17] This battalion had led the advance into Kosovo when it was part of the now disbanded 5 Airborne Brigade. Quite by chance it was the duty Spearhead battalion at the time the Sierra Leone crisis broke.

[18] *HMS Illustrious* was taking part in Exercise Linked Seas off the Iberian Peninsula, therefore she was closer to Freetown than the *HMS Ocean* Group which had to revictual at Gibraltar. *Illustrious* arrived off Freetown on 11 May and the *HMS Ocean* Group on 14 May.

[19] *The Times,* 10 May 2000.

[20] *The Times,* 13 May 2000.

[21] *Daily Telegraph,* 24 May 2000.

[22] Conversation Richards/Connaughton, PJHQ, 19 July 2000.

[23] Contributors of Force Troops were: Bangladesh, Ghana, Guinea, India, Jordan, Kenya, Nigeria, Russian Federation and Zambia.

[24] Contributors of Military Observers were: Bangladesh, Bolivia, Canada, China, Croatia, Czech Republic, Denmark, Egypt, France, Gambia, Ghana, Guinea, India, Indonesia, Jordan, Kenya, Kyrgyzstan, Malaysia, Mali, Nepal, New Zealand, Nigeria, Norway, Pakistan, Russian Federation, Slovakia, Sweden, Thailand, United Kingdom, United Republic of Tanzania, Uruguay, Zambia.

[25] Contributors of Civilian Police Personnel were: Bangladesh, Gambia, Ghana, India, Jordan, Kenya, Malaysia, Mali, Namibia, Nepal, Norway, Senegal, Zimbabwe.

[26] *Sunday Telegraph*, 17 September 2000.

[27] On this operation, Operation Barass, one British soldier was killed and 10 wounded, two seriously.

[28] BBC News Online. Africa. Thursday, 16 November 2000, 16:46 GMT.

[29] Joshua Cooper Ramo. 'The Five Virtues of Kofi Annan'. *Time,* 4 September 2000.

[30] Michael Hirsh. *Foreign Affairs,* Volume 781 No.6. November/December 1999. 8.

Index

1st (UK) Battalion the Parachute Regiment, 228-229, 255
2nd (UK) Royal Gurkha Rifles, 69
4th (UK) Armoured Brigade, 228, 230
5 (UK) Airborne Brigade, 227-229
10th (US) Mountain Division, 117, 127, 130
42 Commando Royal Marines, 255-256
ABCA, 162
Abshir, Mohammed, 121
Abu Abbas, 96
Abu Nidal, 96
Abyssinia, 7
ACE Rapid Reaction Corps, 211
Aceh, 242
Acheson, Dean, 20, 24
Adams, Gerry, 208
Addis Ababa Conference, 120
Adeniji, Oluyemi, 260
Advanced Warfighting Experiment (USA), 33
Afghanistan, 24, 27, 46, 102
Africa, 54, 69, 104, 106, 161, 165, 167, 177, 180, 249, 252-253, 258, 262
Aggravated Peacekeeping, 51
AH-64 Apache attack helicopters, 35, 68, 105
Ahtissari, Martti, 221
Aideed, General Mohammed, 21, 37-38, 56, 108-109, 112, 115-119, 121-123, 126-129, 132-134, 136, 209
Akashi, Yasushi, 195
Albania, 65, 69, 73, 203, 217, 219, 228-229, 232, 234
Albanians, 160, 172, 185, 200-205, 208, 211, 215, 222, 224, 230-231, 233, 235
Albright, Madeleine, 17, 21, 38, 42, 49, 60, 64, 75, 77, 124, 132, 134-137, 150, 154, 193-195, 199-202, 207-209, 211, 238, 255
Algeria, 22
Al-Jumhuriya, 83
Allison, Graham, 23, 195
al-Sabah family, 82
Amahoro Stadium, 152
America, 4, 6, 17, 19, 24-26, 32-33, 35-36, 56-60, 63-64, 70, 77, 93, 102, 113, 126, 131, 136, 162, 184, 186-187, 192-196, 200, 207-208, 210, 215, 217, 221, 223, 234-235, 238, 245
Amman, 86
Amnesty International, 86
Amphibious Ready Group (UK), 255
Angola, 197, 249
Annan Doctrine, 74
Annan, Kofi, 44, 74, 118, 137, 216, 221, 236, 244, 253-254, 262
Arab League, 81, 83
Arab Liberation Front, 96
Arnett, James, 78
Arusha Peace Agreement, 143-145
Asia, 241
Aspen, Colorado, 103
Aspin, Les, 131, 134
Association of South East Asian Nations (ASEAN), ix, 241, 248
Aswan Dam, 21
Athens/Sparta, 1
Atlantic Charter 1941, 4
Attlee, Clement, 20
Australia, 45, 87, 162, 165, 241-242, 244-246
Australia's First Division and Deployable Force Headquarters, 246
Austria, 63, 105, 144
Ayatollah Khomeini, 86
Aziz, Tariq, 81, 83

B-2 bomber, 215
B-52 bomber, 101, 215
Baath Party, 96

Badinter, Robert, 192
Baghdad, 21, 78, 81-83, 85-86, 88, 96, 126
Baghdad Pact, 21
Baidoa, 112
Bakara Market, 128-129
Balkans, 44-45, 59-60, 126, 192-193, 195, 206, 211, 220, 241
Baltics, 65
Bangladesh, 144, 147
Baril, Major-General Maurice, 146
Barnett, Correlli, 10, 210
Barre, Mohammed Siad, 111-112, 116
Basra, 98
Bazoft, Farzad, 86
BBC, 78, 87, 196, 203, 215, 262
Beecroft, Bob, 198
Beirut, v, 36, 56, 111, 113, 136
Belgians, 38, 42, 145, 148-150, 258
Belgium, x, 63, 144
Belgrade, 57, 76, 78, 204-205, 208, 213, 215, 219-221, 224, 227, 242
Belgrano, 36
Bell, Martin, 43
Bentham, Jeremy, 1-3
Berger, Sandy, 75, 209
Berlin, 23, 56, 59, 212
Bihac, 42
Bildt, Carl, 195
Bir, General Cevik, 117, 121
Black Watch, 101
Blair, Tony, 61-62, 79, 203, 206, 210, 216-218, 234
Booh-Booh, Jacques-Roger, 144, 149
Bosnia, viii, x-xi, 37-38, 40-43, 49-51, 53, 56, 58, 60, 71, 80, 90, 94, 125-126, 133, 160, 175, 186-187, 193-198, 205, 207-209, 212, 224, 227, 229, 231-233, 235-236, 268
Bosnia-Herzegovina, 193, 196
Boutros Boutros-Ghali, v, 21, 74, 77, 113, 120, 135-136, 139, 154, 158, 193, 195
Boyd, General Charles G., 196
Brazil, 6, 246
Brezhnev Doctrine, 24
Brezhnev, Leonid, 24
Briand Kellogg Pact, 7
Brisbane, 246-247
Brunei, 45, 248
Brussels, 65, 150, 216, 228-229
Bubiyan Island, 88
Bucyana, Martin, 148
Bujumbura, 168-169
Bukavu, 166, 168, 177
Bulgaria, 65, 203, 229
Burundi, viii, 143, 148
Bush, George, 21, 38, 89, 94, 98, 103, 113-115, 117, 121, 131, 137, 194, 217
Bush, George W., 265
Butare, 153, 170-171
Byrd, Senator Robert, 131
Byrnes, Sean, 205

C-130 Hercules, 61
Cairo, 16-17, 21, 81
Cairo Declaration 1964, 16
Cambodia, 197
Cambridge University, vii, 155, 208, 267
Canada, 72, 87, 105, 144, 162, 165, 181, 246
Canberra, 242, 244, 246
Care, 169
Caritas, 169
Caroline Incident, 72
Carr, E.H., 11
Carrington, Lord, 60, 88, 193
Casper, Colonel Lawrence E., 128, 130
Cassels, Major-General A.J.H., 225
Castro, 21
Casualty aversion, 32, 35, 57, 207, 227, 235, 260
Ceku, Agim, 219, 223
Cellule de Crise, 168
Central and Eastern Europe (CEE), 13, 72
Chad, 165
Chalker, Linda, 153
Chechnya, 27, 49, 55, 57, 238
Chernomyrdin, Viktor, 221
Chiang Kai Shek, 10, 18
China, 10, 19-20, 25, 27, 72, 199, 214-215, 235, 237-239, 241, 246, 265
Chinook helicopter, 227
Chirac, Jacques, 61
Christian, 2, 83, 113, 241-242

Christopher, Warren, 195
Civil Military Cooperation (CIMIC), ix, 157
Claes, Willy, 77
Clark, General Wesley, 76, 79, 203, 236-237, 217, 226-228, 236
Clausewitz, 2
Clinton, Bill, v, 42, 58-59, 61, 70, 77, 113, 131, 135, 150, 154, 176-177, 187, 191, 193, 200, 202-203, 210, 216-217, 221, 235, 238
Clinton Doctrine, 78
CMOC, ix, 180-182
CNN, 75, 78
Cohen, William, 57, 75, 209, 217, 225, 270
Cold War, 1, 16, 20, 26, 33-35, 42, 46, 49, 60, 70, 77, 83, 92, 119, 189, 238, 257
Colombia, 15
Committee for Security and Cooperation in Europe, 192
Concert of Europe, 3, 208
Congo, 16, 28, 69, 98, 144, 160, 165, 210
Congress (US), viii, 24, 59-60, 77, 87, 102, 113, 125, 131-132, 135-136, 177-178, 184, 210, 212, 215, 235, 238, 265, 267
consent, 3, 16, 28, 40-41, 44-47, 51, 70, 80, 103-104, 113, 139, 154, 173, 176, 231, 244-245, 251-252, 254, 264
Contact Group on Yugoslavia, 200
Convention on Genocide 1949, 151, 234
Cook, Robin, 58, 201, 204, 208, 210, 250, 253, 255-256
Corley, Brigadier-General John, 237
Cosgrove, Major-General Peter, 246-248
Croatia, viii, 40, 192, 195, 210, 219-220
Croats, 160, 193, 195, 231
Crucé, Emeric, 1
Cuba, 23-25
Cuban Missile Crisis, 23, 25, 195, 267
Cyangugu, 169
Czech Republic, 63, 72, 212, 237
Czechoslovakia, 15

Dakar, 255
D'Alema, Massimo, 62
Dallaire, General Romeo A., 144-147, 149, 151-160, 162, 164-165, 169, 174, 181-182, 184, 188
Dannatt, Major-General Richard, 225
Dante, 1
DART, ix, 180
Darwin, 44, 242, 246-247
Dasman Palace, 82
David, Lieutenant-Colonel Bill, 129-130
Dayton Peace Settlement, 41-42, 49, 191, 194, 196-197, 201, 265
de Gaulle, Charles, 10
Delors, Jacques, 91
Democratic League of Kosovo, 202
Denmark, 105
Department of Peacekeeping Operations (DPKO), ix, 28, 105, 254
Department of State, 197
Destexhe, Alain, 139
Dili, 242, 246-247
di Mello, Sergio, 233
Djakovica convoy, 79, 218
doctrine, vii, 2, 12, 17, 29, 31-32, 39-40, 43-45, 47, 49-50, 57, 73, 84, 104, 115, 119, 130, 136, 150, 181, 191, 231, 237, 257, 264
Dole, Bob, 202
Dominican Republic, 25, 46-47, 54
Dresden, 92
Drummond, Sir Eric, 5
Drysdale, John, 122-123
Dubois, Pierre, 1
Dulles, John Foster, 9
Dumbarton Oaks, 8, 70
Durant, Warrant Officer Michael, 131
Dutch, 16, 42-43, 77, 163

East Timor, v, vii-xi, 44-45, 53, 57, 68-71, 79, 105, 151, 216, 241-249, 254, 256, 264
EC, 40, 91, 192-193
ECOMOG, ix, 250-251
Eden, Sir Anthony, 21, 90, 206
Egypt, 21-22, 26, 28, 81, 95, 144, 206
Eichmann, Adolf, 73
El Salvador, 197, 199
Entebbe, 178, 180, 183

Eritrea, 210
ERRF, ix, 61-63
ESDI, ix, 60-63, 64-65
ESDP, ix, 65
Ethiopia, 165
EU, ix, 60-65, 74, 77, 139, 158, 192, 195, 200, 204-205, 208, 221, 232, 253
EUCOM, ix, 196
European Court of Human Rights, 63
European Rapid Reaction Force, ix, 61
European Security and Defence Identity, ix, 60
European Security and Defence Policy, ix, 65
Executive Outcomes, 252
Eyskens, Mark, 150

Falklands, 15, 36, 59, 63, 88-89
Farer, Professor Tom, 121
Fatah Revolutionary Council, 96
Fiji, 144
Finland, 7, 63
First World War, 4, 192, 226
Fitzmaurice, Sir Gerald, 22
Force d'Action Rapide (FAR), 107, 167
Foreign and Commonwealth Office (UK), 47, 73, 250
Former Soviet Union (FSU), 27
Fort Hood, Texas, 33, 35
Fort Irwin, 35
France, x, 5, 7-10, 12, 20, 22, 31-32, 38, 41-42, 44, 59, 62-63, 70, 76, 84, 94, 105, 107, 117, 150, 166-167, 169, 176, 187, 194, 200, 206, 218, 223, 246, 253, 265
Franz Ferdinand of Austria, Archduke, 4
Fraticelli, Lieutenant-General Giulio, 254
Freer, Brigadier Adrian, 227-230
Freetown, 250, 252-253, 255, 257-258, 260-262
Fuller, J.F.C., 31, 40
Fulton, Missouri, 212
Future Large Aircraft (FLA), 61, 68

Garba, Brigadier M.A., 261-262
Gatabazi, Felicien, 148
Gelbard, Robert S., 220
General War, 50
Geneva, 27, 74, 92, 155
Geneva Conference 1988, 27
Geneva Convention, 74
Genscher, Hans Dietrich, 192
Georgetown University, 59
Germany, x, 5-7, 9-10, 13, 17, 31, 44, 56, 62-63, 179, 192, 200-201, 218, 220, 223, 246
Ghana, 144, 165
Gibraltar, 255
Gikongoro, 169, 174
Gile, Brigadier-General, 129
Gitarama, 150
Glaspie, April, 88-89, 121-122, 132
Glenny, Misha, 195
Glubb Pasha (Sir John Bagot), 21
Goma, 143, 161, 163, 166, 168, 173, 176-183, 189
Gorazde, 42
Gorbachev, Mikhail, 95, 102, 212
Gore, Al, 194
Gosende, Robert, 121, 134
Gowing, Nik, 196
Graves, General William S., 54
Great Game, 20-21, 24-25
Greece, 16, 63, 192, 194, 211
Grenada, 25, 46-47
Grey Area, 39, 41-43, 48-51
Guinea Bissau, 165
Gulf, vii, 19, 35-36, 39, 50-51, 63, 78-81, 86-89, 92-95, 98-99, 102, 107, 109, 114, 191, 197, 208, 226, 239, 265
Gurkha, 45, 69, 98, 248
Guthrie, General Sir Charles, 210
Gysenia, 182

Habibie Bacharuddin, Jusuf, 242
Habyarimana, Major-General Juvénal, 145-146, 154
Hagglünd, Gustav, 43
Haiti, 184, 235
Halabja, 87
Hammarskjøld, Dag, 39
Hassan al-Majid, Colonel Ali, 82
Hegel, 2
Helms, Jesse, 154
Helsinki Final Act 1975, 73

Hempstone, Smith, v, 111, 113
Henderson, Sir Nicholas, 59
Herzegovina, 125, 133, 193, 195, 197
High Intensity Conflict, x, 49
High Readiness Brigade (SHIRBRIG), 105-106, 254
Hill, Christopher, 199
Hinsley, Sir F.H., 1
Hiroshima, 92
Hitler, Adolf, 7, 21, 84, 89-91, 194-195, 206
HMS Chatham, 255
HMS Glasgow, 69
HMS Illustrious, 255
HMS Ocean, 255, 262
HMS Sheffield, 36
Hoagland, Jim, 132
Hoar, General Joseph, 121
Hobbes, Thomas, 2
Hoffman, Professor Stanley, 244
Holbrooke, Richard, 196-199, 201, 204, 213, 234
Hong Kong, 20
House of Commons Defence Select Committee, 61
Howard, John, 45, 212, 242, 245-246
Howard, Sir Michael, 73
Howe, Admiral Jonathon, 117-118, 120-122, 126, 132, 134
Human Intelligence, x, 127
Hungarian uprising, 22
Hungary, 4, 46, 63, 205, 212, 229, 237
Hussein, Saddam, 21, 75, 81-96, 98-101, 103, 126, 203, 208, 214, 217, 233
Hutu, 42, 141, 143, 145, 148-149, 153, 161, 166, 169-171, 176-177, 182, 245

Iceland, 63
Idealism, 4, 11
IFOR, x, 38, 231
impartiality, 28, 40-41, 44-46, 117, 136, 147, 181, 193, 221, 251, 263-264
Implementation Operations, 33-34, 37, 51-52, 80, 104, 116, 142, 186, 231, 264
Impuzamugambi, 149
Independence, Missouri, 212
India, 93, 98, 114, 241, 251, 260-261, 269, 284
Indonesia, 16, 69-70, 241-245, 247, 249
Indonesian army, 243, 245-248
Interahamwe, 38, 145, 149, 152, 154, 245
InterAid, 113
International Committee of the Red Cross (ICRC), x, 105, 130, 141, 153, 155-156, 162, 169, 179, 185
International Force East Timor (INTERFET), x, 246-248
International Herald Tribune, 172
inter-state conflict, vii, 80, 93, 109, 192
intra-state conflict, vii, 47, 79-80, 93, 264
Iran, 21, 24, 84-86, 98, 100
Iraq, v, vii-viii, 21-22, 36, 42, 73, 75, 80-104, 107, 120, 134, 140-141, 160, 184, 191, 217
Iraqi Army, 91, 97
Ireland, 63, 246
Irian Jaya, 241-242
Irish, 163
Islamabad, 115
Israel, 22, 25-26, 73, 85, 91, 95, 206
Italy, x, 7, 10, 44, 62-63, 76, 117, 199-200, 223, 225, 246

Jackson, General Sir Mike, 190, 223-225, 227-231, 248
Jaggabatra, Major-General Songkitti, 246
Jakarta, 105, 242-243, 245-246
James, Alan, 16
Japan, 7, 9-10, 13, 17, 19, 87
Java, 241
Jeddah, 82
Jetley, Major-General Vijay Kumar, 261
JFHQ (UK), x, 67-69, 257
jihad, 44, 92
Johnson, Boris, 255
Johnson, Lyndon B., 25
Johnston, General Robert, 37, 115, 122
Joint Rapid Reaction Force (UK), x, 67-68, 106
Jordan, 21, 259
Joulwan, General George, 177, 180, 183

JTFC, 255-257
JTFHQ, 67, 253-254, 256
jus ad bellum, 11
jus in bello, 11

Kabbah, Ahmed Tejan, 250
Kacanik, 228
Kagame, Major-General, 155, 159-160, 167, 171
KAMRA, 245
Kant, Immanuel, 1-3, 7
Kashmir, 210
Katanga, 28
KDOM, x, 204-205
Keamanan Rakyat, 245
Keegan, Sir John, 218
Kelly, John, 87
Kennedy, John F., 21, 101
Kenya, 112-113
KFOR, x, 62, 76-77, 157, 164, 185, 211, 222-224, 227-233, 246
Khan, Shaharyar, 149
Khrushchev, Nikita, 23-24
Kibuye, 169
Kigali, 33, 38, 41, 43, 48, 144-145, 147-153, 155-156, 158-160, 162, 166-168, 174, 178, 180-183, 185, 187-188, 256, 258
KIM, 232
King Croesus, 82
Kipper, Judith, 89
Kisangi, 166
Kissinger, Henry, 17, 207, 217
KLA, x, 63, 197, 199-205, 213, 219-223, 233
Kloske, Dennis, 87
Korea, 17-19, 39, 50, 80, 88-89, 92, 107, 131, 225, 246, 267
Kosovo, v, vii-viii, x-xi, 4, 22, 35, 41, 43, 53, 56-58, 60-63, 65, 69, 71, 73-74, 76-79, 90, 105, 107, 134, 139-140, 151, 157, 160, 163-164, 172, 190-191, 197-198, 200-206, 208-209, 211-217, 219-239, 242, 244, 246, 255, 265, 267
Kosovo Contact Group, 201
Kosovo Implementation Mission, 232
Kosovo Polje, 191
Kosovo Verification Mission, x, 198, 232
Kouchner, Bernard, 157
Kouyate, Lansana, 120-121, 251
Krauthammer, Charles, 211
Kremlin, 94
Kukes, 217, 220, 228
Kurds, 87, 134, 160
Kuwait, 69, 81-85, 87-92, 94-98, 100, 107, 117
KVM, x, 198-199, 207, 232

Lafourcade, Major-General, 37, 159-160, 167-175, 178, 188
Lanxade, Admiral, 169
Laskar Jihad, 249
Latin America, 25
League of Nations, 1, 4-8, 12
Lebanon, 56, 117
Leighton Smith, Admiral, 43
Lewinsky, Monica, 202
Liberia, 88, 251, 261-262
Liddell Hart, Basil, 47
Lie, Trygve, 10
Lisbon, 255
Loane, Geoff, 162
Locarno Treaty, 7
Loi, General Bruno, 118
Lomé Agreement, 144, 251-252, 258
London Declaration, 49
Low Intensity Conflict, x, 49
Lubbers, Ruud, 77
Lungi, 255

MacArthur, General Douglas, 18
Macedonia, 65, 163, 192, 199-200, 205, 211, 215, 221, 232
Maginot, 97
Major, John, 99, 242, 245-246
Major Regional Conflicts (MRC), 33
Malawi, 145, 165
Malaya Emergency, 257
Malaysia, 245-246
Mali, 145
Malik, Jakob, 19
Malu, General Victor, 261
Maluccu, 242, 249
Manchuria, 7, 18

Manila, 36
Mao Tse Dong, 10
Marchal, Colonel Luc, 145-147, 271, 276
Markovic, Ratko, 201
Marseilles, 255
Marx, Karl, 2
Maryland University, 37, 216
Mauritania, 255
McCreery, General R.L., 12
McKnight, Lieutenant-Colonel Danny, 128
Médécins sans Frontières, 124, 141, 151, 153
Mid Intensity Conflict, x, 49
Middle East, 20-22, 25, 68-69, 81, 84, 86-87, 90, 96, 104, 106
Military Professional Resources Inc, x, 196, 220
Military Staff Committee (MSC), x, 12, 19, 70-71, 125, 134, 188
Military Technical Agreement Kumanovo, x, 222, 224-225, 231, 248
Milletts, Lord, 73
Milosevic, Slobodan, 21-22, 56, 76, 90, 126, 187, 191, 194-195, 197-199, 201-204, 206-209, 211, 213-214, 216-217, 220-221, 225, 227, 231-233, 237, 250
Mitrovica, 172
Mitterand, François, 167
Miyet, Bernard, 254
Mobutu, Marshal, 166
Mogadishu, 37-38, 48, 50-51, 56, 60, 77-78, 109, 111-113, 116, 118-124, 126-128, 131, 133-136, 149, 154, 188, 197, 253, 256
Monroe Doctrine, 23
Montgomery, Major-General Thomas, 117, 121, 127
Moore, Molly, 230
Morgenthau, Hans, 11, 17
Morillon, General Phillipe, 33, 265
Moscow, 85, 94, 102, 221, 231, 238
Mossadeq, Mohammed, 21
Mount Pastrik, 218
Mozambique, 69, 146, 197, 253
MRND, 145, 154
MSF, 141, 153, 179, 268
Mubarak, Hosni, 81
Mujahadeen, 27, 102
Munitions Effectiveness Assessment Team, 236
Muslim, 24, 41, 43-44, 115, 193-196, 200, 203, 208, 241-242, 245
Muslim-Croat Federation, 194
Muslims, 43, 57, 160, 193, 195, 199-200, 231
Mussolini, 21

Nagorno Karabakh, 198
Nagy, Imré, 46
Nairobi, 122, 162
Napoleon Bonaparte, 100-101
Napoleon's Imperial Guard, 100
Narodna Odbrana, 4
Nasser, Gamel Abdel, 21-22, 55, 90, 95, 206
National Patriotic Front, 249
Nationalist China, 9
NATO, x-xi, 12-13, 25, 33, 36, 38, 42-44, 49, 58, 60-67, 71-74, 76-77, 79, 93, 98, 107, 130, 151, 160, 163, 187-188, 190, 192, 194-195, 197-198, 200-202, 204-205, 207, 209, 210-229, 231-233, 235-239, 259, 265, 268
NATO Russia Founding Act 1997, 237
Ndasingura, Lando, 149
Near East, 20, 88
Netherlands, x, 42, 44, 105, 145
New York, 8, 19, 38, 40-41, 69, 71, 88, 99, 115, 118-119, 121, 124-125, 135-136, 146, 148, 152, 154, 187, 195, 233, 251, 261, 267
New York Post, 99
New York Times, 88, 135, 281, 283
New Zealand, 245-246
Newsweek, 216
NGO, x, 37, 141, 147, 155, 158, 164, 183, 185, 235, 268
Niger, 165
Nigeria, 112, 145, 165, 260-261, 264
Nigerian Army, 261
Nixon, Richard, 24, 95, 227
Nobel Prize, 141
Non-Combatant Evacuation Operations (NEO), 253, 255-256

North Atlantic Council, x, 76
Northern Iraq, 103
Northern Ireland, 45, 53
Norway, 63, 105, 246
Ntaryamira, President, 148
nuclear, biological and chemical (nbc), 75, 100
Nutting, Anthony, 22

Oakley, Robert, 121-122, 134-135
Observer, 86
O'Daniel, Lieutenant-General J.W., 225
Ohio State University, 75
Opande, Lieutenant-General Daniel Ishmael, 261
OPEC, x, 81
Operation Amaryllis, 149
Operation B-Minus, 207
Operation Continue Hope, 111
Operation Desert Storm, 90, 93, 107
Operation Gabriel, 162
Operation Horseshoe, 203-204, 211, 257
Operation Langar, 69
Operation Palliser, 69, 256-259
Operation Provide Comfort, 107, 134
Operation Restore Hope, 111-112, 114, 116, 118
Operation Retour, 166
Operation Support Hope, 143, 161, 175, 177, 184
Operation Turquoise, 141-143, 161-162, 166-169, 171-173, 175-176, 185, 188, 190
Operational Liaison and Reconnaissance Team, x, 69, 253, 255-256
Operations Other Than War (OOTW), 34
Organisation of African Unity (OAU), x, 153, 258
Organisation of American States (OAS), 25
OSCE, x, 46, 67, 77, 158, 163, 192, 198-200, 203-205, 227, 232-233
Osiraq, 90
Owen, Lord, 193-194
Oxfam, 165, 179

Pacific, 13, 27, 241
Pahlawanan Rakyat, 245
Pakistan, 21, 93, 116-117, 149
Palestine Liberation Front, 96
Panama, 15, 37
Paris, 4, 7, 21, 32, 65, 167, 185, 201, 206, 208
Paris Peace Conference 1919, 4
Partnership for Peace, 238
Pax Americana, 25, 92, 197
Peace Support Operations, 15, 40, 46-48, 50-51, 267
Pell, Claiborne, 86, 89
Pentagon, 19, 35, 56, 59, 79, 99, 111, 125, 195, 197, 210, 215
Pérez de Cuellar, Javier, 93
Permanent Joint Headquarters (PJHQ), x, 65, 68, 249, 254, 257-258
Philippines, 36, 246
Poland, 63, 105, 145, 212, 237
Port Loko, 260
Portugal, 243, 245
Potsdam Proclamation, 17
Powell, Colin, 38, 129
Presidential Decision Directives, x, 150, 236
Primakov, Yevgeni, 21
Princip, Gavrilo, 4
Pristina, 62, 94, 157, 172, 185, 215, 224, 227-228, 232, 235
Prizren, 224, 232
Punjab, 123
Putin, Vladimir, 55

Qaibdid, Colonel, 123
Qosja, Reschep, 202

Rabochaya Tribuna, 85
Racak, 199-200, 215
Radio Rwanda, 146
Radio Télévision Libre des Mille Collines, 146, 148-149, 153, 172
Ralston, General Joseph W., 225
Rambouillet, 201, 202, 204-205, 207-209, 221, 232
Rangers (US), 126-129, 130-131
Reagan administration, 86
Realism, 1, 4, 11, 17
Republican Guard, 82, 99-101

Riau, 242
Richards, Brigadier David, 253, 255-256, 258
Roberts, Adam, 226
Robertson, George, 61-62, 74, 78, 210, 213
Romania, 65, 145
Roosevelt, F.D., 8, 10, 27
Rose, General Sir Michael, 50, 58
Rothstein, Robert, 11, 285
Rousseau, Jean-Jacques, 2
Royal Fleet Auxiliary (RFA), xi, 68, 225
Royal Marines, xi, 68, 141, 262
RPF, x, 143, 145, 148-151, 154-155, 158-161, 166-167, 170-171, 173-174, 182, 188
Rubin, James P., 137, 202, 207
RUF, xi, 249-253, 255, 257, 259-262
Rugova, Ibrahim, 202
Ruhengeri, 182
Russia, 10, 20, 44, 49, 57, 63, 65, 70, 72, 100, 199-200, 212, 214-215, 221, 223, 225, 227, 235, 237-239, 246, 265
Russian Congress of People's Deputies, 102
Russian Federation, 102, 145
Russo-Japanese War 1904-05, 2
Rwanda, v, vii-viii, xi, 33, 37, 41, 56, 79, 105, 139, 141-150, 153-155, 157-164, 166-169, 171-173, 175-190, 210-211, 234-235, 245, 253-254, 256, 259, 267-268
Rwandan Government Forces (RGF), 145, 149-151, 154-155, 159, 161, 166-167, 173, 175
Rwandese Patriotic Front, xi, 143

SACEUR, xi, 76, 214, 225, 236
Sadat, Anwar, 26
safe areas, 42, 158, 194, 231
Safe Haven, 42
Sahnoun, Mohammed, 116
Salim, Salim Ahmed, 153
San Francisco, 8, 70, 131
Sandline International, 250, 252-253
Sankoh, Foday, 249-250, 252-253, 258, 261
Sarajevo, 4, 37, 42, 49, 58, 111, 193, 195, 200, 205
Saudi Arabia, 78, 82, 85, 87, 96, 99, 103, 117
Save the Children, 155
Schröder, Gerhard, 56-57, 62, 216
Schroeder, Lieutenant-General Daniel, 177-178, 180-184
Schwarzkopf, General Norman, 78
Scotland, 249
Second World War, 5, 8-9, 11, 17, 27, 38, 51, 122, 192, 226, 234
Senate Foreign Relations Committee, 86-88
Senegal, 145, 165
Serb, 4, 40, 42-44, 111, 126, 160, 172, 191-197, 199, 200-205, 207, 213-214, 219-220, 222-227, 229, 231-235
Sessay, Issa, 261
Sèvres, 22, 206
SFOR, xi, 38, 224, 231
Shea, Jamie, 229
Shelton, General Henry, 209, 212, 217, 225
Shinseki, General Eric, 106
Short, Clare, 211
Short, Lieutenant-General Michael C., 76, 226
Siberia, 54
Sierra Leone, v, vii-viii, xi, 68-69, 79, 105, 144, 201, 210, 241, 245, 249-259, 261-262, 264
Sierra Leone Army, 262
Sierra Leonean Government, 262
Simpson, John, 78
Singapore, 246
Six Day War, 90
Skopje, 220, 232
Slim, Field Marshal Sir William, 119
Smith, Christopher, 59
Smuts, Field Marshal Jan, 6
social Darwinism, 1
Solana, Javier, 62, 77, 216, 221
Solidarités, 169
Somalia, v, vii-viii, xi, 21, 37, 41, 64, 73, 79, 93, 108-109, 111-122, 124-127, 131-137, 141, 145, 147, 149-150, 154-155, 169, 177, 186, 197, 209, 235, 265
South Africa, 6, 161
South China Sea, 20

South East Asia, 26, 241
Soviet Union, 6-7, 9-10, 12-13, 17, 19-23, 25-27, 71, 77, 83-84, 89, 101-102
Spain, x, 6, 63
Spanish Civil War, 7, 15
Spearhead Land Element, 255
Srebrenica, 42-44, 48-49, 267
St Malo, 61, 67
Stalin, Joseph, 10, 194-195
Stalingrad, 108
State Department, 59, 87-88, 90, 113, 120, 151, 186, 195, 197, 202-203, 209, 221, 234-235
Stealth fighter, 215
Sudan, 210
Suez Canal, 21-22
Suharto, President, 241-242
Sulawesi, 249
Sully, Duc de, 1
Sunday Times, 38, 271, 281
Sunni, 100, 241
Surroi, Veton, 202
Sweden, 63, 105

Taft, William Howard, 4
Talbott, Strobe, 221, 233
Tamil Tigers, 108
Tampa, Florida, 106, 127
Tass, 85
Taylor, Charles, 249, 251, 261-262
Tehran, 86
Tenerife, 255
Tenet, George, 108, 209
Thaci, Hashim, 202, 208
Thailand, 241, 246
The Charter paradigm, 11
The Economist, 220, 242, 249, 279, 281-283
The Spectator, 255, 275, 280-281
The Times, 58, 61, 87, 252, 256, 271-274, 276, 278, 280
The United Nations Observer Mission Uganda-Rwanda, 158
Third Way, 71-74
Thirty Years War, 1
Thompson, Sir Robert, 24
Tienanmen Square, 215
Time Magazine, 59, 262, 271-272, 280-282, 284
Tito, Josip Broz, 192
Togo, 145, 250
Tomahawk Cruise missiles, 92
Tousignant, Major-General Guy, 165
Treaty of Versailles, 4, 285
Trinidad, 88
Trocaire, 169
Truman, Harry S., 10, 18, 211
Tsar Nicholas II, 2
Tudjman, Franjo, 195
Tunisia, 145, 165
Turkey, 21, 24, 36, 63, 194, 210
Tutsi, 141, 143, 145, 148-149, 153, 155, 159, 161, 168-170, 174-176
Tuzla, 42, 196

Uganda, xi, 158, 165, 180
UN Charter, vii, 12-13, 17, 51, 70-71, 73, 80, 92, 104, 113, 248, 254
UN Charter Articles
  Article 2(4). 9
  Article 2(7). 9
  Article 42. 119, 285
  Article 43. 92
  Article 47. 70
  Article 51. 9, 71, 80
UN Commission on Human Rights, 86
UN Development Programme, xi, 147
UN Security Council, 3, 5, 9-12, 18-20, 26, 28, 42, 44, 70-73, 79-80, 83, 86, 89, 92, 94-95, 97, 102, 104, 111, 113-115, 119-120, 123-125, 132, 143-144, 148, 150, 152, 154, 158-159, 161, 166, 171, 186-187, 195, 198, 201, 213-215, 222, 231, 239, 246, 248, 250-251, 258, 263, 265
    Resolution 82. 18
    Resolution 598. 86
    Resolution 660. 83, 96-97, 101
    Resolution 678. 97, 102
    Resolution 688. 104
    Resolution 751. 111
    Resolution 794. 111, 114, 119
    Resolution 814. 120, 125
    Resolution 837. 125, 132
    Resolution 872. 143-144

Resolution 912. 152
Resolution 918. 158-159
Resolution 925. 159
Resolution 929. 166
Resolution 935. 159
Resolution 965. 166
Resolution 1244. 222, 231
Resolution 1270. 251-252
Resolution 1272. 248
UN Standby Arrangement System (UNSAS), 254
UNAMET, xi, 243, 247-248
UNAMIR, xi, 41, 141-144, 146-155, 157-159, 161, 163, 165-169, 174-176, 179, 181, 188
UNAMSIL, xi, 251-252, 254, 258-262
UNDP, xi, 126-127, 147
UNFICYP, 28, 80
UNHCR, xi, 158, 160, 164, 169, 172-173, 179, 182-183, 203, 211, 231-232
UNITAF, 37, 111-114, 116, 118, 122, 124, 133
United Kingdom, xi, 5, 8-10, 20-22, 31-32, 38, 40, 42, 44-45, 50, 58, 61-63, 65-68, 72, 76, 87-89, 94, 105-107, 117, 133, 150, 162, 165, 176, 187, 193-194, 200, 203, 206, 210, 228, 244-247, 249-250, 252-253, 257-262, 265, 268
United Nations,
Chapter VI, 13, 28, 33, 39, 41, 48, 50-51, 117, 123, 142-144, 146, 154, 158, 161, 175-176, 244, 252, 254
Chapter (VI½), 39, 47, 51, 117, 186
Chapter VII, 8-9, 33, 39, 41, 48, 50-51, 73, 93, 104, 117, 119, 123, 142-143, 147, 161, 175-176, 244-245, 248, 251-252, 254
United States, viii-ix, xi, 5-13, 15, 17-27, 32-33, 35-38, 41-42, 44, 46-47, 53, 54-57, 59-60, 64-66, 70, 72, 76-78, 81-89, 91, 93-96, 98-99, 101, 103, 105-107, 109, 111-114, 116-118, 120-122, 124-126, 128-129, 131-137, 143, 150-151, 154, 159, 161, 168, 174, 176-187, 189, 192, 194, 196-197, 199-200, 204-205, 207, 209, 212, 215-216, 218, 220, 230, 232, 234-235, 241, 246 253, 262, 264-265, 268
Uniting For Peace Resolution, 19
University of Maryland, 216
UNMIK, xi, 157, 223
UNOMSIL, 250-251
UNOMUR, xi, 158
UNOSOM, xi, 37, 41, 108, 111-112, 116-123, 125, 127-128, 131, 134, 167
UNOSOM I. 111-112, 116, 123
UNOSOM II. 37, 41, 108, 111, 116-120, 125, 127, 134
UNPROFOR, xi, 43, 50, 52, 58, 141, 193-194
UNREO, xi, 142, 153, 157, 169, 181-182, 187, 189
UNTAET, xi, 248
Urquhart, Sir Brian, 39-40
Uruguay, 145
US Central Command, 106, 121
USAID, 178
USCENTCOM, 106, 121, 127
Ushtria Çlirimtare e Kosovës (UCK), 197
USMC, xi, 36
USS Stark, 86
USSR, 24, 46
Utopianism, 4
Uwilingiyimana, Agathe,148

Vance, Cyrus, 193-194
Vattel, Emmerick de, 1-3
Védrine, Hubert, 201, 212
Versailles, 7
Vicenza, 225
Vichy, 10
Vietnam, 15, 26, 36, 56, 60, 64, 80, 91, 98, 101-102, 107, 131, 133, 208, 216, 222, 229, 246-247
VJ Day, 8
Voice of America, 86

Wales, 41, 217
Walker, William, 199-200, 204-205
WANRA, 245
War Crimes Tribunal, 160, 221, 227, 261
War Powers Act, 90
Warba Island, 88
Warner, John, 225

Warsaw Treaty, 13
Washington, 6, 19, 21, 23, 26, 33, 35, 37, 39, 56-59, 61, 64-65, 70, 75, 85-88, 90, 95, 114, 116, 119, 126, 132-134, 136, 154, 177-178, 184, 186, 187, 194-197, 199, 201-203, 205-206, 210, 216-217, 225, 230-231, 236, 238-239, 265, 267-268, 285
Washington Post, 35, 37, 88, 114, 132, 230, 270, 275, 281
Waterloo, 101, 255
weapons of mass destruction, 49, 80-81, 108, 212
Weinberger, Caspar, 36, 64
West Point, 33, 37
West Timor, 245, 247
Westmoreland, General William C., 133
Westphalian concept, 1
WEU, xi, 61, 67
Wharton, Clifton, 134
White House, 19, 35, 59, 78, 87, 115, 125-126, 193, 195, 217, 235
Wider Peacekeeping, 40, 46-47, 50-51
Wilson, Harold, 135
Wilson, President Woodrow, 4
World Food Programme, 179

Yalu River, 20
Yeltsin, Boris, 55, 221
Yom Kippur, 26, 28
Yugoslav Army, 198-200, 204, 213, 217, 219, 222-223, 228, 248

Zagreb, 195
Zaire, 69, 143, 145, 159-161, 166-168, 170, 172, 174-175, 180
Zambia, 165
Zepa, 42, 49
Zimbabwe, 145, 253, 256, 258